Project Director
**Patricia F. Kane**

Project Coordinator
**Dale A. Rosselet**

Authors
**Patricia F. Kane**
**Dale A. Rosselet**
**Karl Anderson (Habitats of New Jersey)**
**Jerry T. Schierloh**

Artwork
**Carol A. Decker**

Graphics and Layout Design
**Joan Rogers Snider of Master Design Studio, Inc.**

Printing
**Alcom Printing Group, Inc., Harleysville, PA**

BOARD OF EDITORS

Education and Science
**Elliott Blaustein - Author, Science Consultant**
**Rose Blaustein - Science Consultant**
**Beryl Robichaud Collins - Research Scholar; Rutgers University Center for
          Coastal and Environmental Studies**
**Richard P. Kane - Former Vice President for Conservation and Stewardship,
          New Jersey Audubon Society**
**Lester A. Ray - K-12 North East Development Executive, Apple**
**Gordon K. Schultze - Former Director; Lorrimer Sanctuary;
          New Jersey Audubon Society**

Copy
**Karen Parrish - Editorial Consultant**
**Dorothy Clair - Editorial Consultant, revised edition**
**Candy Mitchell - Proofreader, revised edition**

New Jersey Audubon Society — 1992
Revised edition 2003

# BRIDGES TO THE NATURAL WORLD

Revised Edition

*A Natural History Guide for Teachers of Grades Pre-K through 6*

Printed in the United States of America

Original edition ISBN # 0-9624065-1-1
Revised edition ISBN # 0-9624065-4-6

Library of Congress Control Number:   2002115359

First printing - October 1992
Second printing - December 1992
Third printing - January 1994
Fourth printing - May 1996
Revised edition - May 2003

Kane, Patricia F., 1937-
        Bridges to the natural world : a natural history guide for
teachers of grades pre-k through 6 /  authors, Patricia F. Kane,
Dale A. Rosselet, Karl Anderson, Jerry T. Schierloh; artwork, Carol A.
Decker.
        p.    cm.
        Includes bibliographical references and index.
        ISBN 0-9624065-4-6
        1. Natural history—Study and teaching (Elementary)—New Jersey.
2. Nature study—New Jersey. 3. Natural history—Study and teaching
(Elementary) 4. Nature study. I. Rosselet, Dale A. (Dale Allyn), 1957-   .
II. Anderson, Karl, 1938-    . III. Schierloh, Jerry T. 1942-    . IV. Title.
QH51.A53  1992
372.3'57—dc20                                          92-2830
                                                         CIP

*To the child in all of us who is reawakened by the simple wonders of the natural world.*

About the cover:

New Jersey boasts of broad diversity not only in wildlife and botanical habitats, but also in cultural and racial composition. The bridge connecting us to the natural world can also unite us as a people, who can learn to share with understanding and gratitude the portion of earth that sustains our lives.

Printed on recycled paper with water-based inks. High-resolution electronic plates were utilized for the print production of this book, keeping the acetate-based negatives out of our landfills.

# ACKNOWLEDGMENTS

The New Jersey Audubon Society would like to thank the following foundations, corporations, and individuals whose generosity has made this publication and our Bridges to the Natural World program possible:

First Edition:
      The Geraldine R. Dodge Foundation
      The Victoria Foundation
      The Schumann Fund for New Jersey
      Church & Dwight Co., Inc.
      The Manny and Ruthy Cohen Foundation
      The Clarence & Anne Dillon Dunwalke Trust
      Herman M. Rosenberg Foundation
      Thanksgiving Foundation, Inc.
      The New York Times Company Foundation
      The Jockey Hollow Foundation
      Ernest Christian Klipstein Foundation
      Subaru of America Foundation
      The Estate of Ernest Sansotera
      The Ann E. Talcott Fund

Revised Edition:
      The Geraldine R. Dodge Foundation

# Additional contributions of time and expertise have been made by:

New Jersey Audubon Society Education Committee:

    Jerry T. Schierloh, Chair, Karl Anderson, R. Michael Anderson, Pete Bacinski, Mary Belko, Scott Barnes, Rose Blaustein, Barbara Brummer, John E. Courtney, Philip DeRea, Linda Dill, Gretchen Ferrante, Don Freiday, Mark Garland, Patricia Kane, Mark Levy, Randolph S. Little, Tara Miller, Karla Risdon, Dale A. Rosselet, Sue Slotterback, Patricia Sutton, and Brian Vernachio

Alicia D. Bass — Teacher Grades 7 & 8, Jersey City School District
Jane T. Brady — Former Director of Development, New Jersey Audubon Society
Audrey Brainard — Science Consultant; Hands-On-Nature, Virginia.
John Carno — Vice President for Development; New Jersey Audubon Society
Loris Chen — Teacher, Wyckoff School District
Denis Cleary — Store Manager, New Jersey Audubon Society
Kathleen Devine — Education Consultant
Peter J. Dunne — Vice President of Natural History Information, New Jersey Audubon Society
Paula Mueller Farris — Music Teacher
Don Freiday — Sanctuary Director, New Jersey Audubon Society
Jennifer Gaus — Environmental Educator
Thomas J. Gilmore — President, New Jersey Audubon Society
Susannah Graedel — Teacher/Naturalist
Greenkill Nature Center — Huguenot, New York
William Haines — Teacher, North Arlington Middle School
Angela Henderson — Special Education Teacher Grade 2, Bayonne School District
Carrie Jacobson — In-Class Support Teacher Grade 4, Manalapan-Englishtown School District
Karen Koenig — Teacher/Naturalist; Franklin County Conservation Board, Hampton, Iowa
Walter A. Koenig — Membership Coordinator; New Jersey Audubon Society
Bruce Marganoff — Education Consultant
Patricia Mazzone — Teacher, North Bergen School District
Arthur Mitchell — New Jersey Department of Education
Mary Mayer — Teacher/Naturalist, Closter Nature Center, Closter, New Jersey
Sharon Moore — Teacher, Central School, Glen Rock, New Jersey
Brian Moscatello — Director, Tenafly Nature Center, Tenafly, New Jersey
Janice McDowell — Teacher Grade 4, Manalapan-Englishtown School District
Jack Padalino — Former Director; Pocono Environmental Education Center, Dingmans Ferry, Pennsylvania
Sharon Peisecki — Teacher Grade 1, North Brunswick School District
Patti Pfeiffer — Winfield Park Elementary School
Linn Pierson — Editorial Consultant
Cindy Rista — Inclusion Support Teacher, Bayonne School District
Patricia Sacco — Teacher Grade 5, North Brunswick School District
Charlene D. Shariff — Teacher of the Handicapped Grade 8, Jersey City School District
Shanna M. Spence — Resource Center Teacher Grade 6, South Brunswick School District
Merle Tanis — Teacher, Sussex County
Karen A. Timmons — Teacher, Watchung School, Montclair, New Jersey
Lisa Wargo — Teacher, Theodore Schor Middle School, Piscataway, New Jersey

# New Jersey Audubon Society

### Headquarters
9 Hardscrabble Road
P.O. Box 126
Bernardsville, N.J. 07924-9971
Phone (908) 204 - 8998
Fax (908) 204 - 8960
Web Site: www.njaudubon.org

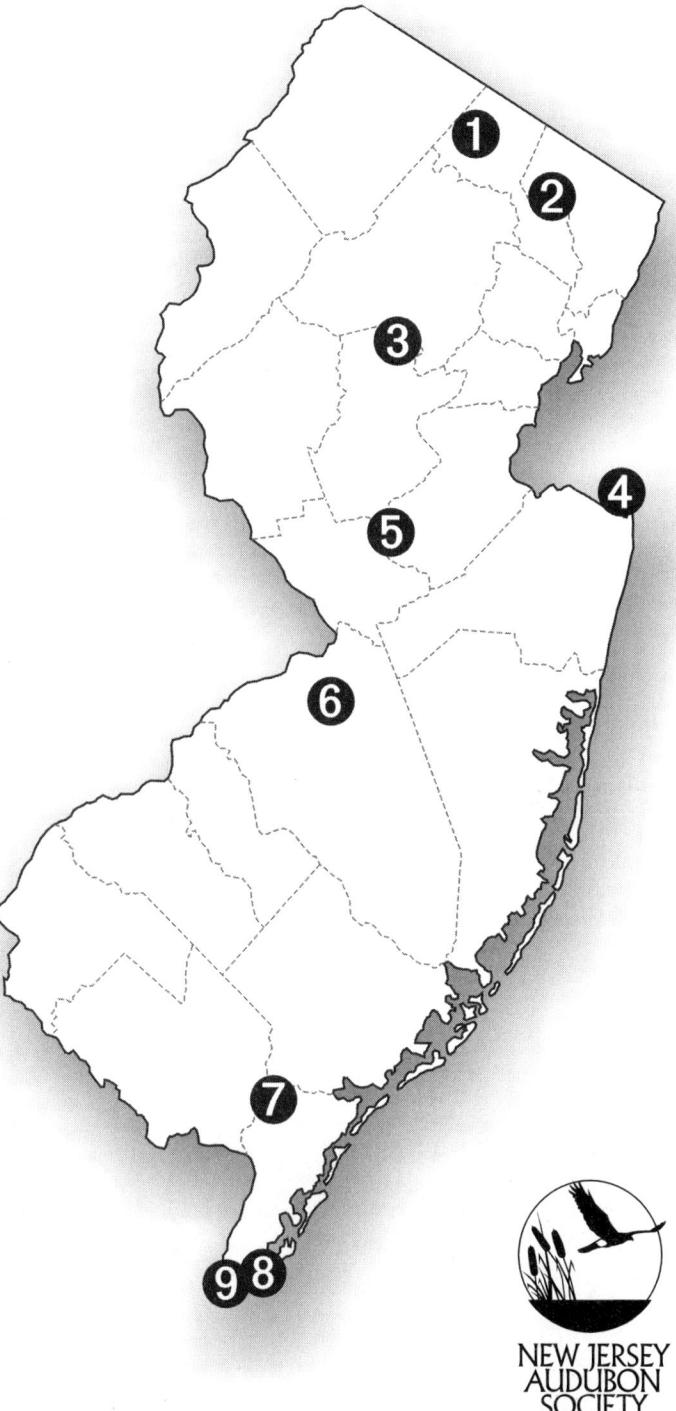

**1 Weis Ecology Center**
150 Snake Den Road, Ringwood, NJ 07456
Phone (973) 835-2160
Fax (973) 835-8986
Email: weis@njaudubon.org

**2 Lorrimer Sanctuary**
790 Ewing Avenue, P.O. Box 125
Franklin Lakes, NJ 07417-2271
Phone (201) 891-2185
Fax (201) 848-8473
Email: lorrimer@njaudubon.org

**3 Scherman-Hoffman Wildlife Sanctuary**
11 Hardscrabble Road, P.O. Box 693
Bernardsville, NJ 07924
Phone (908) 766-5787
Fax (908) 766-7775
Email: scherman-hoffman@njaudubon.org

**4 Sandy Hook Bird Observatory**
20 Hartshorne Drive, P.O. Box 553
Fort Hancock, N.J. 07732
Phone (732) 872 -2500
Fax (732) 872-2577
Email: shbo@njaudubon.org

**5 Plainsboro Preserve**
80 Scotts Corner Road, P.O. Box 446
Plainsboro, N.J. 08536
Phone (609) 897-9400
Email: plainsboro@njaudubon.org

**6 Rancocas Nature Center**
794 Rancocas Road, Mount Holly, NJ 08060
Phone (609) 261-2495
Fax (609) 261-9916
Email: rancocas@njaudubon.org

**7 Cape May Bird Observatory**
**Center for Research and Education**
600 Route 47 North
Cape May Court House, NJ 08210
Phone (609) 861- 0700
Fax (609) 861-1651
Email: cmbo2@njaudubon.org

**8 Nature Center of Cape May**
1600 Delaware Avenue, Cape May, NJ 08204
Phone (609) 898-8848
Fax (609) 898-8512
Email: nccm@njaudubon.org

**9 Cape May Bird Observatory**
**Northwood Center**
707 East Lake Drive, P.O. Box 3
Cape May Point, NJ 08212
Phone (609) 884-2736
Fax (609) 884-6052
Email: cmbo@njaudubon.org

NEW JERSEY
AUDUBON
SOCIETY

# NEW JERSEY AUDUBON SOCIETY

The New Jersey Audubon Society (NJAS) is a privately supported, not-for-profit, statewide membership organization. Founded in 1897 and one of the oldest Audubon societies, NJAS is independent of the National Audubon Society.

The New Jersey Audubon Society has a threefold mission of conservation, education, and research. It fosters environmental awareness and a conservation ethic among New Jersey citizens. The Society is committed to the preservation of New Jersey's natural habitats and the protection of its birds, mammals, other animals, and plants, especially endangered and threatened species.

New Jersey Audubon Society education services include:
- field trips
- assembly programs
- classroom presentations
- natural history slide presentations
- professional development for teachers
- environmental education consulting

These programs are offered at the school site or at a NJAS nature center or sanctuary.

# A View from the Bridge

Dear Educators,

The revised edition of *Bridges to the Natural World* (*Bridges*) comes to you just as New Jersey Audubon Society (NJAS) stands at the threshold of a new and promising era. Our membership is at an all-time high. Our successful capital campaign has provided the resources that will significantly expand our outreach services to schools and communities proximate to our nine staffed centers throughout the state. Two companion NJAS teacher guides, *New Jersey WATERS: A Watershed Approach to Teaching the Ecology of Regional Systems* and *At the Crossroads of Migration* round out our overall school-targeted educational program. These tools give teachers the opportunity to infuse ecological, place-based learning experiences throughout New Jersey's K to 12 school curricula. Our teaching staff will serve local and regional constituents in new and innovative ways.

The founders of New Jersey Audubon Society had a vision - to preserve natural habitats and wildlife diversity within the state. Today, we carry out that quest through our threefold mission of conservation, education, and research. In the revised edition of *Bridges*, we invite teachers and students to take part in that mission. We believe that every citizen has the right to know and understand the great natural treasures that are their heritage. With that knowledge, they can develop the values and learn the skills necessary to participate in research and conservation activities that mirror our own statewide efforts. Educating the citizen-scientist assures that future generations will enjoy the same beauty in wild areas: the clear, free-running streams; the wetlands, teaming with wildlife; the forests sounding a chorus of birdsong.

New Jersey is a rapidly growing state with a constant flow of people arriving from all parts of the world. For many, the land is strange and the wildlife unfamiliar. A critical component of their transition to a new land is to understand the needs and requirements of nature in this place. Understanding fosters a sense of belonging. A sense of place is important for all citizens, be they new to the land or able to claim generations of connection. Children in each new generation must travel that bridge which connects them to those natural systems that sustain their lives and the myriad of living things that share this planet. Knowledge is power and a force for change. Students empowered with the knowledge of how nature works become the citizen-scientists who learn to value our natural treasures.

We at New Jersey Audubon invite you then, to join us in our efforts of conservation, education and research. Help to preserve what is the right of every New Jersey citizen. Be part of this great effort in educating future generations to become stewards of their natural heritage.

Sincerely,

Thomas J. Gilmore
President, New Jersey Audubon Society

NEW JERSEY
AUDUBON
SOCIETY

# PREFACE

Dear Educators,

In 1992 New Jersey Audubon Society (NJAS) introduced *Bridges to the Natural World* (*Bridges*) for the first time. Since then 6,000 copies have been distributed to teachers and nonformal educators. The strength and effectiveness of the instructional activities held within the guide helped teachers and students gain a strong ecological foundation for understanding basic natural communities in New Jersey.

Why then, do we need a revised edition of such a strong tool? There are many answers to this question.

After ten years of experience working with teachers and school districts, we have honed our own skills in understanding new learning strategies for including the broadest diversity in learning styles. It is important for each child to participate and take ownership of personal learning. This is a critical component in empowering the student to become capable of making informed decisions concerning habitat preservation in a rapidly developing state.

Second, by rearranging the lessons and activities it draws attention to the primary ecological principles – habitats, natural communities, and ecosystems. Habitats provide the elements that support a single species throughout its lifetime whereas natural communities are comprised of plant and animal entities that depend on one another while ecosystems incorporate a variety of habitats and natural communities and abiotic factors to create a stable, yet ever-changing system. Students learn to recognize these relationships as similar to their own households and human communities. Our activities begin with the support of a single species; just as the young child's primary interest is self-interest. As the child grows and interaction with other social systems expands, interrelationships and interdependencies are expressed in human communities just as in the natural world.

This revised edition of *Bridges* calls to the curiosity within each human heart. The earth is our home. The secrets held in flowering grasses or a bird's song await discovery. Adventures are mapped out in the tide lines along our beaches, pathways through our forests, or even cracks in urban sidewalks. Investigation of the natural world is what gives us our sense of belonging. It is an integral part of our humanity.

As we become more familiar with different natural communities, recognize the various plant and animal species, and observe the seasonal changes, our acquired knowledge and understanding give us work to do. It is the job of every citizen to monitor the local natural communities because it is the health of these ecosystems that determines the well-being of all living things, including ourselves.

*Dale Rosselet*

Dale A. Rosselet,
NJAS Vice President for Education

NEW JERSEY
AUDUBON
SOCIETY

**Bridges to the Natural World**

# INTRODUCTION

## BUILDING THE BRIDGE

The very first bridges were utilized when some creature encountered an obstacle to its progress. It may have crossed a rock jumble in a swift flowing stream to reach the other side or walked a fallen log over a deep chasm. Human imagination, determination, and skill also build bridges to span separations. These bring people together and make what was impossible, attainable. As a metaphor, bridges of knowledge and changed attitudes can dissolve separations caused by ignorance and indifference.

*Bridges to the Natural World* (*Bridges*) is such a metaphor. With it we look to join unconnected communities – those of formal classroom teachers with the nonformal educators. We aim to reconnect adults with the wonder and curiosity of childhood and we endeavor to reflect the scientific world in our everyday lives. In building this bridge, New Jersey Audubon Society (NJAS), invites all to participate in the Society's three mission domains of conservation, education and research. This threefold mission has served the citizens of New Jersey for more than one hundred years in preserving critical habitat that supports over 600 species of wildlife.

*Bridges* becomes a tool for parents, teachers, and all educators to experience the natural world firsthand and to learn how it works. It enables adults to become comfortable enough with the natural world so they can facilitate explorations with children. Investigation skills honed through personal research help increase understanding and educate a corps of citizen-scientists. People who understand the intricate systems of nature are capable of recognizing how important it is to preserve a reasonable balance between development and conservation.

Likewise, a bridge is built to carry and to support all that we bring. *Bridges* is a support for a child's innate curiosity for the natural world. Children bring so many different methods for investigation and discovery – some process their experiences through complete and total immersion with a why-not perspective, while others are more reflective, imagining the why's and what-if's of what they see. The natural world provides a setting where children learn from each other while the teacher provides the tools and the map.

Finally, this bridge can be viewed as a connector between the built community created by humans and the natural communities with all their life-support elements. As we become more of a society motivated and controlled by technology, there is a tendency to become insulated and isolated from those natural systems that support all life forms. A new definition of stewardship shifts the present paradigm from human consumption and manipulation to one where people take responsibility for their behavior toward natural systems to demonstrate the belief that they share this planet with many life forms.

Familiarity through personal investigation offers a holistic base for learning. Ecosystems, with their unique structure, species indicators, and narrow range of preferences provide a sense of place and of belonging for each living thing. This placebased learning, experienced in the living laboratory provides educational enrichment for which there is no substitute.

NEW JERSEY
AUDUBON
SOCIETY

# CROSSING THE BRIDGE

The format of *Bridges* makes it easy for anyone to use. Classroom teachers will find that the lessons and activities are all fully aligned with the New Jersey Core Curriculum Content Standards. All are strong in science, social studies, and language, but many extend to other content areas of the curriculum. A teacher supplement to *Bridges* lists each lesson with the subject, core standards, and indicators that apply. This supplement as well as other support lessons and materials may be found on the NJAS web site: www.njaudubon.org

Parents and grandparents will find *Bridges* an excellent reference and wonderful resource for teaching their own children and grandchildren. Here is a recipe for a very special birthday party as well as weekend and summer adventures. Learn with your children how exciting the wonders of the natural world can be.

Each year NJAS offers workshops to demonstrate how to use activities and programs as contained in *Bridges*. Make inquiries of the next available workshop by calling any of the NJAS centers, and/or by being placed on the Education Department mailing list. The NJAS teaching staff also offers in-service days to school districts. Arrangements for a date and fees can be obtained through any NJAS center. Workshops presented on the school grounds offer teachers the advantage of learning to integrate the local natural areas into the lessons, making the experience more relevant. Repeated experience by the students fosters depth of understanding and opportunities to observe seasonal change.

*Dale Rosselet*

Dale A. Rosselet,
NJAS Vice President for Education

## HOW TO USE THIS BOOK

***BRIDGES TO THE NATURAL WORLD*** was developed to help New Jersey teachers, parents, caregivers, and group leaders lead children to a better understanding of their local natural environment. The four major sections are designed to facilitate the transition from classroom or indoor teaching to an outdoor learning experience.

## SECTION ONE: HABITATS OF NEW JERSEY

Geographically, New Jersey is divided into five regions. Within those regions, there are unique habitats and natural communities that support a great diversity of plant and animal life. ***BRIDGES TO THE NATURAL WORLD*** features sixteen of these distinct, but common, habitats. A supplement at the end of the section describes intermittent wetlands that are found seasonally or during excessively wet cycles.

### HABITAT/NATURAL COMMUNITIES CHAPTERS

New Jersey is justifiably called The Garden State. Each habitat chapter contains a description of the habitat or natural community and a full-page drawing of a typical scene within the habitat. To assist in the process of identifying flora and fauna, lists of the most common plants and animals are included. Duplications of these pictures may be made for student use without violation of copyright. We do not recommend that these illustrations become part of the student journal (see pg. 297), but that they are used for class discussion.

### HABITAT LOCATION MATRIX

When the areas described in this guide are not near school property, field trips can be planned to other sites. Each chapter has a small map of New Jersey in which shaded areas indicate statewide locations of the habitats. At the back of Section One is a matrix of parks and nature centers that provide staff and nature study or environmental education programs.

### AWARDS – THE HABITAT PASSPORT CONNECTION

NJAS encourages school administrators and teachers to use the outdoors as a learning laboratory. In recognition of those who facilitate this type of learning, NJAS extends the Natural Science Award for schools and teachers. Additionally, students who explore a variety of habitats or a single habitat over a period of time are eligible to receive the Junior Naturalist Award.

## SECTION TWO: NATURAL HISTORY LESSONS

What is it like to fly on a 15,000-mile migration, twice a year? How is a berry or a leaf like a crayon? Which streams or rivers in your town are connected to storm drains?

All of these questions could be answered through pictures or library research, but experience leads to better understanding. Experience also has a stronger impact. This section leads students through activities and simulations that concentrate on five concepts: **Habitats, Natural Communities, Ecosystems, Human Ecological Impacts, and Human Land Stewardship Practices.** These concept areas were chosen because they take the students from an awareness of the fundamental functions

*NB: Photocopying for the purpose of student participation in this activity does not violate copyright.

NEW JERSEY AUDUBON SOCIETY

within ecosystems to the complexities of interdependence and the effects of human behavior on the earth. In the revised edition of *Bridges*, students are invited to take action through a stewardship role in preserving natural systems and wildlife habitats. These activities nurture a sense of responsibility for those life forms that share this planet with the human family. Most lessons are designed for outdoors, but if circumstances are not favorable, they may be run in a classroom or all-purpose room.

Each activity is prefaced with information to help the teacher choose the appropriate grade level. Background information gives the teacher a broader understanding of the natural history concept treated. While the grade level and activity may be written for lower elementary grades, teachers should not disqualify the lessons for use in upper grades. Some activities are fun for all ages and can be used at any level. Watch for expansions and other versions explained at the end of each activity.

## SECTION THREE: NATURE ORIENTATION AND SKILL BUILDING ACTIVITIES

Making the transition from traditional classroom teaching to teaching in the outdoors can be difficult. Usually students associate the schoolyard with a place of recreation rather than study. However, opening the doors can open minds and hearts to a wealth of valuable experiences. There are endless opportunities for education beyond the limits of the four walls. In this section, the teacher will find:
- activities to facilitate the transition from indoor to outdoor instruction
- techniques to focus the students' attention
- methods of exploring a habitat.

## SECTION FOUR: HELPFUL HINTS FOR OUTDOOR NATURE AND ECOLOGY INVESTIGATIONS

HOW TO USE THE SCHOOL GROUNDS AS AN OUTDOOR CLASSROOM – Step-by-step instruction, leading students from the indoor classroom to learning in the outdoors.

NATURAL COMMUNITY LEARNING LOOPS – Inquiry skills are developed through posing problems, exploration, and experimentation. This framework provides the teacher with a design for successful learning. Instead of executing a series of disjointed and independent activities, the outline acts as a template for leading students to a deeper understanding of the interdependencies and interconnections within a natural community.

HOW TO KEEP A JOURNAL – The journal is an informal reflection of an individual's observations and experiences. Drawing or writing in nature provides a personal, illustrated record of a special event in the student's life and reinforces a sense of place and belonging.

NEW JERSEY
AUDUBON
SOCIETY

**Bridges to the Natural World**

SAFETY IN THE OUTDOOR CLASSROOM – Simple precautions make the outdoor experience as safe as any classroom. Preparation is the best prevention of problems in the outdoors.

MAKING FIELD STUDY AND NATURE INVESTIGATION TOOLS – Our primary tools for investigation are our senses, but simple tools made from kitchen items that would normally be discarded can enhance the learning as well as foster a habit of reusing throw-aways.

ASSESSMENT TOOLS – RUBRICS FOR LEARNING OUTDOORS – Each of the lessons and activities has built-in assessment either through teacher-student discussion or worksheets. This form of assessment helps the teacher determine how well the students learned the content of individual lessons. What criteria do we use to measure the overall effectiveness of the outdoor classroom? How does a teacher demonstrate that these experiences serve the learning process of each child? How do students measure growth in their own inquiry skills? How do students recognize their ability to take charge of their own learning? The rubrics in this section offer samples of how this measurement can be taken.

TECHNO-TIPS – Today's technologies, as tools for learning, far outstrip anything we have experienced in the last twenty-five years. Students have access to photographic tools and computer programs that can serve as excellent recorders of personal experiences. It is critical in a child's development that they learn to rely on their own senses first, then use these tools to enhance their firsthand experience and/or share the experience with others. This section offers ideas for creating records of personal experiences.

# SECTION FIVE: APPENDICES AND REFERENCES

GLOSSARY
Words printed in bold throughout the book are defined in the glossary.

THREATENED AND ENDANGERED WILDLIFE SPECIES OF NEW JERSEY
This is the most up-to-date listing of threatened and endangered species as compiled by the Endangered and Nongame Species Program of the New Jersey Department of Fish and Wildlife. (www.state.nj.us/dep/fgw)

ABOUT ORPHANED AND INJURED WILDLIFE
This appendix answers your students' and your own questions on dealing with those animals that are found injured or young animals that seem to be orphaned or abandoned.

CREATING A HABITAT FOR WILDLIFE – This section offers a list of the plantings that are most helpful to wildlife and to natural systems of the region. It also outlines the how-to's and why's of the backyard or schoolyard habitat.

BIBLIOGRAPHY AND RESOURCE LIST – In Section Two there is a list of recommended resources at the end of each activity which relates specifically to the concept covered by the lesson. The expanded bibliography in the appendix provides a broader range of reference materials for teachers and group leaders.

NEW JERSEY
AUDUBON
SOCIETY

# TABLE OF CONTENTS

NEW JERSEY
AUDUBON
SOCIETY

# Section Two: NATURAL HISTORY LESSONS ....................... 111

## HABITATS
*Every living organism within a natural community requires a habitat consisting of food, water, shelter and space in an arrangement that allows the organism to live its full life cycle and reproduce its own kind.*

## NATURAL COMMUNITIES
*Natural land areas support associations of plants and animals called communities. These plants and animals inhabit common environments, interact with one another, and occupy specific niches within their community. In a broad sense, they are also referred to as habitats because they are unique areas defined by indicator species.*

NEW JERSEY
AUDUBON
SOCIETY

## ECOSYSTEMS

*In natural communities, discrete units of biotic and abiotic parts exist that interact to form a stable, yet ever changing system. These self-sustaining units are called ecosystems and their interactions include food chains, energy flow, nutrient exchange, and numerous cycles.*

## HUMAN ECOLOGICAL IMPACTS

*All species affect their natural environment through the food they consume, the nutrients they cycle, the waste they produce, and the space they occupy. Humans, however, have the greatest capacity to exert significant impacts on local and regional ecosystems through personal and collective behavior.*

NEW JERSEY
AUDUBON
SOCIETY

**HUMAN LAND STEWARDSHIP PRACTICES**
*Humans who are sensitive to the various impacts they have on local and regional ecosystems may be better motivated to support improvements to those ecosystems.*

# Section Three:
# NATURE ORIENTATION AND SKILLS ACTIVITIES

**INDOORS-TO-OUTDOORS TRANSITIONAL ACTIVITIES**
*Initial engagements with the outdoor classroom.*

## DISCOVERY–AWARENESS ACTIVITIES
*Sensory investigations that hone observation and thinking skills.*

## CLASSIFICATION ACTIVITIES
*Learning the indicator species of natural communities.*

NEW JERSEY
AUDUBON
SOCIETY

**DEVELOPING AN ENVIRONMENTAL ETHIC**
*Taking responsibility for personal interactions with natural systems.*

# Section Four: HELPFUL HINTS FOR OUTDOOR NATURE AND ECOLOGY INVESTIGATIONS

NEW JERSEY
AUDUBON
SOCIETY

## Section Five: APPENDICES
## TOOLS FOR BUILDING 'BRIDGES' OF
## UNDERSTANDING AND REFERENCES

NEW JERSEY
AUDUBON
SOCIETY

*Bridges to the Natural World*

NEW JERSEY
AUDUBON
SOCIETY

Section

1

# HABITATS OF NEW JERSEY

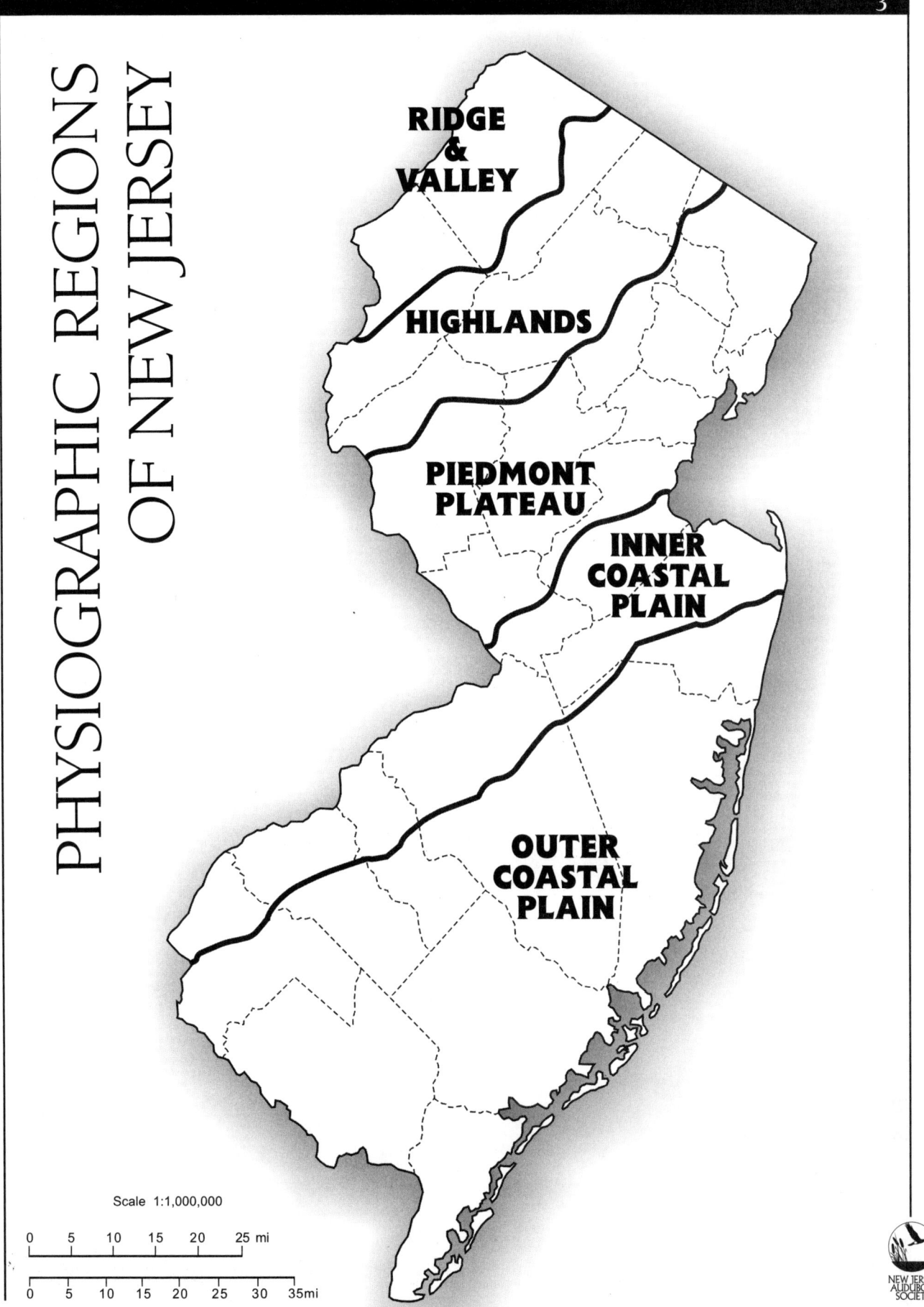

# PHYSIOGRAPHIC REGIONS OF NEW JERSEY

**RIDGE & VALLEY**

**HIGHLANDS**

**PIEDMONT PLATEAU**

**INNER COASTAL PLAIN**

**OUTER COASTAL PLAIN**

Scale 1:1,000,000

| 0 | 5 | 10 | 15 | 20 | 25 mi |

| 0 | 5 | 10 | 15 | 20 | 25 | 30 | 35mi |

NEW JERSEY AUDUBON SOCIETY

# GEOLOGIC HISTORY
# OF NEW JERSEY'S DIVERSITY

New Jersey's place in natural history began over 300 million years ago with the uplift of the Appalachian Mountains in a region of long-buried igneous and sedimentary rocks. The several major episodes of erosion, uplift, volcanic activity, and faulting which followed created a foundation for the varied landscapes of today's New Jersey, with its five **physiographic regions: Ridge and Valley, Highlands, Piedmont Plateau, Inner Coastal Plain,** and **Outer Coastal Plain.**

In the last 700,000 years at least four sheets of ice buried the land, the last being the Wisconsin Glacier that covered the northern half of the state. As the glacier advanced it wore down the mountains of northern New Jersey. As it receded it left behind a changed landscape that included two glacial lakes: Hackensack and Passaic. After the final melting 12,000 years ago, wind, rain, and the battering of the sea molded the surface of New Jersey.

Within the physiographic regions there is a diversity of soil quality and water supplies. These unique arrangements evolved into distinct habitats that support specific species of flora and fauna. ***BRIDGES TO THE NATU-RAL WORLD*** features sixteen of these distinctive habitats as well as a section on incidental wetlands. While this does not exhaust the list of natural habitats found in the state, it provides a showcase for those that cover the largest portion of the state and are available for study at public and private facilities. In this revised edition, we have added two new chapters. One describes the small landscaped areas in urban neighborhoods. These patches of open space can be havens for many species of wildlife by providing food and shelter in all seasons. The second addition describes distinct wetland communities. These habitats are no less important for sustaining the life cycle of certain species. They occur occasionally in various parts of the state and are excellent study areas for anyone who has access to them.

# HOW TO USE THIS SECTION

## Visiting New Jersey's Habitats

The habitat types described in this section are the primary focus of all outdoor studies. New Jersey Audubon Society invites every person to participate in our conservation and research missions by learning to monitor these areas. Exploring the diversity found in each habitat provides a unique opportunity to experience our natural heritage in this densely populated state. Citizens who understand the ecological niche of indicator plants and animals will be more apt to value these treasures and preserve them for future generations.

The habitat descriptions consider how ecological events and circumstances created unique natural areas. By studying a specific habitat type, or natural community, one can predict the plants, animals, and interactions that should be present in a similar habitat type somewhere else in the state or region. For example, the aquatic painted turtle has specific requirements for its habitat: ample food and water, an appropriate substrate for shelter and for hibernating, and a large enough area to support individuals as well as a population of turtles. The habitat type or natural community in which a painted turtle lives supports a broad diversity of organisms. All the ponds throughout New Jersey and the region exhibit a similar dynamic. Generalizations can be made, therefore, about the countless interrelationships found in all pond habitats, and where painted turtles are likely to be found. Use the habitat information as background material prior to visiting a particular habitat and to help create pre- and post-field trip activities.

USING THE HABITAT ILLUSTRATIONS AS A LESSON
The omission of people in the drawings is deliberate. The artist invites you, the viewer, to enter the scene and experience what is happening. Listen with your imagination, and hear the sound of the leaves crunching as the mother bear lumbers through the northern New Jersey mixed oak forest with her cubs (p. 57), or the wind moaning softly as it passes through the hemlock forest (p. 51). Each habitat has its own mood, and its own story. Even the smaller pictures throughout the book tell a special story about physical features, behavior, or adaptations of plants and animals. Be sure to include them in the lesson. NB: Photocopying of habitat art for the purpose of student participation in this activity does not violate copyright.

## Awards – The Habitat Passport Connection

New Jersey Audubon Society encourages teachers and students to use the outdoors as a learning laboratory. To recognize the efforts of those schools and teachers who implement this form of nature discovery education, NJAS offers the Natural Science Award. Likewise, a child who fulfills the requirements for documenting outdoor discovery is eligible for the Junior Naturalist Award.

NATURAL SCIENCE AWARD for the SCHOOL
**Using the Habitat Passport**
Send a single class to study at least ten of the described habitats in *Bridges*. Make a class copy of the NJAS Habitat Passport (p. 7) to keep track of the habitats your class visits. At the end of each field trip, fill in the name of the habitat(s) studied and present the passport to the teacher-naturalist of the park or nature center to sign. If the field trip is on the school grounds, neighborhood site, or

NEW JERSEY
AUDUBON
SOCIETY

local natural area where there is no teacher-naturalist, a school administrator or teacher may sign the passport. On completing the requirements, the school should send the passport to the nearest New Jersey Audubon Society center with a request for the award certificate. Optional: Submit student journals (and a typed list of all student names) along with the Habitat Passport.

### Using the Schoolyard or Neighborhood

Engage students in schoolyard and local neighborhood investigations as a regular part of curriculum studies. Spend at least ten days or 50 hours of the school year investigating an outdoor natural area. Keep a Habitat Activity Log (p. 8) for each outdoor investigation with a brief description of the student's investigations. On completing the requirements, the school should send the log to the nearest New Jersey Audubon Society center with a request for the award certificate.

Optional: Submit student journals (and a typed list of all student names) along with the Habitat Passport.

JUNIOR NATURALIST AWARDS for the STUDENT
### Using the Habitat Passport

Students should complete and submit a personal journal (see How to Keep a Journal, p. 297) of their impressions about the uniqueness of at least ten habitats they have visited. The journal should be submitted along with a completed Habitat Passport to the nearest NJAS center. Journals may **not** include duplications of the habitat illustrations taken from *Bridges to the Natural World*. All work must be original or contain original responses to teacher- or parent-led activities.

### Using the Schoolyard or Neighborhood

Students whose investigations reflect a single area are required to keep a journal that documents that site throughout the seasons or during a designated period of time. Journals must contain at least ten pages of reflections but may **not** include duplications of the habitat illustrations taken from *Bridges to the Natural World*. All work must be original or contain original responses to teacher- or parent-led activities.

Note: All journals and certificates will be processed and sent back to students in a timely manner. Send a typed list of the students with a $5.00 check payable to NJAS for postage and handling.

## Field Study Sites

At the back of this section is a matrix of parks and nature centers whose staff has agreed to participate in the ***BRIDGES TO THE NATURAL WORLD*** program. Most of these facilities have teacher/naturalists who provide programs. When you call to arrange a field trip, be sure to mention the habitats you would like to study and ask if a fee will be charged.

# HABITAT PASSPORT

**NEW JERSEY AUDUBON SOCIETY'S**
## BRIDGES TO THE NATURAL WORLD

THIS PASSPORT BELONGS TO: _____

**NEW JERSEY AUDUBON SOCIETY**

| | |
|---|---|
| HABITAT TYPE _____ | HABITAT TYPE _____ |
| FACILITY _____ | FACILITY _____ |
| NATURALIST _____ | NATURALIST _____ |
| DATE _____ | DATE _____ |
| HABITAT TYPE _____ | HABITAT TYPE _____ |
| FACILITY _____ | FACILITY _____ |
| NATURALIST _____ | NATURALIST _____ |
| DATE _____ | DATE _____ |
| HABITAT TYPE _____ | HABITAT TYPE _____ |
| FACILITY _____ | FACILITY _____ |
| NATURALIST _____ | NATURALIST _____ |
| DATE _____ | DATE _____ |
| HABITAT TYPE _____ | HABITAT TYPE _____ |
| FACILITY _____ | FACILITY _____ |
| NATURALIST _____ | NATURALIST _____ |
| DATE _____ | DATE _____ |
| HABITAT TYPE _____ | HABITAT TYPE _____ |
| FACILITY _____ | FACILITY _____ |
| NATURALIST _____ | NATURALIST _____ |
| DATE _____ | DATE _____ |

NEW JERSEY
AUDUBON
SOCIETY

# HABITAT ACTIVITY LOG

NEW JERSEY
AUDUBON
SOCIETY

**NEW JERSEY AUDUBON SOCIETY'S**

## BRIDGES TO THE NATURAL WORLD

THIS ACTIVITY LOG BELONGS TO: _____

Teacher: _____

School: _____

Date of study: _____

Hours spent in the outdoors: _____

Site or area of concentration
(lawn, trees, field, schoolyard garden, etc.):

_____

List of the activities: _____

_____

_____

Date of study: _____

Signature of an administrator: _____

Teacher: _____

School: _____

Date of study: _____

Hours spent in the outdoors: _____

Site or area of concentration
(lawn, trees, field, schoolyard garden, etc.):

_____

List of the activities: _____

_____

_____

Date of study: _____

Signature of an administrator: _____

Teacher: _____

School: _____

Date of study: _____

Hours spent in the outdoors: _____

Site or area of concentration
(lawn, trees, field, schoolyard garden, etc.):

_____

List of the activities: _____

_____

_____

Date of study: _____

Signature of an administrator: _____

Teacher: _____

School: _____

Date of study: _____

Hours spent in the outdoors: _____

Site or area of concentration
(lawn, trees, field, schoolyard garden, etc.):

_____

List of the activities: _____

_____

_____

Date of study: _____

Signature of an administrator: _____

© Carol Decker

# URBAN NEIGHBORHOOD

NEW JERSEY AUDUBON SOCIETY

# URBAN NEIGHBORHOOD

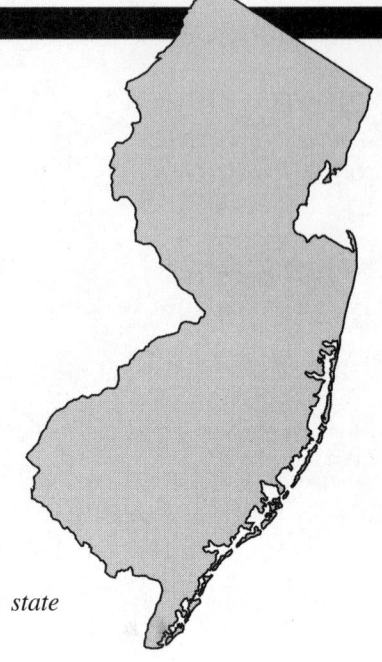

*This habitat is found throughout the state*

The high value of land in urban areas has always operated against the preservation of its natural environment. Most open space in cities is either just temporarily vacant, or it is set aside as parkland. Away from the city center, however, in outskirts not yet urban but no longer suburban, many homes have at least some space for lawns and gardens around them, and streets may be lined with trees. Despite the differences between the city center and its outskirts, there are also ecological similarities: both are intensely managed by humans, and in both there are some plants and animals that resist management.

Perhaps the biggest difference between city open spaces and truly wild areas is that almost all the herbs, shrubs, and trees in the city have been planted; or, if they are native, they have been selected by humans and allowed to remain. These plants have been chosen for beauty, ease of maintenance, ability to grow in poor soil, and resistance to air pollution. Many are non-native, and a list of plants found in a stroll around a neighborhood in the city or its outskirts might easily include species from three continents and a dozen regions. One might find European trees such as London plane, Norway maple, and linden; trees native to North America but not to New Jersey, such as blue spruce, catalpa, and honey locust; and Oriental trees such as princess tree, Japanese maple, and two living fossils, dawn redwood and gingko. Plants from western Europe and the Orient are common in horticulture because the climate of these areas is similar to ours,

> Perhaps the biggest difference between city open spaces and truly wild areas is that almost all the herbs, shrubs, and trees in the city have been planted....

and plants from them adapt well to conditions in New Jersey.

Opossum

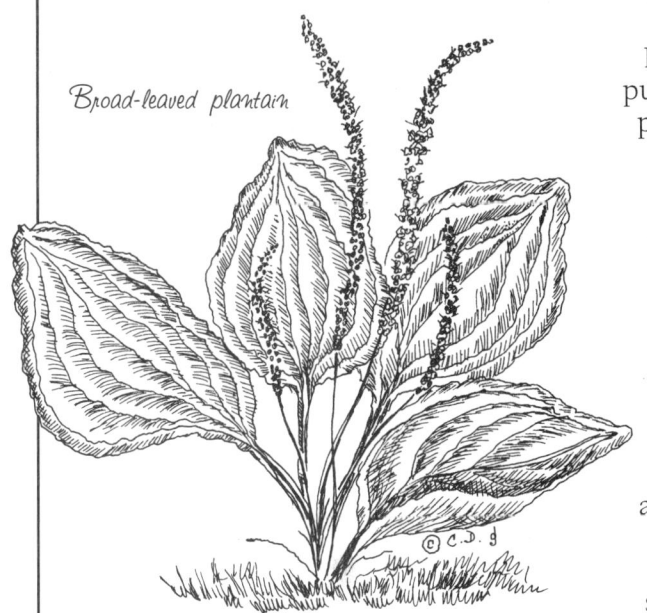

*Broad-leaved plantain*

Knotweed, purslane, and milk purslane are other, unrelated plants with a similar growth habit.

Mosses are also common in sidewalk cracks. One easily found species is silvery bryum, a very low-growing plant that looks silvery when dry. Mosses are non-flowering plants, which reproduce by spores rather than seeds. They are also nonvascular, which means that they absorb water by direct contact, rather than through the intricate system of roots and internal conduits possessed by higher plants. Even in the city center, a search of sidewalk cracks, old brickwork, tree bark, and damp soil will probably turn up several species of mosses. Lichens are another group of nonvascular organisms, but they are not very tolerant of air pollution and only a few species are found in cities. One that is, the so-called mortar lichen, appears as dark gray or yellowish smudges on old concrete; examination with a lens will usually reveal its tiny, orange-rimmed fruits.

In the city center, most open space consists of dedicated parkland, usually with considerable areas of lawn. Lawns are dominated by grasses, which unlike most plants grow upward from the base as well as at the branch tips. They can thus withstand grazing and mowing, and in fact almost any open area, if mowed or grazed regularly but not excessively, will eventually become grass-dominated. In precolonial times, there were no sizable natural grasslands in New Jersey, except for the coastal salt marshes, but early settlers introduced many grass species to serve as food for cattle. Most roadside and lawn grasses in New Jersey today are European species, including Kentucky bluegrass, the most common lawn grass. Lawns have their own complement of weeds. Many are themselves grasses, including goosegrass, sweet vernal grass, large crabgrass, small crabgrass, cheat, and annual bluegrass. Others are plants whose leaves are low-growing and able to escape an occasional mowing, including such plants as white clover, corn speedwell, English plantain, mouse-ear hawkweed, cat's-ear, and dandelion.

Wildlife is dependent on finding food, water, and

But in both the city center and its outskirts, there are some unobtrusive, weedy plants that come up despite human attempts to keep them down. Among the higher plants that occur spontaneously in fragments of open space, many are the same as those that occur in vacant lots. But high-traffic areas have a flora of their own, consisting of very low-growing, mat-forming, drought-resistant species that survive in odd corners and cracks where they are protected from trampling. Common chickweed, mouse-ear chickweed, knawel, and pearlwort are such plants. They survive by being low-growing, so that they are protected by the walls of the sidewalk cracks and crevices in which they are often found, like trees in the bottom of a canyon. Other species have a mat-forming growth habit, with creeping branches radiating in all directions from a single stem. Carpetweed is a good example; it sometimes forms mats a foot across.

suitable cover. In the city center, wildlife is scarce, except for insects, many of which can find a living anywhere. Hundreds of species of insects, as well as spiders and centipedes, can be found in any sizable piece of greenery. But perhaps the most interesting city insect is

## Wildlife is dependent on finding food, water, and suitable cover.

the much-despised cockroach. If nothing else, it deserves credit for survival ability; as a group, cockroaches have been around for about 400 million years. The usual species we see is an immigrant from Europe, which first appeared in New York City in about 1840, but there are many other kinds, including several that are native to North American forests. Like many other animal species that are

able to coexist with man, the cockroach will eat almost anything, is not too particular about where it lives, and reproduces prolifically.

Amphibians and reptiles are very scarce in the city or its outskirts. Most amphibians breed in shallow, temporary ponds, which are almost always filled in as an area becomes settled. With thin, porous skins and eggs that are protected only by a thin gelatinous covering, amphibians are also very vulnerable to water pollution, ultraviolet light, acid rain, and fungus infections, and are in decline worldwide. In city parks and suburban ponds, a few frogs might persist. Reptiles are only slightly more common. A few small, burrowing snakes, such as the brown snake, may survive in parks, cemeteries, and gardens. Ponds and streams, even if rather badly polluted, may still have a few painted, snapping, and red-eared turtles - these last being

individuals once kept as pets, or their descendents. Adult turtles are comparatively safe as long as they stay in the water, but females are subject to a variety of accidents when they leave water to seek egg-laying sites, and hatchlings, in addition, are subject to predation in water and on land. In the city center, resident bird life is limited to such species as house sparrow, starling, rock dove, and house finch, and perhaps an occasional peregrine falcon that might nest on a building ledge or bridge tower. In winter, park ponds may have waterfowl on them, and herring and ring-billed gulls may forage for food scraps at shopping malls and restaurant parking areas. But in the city

## City parkland can be of great importance, however, to migrating birds, both spring and fall, by providing places for them to feed and rest.

outskirts, or in parks that provide adequate cover and food, such hardy birds as blue jay, cardinal, American crow, mockingbird, mourning dove, robin, and house wren, and perhaps a few dozen other species, may nest, though not always successfully. Bird feeders in such places may in winter attract birds like the dark-eyed junco and white-throated sparrow that spend the summer north of us but the winter in New Jersey. City parkland can be of great importance, however, to

Japanese Maple Leaves

NEW JERSEY
AUDUBON
SOCIETY

migrating birds, both spring and fall, by providing places for them to feed and rest.

Mammal life is even less obvious than bird life. Such human commensals as the house mouse and Norway rat are everywhere, but they stay out of sight. In the outskirts of the city, such adaptable native mammals as wood-chuck, chipmunk, opossum, raccoon, and cottontail rabbit may occur. But the most obvious city mammal is the gray squirrel. Given its current abundance, it is hard to believe that, at the turn of the century, this rodent was sometimes thought to be a species that needed special protection. Gray squirrels are omnivorous, feeding on nuts, seeds, fruit, buds, and occa-sional bird's eggs or nestlings. And they are prolific; in New Jersey most female squirrels produce two litters each year, one in early spring and the other in fall, with two or three young in each. Squirrel homes are in hollow trees, which are the preferred maternity site, or in the leaf-covered stick nests that are a familiar sight among the bare tree branches of a winter landscape, in the city as well as the country.

# TYPICAL URBAN NEIGHBORHOOD SPECIES

## TREES
Princess-tree
Ailanthus
Norway maple
Japanese maple
Sugar maple
Pin oak
Willow oak
London plane
Linden
Bradford pear
Catalpa
Honey locust
Norway spruce
Blue spruce
Gingko
Chinese elm

## SHRUBS
Common privet
Forsythia
Lilac
Rose of Sharon
Japanese barberry
Japanese yew

Cardinal

## OTHER PLANTS
Goosegrass
Purslane
Galinsoga
Large crabgrass
Small crabgrass
Milk purslane
Coltsfoot
Pearlwort
Knawel
Common chickweed
Mouse-ear chickweed
English plantain
Broad-leaved plantain
Carpetweed
Knotweed
Sweet vernal grass
Cheat
Annual bluegrass
Corn speedwell
Mouse-ear hawkweed
Cat's-ear
White clover
Dandelion

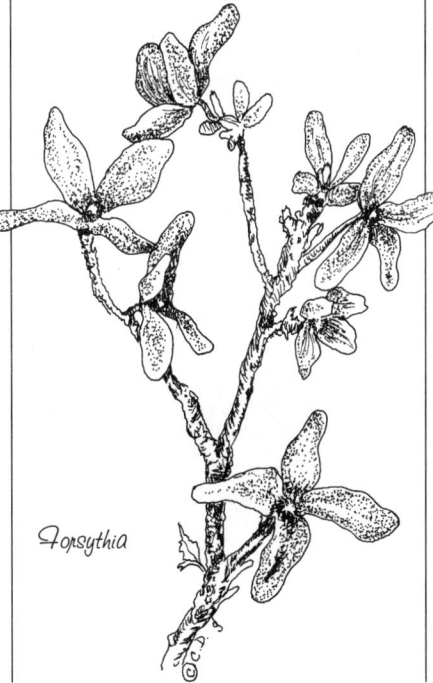

Forsythia

NEW JERSEY
AUDUBON
SOCIETY

# TYPICAL URBAN NEIGHBORHOOD SPECIES (continued)

*Carpetweed*

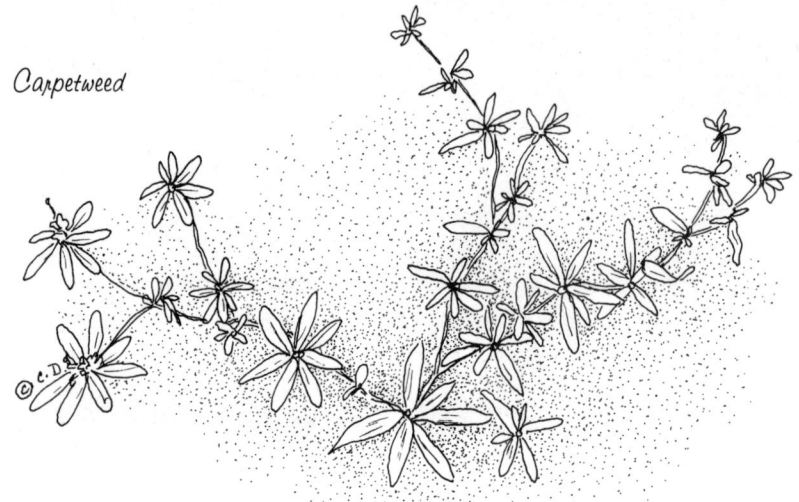

**BIRDS**
House sparrow
European starling
Rock dove
House finch
American crow
Blue jay
Northern cardinal
Song sparrow
Northern mockingbird
American robin
Mallard

**AMPHIBIANS**
Green frog
Bullfrog

**REPTILES**
Brown snake
Painted turtle
Snapping turtle
Red-eared turtle

**MAMMALS**
Norway rat
House mouse
Gray squirrel
Eastern cottontail
Chipmunk
Woodchuck
Raccoon
Opossum
Human

*Gray Squirrel*

NEW JERSEY
AUDUBON
SOCIETY

**Bridges to the Natural World**

VACANT LOT

# VACANT LOT

*This habitat is found throughout the state*

In cities and towns, there are unused open spaces, including not only abandoned building sites, but patches of soil around street trees, edges of railroad rights-of-way, unpaved strips around parking lots, and similar habitats. Although they may seem unpromising as a natural **environment**, they sometimes have surprising plant and animal diversity and provide interesting study.

Whatever their origins, these spots have a lot in common. The soil is usually quite dry, hard-packed, and very poor in **nutrients** – often it is a mix of **subsoil** and cinders, broken brick, plaster, and other construction materials. Also, individual sites may be rather small - some are only a few feet square, and rarely more than an acre or so. Urban real estate is too valuable to let large tracts stay undeveloped, unless they are dedicated as public open space. For the same reason, these sites usually have not been in existence for really long periods of time. One rarely sees large **trees** on them.

Since these sites are often well separated from each other, each site behaves almost like an island. The larger the site, the longer it has been vacant, and the closer it is to seed sources, the more diverse the **flora**. To **colonize** a vacant lot, a plant must have a very efficient means of dispersing its seeds, must be able to grow rapidly, and must be able to tolerate adverse growing conditions. Many vacant lot plants have wind-carried or bird-carried seeds and most are **annuals** or **biennials**. A disproportionate number are of foreign

---

## Since these sites are often well separated from each other, each site behaves almost like an island.

---

origin. The plants of our native forests could not survive in a vacant lot, but plants of dry **habitats** in western and southern Europe, and of the western United States do well here. Overall, about one-fifth of the 2,700 plants that have been found growing wild in New Jersey are of foreign origin. But in urban situations almost half the plants are likely to be **naturalized aliens**.

These immigrant plants came here in various ways: some are escaped garden plants, others entered as

Dandelion

©'89
Carol Decker

seeds mixed with crop seeds, or as seeds in packing material or bulk cargoes such as wool and cotton, and perhaps even in the clothes and belongings of human immigrants. A third group are **ballast plants** that entered as seeds mixed with the dirt or sand that was once used to add stabilizing weight to the hulls of sailing vessels that were sailing without a cargo. This material would have to be shovelled out when the ship arrived in port to take on cargo, and was usually used as landfill. In many cases the first sightings of these plants in New Jersey were at the ports or ballast dumps of Hoboken, Communipaw, and Camden.

Probably the most typical vacant lot tree is the ailanthus, or tree-of-Heaven, which was introduced here from China in the 1860s as a fast-growing shade tree. It grows in almost any kind of soil. In some places it grows with princess-tree, or paulownia, another oriental species. Paulownia is a big-leaved tree, which bears large clusters of purple flowers in May, and was named after princess Anna Paulovna of the Imperial Russian court. A **native** tree that often is found in vacant lots is eastern cottonwood. All of these species have wind-carried seeds. Other trees of vacant lots can include the native black cherry and the white mulberry, which was brought originally to the United States from Europe as a food source for silkworms by entrepreneurs who were trying to create an American silk industry. Both cherry and mulberry have fleshy

fruits that are eaten by birds, which then excrete the undigested seeds.

**Shrubs** are usually few in vacant lot situations, unless they are survivors from plantings. Trees, once they reach a certain size, often are allowed to grow. Shrubs are

---

During migration, however, when vacant lots may appear as green islands to passing birds, almost anything can turn up in lots that afford some cover and food.

---

usually cut back in sporadic attempts at maintenance, and they do not often have the recovery power of annuals and **perennials**. Privet, which is often used as a hedge around city yards,

sometimes survives. Shrubs that occasionally come in on their own include smooth sumac, staghorn sumac, and multiflora rose. A plant that has the aspect of a shrub, although it is not woody, is Japanese knotweed. It has hollow stems, forms dense **thickets**, and can reach a height of ten feet. This giant herb grows up from perennial roots each year and is sometimes common in vacant lots. It was originally a garden plant. Vines that can be found in this habitat include Asiatic bittersweet, poison ivy, porcelain berry, and Japanese honeysuckle. All have fruits that are eaten by birds.

Normally, the **dominant** plants in vacant lots are perennial or annual herbs. Ragweed, mugwort, annual wormwood, wild carrot, small white aster, carpetweed, purslane, common mallow, bladder campion, bouncing bet, chicory, dandelion, evening primrose, horseweed, common chickweed, smartweeds of several kinds, sow-thistles, goldenrods, white and yellow sweetclovers, Mexican tea, and pokeweed are typical **herbaceous** plants. Many kinds of grasses are present also, including large crabgrass, goosegrass, nodding and yellow foxtails,

Cabbage Butterfly

stink-grass, barnyard grass, fall panic grass, switchgrass, and common reed. Not all of these plants are found in all vacant lots, but almost any vacant lot in the northeastern United States will contain some of these plants. Many of them also are found in old fields.

Some of these plants are not without utility, and being "weeds," they usually can be picked freely. A few, including purslane, common chickweed, dandelion, and the young shoots of pokeweed, are edible. Mexican tea has been used as a **vermifuge**. The leaves of bouncing bet, or soapwort, make a green lather when rubbed in water, and once were used in laundering linen. The roots of chicory, roasted and ground, are a coffee substitute or additive. An extract of annual mugwort, a tall, aromatic plant with finely divided **foliage**, recently has been found to cure some quinine-resistant strains of malaria.

Wildlife in vacant lots is minimal. Very small sites will have none. In a truly urban setting, there will be no amphibians and reptiles,

although the brown snake, or cemetery snake, can exist in fairly built-up areas, as can the garter snake. Mammals that are truly resident include the house mouse and the Norway rat, both European species that arrived in the

## Wildlife in vacant lots is minimal.

New World with early settlers and co-exist with humans wherever they live. There are probably as many Norway rats in the United States as there are people, but they are **nocturnal** and burrowing, and adept at keeping out of sight. Their tracks, droppings, and holes may be seen. Stray cats and dogs, and perhaps an occasional gray squirrel or cottontail rabbit, make up the mammal **fauna** of most urban vacant lots.

As one might expect, resident bird life also is scarce in this habitat. Nest sites for tree or cavity-nesting

birds are few and are vulnerable to disturbance. Bird nests on the ground are subject to destruction by dogs, cats, rats, and human traffic. The house sparrow, the starling, the rock dove, and perhaps the house finch, usually can be found. They nest on ledges and in holes and crevices of buildings. Like the Norway rat and the house mouse, the house sparrow, the starling, and the rock dove were originally European species. Occasionally, where shrub thickets have developed around the edges of lots, one might find such birds as robins, mockingbirds, and song sparrows. During migration, however, when vacant lots may appear as green islands to passing birds, almost anything can turn up in lots that afford some cover and food.

One group of animals that can exist in vacant lots is the insects. Even where vegetation is sparse, one can often find ants, grasshoppers, crickets, earwigs, beetles, and butterflies, including the familiar white cabbage butterfly whose larvae feed on the foliage of members of the mustard family. A very large and showy moth, the ailanthus silkworm moth, has larvae that feed exclusively on ailanthus leaves. Other **invertebrates** that usually can be found, even in unpromising habitat, include spiders, centipedes, and isopods, or "sowbugs". Spiders and centipedes are **predators**, but sowbugs are mostly **scavengers**.

Staghorn Sumac

NEW JERSEY
AUDUBON
SOCIETY

# TYPICAL VACANT LOT SPECIES

Ailanthus
(close up)

**TREES**
Ailanthus
Princess-tree
Eastern cottonwood
Black cherry
White mulberry
Norway maple

**SHRUBS**
Smooth sumac
Staghorn sumac
Multiflora rose
Blackberry privet

**OTHER PLANTS**
Asiatic bittersweet
Japanese knotweed
Poison ivy
Japanese honeysuckle
Porcelain berry
Great ragweed
Common ragweed
Mugwort
Annual wormwood
Queen-Anne's lace
Small white aster
Carpetweed
Purslane
Common mallow
Bladder campion
Chicory
Dandelion
Evening primrose
Horseweed
Common chickweed
Nodding smartweed
Long-bristled smartweed
Lady's thumb
Common sow-thistle
Seaside goldenrod
Canada goldenrod

White sweet-clover
Yellow sweet-clover
White clover
Red clover
Pokeberry
Mexican tea
Pigweed
Camphorweed
Common plantain
Pokeweed
Black nightshade
Pilewort
Late-flowering boneset
White snakeroot
Bristly lettuce
Yellow wood sorrel

Chicory

Milk purslane
Wintercress
Shepherd's-purse
Peppergrass
Large crabgrass
Goosegrass
Nodding foxtail
Yellow foxtail
Stink-grass
Combed love-grass

Annual bluegrass
Barnyard grass
Fall panic grass
Switchgrass
Common reed

House Mouse

**MAMMALS**
House mouse
Norway rat
Cat
Dog
Human

House Sparrow

**BIRDS**
European starling
House sparrow
Rock dove
House finch
Common crow
Northern mockingbird
Mourning dove
Song sparrow
American robin

**INSECTS**
Ant
Grasshopper
Cricket
Cabbage butterfly

NEW JERSEY
AUDUBON
SOCIETY

FIELD

New Jersey Audubon Society

Bridges to the Natural World

# FIELD

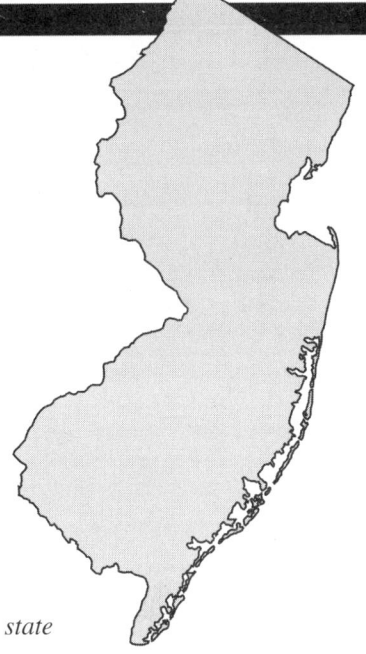

*This habitat is found throughout the state*

Before European settlement, almost all of New Jersey was wooded. The only natural openings in the forest were a few rock outcrops, the salt **marshes** along the coast, and the fresh water marshes in old lake beds and along rivers. Fires, caused by

---

## ...almost all the land in New Jersey has been cleared at one time or another, and most land has been cleared several times.

---

lightning or set by Indians to facilitate hunting and travel, created openings but did not disturb the soil. Man-made clearings were few; the Indians of New Jersey were not numerous and their villages and fields were small.

But today, almost all the land in New Jersey has been cleared at one time or anoth-

er, and most land has been cleared several times. Wherever agriculture was possible, the land has at some time been farmed, eliminating the native plant life and virtually all of the animal life. Land clearing reached its peak in New Jersey around 1850. Since then, because of the abandonment of marginal farmland and for other reasons, some once-cleared land has been reclaimed by forest, and today about 40 percent of New Jersey is wooded. Some old fields throughout the state, no longer farmed or regularly mowed, will also revert to forest.

When a piece of land is cleared, farmed, and abandoned, the first plants to appear on the bare ground grow from seeds that were already present in the soil, or that have come in from nearby areas. Usually, most of these are **annual** plants, that complete their entire life cycle from seed to fruit in one year and then die. These produce many seeds, have efficient mechanisms for seed dispersal, and thrive in full

sun. Many of these plants are of foreign origin. They were adapted to fields in Europe and have now naturalized themselves here.

The particular species of plants found in old fields vary somewhat in different parts of New Jersey, depending on soil, climate, and local seed sources. But some widespread old field annuals are mugwort, common ragweed, field camomile, pilewort, and horseweed, all of which are in the aster family, and such grasses as

*Eastern Bluebird*

NEW JERSEY
AUDUBON
SOCIETY

**Habitats of New Jersey**

nodding foxtail, yellow foxtail, and large crabgrass. When they die and decay, these plants add organic matter to the soil, improving its ability to hold water. They also stabilize the soil surface.

A few years later, **perennial** herbs begin to colonize the old field. These grow more slowly than annual plants,

At some point, perhaps ten to twenty years after the field was abandoned...maximum species diversity is reached.

and have more exacting requirements. But once established, they live for many years, growing each spring from underground parts that survive the winter. They tend to spread radially by vegetative means. By starting growth early in the spring, and by monopolizing soil nutrients and water, these perennials slowly crowd out the annuals. Some typical old field perennials include grasses like broomsedge, orchard grass, little bluestem, and tall redtop, and such other plants as wild bergamot, bush-clovers, and asters.

Goldenrods often are very common in old fields at this stage of **succession**. There are 29 species in New Jersey, but many are woodland plants. The common species in fields are Canada golden-rod, with obvious three-veined leaves; rough-stemmed

goldenrod, with net-veined leaves and a hairy stem; and lance-leaved goldenrod, with a flat-topped flower cluster and very narrow leaves. Despite their reputation, goldenrods usually do not induce hay fever. They are insect-pollinated and produce sticky pollen which does not blow around very much. It is ragweed and late-summer grasses, which are wind pollinated and produce

copious amounts of very fine, dry pollen, that are to blame for most allergies.

Mixed with the perennials in the old field may be **biennials** such as wild carrot, common mullein, and wintercress. These plants finish a life cycle in two years. They develop a strong root system and basal leaves the first year; they flower and fruit the following year, and die. Wild carrot, also called

Red Maple

Queen-Anne's lace and bird's-nest plant, is the ancestor of our domestic carrot. Wintercress, a bitter-tasting yellow-flowered mustard, can turn an old field to a sheet of gold in early spring.

By about ten years after the field has been abandoned, woody plants will have made their appearance. These of course are also perennials, but they have above-ground parts, and not just roots, that persist from year to year. They grow from seeds brought in by wind, water, and animals from nearby woodlands. Again, the species vary somewhat with location within the state, and with the composition of nearby forests.

A few shrubs that fall into this category include arrow-wood, multiflora rose, staghorn and smooth sumac, and several species of blackberries. Red cedar is one tree that often grows abundantly in old fields at this stage of succession. Others include red maple, black cherry, quaking and bigtooth aspen, and gray birch. On southern New Jersey's inner coastal plain, and on the outer coastal plain around the edges of the Pine Barrens, sweet gum, Virginia pine, and persimmon often are found. At some point, perhaps ten to twenty years after the field was abandoned, when annuals, biennials, perennials, shrubs, and small trees are all present in the field, maximum **species diversity** is reached.

By shading the soil surface, trees and shrubs eliminate sun-loving annuals and perennials in their vicinity. But the seedlings of most of these woody plants are not themselves tolerant of shade. As the **pioneer trees** form a closed **canopy**, other trees, whose seedlings can thrive in shade, begin to establish themselves. These eventually displace many of the pioneer trees, forming a forest in which changes are slow and the species mix relatively constant over long periods of time, providing the climate stays the same and barring the occurrence of diseases like the chestnut blight. This is the so-called **climax forest**.

The process of change, by which the final vegetation on a site develops, is called plant succession. The full time, from empty, bare field to a superficially mature forest, varies greatly from site to site depending on such factors as soil fertility, moisture, and the availability of seed sources. But a fair guess on most New Jersey sites is a hundred years or so. Even then, the full **diversity** of plant and animal life that was present in the pre-European forest will not be re-established. Some species take more than a century to become established. Others are **extinct**.

Each stage in this process will have its own associated set of animals; and as the vegetation changes more or less gradually, so will the wildlife. The almost bare field might have such nesting species as grasshopper sparrow, horned lark, and field sparrow. A few years later, when a cover of perennial grasses and young shrubs has formed, these species

All cleared land in New Jersey, if not built upon or artificially managed to benefit old-field species, will undergo succession and eventually revert to forest.

might be replaced by goldfinches, bobolinks, eastern meadowlarks, song sparrows, and northern bobwhite. Still later, when shrubs and young trees become well established, indigo buntings, common yellowthroats, gray catbirds, and mockingbirds

NEW JERSEY
AUDUBON
SOCIETY

will be common. And in turn, these will be replaced eventually by birds of the forest, such as scarlet tanagers, red-eyed vireos, black-and-white warblers, great crested flycatchers, and ruffed grouse.

The change in wildlife with the change in plant cover is perhaps most noticeable when one considers the change in bird life. But the same process affects mammals, reptiles, and insects. In the earlier stages of succession, some mammals of the old field include meadow voles, cottontail rabbits, woodchucks, red foxes, and jumping mice. But as the field grows to forest, these animals are replaced by white-tailed deer, opossums, gray foxes, white-footed mice, gray squirrels, and other forest creatures. Reptiles of the old field include garter snake, brown snake, and smooth green snake, but with time, species like the ring-necked snake and black racer will appear. The butterflies and wasps that were abundant in the sunny, open meadow, can no longer find their food plants, and they will be replaced by a new set of insects. The process is inevitable, although it varies in detail from site to site. All cleared land in New Jersey, if not built upon or artificially managed to benefit old-field species, will undergo succession and eventually revert to forest.

# TYPICAL FIELD SPECIES

## TREES
Black cherry
White mulberry
Red maple
Quaking aspen
Bigtooth aspen
Eastern cottonwood
Gray birch
Ailanthus
Red cedar
Black locust
Sweet gum
Virginia pine
  (southern New Jersey only)
Persimmon
  (southern New Jersey only)

Blackberry

## SHRUBS
Arrowwood
Multiflora rose
Staghorn sumac
Smooth sumac
Blackberry
Panicled dogwood
Silky dogwood

## OTHER PLANTS
Canada goldenrod
Rough-stemmed golden-
  rod
Grass-leaved goldenrod
Small white aster
Bushy aster
Heath aster
Broomsedge
Little bluestem

Timothy
Orchard grass
Switchgrass
Petticoat-climber
Nodding foxtail
Yellow foxtail
Tall redtop
Wild carrot
Common mullein
Chicory
Yarrow
Field thistle
Bull thistle
Canada thistle
Mugwort
Common ragweed
Great ragweed
Pilewort
Late-flowering boneset
Wintercress
Field camomile
Tree-seeded mercury
Dogbane
Red clover
Wild radish
Goat's beard
Lamb's quarters

Broom Sedge ©C.D.

# TYPICAL FIELD SPECIES (continued)

**REPTILES**
Garter snake
Smooth green snake
   (northern New Jersey only)

**BIRDS**
American kestrel
Ring-necked pheasant
Northern bobwhite
Upland sandpiper

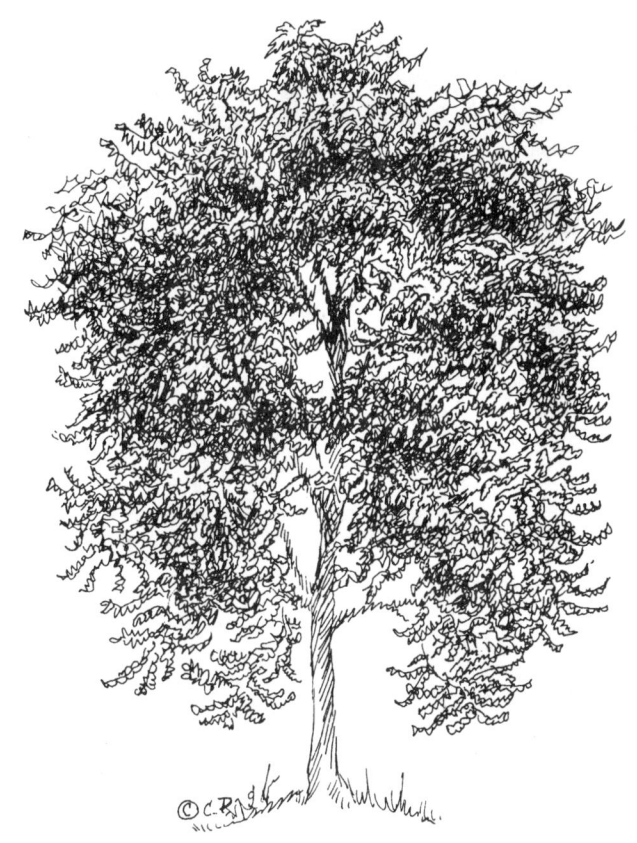

*Ailanthus*

*Eastern Meadowlark*

Killdeer
Mourning dove
Horned lark
Eastern bluebird
Yellow-breasted chat
Common yellowthroat
Indigo bunting
Field sparrow
Chipping sparrow
Song sparrow
Vesper sparrow
Bobolink
Eastern meadowlark
American goldfinch

**MAMMALS**
Eastern cottontail rabbit
Meadow vole
Meadow jumping mouse
Woodchuck
Red fox

*Eastern Cottontail Rabbit*

POND AND LAKE

Bridges to the Natural World

# POND AND LAKE

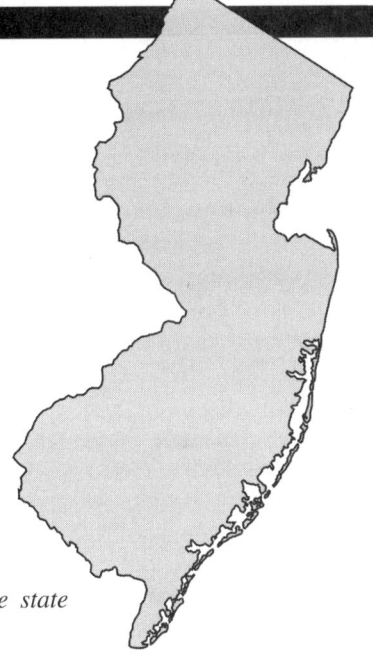

*This habitat is found throughout the state*

There are over 800 ponds and lakes in New Jersey. Some are natural, but the majority are man-made. Of those that are natural, almost all are in northern New Jersey and were created by glacial action during the last ice age, some 15,000 years ago, as **glaciers** deepened valleys parallel to their line of advance, dammed streams with rocks and earth, and left huge ice blocks embedded in the soil to form **kettle hole** ponds. Man-made ponds and lakes include reservoirs and recreational lakes formed by damming streams, ponds built by farmers to provide water for irrigation and livestock, mill ponds, and ponds that form in abandoned quarries and clay and sand pits.

Ponds and lakes are alike in being essentially non-moving water, although small ponds created by damming streams often will have a perceptible flow through them. One technical difference between ponds and lakes is that ponds are shallow enough that

---

### Sixteen species of frogs and toads and eighteen species of salamanders occur in New Jersey...

---

rooted **aquatic** vegetation can survive on the entire bottom. Lakes have some parts too deep and dark for aquatic vegetation. The depth at which this occurs varies with water quality, being less in **turbid** water than in clear water. In ponds, because of their limited water volume, water temperature parallels that of the air. In lakes, the bottom waters stay cooler in summer and warmer in winter than surface waters. Dissolved oxygen content is more variable, both daily and seasonally, in ponds than in lakes. Small ponds may freeze to the bottom in winter; lakes do not.

But these **habitats** often merge into each other. Almost all lakes, and many streams and rivers, have sun-warmed shallows and bays, rich with aquatic life, in which conditions are pond-like. Marshes, with **emergent vegetation**, may form in shallows along the shore. In somewhat deeper water, plants with floating leaves, like pond lily and

*Bullfrog*    ©CD.

water shield, may be abundant. Farther from shore one finds aquatic plants that grow completely submerged, although many have flowers, and perhaps a few leaves, that are raised to the surface. Plants in this category include the pondweeds, of which there are 24 **species** in New Jersey; water stargrass, a plant with narrow, somewhat grasslike leaves that bears star-shaped yellow flowers; water milfoil; and wild celery, or *Vallisneria*, which has female flowers that reach the surface on a long stem, but male flowers that break free and float.

Some plants can grow in even deeper water, and do not reach the surface. Among these are elodea, fanwort, water-weed, and hornwort. There are also free-floating aquatics like duckweed, which forms a green layer on quiet, nutrient-rich ponds. Another group of free-floating plants are the water-meals, or wolffias. These are New Jersey's smallest flowering plants, and each consists of a tiny oval plant body less than one sixteenth of an inch long. Despite their individual small size, water-meals, like duck-weeds, can completely cover the surface of small ponds.

By far the most numerous animal inhabitants of the underwater world are the insects and their **larvae**. Almost any collection will include larvae of damselflies and dragonflies. Although these insects are rather closely related, damselfly larvae are slender-bodied and have three leaf-shaped gills projecting from the end of the abdomen, while dragonfly larvae are chunky and lack the gills.

---

## By far the most numerous animal inhabitants of the underwater world are the insects and their larvae.

---

Both kinds of larvae are **predators**, feeding on almost anything of reasonable size. They catch food by means of an extensible, hooked lower lip, or labium. Adult dragon-flies and damselflies feed on small flying insects such as mosquitoes and gnats, which

they capture in the air. Drag-onflies hold their wings extended horizontally when they alight whereas damsel-flies fold their wings above the abdomen.

Other common insects in this habitat are the water boatmen, medium-sized true bugs, with long legs modified into oar-like structures for swimming. Water scorpions, which despite the name are not related to **terrestrial** scorpions, are thin-bodied, long-legged insects. They have grasping front legs like the praying mantis, with which they catch insect **prey**. The largest insect of the pond is the giant water bug, a two-inch long predator that feeds not only on other insects but on tadpoles and small fish. Some other often-seen insects include water striders, also predatory, which walk on the surface film, upheld by surface tension;

©Carol Decker

backswimmers, that swim submerged and upside-down; and the black, shiny whirligig beetles that swim in arcs at the water surface. Whirligig beetles have eyes that are divided horizontally, so that in effect they have four eyes, one pair for looking up and one pair for looking down into the water. Most of these insect groups contain numerous species that are identifiable only by microscopic characteristics.

There are a variety of miscellaneous creatures of other groups that are common in ponds. Leeches of several species often are found, either free-swimming among vegetation or attached to rocks or the shells of turtles. Crayfish stalk the underwater world. They eat almost any kind of animal food. The fresh water **isopod**, *Asellus*, is a **scavenger**. In late summer, football-sized translucent colonies of the **bryozoan**, *Pectinatella*, may be found attached to submerged branches. There are many kinds of worms. There are several species of **mollusks**, including freshwater clams and snails of several species and various shapes. Of course, there are fish in ponds. Some of the species often visible from shore include: pumpkinseed, which has a bright red spot on each gill cover, bluegill sunfish, largemouth bass, and bullhead catfish. Eels are common, but are **nocturnal**. Young chain pickerel often hide in the weed beds, from which they venture forth to prey on passing insects and small fish.

Amphibians and their larvae are likely to be numerous in the pond. Sixteen species of

frogs and toads and eighteen species of salamanders occur in New Jersey, and most of them frequent pond edges for breeding. The distinctive calls of frogs and toads are made only by the males, and they serve to attract females to breeding areas. Salamanders are voiceless. Frog tadpoles are big-headed and initially legless, with internal gills, and are scavengers and **herbivores**, feeding mostly on green **algae**. Salamander larvae have external gills, functional legs, and are predators. Identification of species of larval amphibians is difficult, but possible, with the help of technical manuals.

Turtles are the most typical reptiles of ponds and lakes. We have thirteen species in New Jersey, and all but two or three are inhabitants of ponds and lakes, at least seasonally. Some idea of the extent to which a species is adapted for swimming can be gotten by looking at the hind feet. Species like the spotted turtle favor shallow water; hence, it

---

## Most natural ponds in New Jersey that were not ice-formed were created by beavers.

---

has almost unwebbed feet. The feet of really aquatic species like the painted turtle are modified into broad, heavily-webbed paddles.

Few mammals are truly at home in this habitat. One exception is the beaver. Once **extinct** in New Jersey, it has been reintroduced and is now almost too numerous. Most

natural ponds in New Jersey that were not ice-formed were created by beavers. Observers by a beaver pond will sooner or later see the animals, especially at dawn or dusk. The river otter occurs in New Jersey, but it is seldom seen. Muskrats may frequent the marshes around pond and lake margins, but rarely venture out into open water.

Relatively few birds are seen on open water in New Jersey ponds and lakes during the breeding season. Ospreys hunt over inland waters, especially during fall and spring, but during summer, our ospreys are found mostly along the coast. The same pattern holds for water birds. During migration, and in winter, many are found in New Jersey. These include common and red-throated loons, pied-billed and horned grebes, double-crested cormorant, American coot, ring-billed gull, Canada goose, mute swan, tundra swan, and about twenty-nine species of ducks. But of these, only the Canada goose, mute swan (which is not a **native** species), American coot, pied-billed grebe, and mallard, black, and wood ducks nest regularly on New Jersey ponds and lakes.

NEW JERSEY
AUDUBON
SOCIETY

# TYPICAL POND AND LAKE SPECIES

**PLANTS**
Pond lily
White water lily
Water shield
Ten-angled pipewort
Bayonet rush
Floating bladderwort
Curly pondweed
Water stargrass
Water milfoil
Wild celery
Fanwort
Water-weed
Hornwort
Greater duckweed
Lesser duckweed
Water-meal

**INSECTS**
Damselfly
Dragonfly
Water boatman
Backswimmer
Water strider
Water scorpion
Water measurer
Giant water bug
Whirligig beetle
Diving beetle
Water scavenger beetle
Mayfly
Blackfly

**OTHER ORGANISMS**
Pond crayfish
Asellus
Freshwater clam

Pectinatella
Orb snail
Left-handed pond snail
Leech
Flatworm

**FISH**
Pumpkinseed
Bluegill sunfish
Largemouth bass
Smallmouth bass
Carp
Brown bullhead
Chain pickerel
American eel
Common shiner
Golden shiner

**AMPHIBIANS**
Bullfrog
Green frog
Southern leopard frog
Pickerel frog
Spotted salamander
Red-spotted newt
Two-lined salamander

**REPTILES**
Snapping turtle
Musk turtle
Mud turtle
Painted turtle
Red-bellied turtle
Spotted turtle
Northern water snake

**MAMMALS**
Beaver
River Otter
Muskrat

Mute Swan

**BIRDS**
Common loon
Red-throated loon
Pied-billed grebe
Horned grebe
Mute swan
Tundra swan
Mallard
American black duck
Northern pintail
Blue-winged teal
American wigeon
Ring-necked duck
Bufflehead
Hooded merganser
Common merganser
American coot
Belted kingfisher
Double-crested cormorant
Ring-billed gull
Osprey

Water Strider

Painted Turtle

River Otter

© Carol Decker

# RIVER AND STREAM

# RIVER AND STREAM

*This habitat is found throughout the state*

Fast-flowing streams are common in northern New Jersey's **uplands**, and are found also, though much less often, in southern New Jersey. They occupy a tiny percentage of the state's area, but they loom large in aesthetic appeal. The plants, animals, and overall ecology of these waters generally are similar to those of ponds and lakes, but there are many differences in detail. Creatures of moving water must have a means of attachment, or a means of responding to water flow, that will prevent them from being swept downstream by the current. Fish that are typical of moving waters often instinctively face into the current and swim against it to stay in place. With some species this can be demonstrated convincingly in an aquarium. Many insects, insect **larvae**, freshwater clams, worms, and other **invertebrates** solve the problem of staying in place by either burrowing into the stream bed, or anchoring themselves, sometimes

permanently, to rocks and other fixed objects. Many creatures seek both shelter and calm water between and under streambed rocks, tree roots, and submerged logs.

Oxygen content is high in moving streams, partly because the agitated, shallow water exposes a large surface to the air, partly because

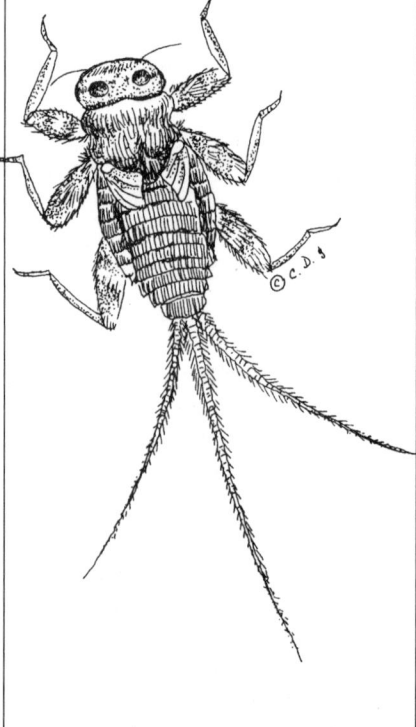

*Mayfly Nymph*

oxygen-consuming **organic** debris is washed away, and partly because the water is cold. Cold water dissolves gases more readily than warm

---

Streams, unlike shallow ponds, usually remain unfrozen and highly oxygenated during the winter.

---

water. Streams, unlike shallow ponds, usually remain unfrozen and highly oxygenated during the winter. But on the other hand, many small streams dry up, at least partly, during the summer months. The mere fact that a stream is clear and cool does not mean that the water is safe to drink. **Toxic** chemicals, heavy metals, **pathogenic** bacteria, and a variety of **amoeboid** and **protozoan parasites** or their eggs and cysts could be present in almost any water. One widespread protozoan, *Giardia*, causes "beaver fever" or giardiasis, an occasionally-

NEW JERSEY
AUDUBON
SOCIETY

© Carol Decker

fatal disease characterized by long-lasting intestinal distress and fever.

Few rooted plants can become established in fast-flowing streams, except in **backwaters** and other places where the current slows and deposits of sand and gravel can accumulate. Here the plant life is much the same as in ponds and lakes, with such species as wild celery, fanwort, pondweeds, and water stargrass. One plant that is somewhat typical of moving water is watercress, a European member of the mustard family that has become thoroughly established here. It sometimes forms dense beds along the edges of small streams, providing good **habitat** for small **vertebrates** and invertebrates. Water starwort, a rooted plant with small, floating leaves, is found often. Water carpet, with

oval, opposite leaves and tiny four-petalled flowers, grows where water trickles over rocks. Threadfoot, a rubbery, much-branched plant that looks more like a marine **alga** than the flowering plant it is, attaches to submerged rocks by holdfast-like roots.

Mosses and other **non-vascular** plants often are abundant, however. The

---

By far the most visible life forms in most streams are the invertebrates, from worms and leeches to insects.

---

willow-moss, *fontinalis*, may coat submerged rocks and send long streamers out into the current. Sphagnum mosses are common along the

banks of many small steams. These are usually different **species** from those found in Pine Barrens cedar **swamps** or northern **bogs**. Liverworts, relatives of mosses, but with a slightly different life cycle, can be found, sometimes covering streamside rocks.

By far the most visible life forms in most streams are the invertebrates, from worms and leeches to insects. Planarians, famous for their ability to regenerate lost body parts, can be found clinging to the undersides of rocks. Several kinds of leeches occur. Most are **predators** or **scavengers**, although a few feed on vertebrate blood. Crayfish hide under rocks during the day, emerging at night to feed. The larvae of blackflies attach themselves to rocks and submerged wood by means of minute barbs on the end of the abdomen. They may occur in enormous numbers. The larvae of dragonflies, damselflies, and beetles are frequent, as they are in pond habitats. Caddis fly larvae usually build protective tubes, or "cases" around themselves. These tubes are made from sand grains or bits of wood or algae cemented together with silk. The cases vary in size, shape, and material depending on the species of caddis fly that made them. The larvae of alder flies, and the related dobson flies, are big-headed, many-legged, grub-like creatures which may reach a length of several inches. Stonefly and mayfly larvae are long-tailed. Stonefly larvae have two tails, mayflies have two or three, and both are often abundant in non-polluted streams.

NEW JERSEY
AUDUBON
SOCIETY

All of these insects and larvae are important foods for fish, the best known, even if not the most abundant, stream inhabitants. New Jersey has only one native trout, the brook trout, and it still survives in some New Jersey streams. Rainbow trout and brown trout have been introduced. White suckers, and northern hog suckers, are found in some streams. These fish forage on the streambed for insect larvae and other animal food. A variety of small fish, including river chub, satinfin shiner, common shiner, creek chub, and blacknose dace, fill intermediate positions in the food chain. They are big enough to eat insects, but small enough to be eaten by trout. Darters, small fish in the perch family, live up to their name. Small and **camouflaged**, they sit quietly until approached, then dart away, faster than the eye can follow. American eels sometimes ascend small streams. They are **nocturnal**. When small streams dry up in summer, most fish retreat to the few pools that still remain.

An occasional ribbon snake or garter snake, and perhaps a turtle or two, might be seen along a small stream. But the only reptile really typical of the habitat is the northern water snake. This medium-sized, dark brown snake often can be found around driftwood piles and around shallows and waterfalls, where it finds easy prey among fish that get trapped in small pools. Water snakes can eat surprisingly large, spiny-finned fish, swallowing them whole and

head-first. It is interesting to watch one of them shift a slippery, struggling fish into position for swallowing. The technique is at least partly learned. Very young water snakes are inept at it.

Amphibians are somewhat more abundant. Bullfrogs, green frogs, and leopard frogs often are common. Salamanders found in streams or among the dripping moss of the stream banks include the two-lined salamander, northern red salamander, dusky salamander, mountain

---

New Jersey has only one native trout, the brook trout, and it still survives in some New Jersey streams.

---

dusky salamander, and occasionally the spring salamander. These are all lungless salamanders. They obtain oxygen through their moist skin and mouth lining. It is thought that this is an adaptation for life in moving water, where the added buoyancy created by air-filled lungs would make it difficult for a small animal like a salamander to remain in place when submerged. Of course, it also limits the distribution of these creatures to well-oxygenated, wet habitats. Eastern North America has more species of lungless salamanders than any other geographic region in the world.

Mammals are not especially typical of this habitat. Where beavers occur, this oversized rodent often disrupts stream

flow by building dams, and making beaver ponds. This creates habitat for some species and destroys it for others. Most other mammals here occur along the stream, rather than in it, and they include raccoon, mink, and occasionally otter, all of which seek food in and around the water.

Birds are likewise not really tied to this habitat. We have no eastern equivalent of the western dipper, which walks under water in the fastest streams, finding food on the bottom. The Louisiana waterthrush does nest along fast-moving streams, in moss-lined holes in the banks and under tree roots. It does not submerge to find food, but instead walks, teetering, along the banks and shallows looking for insects. The unrelated spotted sandpiper, one of New Jersey's very few nesting shorebirds, also feeds along the shallows, and also teeters. Belted kingfishers and green-backed herons find food in streams, and swallows often course low over the water, especially when insect larvae are hatching. The maiden flight of newly emerged mayflies and stoneflies is often their last.

# TYPICAL RIVER AND STREAM SPECIES

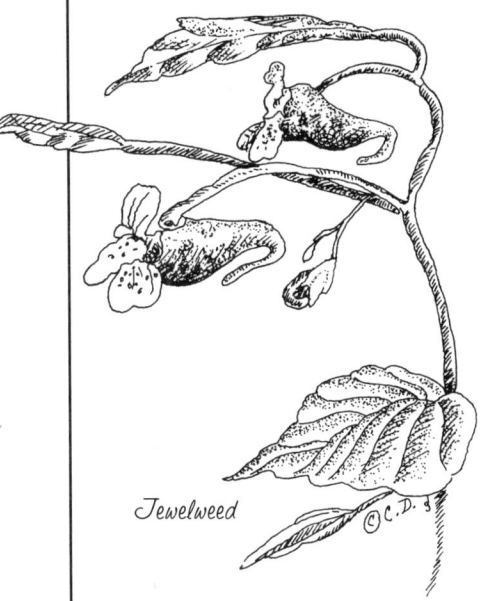

Jewelweed

**PLANTS**
Water starwort
Threadfoot
Watercress
Water carpet
Curly pondweed
Water stargrass
Water milfoil
Wild celery
Fanwort
Water-weed
Hornwort
Sphagnum moss
Willow moss

**INSECTS**
Damselfly
Dragonfly
Water boatman
Backswimmer
Water strider
Water scorpion
Water measurer

Giant water bug
Whirligig beetle
Diving beetle
Water scavenger beetle
Mayfly
Stonefly
Blackfly
Caddis fly
Dobson fly
Alder fly

Crayfish

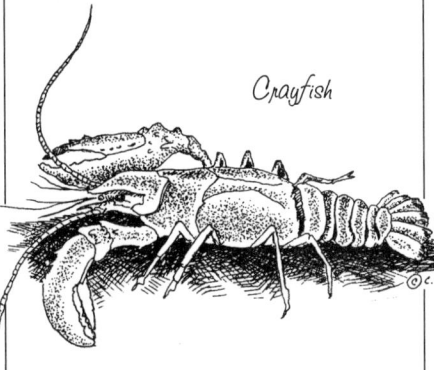

**OTHER ORGANISMS**
Brook crayfish
Leech
Fresh-water sponge
Planarian
Isopod

**FISH**
Brook trout
Rainbow trout
Brown trout
White sucker
Northern hog sucker
River chub
Satinfin shiner
Common shiner
Creek chub
Blacknose dace
Fantail darter
Tesselated darter
American eel

**AMPHIBIANS**
Bullfrog
Green frog
Southern leopard frog

Pickerel frog
Two-lined salamander
Northern red salamander
Spring salamander
Dusky salamander
Mountain dusky
   salamander

**REPTILES**
Northern water snake
Ribbon snake
Wood turtle

**MAMMALS**
Beaver
Mink
River otter
Raccoon

**BIRDS**
Louisiana waterthrush
Northern waterthrush
Spotted sandpiper
Belted kingfisher
Mallard
Barn swallow
Bank swallow
Rough-winged swallow
Green Heron

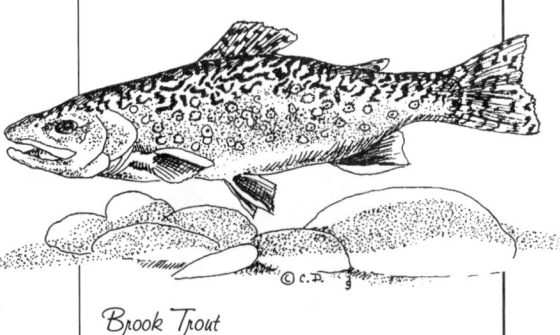

Brook Trout

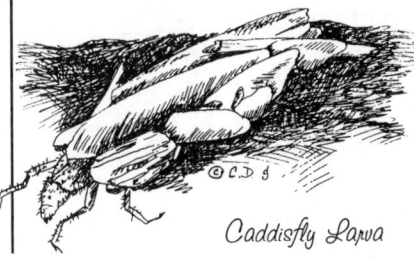

Caddisfly Larva

NEW JERSEY
AUDUBON
SOCIETY

© Carol Decker
'91

# FRESHWATER MARSH

NEW JERSEY
AUDUBON
SOCIETY

Bridges to the Natural World

# FRESHWATER MARSH

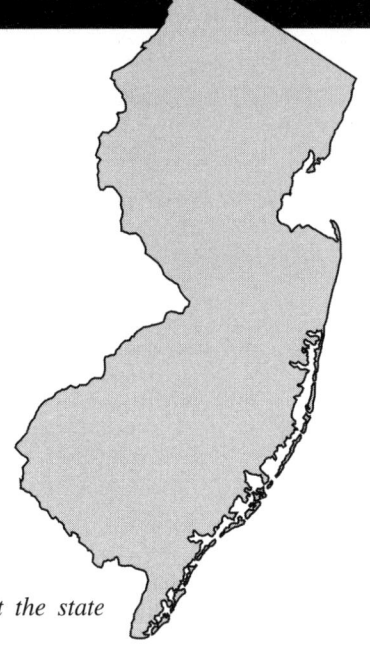

*This habitat is found throughout the state*

Marshes are permanently wet areas with a cover of non-woody vegetation. They can form in almost any shallow depression that is kept wet by streams or **groundwater**. They are found along the shallow edges of ponds and lakes, in old lake beds and abandoned beaver ponds, and along streams in places where the water table is high year-round. In southern New Jersey, most large freshwater marshes are tidal, having formed along rivers that are affected by ocean tides at their mouth. Like salt marshes, and for much the same reasons, freshwater marshes are extremely productive, converting water, sunlight, and minerals to **biomass** at rates much higher than in most dry **ecosystems**.

Marshes differ from swamps by being wet year-round, even if only for a few hours each day or a few days each month, and by being essentially treeless. But marshes, swamps, ponds, and streams often are found together and cannot always be clearly delineated. In some cases, marshes are a **successional** stage. Most ponds, for example, eventually fill completely with **organic** matter and soil and are no longer wet enough to support wetland vegetation, becoming first marshes, then swamps, and finally forests. All of these stages of pond succession sometimes can be seen simultaneously on one site, where open water is surrounded by marsh, while trees and shrubs like black willow, American elder, and smooth alder encroach on the wetland at the drier edges.

Perhaps the most characteristic and best known plant of the typical, unpolluted

---

*…freshwater marshes are extremely productive, converting water, sunlight, and minerals to biomass at rates much higher than in most dry ecosystems.*

---

freshwater marsh is the broad-leaved cattail, which is almost a symbol for the **habitat**. It is one of two New Jersey cattail **species**, the other being the narrow-leaved cattail. The familiar brown "tails" are composed of thousands of tiny female flowers, each consisting of an ovary and six hair-like petals and **sepals**. Early in the season, these

*Blue Flag Iris*

NEW JERSEY
AUDUBON
SOCIETY

spikes of female flowers are surmounted by thinner spikes containing only male flowers, which disintegrate after shedding their pollen to the winds.

Another very abundant marsh plant is common reed, or phragmites, a very tall, feathery-topped grass that grows rapidly, spreads via a fast-growing and wide-ranging network of underground stems, and is almost impossible to eradicate. It is most typical of wetlands that have been somewhat degraded, usually by human activities. It can tolerate disturbance, salinity, and fluctuations in water level better than most wetland plants. Phragmites grows almost world-wide, and it is **native** to North America, but apparently it was not common in New Jersey until the end of the nineteenth century. It has expanded its range tremendously in the last hundred years, for reasons not completely understood.

Many other plants are found in New Jersey's freshwater marshes. Purple loosestrife, a native of Europe, is common in many marshes and makes a lovely sight when it blooms in late summer. Unfortunately, it is **invasive**, and like phragmites tends to crowd out other marsh vegetation. Broad-leaved arrowhead, pickerelweed, bur-reed, and pond lily are emergent plants, growing up from the bottom of shallow water. Swamp loosestrife, larger blue flag, arrow-leaved and halberd-leaved tearthumbs, rice cutgrass, and many species of sedges and rushes can be found around the edges of the marsh.

Humans have obtained food directly from marsh plants. Rice and taro, for instance, are both marsh plants, but neither can grow in New Jersey. Locally, the arrow arum, or tuckahoe as it was called by the Lenape, is common in many New Jersey marshes. The Indians of southern New Jersey used

---

Perhaps the most characteristic and best known plant of the typical, unpolluted freshwater marsh is the broad-leaved cattail.

---

both its starchy roots and its seeds as food. Both roots and seeds are poisonous when fresh, and must be treated before being eaten. The central, white leaves of cattail

are edible, and a flour of sorts can be made, with great labor, from the roots. Broad-leaved arrowhead produces edible starchy tubers on its roots in the late summer. None of these plants is likely to show up on the shelves of the neighborhood supermarket, but wild rice, the seeds of a very tall annual grass that is sometimes abundant in southern New Jersey's tidal freshwater marshes, can be bought. It is expensive! Wild rice is not very closely related to ordinary rice.

The most typical mammal of the marsh is the muskrat, which is well adapted to the habitat. These rodents live in burrows, or in lodges made of marsh plants piled high above the waterline. They feed on vegetation, particularly the roots and stems of cattail, but they also eat fish and freshwater mussels. Muskrats are **preyed** upon by mink, another mammal well-adapted to life in the wetland, and sometimes by otters. The fact that a female muskrat can produce three sets of young each year, with four to nine in each litter, helps maintain the species. One other native mammal that regularly frequents marshes is the raccoon, which finds much of its food in and around water.

Bird life in and around the marsh is often abundant and varied. Where there is open water, ducks such as mallards, wood ducks, and blue-winged teal will stop to feed and perhaps to nest. Herons and egrets are likely to be seen feeding around the marsh edges, but few of them will nest. One exception is the green-backed heron, which builds its platform-shaped

nest in alders and other shrubs, or occasionally on the top of a muskrat lodge. The least bittern, smallest of our herons, builds its nest in similar situations, but the larger American bittern builds a nest on marsh vegetation on the ground. Other marsh birds include Virginia and sora rails, which are likely to be found in larger marshes statewide. Common moorhens are related to rails, and they are expected residents of large marshes with permanent open water. They build their nests of dead cattails and stems of **aquatic** plants in clumps of emergent vegetation.

Other marsh-nesting birds include marsh wrens, which build globular nests around the stems of cattail, and yellow warblers, which nest in willow and alder thickets. But by far the most noticeable songbird of the marsh is the red-winged blackbird. In summer and spring, the males may be seen perched on vegetation, spreading their wings to expose the red **epaulets**. This display, accompanied by song, advertises territorial claims to rival males. Red-wing nests are built of cattail leaves, sedges, grasses, and roots, and are placed in shrubs or among cattail stems. The nests are built completely by the female, a smaller, streaked bird that lacks the red epaulets of the male red-wing. She also incubates the eggs, and does most feeding of the nestlings.

Reptiles can be reasonably common in this habitat. If the marsh includes or adjoins permanent open water, the dense emergent vegetation is

likely to shelter snapping, musk, mud, painted, and perhaps spotted turtles. In northern New Jersey, the wood turtle, a **threatened species** in the state, is sometimes found in marshes. In the **riverine** marshes of southern New Jersey, the big red-bellied turtle often can be seen basking on logs and muskrat lodges. In both north and south, northern water snakes are likely to be found in almost any marsh. Two other snakes that often find food in and near water, the garter snake and the ribbon snake, can be found also. As one might expect, these snakes feed primarily on fish and frogs.

Amphibians are also common in this habitat. Even marshes that do not have standing water in them year-round are likely to have several species of frogs, toads, and salamanders around them. The animals either leave the marsh if it dries, or they burrow into the wet mud to await better times. But marshes that do contain standing water for most of the year are likely to have many more species, especially if there are no **predatory** fish in the water. Fourteen species of frogs and toads occur in New Jersey outside of the Pinelands, and many of them can be found in marshes. The song of the

diminutive spring peeper is one of the first signs of spring, and the strident call of the bullfrog, North America's largest frog, can be heard throughout the summer. Salamanders also frequent marshes. One that is seen year-round is the red-spotted newt, an olive-green aquatic species with two rows of red **dorsal** spots. Others can be found, especially during the spring breeding season.

Green Heron

NEW JERSEY AUDUBON SOCIETY

**Habitats of New Jersey**

# TYPICAL FRESHWATER MARSH SPECIES

### TREES
Black willow
Weeping willow
Pin oak
Sycamore
River birch
Box elder
Red maple

### SHRUBS
Smooth alder
Buttonbush
Common elder
Winterberry
Pussy willow
Highbush blueberry
Silky dogwood
Arrowwood

### OTHER PLANTS
Broad-leaved cattail
Narrow-leaved cattail
Reed
Wild rice
Blue-joint grass
Reed canary grass
Rice cutgrass

Tussock sedge
Sallow sedge
Woolgrass
Dark-green bulrush
Great bulrush
Common rush
Broad-leaved arrowhead
Pickerelweed
Bur-reed
Pond lily
Swamp loosestrife
Larger blue flag
Swamp milkweed
Spotted Joe-pye weed
Boneset
Purple loosestrife
Arrow-leaved tearthumb
Halberd-leaved
tearthumb
Water willow
New York ironweed
Blue vervain
Sweet flag
Arrow arum
Water hemlock
Marsh fern
Sensitive fern

### REPTILES
Snapping turtle
Musk turtle
Mud turtle
Painted turtle
Spotted turtle
Wood turtle
Red-bellied turtle
Northern water snake
Garter snake
Ribbon snake

### AMPHIBIANS
Spring peeper
Northern cricket frog
Gray treefrog
Bullfrog
Pickerel frog
Green frog
Red-spotted newt
Northern red salamander
Four-toed salamander

### MAMMALS
Muskrat
Mink
River otter
Beaver

*Muskrat*

### BIRDS
Mallard
Wood duck
Blue-winged teal
Great blue heron
American bittern
Least bittern
Green heron
Sora
Virginia rail
Common moorhen
American coot
Spotted sandpiper
Belted kingfisher
Tree swallow
Alder fly-
catcher
Willow
flycatcher
Marsh
wren
Yellow
warbler
Song
sparrow
Swamp
sparrow
Red-winged
blackbird
Common
grackle

*Broad-leaved Cattail*

*Red-winged Blackbird*

© Carol Decker

# CEDAR SWAMP

NEW JERSEY
AUDUBON
SOCIETY

Habitats of New Jersey

Habitats of New Jersey

# CEDAR SWAMP

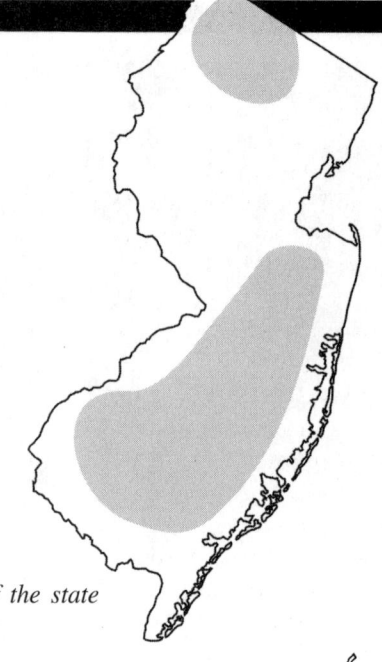

*This habitat is found in these areas of the state*

Forested wetlands, dominated by Atlantic white cedar, are frequent on the flat, sandy coastal plain of southern New Jersey, and also can be found, though much less commonly, in scattered pockets among our northern hills. White cedar, which gives its name to this **habitat**, is found from Mississippi to Maine, always in similar wet places. It is a valuable timber tree. The wood is light, straight-grained, easy to work, and decay-resistant. Wherever

---

White cedars often grow very close together. A young stand can be so dense that it is impossible to squeeze between the trees...

---

it grows, it is eagerly sought for lumber, shingles, poles, boats, and other uses exposed to the weather.

White cedar is still being cut for these purposes in New

*Atlantic White Cedar*

Jersey, and some large stands have been destroyed even in recent years. White cedar also can be killed by flooding, even though it is a wetland **species**. In places where southern New Jersey streams have been dammed to create reservoirs and recreational lakes, dead white cedars sometimes rim the newly-created impoundments. Salt also can kill this tree. The meadows along the lower reaches of the Raritan and Hackensack Rivers once contained extensive cedar swamps, but the cedars died when the upper reaches of the streams were dammed, allowing salt water to enter the meadows. Fires are also a major threat to white cedars, particularly where cedar

swamps are small and surrounded by flammable **upland** forests. In New Jersey, white cedar is much less common today than it was a century or two ago.

White cedars often grow very close together. A young stand can be so dense that it is impossible to squeeze between the trees, and a stand that is forty years old will on the average have about 3,000

NEW JERSEY AUDUBON SOCIETY

trees per acre, or one tree for every thirteen square feet. White cedar stands usually begin to grow from seedlings that sprout after cutting or fire has created an opportunity for them, so the trees in many cedar swamps, especially in southern New Jersey, are approximately equal in age and in size. The trees are slow-growing. A century-old tree is usually only about a foot in diameter.

Few New Jersey forest habitats are so completely **dominated** by a single tree species as a cedar swamp. In most cedar swamps though, wherever they are in New Jersey, one can find individual trees of red maple, sour gum, and pitch pine growing with the cedars and struggling upwards towards sunlight. Southern New Jersey cedar swamps often have sweetbay magnolia growing in and around them. This southern tree has oval, somewhat leathery leaves that are silvery-gray beneath. They are also aromatic when crushed. The flowers, which bloom in late June through July, are extremely fragrant. In northern New Jersey's cedar swamps, one often finds eastern hemlock growing with such northern trees as black spruce and American larch. Around the edges of many cedar swamps, and in openings within them, one can find such shrubs as swamp azalea, dangleberry, fetterbush, maleberry, sheep laurel, great rhododendron, and leatherleaf. All are in the heath family. Other common shrubs in and around cedar swamps are inkberry, a native holly with black fruits; winterberry, a deciduous holly; and sweet

pepperbush, whose spicy, fragrant blossoms in white spikes are conspicuous along Pine Barrens waterways in August.

Highbush blueberry also is found on the edges of white cedar swamps. This is the plant from which the cultivated highbush blueberry was developed, and much of the work was done at Whitesbog, New Jersey, between 1910 and 1916. F.V. Colville, of

---

Almost always, the ground in the swamps is covered with a thick mat of sphagnum mosses, which holds water and often creates the illusion of firm footing which does not exist.

---

the U.S. Department of Agriculture, and Elizabeth White, of Whitesbog, cross-bred selected wild plants from New Jersey's Pine Barrens and from New Hampshire to get high yield and large berry size. Today about 6,000 acres in New Jersey are devoted to this crop.

The forest floor in a cedar swamp is invariably damp, often with pools of standing water, and light levels are low because of the dense tree growth. Few species of higher plants can thrive here. Some specialized orchids, sedges, grasses, rushes, and a few other unusual and often rare plants are sometimes found. Ferns of several kinds, including netted chain fern, bog fern, cinnamon fern, and royal

fern can be common. In the cedar swamps of southern New Jersey, one finds the rare curly-grass fern, a northern plant that in the United States is found only in New Jersey and at a few sites on Long Island and in Delaware.

Mosses, liverworts, and a few lichens may grow on higher ground in the cedar swamps and on the bases and trunks of trees. Almost always, the ground in the swamps is covered with a thick mat of sphagnum mosses, which holds water and often creates the illusion of firm footing which does not exist. Many sphagnum mosses, or peat mosses, are able to grow as a floating mat in water, and they will often fill a small pond completely with their half-decayed stems, changing it to swampland. Peat moss has value to gardeners as a soil conditioner, and to nursery owners as a rooting medium and packing material for plants. During the first World War, sphagnum sometimes was used as a wound dressing instead of cotton, which was being used to make explosives. Moss gathering was once a minor industry in the Pine Barrens of southern New Jersey.

The water in cedar swamps is always highly acid, partly due to the **tannic acids** that leach from fallen leaves and conifer needles. It is also characteristically brown, for the same reason. Derived from rain water percolating through sand or peat moss, these waters are also very low in nitrogen, most minerals, and other **nutrients**, and they are naturally almost bacteria-free. In colonial times, cedar water was prized as ships'

© Carol Decker

drinking water by sea captains, who found that it did not become foul when kept in wooden casks during a long voyage.

To survive in the mineral-poor environment of the cedar swamps, a number of plant species, including round-leaved and spatulate-leaved sundews, pitcher plant, and a dozen kinds of bladderworts, have evolved methods for capturing insects and other small organisms to obtain needed minerals from their bodies. Sundews, small plants with leaves growing in rosettes, catch **prey** with hair-like structures on their leaves that are tipped with droplets of an extremely sticky liquid. Pitcher plants entrap insects in pitcher-shaped structures formed by tubular leaves filled with a mixture of rain water and plant secretions.

Bladderworts, most of which are floating plants, catch small **aquatic** life in bladders on their roots, which pop

---

In colonial times, cedar water was prized as ships' drinking water by sea captains, who found that it did not become foul when kept in wooden casks during a long voyage.

---

open when touched and suck in a droplet of water containing the prey.

In general, though, cedar water makes poor habitat for aquatic vegetation, most insect **larvae** and other **invertebrate** life, and for many fish and amphibians.

Mammal, bird, and reptile life in most cedar swamps is also comparatively sparse. In a habitat dominated by a few plant species, food is not usually plentiful. Amphibians of southern New Jersey's cedar swamps include southern leopard frog, carpenter frog, and the endangered Pine Barrens tree frog. Resident birds of cedar swamps tend to be insect-eating species, including eastern wood-pewee, white-eyed vireo, American redstart, black-throated green warbler, black-and-white warbler, wood thrush, and Carolina chickadee in southern New Jersey or black-capped chickadee in northern New Jersey. Small mammals are likewise few, again because food is scarce. One typical species is the red-backed vole. Weasels, raccoons, and other **predators**,

NEW JERSEY
AUDUBON
SOCIETY

however, follow waterways in search of food and can be found anyplace.

Although cedar swamps provide little food, the dense tree growth and the presence of water creates a **microclimate** in them which is cooler in summer, and warmer in winter, than surrounding uplands. Cedar swamps often shelter birds and mammals in winter. White-tailed deer often yard up in cedar swamps, where they browse on cedar twigs and seedlings. In fact, because of intensive browsing by deer, many stands of white cedar are unable to regenerate after logging or fire, and are replaced by hardwood trees and shrubs.

# TYPICAL CEDAR SWAMP SPECIES

*Pitcher Plant*

**TREES**
White cedar
Pitch pine
Sour gum
Red maple
Sweetbay magnolia
    (southern New Jersey only)
Eastern hemlock
    (northern New Jersey only)
Black spruce
    (northern New Jersey only)
American larch
    (northern New Jersey only)

**SHRUBS**
Highbush blueberry
Black blueberry
Swamp azalea
Leatherleaf
Maleberry
Fetterbush
Dangleberry
Sheep laurel
Winterberry

*Sweet Pepperbush*

Sweet pepperbush
Poison sumac
Naked withe-rod
    (southern New Jersey only)
Inkberry
    (southern New Jersey only)
Mountain holly
    (northern New Jersey only)
Great rhododendron
    (northern New Jersey only)

**OTHER PLANTS**
Royal fern
Cinnamon fern
Virginia chain fern
Bog fern
Collin's sedge
Long sedge
Three-way sedge
Pitcher plant
Round-leaved sundew
Spatulate-leaved sundew
Large cranberry
Starflower
Partridgeberry
Golden club
Horned bladderwort
Sphagnum mosses
Arethusa
    (southern New Jersey only)
Netted chain fern
    (southern New Jersey only)
Curly-grass fern
    (southern New Jersey only)
Goldthread
    (northern New Jersey only)
Wild calla
    (northern New Jersey only)

NEW JERSEY
AUDUBON
SOCIETY

# TYPICAL CEDAR SWAMP SPECIES (continued)

**AMPHIBIANS**
Pine Barrens treefrog
   (southern New Jersey only)
Carpenter frog
   (southern New Jersey only)
Southern leopard frog
Four-toed salamander

**REPTILES**
Red-bellied snake
Spotted turtle
Painted turtle

**MAMMALS**
Common shrew
Red-backed vole
Long-tailed weasel
Raccoon

**BIRDS**
Wood thrush
Eastern wood-pewee
White-eyed vireo
Black-throated green
   warbler
Black-and-white warbler
American redstart
Gray catbird
Carolina chickadee
   (southern New Jersey only)
Blue-headed vireo
   (northern New Jersey only)
Black-capped chickadee
   (northern New Jersey only)

*Pine Barrens Treefrog*

*Black-throated Green Warbler*

NEW JERSEY AUDUBON SOCIETY

# SUGAR MAPLE/MIXED HARDWOOD FOREST

NEW JERSEY
AUDUBON
SOCIETY

# SUGAR MAPLE/MIXED HARDWOOD FOREST

*This habitat is found in this area of the state*

The sugar maple/ mixed **hardwood** forest contains more plant and animal **species** than any other in New Jersey, and more than most **temperate zone** forests worldwide. It is found at its best in fertile, deep, well-drained soils overlying limestone in the valleys of northern and western New Jersey, but scattered pockets can be found elsewhere in the state. At one time, this forest type made up a greater percentage of New Jersey's forested lands than it does today. The places in which it grew best were desirable lands for farming; hence, they were cleared early in our state's history, and often remain under cultivation today. Even where this forest type now covers the ground, old stone walls and stone-lined cellar holes often show that it had been cleared in the past.

The sugar maple/mixed hardwood forest is a **climax** type, but the exact composition it had on a particular site

before European settlement, or will have at some indeterminate future, is open to discussion. Some mixed oak forests in New Jersey seem to be changing gradually to sugar maple/mixed hardwood forests as they mature, but it may take centuries before

---

...in good seed years as many as eight-million seeds per acre can fall on the forest floor under old-growth sugar maple stands.

---

the transition is complete, if it ever is. On these time scales, external factors like climate changes, acid rain, and the random effects of fire, plant diseases, and insects may influence plant **succession**.

Sugar maple itself is easy to recognize. The spaces between the leaf **lobes** are U-shaped, and the leaf underside

is pale green. In red maple, our other common native species, the spaces between the leaf lobes are V-shaped. In Norway maple, a European tree that sometimes escapes into the woods, the spaces between the leaf lobes are U-shaped, but the leaf undersides are dark green and shiny. Maple syrup can be made from any kind of maple, but sugar maple sap has a higher sugar content, and the trees grow larger and produce more sap than other species. The trees are tapped in the very early spring, before the buds begin to open. The sap as it comes from the tree has very little taste, and it must be boiled down and concentrated. It takes between 20 and 40 gallons of sap to make one gallon of syrup.

More species of trees are found in the sugar maple/ mixed hardwood forest, and its composition is more evenly distributed among the species, than in the mixed oak forests and hemlock forests with which it associates and with which it intergrades.

NEW JERSEY
AUDUBON
SOCIETY

Wood Thrush

Sugar maple is usually the most abundant and obvious tree, but it is joined by white ash, tulip tree, black and yellow birches, basswood, shagbark and pignut hickories, black walnut, red maple, beech, sassafras, and several other trees. White, red, scarlet, black, and chestnut oaks also occur within this forest type, but they are scattered. American chestnut was once common, but today usually is found only as stump sprouts.

Sugar maple-dominated forests usually have a well-developed **understory** of shrubs and small trees. Flowering dogwood, hop hornbeam, and ironwood are typical understory trees. Shrubs include spicebush, arrowwood, black haw, mapleleaf viburnum, witch hazel, alternate-leaf dogwood, and beaked hazel, to name just a few; but the blueberries and huckleberries typical of the mixed oak forest are not much in evidence. Vines include Virginia creeper, several species of wild grape, and poison ivy. Typically, there are many saplings of sugar maple. This is not surprising, since in good seed years as many as 8 million seeds per acre can fall on the forest floor under old-growth sugar maple stands. The seedlings are extremely shade tolerant, as one might expect of a climax forest tree. Mixed with the young sugar maples are scattered saplings of the other canopy trees.

In early spring the floor of many of these forests is a beautiful garden of many species of wildflowers. The early-blooming habit is not accidental. These plants emerge and flower when they do because sunlight is available to them only before the canopy trees are fully leafed

---

**In early spring the floor of many of these forests is a beautiful garden of many species of wildflowers.**

---

out. By midsummer even the **foliage** of some of these wildflowers has withered and disappeared. Flowering early as they do, before many insects are active, some of these spring **ephemerals** have evolved strategies to reduce dependence on the usual bees and wasps for pollination. Wake-robin, or red trillium, has carrion-scented flowers that attract flies; wild ginger has flowers at ground level that are pollinated by beetles;

violets are largely self-pollinated; and many species bloom sparingly, depending primarily on vegetative means of **propagation**.

Some typical wildflowers of these forests are Jack-in-the-pulpit, trout lily, perfoliate bellwort, Solomon's seal, false Solomon's seal, nodding trillium, wakerobin, bloodroot, mayapple, common blue violet, round-leaved yellow violet, wild ginger, wood anemone, Dutchman's breeches, spring beauty, blue cohosh, and black snakeroot. Ferns are abundant also. New York fern, hay-scented fern, several species of wood ferns, maidenhair fern, and Christmas fern are typical. Christmas fern is so named because it is evergreen, but coincidentally, it has leaflets that are shaped somewhat like a Christmas stocking. Where limestone **outcrops** occur, such lime-loving ferns as walking fern, maidenhair, spleenwort, and blunt-lobed woodsia may be found.

Mammal life is abundant in these forests, although no species is confined to them. Mammals include gray and flying squirrels, eastern chipmunk, white-footed mouse, common shrew, big short-tailed shrew, gray fox, long-tailed weasel, striped skunk, raccoon, and opossum. Porcupines may be found in northwestern New Jersey. This species was almost **extirpated** from the state, but it is now expanding its range. White-tailed deer, another animal that was virtually

NEW JERSEY AUDUBON SOCIETY

**extinct** in New Jersey at the turn of the century, has been re-established. Today, its numbers in some parts of New Jersey are excessive. Red foxes and woodchucks

White-tailed deer, another animal that was virtually extinct in New Jersey at the turn of the century, has been re-established.

can be found where forests are interspersed with open fields.

Reptiles are not rare in these forests, but as usual they are not seen often. In addition to the black racer, black rat snake, and garter snake, all of which can be found almost anyplace in New Jersey, some reptiles of the rich forest include the ring-necked snake, a small but attractive species that feeds on insects, earthworms, and salamanders; and the brown snake, another small, secretive species. The only turtles that are likely to be found in **upland** forests are the eastern box turtle and the wood turtle. This last species spends much of its time near water but wanders far out into surrounding woodlands in search of food. The only lizard native to northern New Jersey is the five-lined skink, and occasionally it might be found around old stone walls and rock piles.

Amphibians are not especially common in this dry **habitat**. As in the oak forest, red-backed salamanders can

be found by diligent searching under rocks and logs. **Vernal ponds** in this forest may be breeding places for red-spotted newts, and for spotted and Jefferson salamanders, and small streams may harbor such species as dusky, four-toed, and two-lined salamanders. Wood frogs, American toads, and gray tree frogs may be found in the upland forests after their spring and early summer breeding season.

Bird life, however, is both abundant and varied in this rich habitat. Many birds nest here, and in spring and fall migration, many additional species can be seen as transients. To some extent, the distribution of bird species follows the **vertical zonation** of the forest. In the **canopy**, birds such as American redstarts, black-and-white warblers, rose-breasted grosbeaks, northern orioles,

and yellow-billed and black-billed cuckoos forage for their food. Blue jays, common crows, and broad-winged hawks nest high up, but find food elsewhere. The great horned owl nests in a tree cavity, or appropriates the old nest of a crow or other large bird. House wrens, wood thrushes, red-eyed vireos, and hooded warblers nest among the understory shrubs. On the forest floor veeries, ovenbirds, rufous-sided towhees, woodcock, and ruffed grouse are typical. And such cavity-nesting birds as tufted titmice, black-capped chickadees, and hairy and downy woodpeckers are common throughout.

# TYPICAL SUGAR MAPLE/
# MIXED HARDWOOD FOREST SPECIES

*Sugar Maple*

## TREES
Sugar maple
Red maple
White ash
Tulip tree
Black birch
Yellow birch
Gray birch
Basswood
Shagbark hickory
Pignut hickory
Black walnut
Beech
Sassafras
Black cherry
American chestnut
White oak
Scarlet oak
Red oak
Black oak
Chestnut oak
Chinquapin oak
White pine
Flowering dogwood
Ironwood
Downy juneberry
Hop hornbeam

## SHRUBS
Spicebush
Maple-leaf viburnum
Arrowwood

Black haw
Alternate-leaf dogwood
Round-leaf dogwood
Witch hazel
Beaked hazel
Pinxter flower

## OTHER PLANTS
Poison ivy
Fox grape
Virginia creeper
Lady fern
Silvery glade fern
New York fern
Hay-scented fern
Marginal wood fern
Spinulose wood fern
Intermediate wood fern
Maidenhair fern
Christmas fern
Broad beech fern
Wild ginger
Rue anemone
Wood anemone
Spring beauty
White baneberry
Black snakeroot

*Christmas Fern*

Blue cohosh
Mayapple
Dutchman's breeches
Jack-in-the-pulpit
Solomon's seal
Canada mayflower
Common blue violet
Round-leaved yellow
    violet
Trout lily
Perfoliate bellwort
False solomon's seal
Nodding trillium
Wake-robin
Bloodroot

*Wood Turtle*

## REPTILES
Wood turtle
Ring-necked snake
Brown snake

## AMPHIBIANS
Red-backed salamander
Jefferson salamander
Spotted salamander

## MAMMALS
White-tailed deer
Raccoon
Eastern chipmunk
Striped skunk

## BIRDS
Great horned owl
Broad-winged hawk
Common crow
Blue jay
Black-and-white warbler
Hooded warbler
Ovenbird

NEW JERSEY
AUDUBON
SOCIETY

Habitats of New Jersey

# TYPICAL SUGAR MAPLE/
# MIXED HARDWOOD FOREST SPECIES (continued)

American redstart
Wood thrush
American robin
Veery
Rose-breasted grosbeak
Baltimore oriole
Red-eyed vireo
Black-capped chickadee

Black-and-White Warbler

NEW JERSEY
AUDUBON
SOCIETY

**Bridges to the Natural World**

© Carol Decker
91

# HEMLOCK FOREST

NEW JERSEY
AUDUBON
SOCIETY

Habitats of New Jersey

# HEMLOCK FOREST

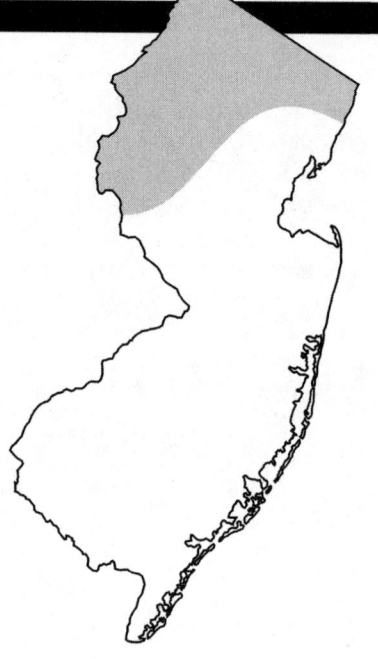

*This habitat is found in this area of the state*

I n some of forests of northern New Jersey, the most abundant tree is eastern hemlock. This is perhaps northern New Jersey's most typical **native** evergreen, and it is identified easily. The needles grow singly rather than in bunches like pine needles, and they are about half an inch long, flat, and rounded at the end. They grow in two opposing ranks, not all the way around the twigs as is true in spruces, for example. This gives each spray of hemlock **foliage** a distinctive flattened appearance.

Individual hemlock trees are found scattered in a variety of **habitats**, but hemlock-dominated forests usually are found in cool **ravines** and basins between rocky ridges. In some areas, hemlock is found in almost every valley. Because of their location, these forests often are associated with streams or bogs. Hemlock seedlings are able to germinate and grow, though slowly, in the shade cast by mature trees. This makes hemlock a **climax forest** tree, and hemlock forests are thus theoretically self-renewing.

An extensive hemlock forest is an impressive place to visit. The shade is very dense and the ground thickly carpeted with the fallen needles. The trees themselves are sometimes quite large as trees go in New Jersey, perhaps two feet or more in diameter and 60 to 70 feet high. This may be because in times past hemlock wood, which is hard to work, had relatively little commercial value, and trees not in areas

suited for agriculture were left uncut. Hemlock was cut where there was local demand for fuel and such rough uses as mine props and railroad ties. In some places, hemlock was cut only for its bark,

---

An extensive hemlock forest is an impressive place to visit. The shade is very dense, and the ground thickly carpeted with the fallen needles.

---

which was stripped off and used in tanning leather. The trunks were left to rot where they fell.

As one might expect, few other trees besides hemlock really thrive in most hemlock woods. The dense shade and the acid conditions created by the decay of hemlock needles inhibit competition. Typically, more than half the mature trees in these forests are hemlocks, and some

hemlock forests are virtually 100 percent hemlock. Some trees often associated with hemlock are yellow birch, which is also a shade-tolerant tree, and occasionally black birch, red maple, sugar maple, and American beech. In some places, at the edges of old glacial lakes that have turned into bogs or swamps, eastern hemlock grows with Atlantic white cedar and even with black spruce, a bog tree

---

*...hemlock forests are cooler in summer and somewhat warmer in winter than surrounding open areas or deciduous woods.*

---

much more typical of New England and Canada than New Jersey.

**Understory** shrubs are rather sparse in most hemlock woods. One species that does occur is great rhododendron, which may form almost impenetrable thickets around the edges and openings of the forest. Mapleleaf viburnum, mountain laurel, and witch hazel occur sparingly on drier sites. Understory herbs are likewise scarce in dry hemlock forests, but if the forests are not too shady, one often can find such acid-loving plants as trailing arbutus, stemless ladies'-slipper, partridgeberry, Canada mayflower, and Indian pipe. Mushrooms and bracket fungi need little light, and often are found here. One very characteristic species is

hemlock shelf fungus, a shiny, red-brown, woody bracket fungus that grows almost exclusively on hemlock logs and stumps.

Wet pockets and intermittent stream channels in hemlock forests may fill with sphagnum moss, and these boggy areas often have an interesting, somewhat northern mix of plants, including goldthread, alpine enchanter's nightshade, and a northern variety of Jack-in-the-pulpit, as well as more common plants like skunk cabbage and cinnamon fern. Such shrubs as highbush blueberry and winterberry may be found here as well.

Somewhat surprisingly, considering the dense shade and the relative lack of **botanical diversity**, wildlife is not uncommon in hemlock forests, although few species feed directly on the trees. Red squirrels do eat both **conifer** seeds and fungi, and this mammal often is associated with hemlock. Porcupines feed on bark, at least in winter, including hemlock bark. This animal is found only in the northwestern part of New Jersey, and being both **nocturnal** and **arboreal**, it is not often seen. But the scars left on trees by their feeding are unmistakable and permanent. Several species of shrews roam the forest

floor in search of insect and **arthropod prey**. Red-backed voles and white-footed mice are common. Mink, long-tailed weasels, and other **predators** seek their prey here, as they do elsewhere.

Like the cedar swamps of the Pine Barrens, hemlock forests are cooler in summer and somewhat warmer in winter than surrounding open areas or deciduous woods. White-tailed deer often seek shelter from human disturbance and from heat on hot summer days in the hemlock thickets, and in winter they commonly congregate in such areas. Deer will eat hemlock twigs and needles, but in a hard winter, with deep snow that prevents them from moving about and finding food, some may starve. Their bones are likely to be found in hemlock forests in the spring.

Amphibians and reptiles often can be quite common in hemlock forests, particularly where the forest floor is damp. Red efts, the orange-colored **terrestrial subadult**

*Red-spotted Newt*

NEW JERSEY AUDUBON SOCIETY

stage of the otherwise **aquatic** red-spotted newt, often can be found prowling the forest floor after summer rains. They can afford to be obvious because their skin glands secrete a **toxin** that makes them unpalatable to most predators, and their bright color is a warning to that effect. Wood frogs and spring peepers also can be seen in similar circumstances. In their cases, cryptic coloration makes it possible for them to forage in the open.

Other amphibians of the hemlock forest must be searched for. One species that is almost certain to be found is the red-backed salamander, which is one of the few salamanders that does not have a free-living aquatic **larval** stage. Slimy salamanders and spotted salamanders also may be encountered. Wetlands in hemlock forests are likely to harbor dusky salamanders,

*Great Rhododendron*

> As one might expect, few other trees besides hemlock really thrive in most hemlock woods.

and perhaps northern red and two-lined salamanders. All these species except the spotted salamander are lungless, and get all the oxygen they need through their moist skin. Reptiles

include ring-necked, ribbon, and red-bellied snakes in damp areas, and such ubiquitous species as garter snake, black rat snake, and black racer on the uplands.

Bird life in the hemlock forest also is fairly diverse. In some places a good variety of warblers, small, insect-eating forest birds, can be found nesting, including black-throated green, black-throated blue, Blackburnian, magnolia, and black-and-white warblers. Solitary vireos, brown creepers, black-capped chickadees, and hermit thrushes are seen frequently. Brush tangles along streams occasionally may shelter a family of winter wrens. Cavities in dead and dying trees are home to such birds as downy, hairy, and pileated woodpeckers. In winter, the hemlock forests are good places in which to search for winter visitors like white-winged and red crossbills, both of which feed on hemlock seeds, as well as golden-crowned kinglets,

and long-eared and saw-whet owls.

Flying insects usually are rather scarce in hemlock forests. There is little to attract nectar-seeking or leaf-eating creatures. Burrowing and wood-boring insects may be found. But unfortunately, in recent years an aphid-like Asiatic insect, the woolly adelgid, has become all too numerous in some hemlock forests. Its presence can be detected by its white egg masses, like tiny balls of cotton, on the young growth. The adelgid was first noticed in the eastern United States about thirty years ago, and it has been expanding its range ever since. This insect sucks the sap from hemlock trees, and heavy **infestations** can kill a tree in a year. Although individually planted hemlocks can be protected, there is not now a practical way of controlling this insect in a forest situation. Some large tracts of hemlock forest already have been killed in New Jersey, and others are likely to follow.

NEW JERSEY AUDUBON SOCIETY

# TYPICAL HEMLOCK FOREST SPECIES

Eastern Hemlock

Trailing arbutus
Shinleaf
Striped wintergreen
Stemless ladies'-slipper
Goldthread
Alpine enchanter's night
  shade
Cinnamon fern
Interrupted fern
Christmas fern
Hemlock shelf fungus

Trailing Arbutus

**AMPHIBIANS**
Red-backed salamander
Slimy salamander
Dusky salamander
Northern red salamander
Two-lined salamander

Spotted salamander
Red-spotted newt
Wood frog
Spring peeper
American toad

**REPTILES**
Ring-necked snake
Ribbon snake
Red-bellied snake
Garter snake
Black racer
Black rat snake

Porcupine

**TREES**
Eastern hemlock
Yellow birch
Black birch
White pine
American beech
Sugar maple
Red maple
Red oak
Striped maple
Chestnut oak
White ash

**SHRUBS**
Highbush blueberry
Witch hazel
Mapleleaf viburnum
Spicebush
Great rhododendron
Maleberry
Swamp azalea
Winterberry

**OTHER PLANTS**
Canada mayflower
Wake-robin
Partridgeberry
Indian pipe

Garter Snake

**MAMMALS**
Common shrew
Big short-tailed shrew
Red-backed vole
White-footed mouse
Red squirrel
Porcupine
White-tailed deer

**BIRDS**
Ruffed grouse
Saw-whet owl
Long-eared owl
Downy woodpecker
Hairy woodpecker
Pileated woodpecker
Black-capped chickadee
Brown creeper
Winter wren

NEW JERSEY
AUDUBON
SOCIETY

# TYPICAL HEMLOCK FOREST SPECIES (continued)

Golden-crowned kinglet
Ruby-crowned kinglet
Veery
Hermit thrush
Blue-headed vireo
Magnolia warbler
Black-throated blue
　warbler
Black-throated green
　warbler
Blackburnian warbler
Black-and-white warbler
Purple finch
White-winged crossbill

Pileated Woodpecker

NEW JERSEY
AUDUBON
SOCIETY

# NORTHERN NEW JERSEY MIXED OAK FOREST

# NORTHERN NEW JERSEY MIXED OAK FOREST

*This habitat is found in this area of the state*

The mixed oak forest is the most common forest type on dry sites in northern New Jersey. It varies greatly in composition and in general appearance, depending on such factors as exposure, history of human use or abuse, fire frequency, soil fertility, and moisture. Oak forests **intergrade** with sugar maple/mixed hardwood forests and with ridgetop pitch pine forests, often making it difficult to put a label on a particular piece of woodland. But in general, more than half of the larger trees in oak forests are oaks of one kind or another.

Eighteen species of oaks are **native** to New Jersey. These often are divided into two subgroups; the red oaks and the white oaks. The red oak subgroup, including red, black, scarlet, pin, scrub, blackjack, willow, shingle, water, and Spanish oaks, is characterized by having leaves with pointed, bristle-tipped **lobes**, and acorns that take two years to mature on the tree. The white oak subgroup, including white, chestnut, post, swamp white, chinquapin, basket, overcup, and dwarf chestnut oaks, has leaves with rounded lobes, and acorns that mature in one year. Within each group, hybrids sometimes occur, and individual variation is great. Oaks can be notoriously difficult to identify.

Not all of these oaks are components of the mixed oak forest. Pin oak, swamp white oak, basket oak, willow oak, and water oak, for instance, are wetland trees. In northern New Jersey's upland oak-dominated woodlands, one usually finds just five oak species growing as large trees: red oak, black oak, white oak, chestnut oak, and scarlet oak. Scarlet oak is somewhat more common on moist, fertile sites. Chestnut oak favors, or at least can live on, more exposed, drier, fire-prone sites, and on the driest, most rocky

mountain slopes often will make up more than half of the forest **canopy**.

The mixed oak forest is botanically more diverse than most New Jersey forest types. Within it, especially on better sites, one usually finds many other trees, including shagbark and pignut hickories, sugar and red maples, white ash, beech, black birch, and sassafras. Black birch, also called sweet birch, has twigs and bark that are strongly flavored with wintergreen, and was once a commercial source of the oil of wintergreen used as a flavoring in candy and chewing gum. The fermented sap of this tree was the original birch beer. On some sites, particularly on dry ridgetops,

## Eighteen species of oaks are native to New Jersey.

one often finds pitch pine, usually associated with chestnut oak. Before the 1930s, American chestnut was abundant in this forest, making up as much as one-third of the canopy, and in fact this forest type was then called the oak-chestnut forest; but a fungus disease, accidentally introduced from Asia in 1904, has practically eliminated this species.

Beneath the canopy formed by mature trees in the oak forest, there is usually an **underlayer** of small trees and tall shrubs. Flowering dogwood is common, as is witch hazel, mountain laurel, mapleleaf vibur-

num, arrowwood, black haw, ironwood, and sprouts of American chestnut which grow from old roots. These chestnut sprouts may get big enough to flower and bear a few nuts before the blight infects and kills them. Scrub oak sometimes is found in the **understory**, especially on ridgetop sites. In many oak forests, young oak saplings are few, and saplings of such species as sugar maple and beech are common. It may be that some of the modern-day mixed oak forests on better soils are a long-lived **successional** stage, and that the areas they occupy would, if left alone long enough, become sugar maple/mixed hardwood forests.

The forest floor in most oak forests supports a healthy layer of low shrubs and **herbaceous** plants. Plants in the heath family, such as early lowbush blueberry, late lowbush blueberry, deerberry, and black huckleberry, are common. Herbs include wild sarsaparilla and mayapple, each of which may carpet large areas, as well as bracken fern, New York fern, and

*Wild Turkey*

'91 © Carol Decker

poison ivy. Ripe fruits of mayapple are edible, and they taste something like weak lemonade, but unripe fruits and the rest of the plant are poisonous. On fertile sites, there is often a good growth of spring wildflowers, including Dutchman's breeches, Jack-in-the-pulpit, Solomon's seal, Canada mayflower, blue and yellow violets, hepatica,

## The mixed oak forest is botanically more diverse than most New Jersey forest types.

and wood anemone. Open, dry areas may support a lawn of such plants as tufted hairgrass, Pennsylvania sedge, and poverty grass.

Wildlife often is abundant in these mixed oak forests. Acorns, hickory nuts, and beech nuts are all excellent wildlife foods, as are the fruits of viburnums, wild grapes, huckleberries, and blueberries. Nesting birds include pileated woodpecker, hairy woodpecker, downy woodpecker, ruffed grouse, great crested flycatcher, wood-pewee, blue jay, black-capped chickadee, tufted titmouse, wood thrush, red-eyed vireo, scarlet tanager, rufous-sided towhee, hooded and black-and-white warblers, and ovenbird.

The ovenbird gets its name from its nest, which is built on the ground and covered with a domed roof of leaves, making a

NEW JERSEY
AUDUBON
SOCIETY

structure shaped like a colonial-era outdoor bread oven. Its song, a much-repeated tea-cher-tea-cher, is a familiar spring sound in New Jersey forests. In recent years populations of this six-inch-long insect-eating bird have declined sharply, in part because of **forest fragmentation** in North America, and in part because of the destruction of tropical rainforests where it spends the winter months.

A few of the mammals of this habitat are white-tailed

deer, gray squirrel, chipmunk, flying squirrel, white-footed mouse, common shrew, and such widespread **predators** and **omnivores** as striped skunk, long-tailed weasel, and raccoon. In the northwestern corner of New Jersey, one might even be lucky enough to find a black bear in this habitat. Both blueberries and acorns, as well as rodents and insects, are eaten by this mammal.

In these dry forests, amphibian life is scarce, although wood frogs, American toads, and spring peepers may emerge from hiding places after a rain. Red-backed salamanders and a few other species can be found by diligent searching. Red-backs are one exception to the rule that amphibians have a free-living **aquatic larval** stage. They lay their eggs in moist soil, under logs or rocks, and the larval development takes place completely within the eggs, which hatch into inch-long miniatures of their parents.

Reptiles are somewhat more abundant than amphibians. Although turtles and lizards are few, snakes such as the black rat snake, black racer, garter snake, and ring-necked snake usually are present. All are harmless to people, and feed mostly on the small animal life of the forest floor, although the black rat snake will sometimes climb to a bird's nest to eat eggs or **nestlings**. In some places, often near rock ledges that provide shelter and winter den sites, the eastern copper-head can be found. Although **venomous**, this snake is sluggish and inoffensive. It relies on immobility and its

dead-leaf pattern to escape detection by predators.

Insect life often is abundant in these forests. One species that sometimes seems too abundant is the gypsy moth, an insect that was introduced accidentally into the United States from Europe in 1869. Its larvae prefer oaks as a food, and at one stage in their early life, they balloon from

---

Wildlife often is abundant in these mixed oak forests. Acorns, hickory nuts, and beech nuts are all excellent wildlife foods...

---

place to place on wind currents, often landing on mountain slopes covered with oak forests. Gypsy moth populations are **cyclic**, and in some years the insect occurs in large enough numbers that extensive **defoliation** of oaks and other trees in these forests takes place. Most trees recover easily, but some die, particularly if they are defoliated for several successive years. The loss of a few trees does not affect the overall health of the forest, and the dead trunks provide nesting and feeding places for woodpeckers and other cavity-nesting birds and animals, while the increase in light reaching the forest floor is likely to enhance the growth of the understory and increase berry crops.

# TYPICAL NORTHERN NEW JERSEY MIXED OAK FOREST SPECIES

**TREES**
Red oak
Black oak
White oak
Scarlet oak
Chestnut oak
Shagbark hickory
Sugar maple
Red maple
White ash
American beech
Sassafras
Black birch
Gray birch
Pitch pine
Sour gum
Tulip tree
Black cherry
American chestnut
Flowering dogwood
Ironwood

Eastern Chipmunk

Mayapple

**SHRUBS**
Scrub oak
Mapleleaf viburnum
Arrowwood
Early lowbush blueberry

Late lowbush blueberry
Deerberry
Black huckleberry
Sweet fern
Mountain laurel
Pinxter flower

**OTHER PLANTS**
Wild sarsaparilla
Mayapple
Bracken fern
New York fern
Christmas fern
Hay-scented fern

Ring-necked Snake

Poison ivy
Dutchman's breeches
Jack-in-the-pulpit
Solomon's seal
Canada mayflower
Common blue violet
Hepatica
Trailing arbutus
Striped wintergreen
Whorled aster
White wood aster
Tufted hairgrass
Poverty grass
Pennsylvania sedge

**REPTILES**
Ring-necked snake
Black racer
Eastern copperhead

**AMPHIBIANS**
Red-backed salamander
Wood frog
American toad

**MAMMALS**
White-tailed deer
Gray squirrel
Eastern chipmunk

NEW JERSEY
AUDUBON
SOCIETY

**Habitats of New Jersey**

# TYPICAL NORTHERN NEW JERSEY
# MIXED OAK FOREST SPECIES (continued)

Flying squirrel
White-footed mouse
Common shrew
Long-tailed weasel
Striped skunk
Gray fox
Raccoon

**BIRDS**
Black-billed cuckoo
Yellow-billed cuckoo
Pileated woodpecker
Hairy woodpecker
Downy woodpecker
Great-crested flycatcher
Eastern wood-pewee
Common crow
Blue jay
Tufted titmouse
White-breasted nuthatch
Black-capped chickadee
Wood thrush
Veery
American robin
Red-eyed vireo
Ovenbird
Black-and-white warbler
American redstart
Hooded warbler
Scarlet tanager
Rose-breasted grosbeak

Blue Jay

©'91 Carol Decker

# HARDWOOD SWAMP

NEW JERSEY
AUDUBON
SOCIETY

**Habitats of New Jersey**

# HARDWOOD SWAMP

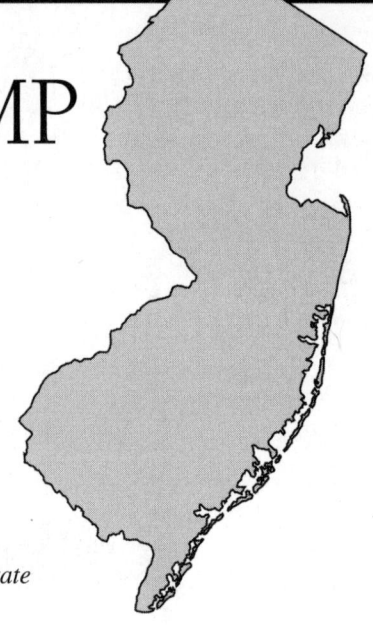

*This habitat is found throughout the state*

Swamps are forested wetlands which are wet only at certain times of the year, usually in spring and fall. Surface drainage is slow or nonexistent. The saturated soil is oxygen-deficient, and trees growing in swamps typically have root systems that spread along the soil surface to make the most of whatever oxygen is available.

---

Skunk cabbage...generates heat as it grows, melting its way through frozen soil to emerge very early in the spring.

---

In the summer many swamps dry completely, but they can still be recognized by these spreading tree roots, their vegetation, and by watermarks on standing trees.

New Jersey swamps vary in origin. Some are the remains of old lakes and bogs, which through the natural processes of pond **succession** have filled with **organic** matter and with soil washed in from surrounding uplands, and have almost but not quite become dry land. Other swamps are formed in **floodplains** when water overflows and is trapped behind the naturally raised river banks. In the sandy soils of southern New Jersey, swamps occur where depressions in the soil surface dip close to or below the level of the seasonal water table.

Some species of plants and animals are present in northern New Jersey swamps, but not in southern New Jersey, and vice versa. But one species that is common and characteristic of wetlands north and south is red maple. Although this tree grows well in dry soil, it is most typical of wet locations. Another wetland tree found statewide is black gum, or sour gum. Its oval, shiny leaves turn bright red or purple very early in the autumn, making it easy to recognize. Sour gum fruits are oval, thin-fleshed, purple berries, and about one-half inch long. They are eaten by many birds.

In the swamps of northern and central New Jersey, the trees noted above are joined by such trees as silver maple, with deeply cut leaves that are whitish below; box elder, a maple with **compound leaves**; and river birch, a tree which, when young, has peeling, reddish bark. Sycamore, with outer bark that flakes off

Cinnamon Fern

NEW JERSEY
AUDUBON
SOCIETY

in patches to expose the cream-colored inner bark, is common in this **habitat**. It is one of the ancestors of the hybrid London plane trees that are sometimes planted on city streets. Pin oak, whose drooping lower branches make it easy to recognize at a distance, is a very typical swamp tree, but it also grows well when planted on **upland** sites.

Farther south, on the inner coastal plain, sweet gum is perhaps the commonest tree in this habitat, although like red maple it also can thrive on upland sites. Sweet gum is identified by its star-shaped leaves and spiny round fruits. Its name is derived from a fragrant resin that seeps from injuries to the bark. Two trees of southern affinity, the willow oak and the basket oak, also occur in southern New Jersey swamps. White cedar is sometimes found. A very common small tree in southern New Jersey swamps is sweetbay magnolia, whose cup-shaped, cream-colored, extremely fragrant flowers bloom from late June to early August.

Several species of shrubs are typical to swamps. Highbush blueberry and winterberry are found statewide. Spicebush, whose tiny yellow flowers are a welcome sign of spring in the wet woodlands, is common in northern New Jersey,

and moderately common in the inner coastal plain, but rare in the outer coastal plain. Spicebush is related to sassafras, and like sassafras its bark is pleasantly fragrant, as are its shiny red berries. Spicebush

often grows with arrowwood, a shrub with coarsely toothed leaves that grow opposite each other along the stem. Fetterbush and sweet pepperbush are common in hardwood swamps of southern New Jersey. Poison sumac sometimes is found, north and south. This uncommon wetland shrub has compound leaves with conspicuous red stems, and bears white berries in loose clusters from the upper **leaf axils**.

Some of our finest displays of spring wildflowers are found in hardwood swamps, especially in northern New Jersey, where some plants include spring beauty, wood

anemone, Virginia bluebells, Jack-in-the-pulpit, and violets of many species. Skunk cabbage, whose oversized, ill-smelling leaves are familiar to many people, is typical of the habitat. Skunk cabbage flowers are borne in a squat club-like spike, which in turn is surrounded by a greenish or purple fleshy **spathe**. This plant actually generates heat as it grows, melting its way through frozen soil to emerge very early in the spring. In the wooded swamps of southern New Jersey the **botanical diversity** is usually somewhat less, although there are a few local specialties. One is the **endangered** swamp pink, which is now almost a New Jersey **endemic**.

Ferns often are abundant in hardwood swamps. Ostrich fern and crested fern are found in some northern New Jersey swamps, while netted chain fern and Virginia chain fern are more typical of swamps in southern New Jersey. Royal fern, sensitive fern, and cinnamon fern are common statewide. Cinnamon fern has large fronds that grow in neat rosettes from a long-lived, hairy-looking underground stem. When the fronds emerge in the spring they are covered with a loose brownish fuzz, which is used as nesting material by hum-

NEW JERSEY
AUDUBON
SOCIETY

mingbirds and other small birds.

Slow-moving, temporary woodland pools, containing no **carnivorous** fish and few other **predators**, are good breeding places for mosquitoes and other insects with an **aquatic larval** stage. In turn, these insects are food for many small birds, and hardwood swamps in the early spring are good places in which to see migrant warblers and other birds. Many birds nest in this habitat. Kentucky warbler, black-and-white warbler, American redstart, red-eyed vireo, swamp sparrow, veery, and wood thrush are just a few of them. One of the most characteristic birds of southern swamps, the prothonotary warbler, is found only rarely in northern New Jersey, but nests regularly in the south. It is our only warbler to nest in tree cavities. Wood ducks also nest in tree cavities, and frequent wooded swamps.

---

## Swamps are good amphibian habitat, and in the spring they may resound with the calls of frogs and toads.

---

An uncommon but widely distributed bird of the swamp forest is the barred owl, whose distinctive call of "who-cooks-for-you" makes its presence known.

Swamps are good amphibian habitat, and in the spring they may resound with the calls of frogs and toads. In the Pine Barrens of southern New Jersey, one can hear the

snore of the leopard frog and the "thunkathunk" of the carpenter frog most frequently, but outside of the Pine Barrens, the calls of the pickerel frog, green frog, American toad, and gray treefrog are more likely to be heard. The earliest true frog to call is usually the wood frog, a light brown amphibian with a dark mask on each side of the head. Its call, which sounds like the rapid quacking of a small duck, can be heard even before the ice is melted completely on woodland pools. Salamanders also breed in these pools. One, the aptly named spotted salamander, wanders far from water in the summer but returns to the breeding pools each year in the early spring. Females lay eggs in jelly-covered masses, like frog's eggs, with each mass containing as many as 200 eggs.

Some species of reptiles are not uncommon in hardwood swamps. Northern water snakes are frequent. They feed on fish, tadpoles, frogs, salamanders, and crayfish. Ribbon snakes, and the similarly marked garter snakes, also forage in water. In southern New Jersey, the king snake can be found. It feeds on other snakes, lizards, and rodents. Spotted turtles are somewhat characteristic of woodland pools. When the pools dry, they may burrow into

the mud to await the next wet season. Wood turtles are found mostly in northern New Jersey. They find some of their food in water, and **hibernate** underwater, but they also wander far out into surrounding uplands. Painted turtles and snapping turtles also are found.

Mammals of the swamp include such species as raccoon, mink, and occasionally river otter, all of which find much of their food in the water. White-tailed deer come to woodland pools to drink, and they feed on the tender plants of the forest floor. In winter, they may shelter in these swamps, and feed on the twigs of red maple. In past centuries, the hard-to-penetrate hardwood swamps were sometimes last refuges for mammals that had been killed off in more accessible places. Local place names like Bear Swamp and Cat Swamp memorialize these animals.

American Toad

NEW JERSEY
AUDUBON
SOCIETY

# TYPICAL HARDWOOD SWAMP SPECIES

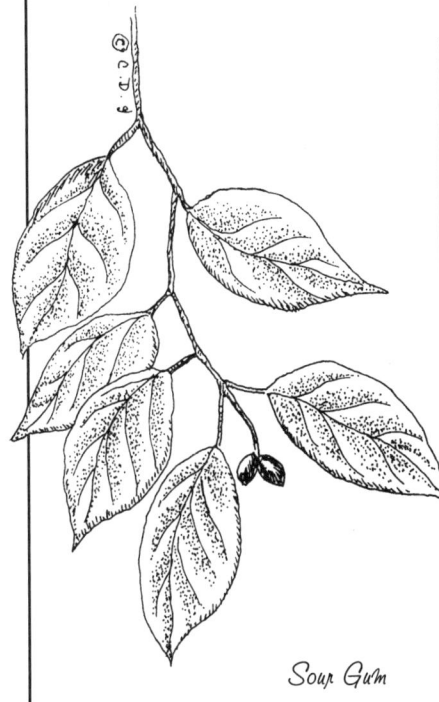

*Sour Gum*

## TREES
Red maple
Silver maple
Box elder
Sour gum
American elm
Pin oak
Swamp white oak
River birch
Black willow
Sycamore
White ash
Sweet gum
Willow oak
    (southern New Jersey only)
Spanish oak
    (southern New Jersey only)
American holly
    (southern New Jersey only)
Sweetbay magnolia
    (southern New Jersey only)

## SHRUBS
Spicebush
Arrowwood
Buttonbush
Winterberry

Sweet pepperbush
Swamp azalea
Highbush blueberry
Maleberry
Smooth alder
Silky dogwood
American elder
Poison sumac

## OTHER PLANTS
Skunk cabbage
White hellebore
Jack-in-the-pulpit
Trout lily
Canada mayflower
Spring beauty
Cardinal flower
Marsh marigold
Virginia bluebells
Marsh violet
Smooth yellow violet
Poison ivy
Sensitive fern
Crested fern
Cinnamon fern
Royal fern
False nettle
Tussock sedge
Wood-reed

*Jack-in-the-Pulpit*

Netted chain fern
    (southern New Jersey only)
Swamp pink
    (southern New Jersey only)

## AMPHIBIANS
Red-spotted newt
Spotted salamander
Leopard frog
Pickerel frog
Green frog
Spring peeper
Gray treefrog
American toad
Carpenter frog
    (southern New Jersey only)

## REPTILES:
Spotted turtle
Painted turtle
Snapping turtle
Wood turtle
Ribbon snake
Northern water snake

*Wood Duck*

## BIRDS
Green heron
Wood duck
Red-shouldered hawk
Spotted sandpiper
Barred owl
Acadian flycatcher
Black-capped chickadee
Veery
White-eyed vireo
Northern waterthrush
Kentucky warbler

# TYPICAL HARDWOOD SWAMP SPECIES (continued)

Canada warbler
American redstart
Swamp sparrow
Song sparrow
Prothonotary warbler
  (southern New Jersey only)

**MAMMALS**
Raccoon
Mink

Raccoon

SOUTHERN NEW JERSEY OAK FOREST

NEW JERSEY
AUDUBON
SOCIETY

# SOUTHERN NEW JERSEY OAK FOREST

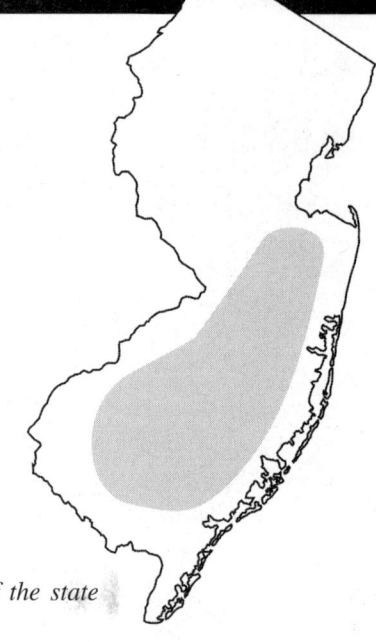

*This habitat is found in this area of the state*

About half of the **upland** forests of southern New Jersey's coastal plain are **dominated** by several **species** of oaks. As one might expect in this area, they often are mixed with pitch pine and shortleaf pine, and in fact there is a continuum from forests of almost all oak, through mixtures of oaks and pines, to almost pure pine forests that give their name to the Pine Barrens. In general, the oaks are most common on upland sites where fires have been more or less suppressed. Although some oaks sprout readily from unburned root crowns after a burn, producing multiple-stemmed trees that are good evidence of past fires, most species are not as fire-tolerant as pitch pine. More important in the development of an oak forest is the fact that acorns can sprout and grow in **leaf litter** beneath an existing forest **canopy**, whereas the small seeds of pine cannot.

Most of the forest canopy in southern New Jersey oak

In addition to the oaks, pitch pine, shortleaf pine, and sassafras grow in these dry upland forests.

forests is made up of five species: these are white, chestnut, black, scarlet, and post oaks. Of these, the first four are common in northern New Jersey's mixed oak forests, but post oak is a southern and coastal species that reaches its northern limit of range on Long Island and is not found inland in northern New Jersey. Post oak is in the white oak subgroup, and like the other members of its group it has rounded leaf **lobes**.

In addition to the oaks, pitch pine, shortleaf pine, and sassafras grow in these dry

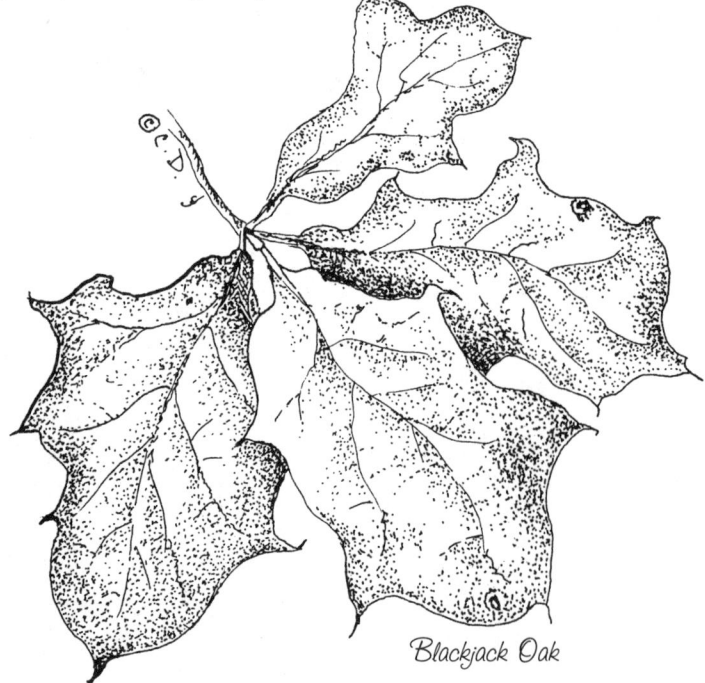

*Blackjack Oak*

NEW JERSEY
AUDUBON
SOCIETY

upland forests. Sweet gum, American beech, persimmon, and Virginia pine are present around the edges of the Pine Barrens and in the inner coastal plain. Sassafras usually, but not always, has leaves of different shapes, either three-lobed or mitten-shaped or oval, on the same tree. But it is easy to recognize without the leaves; the twigs stay green year-round and the bark has a characteristic spicy aroma. Sassafras bark, particularly the root bark, has long been used to make sassafras tea and it was once a flavoring ingredient of root beer. This bark, which in the 18th century was thought to be medicinal, was one of the earliest imports from North America to Europe.

Even though many of the common trees of the oak forests of southern New Jersey's outer coastal plain are found in northern New Jersey, the flat, sandy terrain, and the different associated plants make this a very different forest type from most oak forests found in northern New Jersey. Also, tree **species diversity** is much lower in the south than in the north. Red oak, very common in the north and our state tree, is almost never found on the outer coastal plain. Such trees as black birch, white ash, shagbark hickory, pignut hickory, sugar maple, and American chestnut are found only rarely, if at all, and are by no means typical of the **habitat**.

The **understory** of southern New Jersey's oak forests is, like the understory in the nearby pine forests, likely to be largely composed of shrubs in the heath family. Black huckleberry, late lowbush blueberry, and staggerbush are the most common species. Mountain laurel is locally abundant, and in June its blooms are a delight to the eye. Its scientific name, *Kalmia*, commemorates Swedish botanist Peter Kalm, who in the 1750s was one of the first scientists to look at the plants of southern New Jersey. Several low-growing oaks are also common. These include scrub oak, or bear oak, and sometimes dwarf chestnut oak, which rarely gets to be as much as six feet tall. Another oak, with much the same range in our area as post oak, is blackjack oak. It can grow into a medium-sized tree, but usually is found growing as an understory shrub. It is quite resistant to fire, sprouting readily after a burn, and it is often abundant in areas where fires are frequent. Blackjack oak is in the red oak subfamily, and has leathery leaves that are somewhat yellowish-green beneath. The leaves, though very variable in shape, are often triangular in general outline and almost unlobed. Bayberry, which one associates with the seacoast, is not uncommon, and its relative, sweet fern, also occurs.

**Herbaceous** plants of the southern New Jersey oak forest include bracken fern,

---

Mountain laurel is locally abundant, and in June its blooms are a delight to the eye.

---

golden heather, Pine Barrens sandwort, pyxie moss, trailing arbutus, goat's-rue, wild indigo, pink ladies'-slipper, Pennsylvania sedge, bearberry, cow-wheat, rattlesnake weed, black oat-grass, and little bluestem, to name just a few. Most of these herbs also can be found in adjacent pine forests. In autumn, one can

NEW JERSEY AUDUBON SOCIETY

find grass-leaved blazing star, fern-leaved false foxglove, stiff aster, purple gerardia, downy goldenrod, and sweet goldenrod here. Goldenrods usually are rather difficult to identify, but sweet goldenrod is easy. Its smooth, untoothed leaves smell of anise and can make an interesting herbal tea.

In many of these forests the ground is carpeted with **nonvascular** plants. Lichens, composite organisms containing both a dominant fungus partner and cells of a **subordinate** green **algae**, are able to grow on some very unpromising **substrates** which higher plants cannot colonize, and they do very well in the rather open, sunlit, oak woods. The green algae manufactures starches and sugars, and the fungus provides mechanical attachment and protects the algae from drying. One species, thorn lichen, spreads a fragile yellow-green mat over large areas. Three species of many-branched reindeer lichens form cushions on the forest floor. Nipple lichen, the red-tipped British soldier, and goblet-shaped pixie cup lichens are frequent. Tar lichen, like patches of spilled black paint, forms a crust on roadside sands. Many species of lichens also are found growing on the trunks of trees, particularly oaks. Mosses are also abundant. Some that are found often are the common haircap moss, juniper haircap, broom moss, and silvery pincushion moss.

Some of the birds of this forest habitat nest in tree cavities. These include Carolina chickadee, great crested flycatcher, screech owl, downy and hairy wood-

peckers, northern flicker, and eastern bluebird. The tall stumps of old, fire-killed oaks often are favored nest sites. In some places, the red-headed woodpecker is found. This beautiful bird is rare in New Jersey, but seems to favor oak forests. Such birds as blue jay, scarlet tanager, wood pewee, brown thrasher, northern mockingbird, and

---

## Some of the birds of this forest habitat nest in tree cavities.

---

red-eyed vireo build nests in trees or shrubs. A surprising number of birds, however, nest on the ground. In the oak forests, these include rufous-sided towhee, ovenbird, common nighthawk, and whip-poor-will. The wild turkey has been reintroduced into some of the southern New Jersey forests and seems to be well established. It is a shy and wary bird, seldom seen despite its large size.

Mammal life is somewhat more abundant in oak woods in southern New Jersey than it is in adjacent pinelands, but the species are about the same. White-tailed deer can be quite abundant in some oak woodlands. The gray squirrel is not uncommon. Like the deer, it feeds on acorns. Red squirrels are found also. The southern flying squirrel also lives in these forests. This animal is smaller than a chipmunk and is strictly **nocturnal**. It is not often seen but is probably not uncommon. It eats insects and birds' eggs as well as acorns, nuts, and seeds.

Other mammals of the area are gray fox, raccoon, opossum, pine vole, and white-footed mouse.

Reptiles of these forests are not different from those of nearby pine woods, and include the same southern species. Corn and pine snakes feed on white-footed mice and other small rodents, but do not disdain an occasional bird. Fence lizards scuttle along old stumps in search of insect food. Males have bright blue flanks, which they use in a territorial display. Amphibian species are few, although in damp weather Fowler's toads may emerge in some numbers from hiding places beneath logs and leaf litter. The eastern spadefoot, a burrowing toadlike amphibian, spends most of its life underground, emerging only to feed and breed. Its voice, which sounds like the bleating of a sheep, can sometimes be heard from temporary ponds after heavy summer rains.

Downy Woodpecker

# TYPICAL SOUTHERN NEW JERSEY OAK FOREST SPECIES

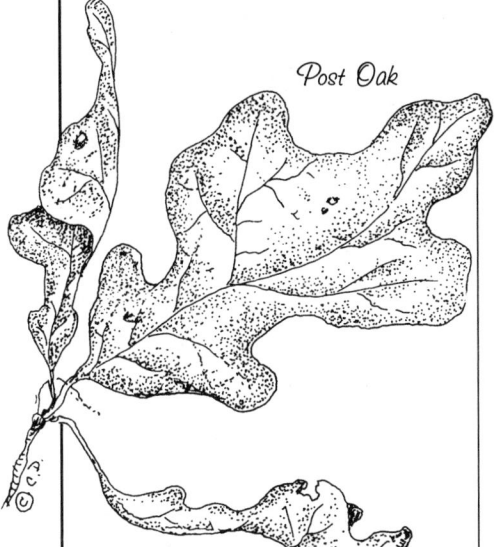

Post Oak

Bracken fern
Sweet goldenrod
Downy goldenrod
Gray goldenrod
Wintergreen
Trailing arbutus
Pine Barrens sandwort
Golden heather
Pyxie moss
Maryland golden-aster
Grass-leaved blazing star
Hairy hawkweed
Rattlesnake weed
Stiff aster
Hyssop-leaved boneset
Blunt-leaved milkweed
Turkeybeard
Bearberry Saint Andrew's
  cross
Goat's-rue
Wild indigo
Wild lupine
Prickly pear
False reindeer lichen
Mealy pixie cup cladonia
Atlantic cladonia
British soldier cladonia
Thorn lichen

Gray Fox

**TREES**
Black oak
Post oak
Scarlet oak
Chestnut oak
White oak
Blackjack oak
Sassafras
Sweet gum
Pitch pine
Shortleaf pine
Virginia pine
Black cherry

**SHRUBS**
Scrub oak
Dwarf chestnut oak
Late lowbush blueberry
Black huckleberry
Dangleberry
Mountain laurel
Sheep laurel
Staggerbush
Sand myrtle
Bayberry
Sweet fern

**OTHER PLANTS**
Pennsylvania sedge
Cow-wheat
Little bluestem
Black oat-grass
Poverty grass
Switchgrass
Common greenbrier

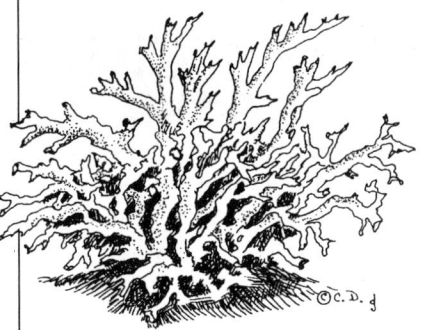

Thorn Lichen

**REPTILES**
Corn snake
Pine snake
Hognosed snake
Fence lizard

**AMPHIBIANS**
Fowler's toad
Eastern spadefoot

**MAMMALS**
Gray fox
Red squirrel
Gray squirrel
Flying squirrel
White-footed mouse
Pine vole
White-tailed deer

**BIRDS**
Wild turkey
Yellow-billed cuckoo
Whip-poor-will
Red-headed woodpecker
Hairy woodpecker
Downy woodpecker
Northern flicker
Carolina chickadee
Tufted titmouse
Eastern bluebird
Brown thrasher
Northern mockingbird
Gray catbird
Scarlet tanager
Black-and-white warbler
Ovenbird
Red-eyed vireo

NEW JERSEY
AUDUBON
SOCIETY

© Carol Decker

PINE FOREST

# PINE FOREST

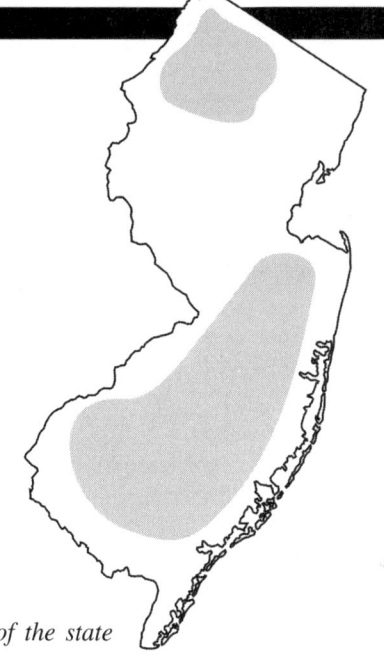

*This habitat is found in these areas of the state*

Natural pine forests in New Jersey occur primarily in the outer coastal plain, where they give their name to the Pine Barrens, or Pinelands. Pine forests also can be found on some of the drier ridgetops in the northwestern part of the state. By far the commonest and

---

Pitch pine...is one of the few pines that, after it has been burned, can regenerate from dormant buds below the bark and on the roots below the soil surface.

---

most typical pine in these forests is pitch pine, although shortleaf pine and Virginia pine are fairly common in southern New Jersey. The needles of pines grow in bunches, and the number of needles per bunch helps

identify the **species**. Pitch pine has rather long needles that grow in bunches of three, shortleaf pine has medium length needles in bunches of two, and Virginia pine has short, twisted needles in bunches of two. White pine, red pine, loblolly pine, pond pine, and Table Mountain pine also are found in New Jersey, but all except white pine are rare as **native** trees, and none makes extensive pure stands here naturally. Red and white pines, however, have been widely planted, especially in northern New Jersey, as have the introduced Austrian, Japanese black, and Scotch pines in various locations.

Pines in general are not **climax forest** trees. Their seeds need disturbed, bare, soil in which to germinate, and their seedlings require more light to grow than they can

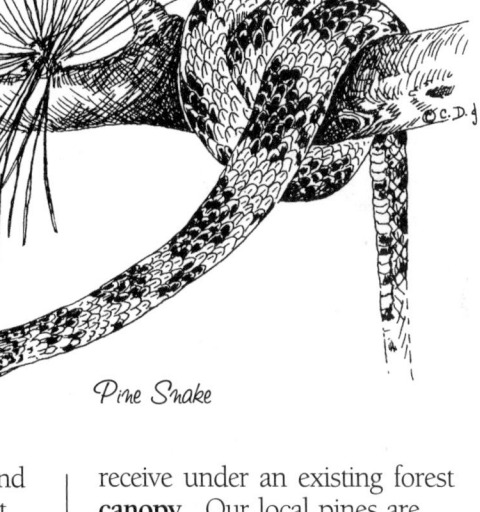

*Pine Snake*

receive under an existing forest **canopy**. Our local pines are no exception. Pitch pine thrives on frequent fires, which remove competition, release mineral **nutrients** from **leaf litter**, and expose bare soil. It is one of the few pines that, after it has been burned, can **regenerate** from **dormant** buds below the bark and on the roots below the soil surface. A pitch pine forest that has been burned and given a year or so to recover provides many opportunities to observe this regeneration. New growth will be seen sprouting from

NEW JERSEY
AUDUBON
SOCIETY

the bases of charred stumps, directly from the blackened bark on half-burned trunks, and growing up from the forest floor along with new seedlings.

Fires are no new thing in our landscape. Before there were people in New Jersey, fires were caused by lightning; and on the dry, sandy outer coastal plain of New Jersey such fires would burn large areas. The Indians of New Jersey, at least at the time of first contact with Europeans, burned woodlands regularly to clear underbrush, facilitate travel, and make hunting easier. After European settlement in New Jersey, fires became much more frequent, but it was two hundred years before anybody thought very seriously about even trying to put out forest fires. Today, in addition to fires from other causes, including lightning, arson, and sparks from campfires, southern New Jersey pine forests are subject to controlled burning by state foresters. This burning, done in wintertime, reduces the amount of inflammable litter on the forest floor and thus reduces the seriousness of summer fires.

It is not clear that the present-day fire regime, with many small, rather cool fires, has the same effect on Pine

---

## In general, a fire frequency of once every twenty years or so seems to maintain pitch pine forests free of competition.

---

Barrens ecology as fires in the past, which were probably hotter and larger, but less frequent. But it is fairly clear that if fires were suppressed completely in most pitch pine-**dominated** areas, north and south, the pines eventually would be replaced by oaks, which grow well in leaf litter from large seeds. In general, a fire frequency of once every twenty years or so seems to maintain pitch pine forests free of competition. In areas where fire frequency is much greater than this, a "pygmy forest" type of vegetation may develop, in which almost all tree species have been eliminated except pitch pine and stunted scrub or blackjack oak. Indeed, in this situation, pitch pine varieties have evolved that are dwarfed, mature early, and have cones that do not open and release seeds until they have been exposed to heat. All the plant species native to southern New Jersey's Pine Barrens are more or less tolerant of fire, and many of them actually require fire to create favorable **habitat**.

NEW JERSEY AUDUBON SOCIETY

In addition to the pines, several species of oaks can be found in New Jersey's native pine forests, including white, chestnut, scrub, black, dwarf chestnut, red, and post oak. The first five of these can be found in northern New Jersey's ridgetop pine forests as well as in the Pine Barrens, but red oak is not found in the Pine Barrens, while post oak is found in New Jersey only on the coastal plain. Sassafras and sour gum are found as well. The ridgetop pine forests also are likely to contain specimens of black birch, gray birch, red maple, and serviceberry.

Shrubs in the heath family, including mountain laurel, sheep laurel, black huckleberry, and lowbush blueberry, usually early lowbush blueberry in southern New Jersey, but more likely late lowbush blueberry in northern New Jersey, often will form an almost continuous **understory** in both northern and southern pine forests. Both huckleberries and blueberries are edible, but the true blueberries have numerous very small seeds that go unnoticed in muffins and pancakes while huckleberries have ten large seeds. Bracken fern, and Pennsylvania sedge, one of the few **upland** members of this group of grasslike plants, also are common to both regions. In the pine forests of southern New Jersey one can find additional Pine Barrens specialties such as turkeybeard, sand myrtle, Pine Barrens sandwort, Pine Barrens reed-grass, goat's-rue, staggerbush, pyxie moss, and broom crowberry. Some of these plants are southern species at or near their

*Bracken Fern*

northern limit of range here, but the broom crowberry is an arctic plant. Its presence in the Pine Barrens, the only part of New Jersey in which it is found, suggests that it is a survivor here from the time of the last ice age when **tundra**-like conditions must have prevailed on the coastal plain.

The most characteristic bird of the pine forest is the pine warbler, whose song, a

---

The most characteristic bird of the pine forest is the pine warbler, whose song, a long trill, like a sewing machine in the woods, can be heard from early April on.

---

long trill, like a sewing machine in the woods, can be heard from early April on. This is the earliest warbler to nest in New Jersey, and it

nests only in pines, although it is not very particular about the species. Dense new growths of pines and the stunted pines of frequently burned areas are favored nesting sites for prairie warblers, whose song, a series of buzzy notes on a rising scale, is easy to recognize once it has been learned. Carolina chickadees **forage** impartially in pines and oaks in southern New Jersey, as do black-capped chickadees in northern New Jersey. Eastern wood-pewees, downy woodpeckers, brown thrashers, northern mockingbirds, rufous-sided towhees, and whip-poor-wills are common. Eastern bluebirds sometimes can be found nesting in old woodpecker holes on the edges of clearings and recent burns, where they forage for insects on the newly-bare ground. In general, however, bird life in pure stands of pine of any species is likely to be somewhat sparse, as it is in any habitat dominated by a single plant.

Mammal life is likewise somewhat scarce, at least in extensive pine forests. The largest and most conspicuous mammal of this habitat, north or south, is the white-tailed deer. However, it feeds on acorns and on twigs of **deciduous** trees, and so is not really dependent on pines for survival. The red squirrel, on the other hand, eats pine seeds, and its feeding places are marked by piles of torn-apart cones. Southern New Jersey has pine voles, and both northern and southern New Jersey have such ubiquitous small mammals as the white-footed mouse and short-tailed shrew. Such

generalized feeders as opossum and raccoon can be found anyplace. The gray fox is common in southern New Jersey's Pine Barrens. It is mostly **nocturnal**, and one of the few members of the dog family that will climb a tree to get away from danger.

Reptiles of the southern New Jersey Pine Barrens include some southern species that reach the northern limit of their ranges here. These include pine snake, corn snake, scarlet snake, rough green snake, and king snake. Of these, the pine, corn, and scarlet snakes are burrowing species which find the sandy soil of the outer coastal plain suitable habitat. The habit of burrowing also helps them escape fires. Other reptiles include hog-nosed snake, black racer, black rat snake, milk snake, box turtle, and fence lizard. Almost the only amphibians are Fowler's toad and eastern spadefoot. Northern New Jersey pine forests, which are typically on rocky upland sites, lack the burrowing species, but may have black racer, black rat snake, copperhead, and occasionally five-lined skink, an attractive lizard that finds safety from **predators** in rock crevices. The timber rattlesnake, an **endangered species** in New Jersey, also is seen occasionally on these rocky uplands, as well as in a few Pine Barrens localities.

# TYPICAL PINE FOREST SPECIES

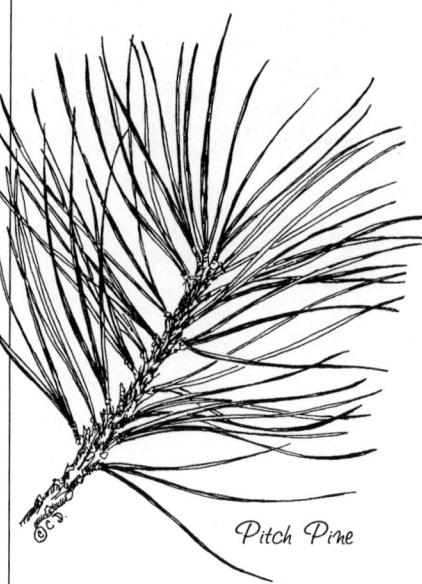

*Pitch Pine*

**TREES**
Pitch pine
White oak
Black oak
Virginia pine
   (southern New Jersey only)
Shortleaf pine
   (southern New Jersey only)
Blackjack oak
   (southern New Jersey only)

**SHRUBS**
Scrub oak
Late lowbush blueberry
Early lowbush blueberry

*Late Lowbush Blueberry*

Black huckleberry
Sheep laurel
Mountain laurel
Sweet fern
Dwarf chestnut oak
Staggerbush
   (southern New Jersey only)
Sand myrtle
   (southern New Jersey only)

**OTHER PLANTS**
Pennsylvania sedge
Cow-wheat
Bracken fern
Little bluestem
Glaucous greenbrier
Poverty grass
Sweet goldenrod
Downy goldenrod
Wintergreen
Spotted wintergreen
Pine Barrens sandwort
   (southern New Jersey only)
Pine Barrens reed-grass
   (southern New Jersey only)
Pursh's millet-grass
   (southern New Jersey only)
Broom crowberry
   (southern New Jersey only)
Pyxie moss
   (southern New Jersey only)
Maryland golden-aster
   (southern New Jersey only)
Grass-leaved blazing star
   (southern New Jersey only)
Hairy hawkweed
   (southern New Jersey only)
Golden heather
   (southern New Jersey only)
Turkeybeard
   (southern New Jersey only)
Bearberry
   (southern New Jersey only)

# TYPICAL PINE FOREST SPECIES (continued)

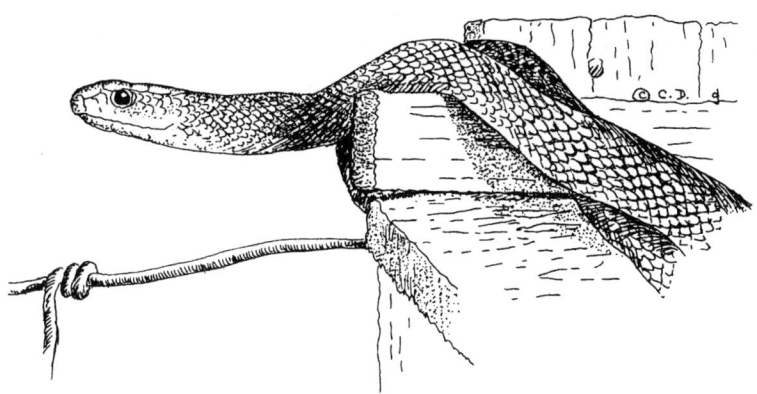

*Black Rat Snake*

**REPTILES**
Black rat snake
Corn snake
   (southern New Jersey only)
King snake
   (southern New Jersey only)
Pine snake
   (southern New Jersey only)
Fence lizard
   (southern New Jersey only)
Five-lined skink
   (northern New Jersey only)

**MAMMALS**
Gray fox
White-footed mouse
Red squirrel
Pine vole
   (southern New Jersey only)

**BIRDS**
Eastern wood-pewee
Tufted titmouse
Downy woodpecker
Brown thrasher
Northern mockingbird
Gray catbird
Whip-poor-will
Common nighthawk
Eastern bluebird
Pine warbler
Prairie warbler

Blue-winged warbler
Common yellowthroat
Eastern towhee
Carolina chickadee
   (southern New Jersey only)
Black-capped chickadee
   (northern New Jersey only)

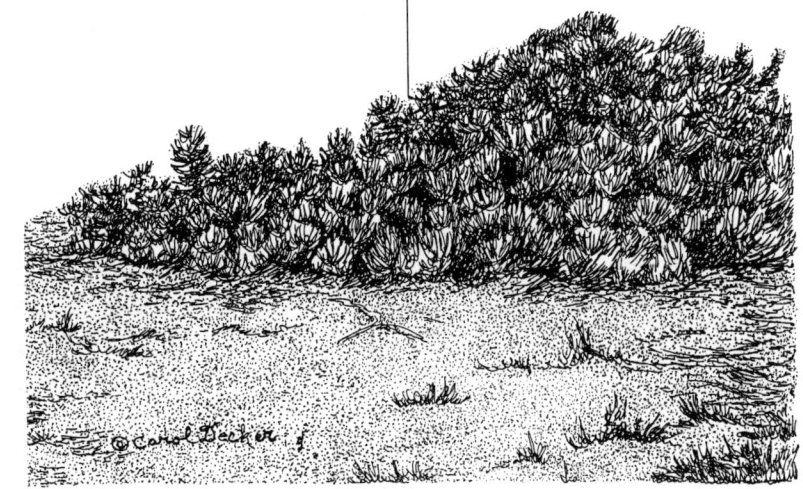

© '91 Carol Decker

# COASTAL DUNES AND FOREST

# COASTAL DUNES AND FOREST

*This habitat is found in this area of the state*

The shores of New Jersey, from Raritan Bay south to Cape May and north along Delaware Bay, are characterized by sandy beaches and offshore islands. In many places, these lands have been completely built upon, despite the fact that they are subject to erosion by winds and waves. But here and there, in state and county parks and in small pockets of private land that are waiting to be developed, the original vegetation and its associated wildlife persist. As is true of the **fauna** and **flora** of the salt marshes, the plants, birds, and mammals of this coastal **habitat** face problems with which inland species do not have to deal. Fresh water is scarce, drying winds are constant, and salt blows inland for considerable distances. The sandy soil itself is unstable, and ocean winds shift it from the shore, moving it inland to form dunes.

Plant species worldwide have evolved various ways in which to deal with dry conditions. Some plants have roots that spread widely and penetrate deeply in search of moisture. Others have leaves that are reduced in area, or that are covered with a waxy

*Bayberry*

---

In many places, these lands have been completely built upon, despite the fact that they are subject to erosion by winds and waves.

---

cuticle, or that are thick and fleshy, to reduce water loss by evaporation. Plant surfaces may be covered with hairs, which create a calm, moist **microclimate** around each plant. Some species simply

NEW JERSEY
AUDUBON
SOCIETY

hug the ground, since winds blow less strongly at ground level than they do even a few feet above it. All of these **adaptations** can be found in New Jersey's coastal plants.

Not all of the plants of the coastal forest face identical conditions. Those on the seaward side of the dunes face the greatest stress from salt spray and shifting sand. Plants on the tops of the dunes must endure very dry, windy conditions. Those that grow between the dunes are sheltered from the winds, and may have considerably more soil moisture available to them than plants on exposed dune surfaces. As a result, the vegetation of this habitat varies considerably from place to place within it. Different areas may be **dominated** by dunegrass, beach heather, shrubs, or trees, but these areas are intermixed and often **intergrade**.

Dunegrass, or beach grass, is a tall clump-forming **perennial** with roots that spread

---

Prickly pear cactus grows here; like most cacti, this plant has carried leaf reduction to its maximum and conducts photosynthesis with its stems.

---

widely, binding the sand surface and stabilizing the dune. It dominates the coastal strip closest to the water, above the highest tide line, on the seaward side of the dunes. This grass is **native**, but it also has been and still is widely planted as

Prickly Pear

© C.D.

shore protection. Plants found growing with the beach grass include beach panic grass, sea rocket, seaside goldenrod, beach pea, orache, cocklebur, and sandbur. Seaside spurge, a creeping plant with milky sap, pink stems, and reduced leaves, sprawls on the dry sand. Saltwort, or Russian thistle, a member of the goosefoot family with leaves that have been reduced to thorn-like structures, is another often-found plant here.

Behind the first dunes, in areas somewhat sheltered from salt spray and the more intense winds, beach heather forms blue-green mats on the sand. This plant rarely grows more than a foot tall, and is a good example of a plant with several adaptations that conserve water. In addition to being low-growing and deep-rooted, it has reduced leaves and surfaces covered with hairs. In mid-May, beach heather is covered for a few

weeks with yellow flowers. The beach heather itself forms most of the plant cover in this area, but dunegrass and some of the plants associated with it are found here also, as are tangles of poison ivy, Virginia creeper, and greenbrier. Prickly pear cactus grows here; like most cacti, this plant has carried leaf reduction to its maximum and conducts **photosynthesis** with its stems. Dusty miller, a gray, woolly, low-growing plant that was originally native to the Pacific coast, is locally common.

In more sheltered spots, usually to the landward side of the beach heather, is the shrub thicket. This is perhaps the most characteristic **community** of woody vegetation of the New Jersey shore, and usually is made up of beach plum, coastal juneberry, winged sumac, highbush blueberry, and bayberry, with some low-growing scrub oak, red cedar, and American holly. Bayberry and some of its close relatives are able to extract nitrogen from the air and convert it to the **soluble nitrates** needed by plants. They can thus grow in very infertile soils. Bayberry candles are made from the wax that covers the small gray bayberry fruits. The wax is obtained by steeping the berries in boiling water and skimming the wax from the water surface, but it takes many pounds of berries to produce a pound of wax.

Poison ivy is very common in these shrub thickets, and often grows in a shrubby form. American bittersweet is sometimes found in the shrub thicket, although it is no-where common. Its orange-hulled red berries are most obvious in winter. The height of the shrub thicket vegeta-tion varies from one to fifteen feet, depending on the amount of salt spray reaching the location. Typically, the tops of these shrubs are sculptured by the wind. Branches on the lee side grow vigorously while branches on the windward side are short, being killed back annually by windborne salt.

Dune woodland grows in the most sheltered locations between and behind the dunes. Typical trees here include American holly, black cherry, red cedar, hackberry, sassafras, and pitch pine, with some Spanish oak, white oak, blackjack oak, and persim-mon. Persimmon is a south-ern species that approaches its northern limit of range in New Jersey. The orange fruits are delicious when they are fully ripe and soft, which usually is not until mid-October or later, but they are

exceedingly astringent when unripe. Vines of several species, including greenbrier, wild grape, and Japanese honeysuckle may form impenetrable tangles between the trees. **Understory** herbs are not common.

The coastal dunes and forests provide variable habitat for wildlife. As in the salt marsh, amphibians are few, although where pools of rain water accumulate be-tween the dunes, Fowler's toads and perhaps a few other amphibians may breed successfully. The toads may be fed upon by garter snakes and hog-nosed snakes, and an occasional king snake that has wandered into this habitat from farther inland, but in general, snakes are few. Fence lizards and box turtles are the likely reptiles of the upland areas. But where the beaches adjoin salt marshes, diamond-

back terrapins, mud turtles, and snapping turtles may be found. All may lay their eggs in the sand of the coastal dunes.

Mammals are limited in number here, perhaps in part because our coastal habitats

---

The height of the shrub thicket vegetation varies from one to fifteen feet, depending on the amount of salt spray reaching the location.

---

are usually rather small in area. There is little room for large mammals, or for those that require a large home range. In New Jersey, no mammal is truly typical of this coastal strip. However, meadow voles, white-footed mice, Norway rats, and eastern cottontails are com-mon enough in the dunegrass and beach heather to be prey for an occasional red or gray fox. Skunks, raccoons, and opossums are not uncommon in thickets and forests.

Bird life, however, can be quite abundant in the coastal forest, although the abun-dance varies with the season. Breeding birds of this habitat are few. Piping plovers and least terns nest on bare or almost-bare sand, and both species are **endangered**, due to human usurpation of beaches. In the shrub thick-ets and dune forests, such familiar birds as robins, catbirds, mockingbirds, brown thrashers, yel-lowthroats, song sparrows, and white-eyed vireos may

nest. But during **migration**, especially fall migration, the shrub thickets and dune woodland can be crowded with birds that migrate along the shore. Included among these migrants are birds of prey. Autumn hawk flights in some places along our shore can be spectacular, with

---

But during migration, especially fall migration, the shrub thickets and dune woodland can be crowded with birds that migrate along the shore.

---

thousands of hawks passing overhead in a single day. In winter, these very dense thickets and coastal forests provide shelter and food for yellow-rumped warblers, savannah sparrows, and other birds. Many of these feed on the fruits of bayberry and poison ivy. There are also winter birds of prey. Red-tailed and rough-legged hawks search the dunes for mice and other food, and a white object on a distant dune may, with luck, turn out to be a snowy owl, a visitor from the Arctic **tundra** that finds congenial surroundings at the winter shore.

# TYPICAL COASTAL DUNES AND FOREST SPECIES

## TREES
American holly
Hackberry
Black cherry
Sassafras
Spanish oak
White oak
Blackjack oak
Willow oak
Persimmon
Red maple
Pitch pine
Red cedar

*Poison Ivy*

*American Holly*

## SHRUBS
Bayberry
Wax myrtle
Beach plum
Winged sumac
Coastal juneberry
Rugosa rose
Highbush blueberry
Scrub oak
Sheep laurel
Inkberry

## OTHER PLANTS
American bittersweet
Virginia creeper
Poison ivy
Common greenbrier
American beach grass
Sea rocket
Seaside goldenrod
Beach pea
Trailing wild bean
Orache
Sandbur
Seaside spurge
Saltwort
Beach heather
Little bluestem
Switchgrass
Prickly pear
Dusty miller

## REPTILES
Hog-nosed snake
Garter snake
Eastern box turtle
Diamondback terrapin
Fence lizard

## AMPHIBIANS
Fowler's toad
Spring peeper

NEW JERSEY AUDUBON SOCIETY

# TYPICAL COASTAL DUNES AND FOREST SPECIES
(continued)

**MAMMALS**
Red fox
Meadow vole
White-footed mouse
Norway rat
Eastern cottontail
Striped skunk
Opossum

Yellow-rumped warbler
Palm warbler
Northern mockingbird
Gray catbird
Brown thrasher
American robin
Fish crow
Horned lark
Snow bunting

*Song Sparrow*

**BIRDS**
Least tern
Common tern
Piping plover
Savannah sparrow
Song sparrow
Seaside sparrow

SALT MARSH

# SALT MARSH

*This habitat is found in this area of the state*

Salt marshes are found along the eastern and western coasts of New Jersey. Small pockets of salt marsh occur along the Hudson River almost as far north as the state line, and they extend up the valleys of the Passaic, Hackensack, and Raritan Rivers. The best development of salt marsh is found along the coast from Monmouth County south, both on the landward sides of offshore islands and on the opposing mainland. Salt marshes fringe the coast all the way to Cape May, and although sparse at Cape May Point itself, they continue on the Delaware Bay shore to Salem County.

Wherever they are, these salt marshes contain much the same **species** of plants and animals, and their **ecology** is ruled by their twice-daily flooding by salt water at high tides. It is a difficult **habitat**, which requires some special **adaptations** by the species that live in it. But for plants and animals with the right adaptations, the endless supply of water, **nutrients**, and sunlight makes salt marshes the most productive environment on earth, converting these raw materials into **biomass** at rates up to ten tons per acre per year, far more than most **terrestrial** environments.

Salt marshes can form wherever shallow, sheltered ocean waters meet a gently sloping coast. If sea levels are stable, the marsh tends to extend itself at its seaward edge. The roots and stems of salt marsh grasses trap sediments carried by the tides, and as this fill accumulates, the grasses grow out into it, creating new marsh. Slow, minor increases in sea level can be accommodated. The marsh grows upward to maintain its surface at a level about equal to the average high tide. But sea levels along the New Jersey shore are rising relatively rapidly because of the melting of glacial ice, so it is more common today to find erosion at the outer margins of salt marshes than to find the marshes extending themselves.

The **flora** of our salt marshes is **dominated** by a very few species, most of them grasses. The wettest areas, exposed to tidal flooding twice daily along the seaward edge of the marshes and along salt water creeks, are covered with cordgrass, which grows to a height of as much as five feet. Higher up in the marsh, salt meadow grass, a much more delicate species, grows no more than two feet tall. Both salt meadow grass and

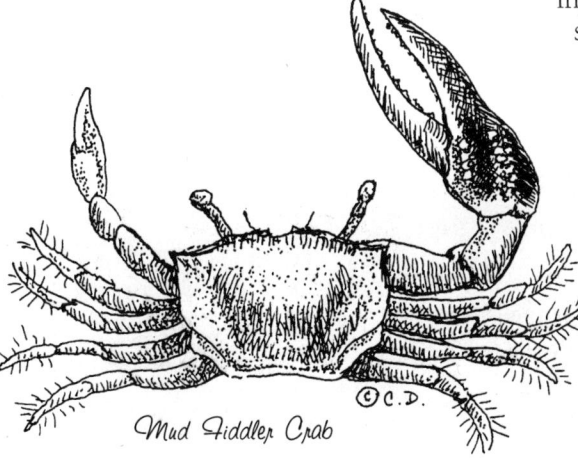

*Mud Fiddler Crab*

© C.D.

NEW JERSEY
AUDUBON
SOCIETY

**Habitats of New Jersey**

cordgrass have mechanisms to excrete excess salt. A search along the leaves with a lens usually will turn up small square crystals of this mineral. Also on the high marsh, which is flooded by only the highest tides, one finds spike grass, a low, rather bushy plant. Black rush, a somewhat grasslike plant, frequently is abundant in the high marsh. Early European settlers along the coast often pastured their cattle on the salt marshes, at the risk of occasionally losing a cow in a tidal creek. Even today, salt meadow grass is harvested in a few places along the New Jersey shore, for use as mulch and animal food and bedding.

Low places within the marsh, which trap sea water after tides and become too salty even for cordgrass, are the domain of the glassworts, fleshy, leafless plants, which turn a fiery red in autumn. Though somewhat fibrous, the several species of these plants are edible, and in colonial times they were sometimes pickled, giving them the alternate name of "pickle plant". Other plants commonly found, especially along the upper edges of the marsh, include salt marsh bulrush, annual and perennial salt marsh asters, sea pink, Walter's cockspur grass, big cordgrass, common reed or phragmites, seaside goldenrod, sea lavender, marsh elder, and groundsel bush. But usually, in terms of area covered, these are minor components.

The most obvious living creatures of the marsh are the birds. Although not too many New Jersey species actually nest in the marsh (some exceptions include osprey,

Salt marshes can form wherever shallow, sheltered ocean waters meet a gently sloping coast.

northern harrier, willet, Forster's tern, laughing gull, clapper rail, and seaside and sharp-tailed sparrows) a great many species find food there. Great blue herons, little blue herons, tricolored herons, green-backed herons, black-

crowned and yellow-crowned night-herons, American bitterns, great egrets, and snowy egrets are easy to find in season in any large salt marsh. Terns and black skimmers patrol creeks and shallows. Herring gulls and laughing gulls can be seen in New Jersey salt marshes at all seasons. Gulls can be told from terns by their manner of flight and feeding. Gulls have relatively short wings, rather slow wingbeats, and feed on the ground or by picking food from the water surface. Terns have rather long, pointed wings, rapid wingbeats, and usually feed by diving, hitting the water with a splash.

In spring and fall, huge flocks of shorebirds may settle down in the salt marsh to feed and rest during their often-lengthy migrations. Most species spend the winter south of New Jersey but nest north of it, many on the arctic **tundra**, where long days and abundant food make it possible for the birds to go through their entire breeding cycle in only a few weeks. Although all shorebirds eat animal food, some species pick it from the surface of the marsh, while others probe into the mud. In this way, different species can feed together in the same area without competing for the same food items.

Although birds are visible, it is the **invertebrate** life in the water and mud that actually keeps the salt marsh functioning. Some of these invertebrates convert plant **detritus** into animal protein, and thus form the bottom of

the food chain that may end in a peregrine falcon or a human. The **larvae** of the fiercely-biting greenhead flies live in the mud throughout the marsh. Mosquito larvae thrive in isolated shallow pools, where they are safe from the killifish that prey on them in ditches exposed to tidal flow. The surfaces of the

Although birds are visible, it is the invertebrate life in the water and mud that actually keeps the salt marsh functioning.

firmer marsh muds often are studded with ribbed mussels, each in its own burrow. These are **filter feeders**, which strain food from incoming tides. Mud snails, common periwinkles, knobbed and channeled whelks, blue mussels, quahogs, oysters, false angel wings, and an enormous variety of less obvious **mollusks**, **crustaceans**, insects, starfish, and other invertebrates make a very varied **fauna**.

Fiddler crabs are familiar invertebrate residents of the salt marsh, and several species usually can be seen in warm weather, foraging for food at low tide and retreating to their burrows at high water to seek safety from **aquatic predators**. They eat both animal and vegetable food. Male fiddler crabs have one claw greatly enlarged. It is used in courtship display and in threatening, but only rarely in fighting other male fiddler crabs. If the big claw should be broken off, the small claw

on the other front leg will grow larger to replace it, and the leg that originally had a big claw eventually will regrow a small one. Thus, although most fiddler males begin with the enlarged claw on the left, many eventually wind up with it on the right.

In contrast to the great variety of birds and invertebrates, other orders and classes of life are rather poorly represented in the salt marsh. There are no amphibians. This group of animals cannot tolerate salt water. There are usually no terrestrial reptiles, but aquatic turtles, including mud turtle, musk turtle, snapping turtle, and even the occasional painted turtle can be found in the ditches and marsh pools. But by far the most characteristic reptile of the New Jersey salt marsh is the diamondback terrapin, which lives and feeds in salt water, **hibernates** in winter in the salt marsh mud, and lays its eggs in sandy banks, road edges, and at the high tide line of the beaches that often border the marsh. These areas are extremely subject to human disturbance and to natural predation by raccoons and other **upland** mammals. As a result, reproduction of diamondbacks is very slow, and like many other creatures of the sandy shore, the species needs all the help it can get from humans.

Mammals are likewise few. Muskrats may build their homes and feed in the marsh, and may fall **prey** to the occasional mink that moves down from higher ground. Meadow voles burrow through the grass of the high marsh, and are food for northern harriers, short-eared owls, and in winter for rough-legged hawks. Rice rats are found in some New Jersey salt marshes. An occasional river otter may take up residence in a hole beneath the bank of a tidal creek. Raccoons seek food in the marsh between the tides, leaving their distinctive footprints in the mud flats to mark their passage.

Willet

# TYPICAL SALT MARSH SPECIES

Laughing Gull

## SHRUBS
Groundsel bush
Marsh elder
Bayberry

Cordgrass

## OTHER PLANTS
Cordgrass
Salt meadow grass
Spike grass
Black rush
Glasswort
Woody glasswort
Sea pink
Annual salt marsh aster
Perennial salt marsh aster

Walter's cockspur grass
Big cordgrass
Common reed
Seaside goldenrod
Sea lavender
Salt marsh bulrush
Saltwort
Orache
Seaside mallow
Salt marsh fleabane
Poison ivy
Hairy sea-blite
Tall sea-blite

## REPTILES
Diamondback terrapin
Snapping turtle
Mud turtle
Musk turtle

## MAMMALS
Meadow vole
Rice rat
Raccoon
River otter

## BIRDS
American bittern
Great blue heron
Great egret
Snowy egret
Little blue heron
Tricolored heron
Green heron
Black-crowned night-heron
Glossy ibis
American black duck
Osprey
Rough-legged hawk
Northern harrier
Clapper rail
Semipalmated plover
American oystercatcher
Greater yellowlegs
Willet
Whimbrel
Laughing gull
Herring gull
Ring-billed gull

Forster's tern
Black skimmer
Short-eared owl
Tree swallow
Marsh wren
Sharp-tailed sparrow
Seaside sparrow
Boat-tailed grackle

## FISH
Banded killifish
Common killifish

## INVERTEBRATES
Blue crab
Mud fiddler crab
Horseshoe crab
Amphipod
Common periwinkle
Mud snail
Blue mussel
Ribbed mussel
Quahog
Oyster
False angel wing
Channeled whelk
Knobbed whelk
Lugworm
Clamworm
Greenhead fly
Salt marsh mosquito

Ribbed Mussel

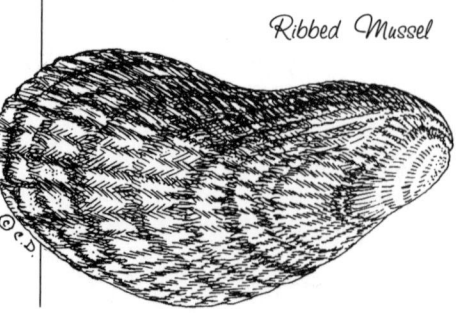

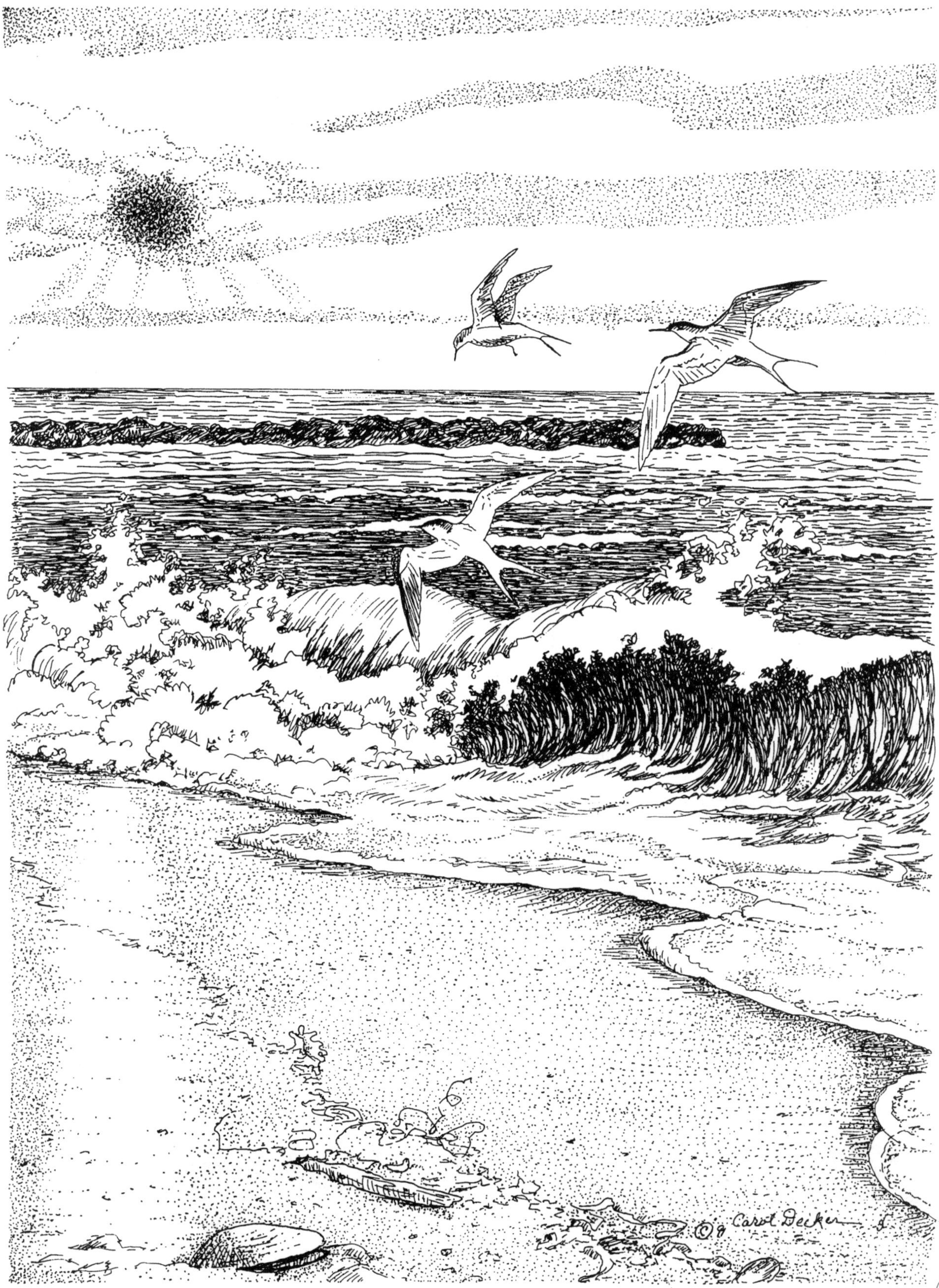

BEACH

Habitats of New Jersey

# BEACH

*This habitat is found in this area of the state*

The sandy shore, from the point reached by the highest tides to a point well below the level of the lowest tides, is a difficult **habitat** for life. As in the salt marsh, **organisms** that live here must cope with the twice-daily rise and fall of the tides. They must endure

---

## ...the greatest problem faced by dwellers on the sandy shore is the instability of the surface on which they live.

---

variation in the salt content of the water, which near shore varies between about 3.2 and 2.5 percent by weight because of freshwater **runoff** from land. Water salinity is critical to marine organisms, and many can not survive even this small variation. Water temperature is variable here as well, from freezing in winter to about 70 degrees F. in summer.

But the greatest problem faced by dwellers on the sandy shore is the instability of the surface on which they live. Sand actually **migrates** along the shore, moved by waves and currents. It also moves inland. The seaward side of **barrier islands** is constantly being eroded by waves and wind, and the sand is deposited in the sheltered bays behind them. Human attempts to prevent this sand movement by the construction of seawalls and jetties may be successful locally but overall lead to the destruction of beaches. Whatever the cause, the shifting sands provide no firm surface to which animals or plants can attach to avoid being swept to sea.

Thus, there are no forests of marine **algae** on the sandy shore. Most seaweeds must attach to something solid, and so are found here only where man-made structures provide an anchorage. They may be common

in sheltered bays or in deeper, calmer offshore waters, where they grow attached to pebbles and shells. A few **species** frequently are found washed onto the beach. These include sea lettuce, a paper-thin bright green algae; rockweeds, a group of similar brown species whose flattened, branching fronds are tipped with swollen fruiting bodies; *enteromorpha*, a bright green, tubular alga that withstands low salinity and often colonizes shallow pools atop jetties; and codium, a dark green, spongy, branching species. Codium is not native to New Jersey,

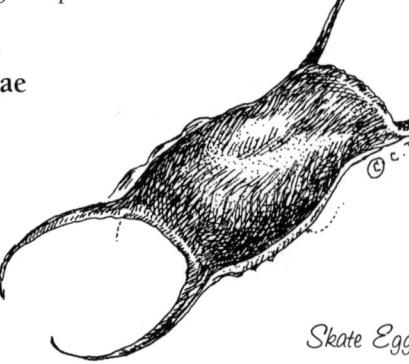

*Skate Egg Case*

NEW JERSEY
AUDUBON
SOCIETY

**Bridges to the Natural World**

but was introduced accidentally in the east coast around 1957, possibly from the North Pacific. It attaches to oysters and clams and is a nuisance to the shellfish industry.

Marine algae are not **vascular** plants, and none produce flowers. In most species, sperms and eggs are

---

The hard-shelled clam so popular as food today was also a favorite food of New Jersey's Indians, as attested by the frequency of its shell in middens along the New Jersey shore.

---

liberated into the water and combine by chance. There are very few vascular, flowering plants that have made the transition from land to marine life, but one, eelgrass, is very common in sheltered waters along the New Jersey coast. Its ribbon-like green leaves often wash ashore. But the absence of large plants does not mean that there is no food here for plant-eating animals, for the water itself, at least in summer, contains countless single-celled plants of many kinds in suspension. Mixed with them are microscopic animals, and the eggs of young fish, crabs, worms, and shellfish. Collectively, these organisms are called **plankton**.

To exploit this resource, many of the creatures of the sandy shore are **filter feeders**; that is, they draw in large

quantities of water, strain out the plankton, and expel the water. Most of them are burrowing species, to resist the movement of the shifting sands. Many species of marine worms fall into this category. So do all our clams and mussels, including the elongated razor clams; the very common, oval-shelled surf clam; the soft-shelled clam; the blue mussels that are found so abundantly on jetties and pilings; and the hard-shelled clam, or quahog. The hard-shelled clam so popular as food today was also a favorite food of New Jersey's Indians, as attested by the frequency of its shell in **middens** along the New Jersey shore.

There are **predators** in the sands as well, feeding on the clams and often on each other. In New Jersey, the commonest **carnivorous** mollusk is the northern moon snail. This large, globular animal burrows just beneath the sand, following scent trails to its **prey**. When it finds a buried clam, it engulfs the animal in its massive foot, drills a hole through the shell with an abrasive-studded tongue, and feeds at leisure. Surf clam shells that are found on the beach, with a neat round hole near the hinge end, show the work of the moon snail. Two other large snails, the channeled whelk and the knobbed whelk, also prey on **bivalves** but are **scavengers** as well. Not all predators are **mollusks**. Starfish, venturing from crevices in jetties and breakwaters, grasp exposed bivalves and gradually pull the valves apart, until they are able to feed on the animal inside.

© Carol Decker

Crabs, some fish, and gulls and shorebirds, all take their toll of the dwellers in the sand.

The shells of mollusks are common on the beach. In addition to those noted above, bivalves include chestnut astarte, blood ark, oyster, jingle shell, ribbed mussel, bay scallop, angel wing, and false angel wing. **Univalves** are likely to include the shells of several species of oyster drills, common periwinkle, and

New England and nassa mud snails. Large empty shells and other hard objects that have been long submerged often have slipper shells attached to them. There are three species: the common slipper, the convex slipper, and the flat slipper.

In addition to mollusk shells and a great variety of human artifacts, the beach drift is likely to contain skate egg cases shaped like rectangular black purses; the remains of several species of crabs and their close relatives; the hard parts of horseshoe crabs, more closely related to spiders than to the true crabs; the bones of fish and seabirds; and the skeletons of sea urchins and starfish. Jellyfish are common at some times of the year. The redbeard sponge is abundant in some places. When alive or freshly washed up, it is a bright orange-red, but soon dries to a dirty brown. Old pieces of driftwood are likely to be covered with acorn barnacles, which are **crustaceans**, not mollusks. They also may be riddled with burrows made by the shipworm, really a tunneling clam, and have **bryozoans**, **tunicates**, **sponges**, and marine algae growing on them. But the beach drift is full of surprises. One can sometimes find whale and dolphin bones, fossils washed from offshore deposits, and occasional seeds from tropical shores.

There are no amphibians, and few reptiles and mammals in this habitat. On sheltered beaches, an occasional diamondback terrapin might turn up, and perhaps lay eggs in the sand well above high tide line. Much less often, a sea turtle, most commonly a loggerhead, will be washed up on shore, usually dead. Offshore, the only mammal which is regularly visible is the bottle-nosed dolphin, which sometimes pursues fish into shallow water. In winter, harbor seals are seen regularly from New Jersey beaches.

Birds, however, are plentiful and conspicuous. Gulls are always present. In summer, the laughing gull is abundant. In winter, most move south. Great black-backed gulls, herring gulls, and ring-billed

---

One can sometimes find whale and dolphin bones, fossils washed from offshore deposits, and occasional seeds from tropical shores.

---

gulls can be seen most of the year. In winter, the small, tern-like Bonaparte's gull is often common, and can be distinguished from our other gulls by flashing white wings, easily visible at a distance. Gulls will eat almost anything, but usually feed at the surface, or on land. Terns, another group of birds, feed primarily on small fish, and often dive for their food. In New Jersey, we see common terns and Forster's terns most frequently, but during migration, Caspian terns and royal terns are seen often. The least tern nests on the beaches, as does the piping plover.

In winter, the waters off New Jersey also harbor a variety of ducks including greater scaup, oldsquaw, three species of scoters, common goldeneye, and red-breasted merganser as well as common and red-throated loons, and horned grebes. Shorebirds also may winter here. Dunlin are likely, and sanderlings patrol the high tide line, running in and out of the surf as they **forage** for food. The lucky observer, staring eastward toward the horizon three miles away, occasionally might glimpse a gannet or a kittiwake, truly **pelagic** birds, that spend their entire lives, except for the breeding season, at sea.

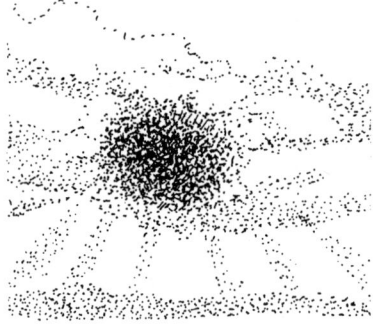

NEW JERSEY
AUDUBON
SOCIETY

# TYPICAL BEACH SPECIES

**MARINE ALGAE**
Sea lettuce
Enteromorpha
Codium
Rockweed
Knotted wrack
Agardhiella

**ARTHROPODS**
Spider crab
Horseshoe crab
Blue crab
Lady crab
Mole crab
Acorn barnacle

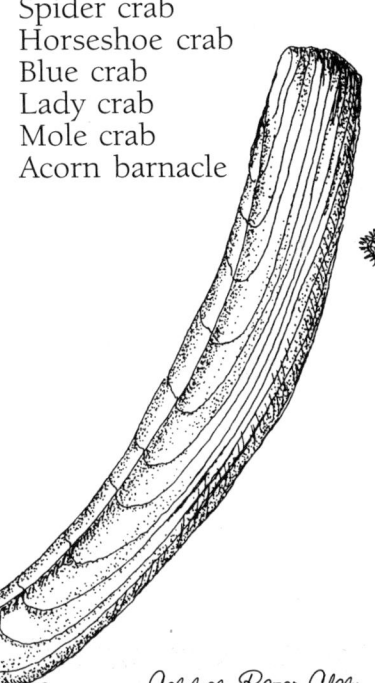

Common Razor Clam

**MOLLUSKS**
Slipper shell
Flat slipper shell
Nassa mud snail
New England mud snail
Common periwinkle
Oyster drill
Thick-lipped oyster drill
Channeled whelk
Knobbed whelk
Northern moon snail
Lobed moon snail
Blue mussel
Ribbed mussel
Jingle shell
Common razor clam
Stout tagelus

Chestnut astarte
Blood ark
Bay scallop
Deep-sea scallop
Angel wing
False angel wing
Shipworm
Hard-shelled clam
Surf clam
Soft-shelled clam
Common oyster

Asteriid Sea Star

**OTHER ORGANISMS**
Redbeard sponge
Common starfish
Green sea urchin
Clam worm
Blood worm
Plumed worm
Parchment worm
Jellyfish

**REPTILES**
Diamondback terrapin
Loggerhead turtle
Green sea turtle

**MAMMALS**
Harbor seal
Bottle-nosed dolphin

**BIRDS**
Herring gull
Laughing gull
Ring-billed gull

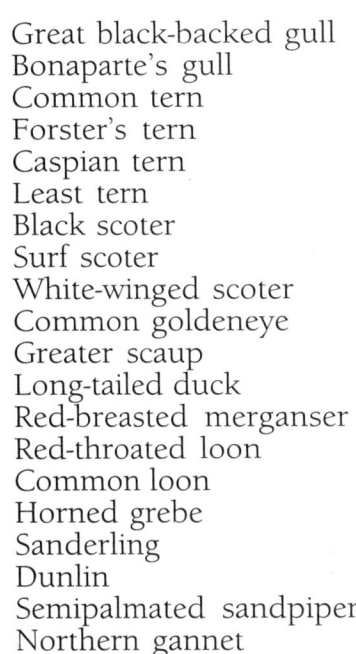

Great Black-backed Gull

Great black-backed gull
Bonaparte's gull
Common tern
Forster's tern
Caspian tern
Least tern
Black scoter
Surf scoter
White-winged scoter
Common goldeneye
Greater scaup
Long-tailed duck
Red-breasted merganser
Red-throated loon
Common loon
Horned grebe
Sanderling
Dunlin
Semipalmated sandpiper
Northern gannet

Bottle-nosed dolphin

NEW JERSEY
AUDUBON
SOCIETY

# WETLANDS HERE AND THERE

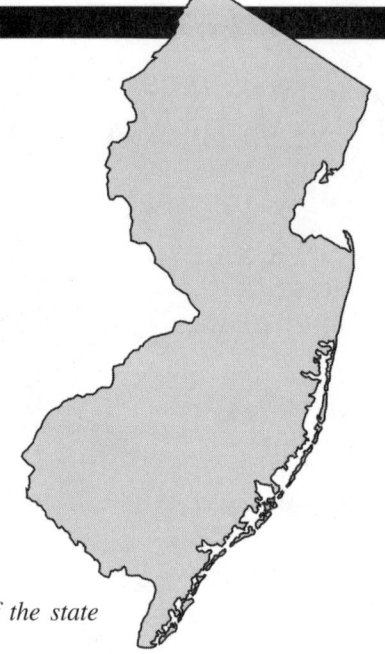

*This habitat is found in this area of the state*

Wetlands come in many forms. Ponds and lakes, rivers, fens, swamps and bogs are obvious, but that does not exhaust the category. Many wetlands, including some that are extremely important for wildlife and rare native plants, are small and temporary. These are the intermittent ponds - sometimes called vernal ponds - that form in shallow ground depressions during protracted periods of wet weather, whether it be after spring or autumn rains or after summer thunderstorms.

Intermittent ponds can form wherever impervious layers of clay, rock, or hardpan slow or prevent subsurface drainage; they can also form in porous soils when the local water table temporarily rises to intersect depressions in the land surface. The depressions themselves may have formed in various ways. Some may be remnants of larger bodies of water, which over millennia have partly filled with sediments in a process of pond succession. Others are remains of old stream channels. Some, such as abandoned sand pits and clay pits, mine holes, and gravel quarries, are man-made and can be found throughout New Jersey in one form or other. In the part of New Jersey that was glaciated during the last ice age - roughly the line of Interstate Route 80, with a dip south from Morristown to the Amboys - some are kettles, formed when huge blocks of ice embedded in glacial debris melted to leave water-filled holes. In the limestone areas of Sussex and Warren counties, some are sinks - depressions in the surface created by collapse of caves in the limestone beneath them. And some ponds in Cape May and Atlantic counties are "bays" - oval ponds of mysterious origin that are scattered from New Jersey to Florida.

Even when they are dry, shallow intermittent ponds can usually be recognized by the vegetation in and around them. Since frequent flooding prevents tree growth, the ponds remain open, although they may be rimmed with water-loving trees such as red maple, sour gum, and pin oak. At the same time, the frequent drying prevents the establishment of truly aquatic plants. Thus the vegetation of the pond itself usually consists of specialized annual or perennial herbs, grasses, sedges, and

*Broad-leaved Cattail*

NEW JERSEY
AUDUBON
SOCIETY

occasional shrubs that can tolerate the cycles of wet and dry. Woolgrass, cattails, common reed, purple loosestrife, blue vervain, and soft rush are just a few typical plants of intermittent ponds in open, sunny areas. Woodland pools are likely to have skunk cabbage, royal fern, buttonbush, water parsnip, tussock sedge as well as other sedges. Floating aquatic plants such as water meal and duckweed may be common in some ponds, forming a green film over the water. Coastal plain ponds may have bladderworts - carnivorous plants that catch small aquatic life in thin-walled traps on their underwater stems. Most of these plants of intermittent wetlands are also found in swamps and marshes. But some intermittent ponds have plants in them that never show themselves or never flower except in dry years, when the pond bottom may become a carpet of plants that are otherwise seldom seen; in wet years the plants remain more or less dormant or persist only as seeds in the mud of the pond bottom. Some examples include rose coreopsis, featherfoil, golden hedge hyssop, mermaid-weed, and sedges and grasses such as bald rush and floating manna-grass.

There are great differences between intermittent ponds in open, sunny, locations and ponds in shaded woodland settings. But whatever their origin and location, these intermittent ponds share some characteristics. Most

Painted Turtle

obviously, they are not permanently wet - in fact, some may be wet only occasionally and briefly. As a result, they do not have fish in them. With no fish to prey on them, insects and insect larvae abound. These ponds are prime breeding areas for dragonflies and damselflies. The adults feed on flying insects, including the mosquitoes and midges that also breed in the ponds, and their eggs, laid in the water, hatch into predatory larvae which feed on aquatic life. Several species of aquatic bugs (with sucking mouth parts) and beetles (with biting mouth parts) also are often found in these ponds. Water boatmen are inch-long bugs with hind legs flattened for swimming. Backswimmers, as the name suggests, swim upside-down; like water boatmen, they have legs flattened into paddles. Giant water bugs, up to three inches long, feed on other insects, tadpoles, and salamander larvae. Predaceous diving beetles of several species are common; both the adults and larvae are carnivorous.

Amphibians are usually the

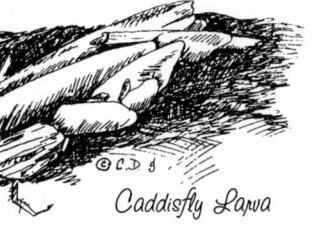

Caddisfly Larva

most obvious vertebrates in intermittent ponds. Like the insects, frogs and toads live and breed successfully in these ponds because fish are absent. Of course, larvae of amphibians that breed in intermittent ponds have to be able to complete the entire cycle from egg to air-breathing adult in one season - which in some ponds can be very short.

Hot dry summers can convert even a rather large pool to a sun-baked mud flat, strewn with dead and dessicated tadpoles and marked with the tracks of foraging scavengers. Wood frogs, American and Fowler's toads, spring peepers, chorus frogs, and cricket frogs manage this; and in the New Jersey Pine Barrens, the rare pine barrens tree frog often breeds in intermittent ponds. Species like the green frog and bullfrog, whose larvae often take several years to mature, don't breed very successfully in these ponds, though the adult frogs may inhabit them. The fastest-maturing tailless amphibian in New Jersey is the eastern spadefoot, a toad-like creature that spends most of its life underground but comes out to feed and breed after heavy summer rains have filled intermittent ponds.

Salamanders, including spotted salamander, eastern tiger salamander, Jefferson salamander, and blue-spotted salamander , also breed in these ponds, often making rather lengthy migrations to reach them. And even outside of the

breeding season, many salamanders, particularly the lungless species such as the red-backed, dusky, slimy, and two-lined salamanders, can often be found among damp debris on woodland pond edges. These salamanders absorb oxygen directly through their skins, which must be wet at all times. Red efts - the orange-colored subadult stage of the red-spotted newt - are often present around woodland pools, especially in northern New Jersey. The adults are aquatic, and mate and lay their eggs in water. The eggs hatch into gilled larvae, which rapidly metamorphose into red efts. These efts are terrestrial; they leave the water and may spend several years roaming the forest floor before returning to water to complete their metamorphosis. As a result, the species manages to colonize every suitable body of water within its range.

Other wildlife may frequent these pools, for as long as they last. Although none of our mammals typically lives in them, white-tailed deer and many other mammals come to drink in woodland pools, and their tracks reveal their comings and goings. Some do more than drink; predators such as raccoons, mink, and skunks find food in them. An occasional green heron or great blue heron may stop by for a meal.

Wood ducks find water, but not usually much food, in them. Spotted sandpipers may occasionally breed near them, and solitary sandpipers and yellowlegs drop in during migration. The abundant insect life is likely to attract other birds, such as yellow warbler, hooded warbler, northern waterthrush, and great crested flycatcher.

Reptiles are not particularly common in these ponds, but painted turtles may be found in almost any body of water, including some intermittent ponds. Spotted turtles often are found in woodland pools, where their pattern provides effective camouflage against a dark pond bottom flecked with spots of sunlight. Both turtle species feed on insects, insect larvae, and amphibian larvae. If the pond dries, the turtles may either leave them or aestivate in the mud of the pond bottom. Garter snakes and ribbon snakes and northern water snakes, all of which feed on amphibians, often can be found.

The small size of these intermittent ponds is often their downfall. Because they are not very obvious in the dry season, they are easy to ignore, easy to fill, and vulnerable to slight changes in drainage patterns. They are often regarded as mosquito-breeding nuisances by land-owners who are unaware of the rich drama of small lives and deaths within them. To farmers, they may be simply a wet spot in a field, to be drained and plowed. Even where there is no interest in filling them, the natural processes of pond succession tend to shrink them - a process accelerated by the lowering of ground water tables that often accompanies development. Aerial photos of farmland often show ghostly outlines of old ponds which are visible at ground level only as areas where crops grow a bit less tall than on adjacent uplands. Similar views of developed areas show houses, lawns, streets, and play areas where deer once drank and amphibians voiced their primeval chorus into the night.

Sour Gum

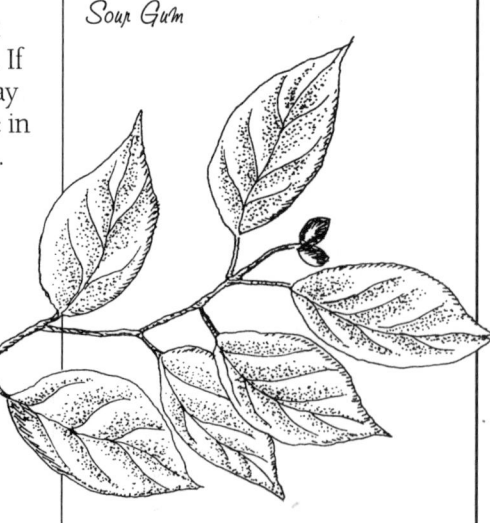

# TYPICAL WETLAND SPECIES

*Red Maple*

**TREES:**
Red maple
Silver maple
Sour gum

**SHRUBS:**
Buttonbush
Winterberry

**OTHER PLANTS:**
Cinnamon fern
Royal fern
Skunk cabbage
Water parsnip
Water purslane
Marsh marigold
Woolgrass
Broad-leaved cattail
Common reed
Purple loosestrife
Blue vervain
Soft rush
Duckweed
Water meal
Rose coreopsis
Featherfoil
Golden hedge hyssop
Mermaid-weed
Bald rush
Horned rush
Floating manna-grass
Humped bladderwort

**AMPHIBIANS:**
Green frog
Wood frog
Gray tree frog
Southern gray tree frog
Pine barrens tree frog
Spring peeper
Cricket frog
American toad
Fowler's toad
Eastern spadefoot
Eastern tiger salamander
Spotted salamander
Jefferson salamander
Marbled salamander
Blue-spotted salamander
Dusky salamander
Two-lined salamander
Slimy salamander
Red-spotted newt

*American Toad*

**REPTILES:**
Spotted turtle
Eastern painted turtle
Northern water snake
Garter snake
Ribbon snake

**BIRDS:**
Great blue heron
Green heron
Northern waterthrush
Spotted sandpiper
Yellow warbler

**MAMMALS:**
Raccoon
Mink
White-tailed deer

*Cinnamon Fern*

*Raccoon*

NEW JERSEY
AUDUBON
SOCIETY

**Habitats of New Jersey**

# NOTES

Y = yes
N = no
P = partial
* = see comments

**AVAILABLE SITES FOR HABITAT STUDY**

| | Urban Landscape | Vacant Lot | Field | Pond and Lake | River and Stream | Freshwater Marsh | Cedar Swamp | Sugar Maple/Mixed Hardwood Forest | Hemlock Forest | Northern New Jersey Mixed Oak Forest | Hardwood Swamp | Southern New Jersey Mixed Oak Forest | Pine Forest | Coastal Dunes and Forest | Salt Marsh | Beach | Bus Parking | Restrooms | Picnic Area | Naturalist Available | Fee for Naturalist | Self-Guided Field Trips | Handicap Accessible | Comments |
|---|---|---|---|---|---|---|---|---|---|---|---|---|---|---|---|---|---|---|---|---|---|---|---|---|
| **ATLANTIC COUNTY** **Atlantic County Park**   **Warren E. Fox Nature Center** 109 St. Hwy. 50, Mays Landing, NJ 08330 609-625-7000 x 5405 | | | X | X | X | X | X | | | | | X | X | X | X | | Y | Y | Y | Y | N | Y | Y | Backyard Habitat Laboratory |
| **Edwin B. Forsythe National Wildlife Refuge**   **Brigantine Division** Great Creek Road, Oceanville, NJ 08231 609-652-1665 | | | X | | | X | | | | | | X | | | X | | Y | Y | Y | P | N | Y | Y | Groups must call ahead. Passports stamped on weekdays only. |
| **BERGEN COUNTY** **Closter Nature Center** P.O. Box 80, Closter, NJ 07624 201-750-2778 | | | | X | X | | | | | X | X | | | | | | Y | Y | Y | Y | Y | Y | P | |
| **Flat Rock Brook Nature Center** 443 Van Nostrand Ave., Englewood, NJ 07631 201-567-1265 | | | X | X | X | | | | | X | | | | | | | Y | Y | Y | Y | Y | Y | Y | |
| **Hackensack Meadowlands Development**   **Commission Environment Center** 2 DeKorte Park Plaza, Lyndhurst, NJ 07071 201-460-8300 | | | X | | | X | | | | | | | | | X | | Y | Y | Y | Y | Y | Y | Y | |
| **James A. McFaul Environment Center** Crescent Avenue, Wyckoff, NJ 07481 201-891-5571 | | | X | X | | | | X | | X | X | | | | | | Y | Y | Y | Y | Y | Y | Y | |
| **New Jersey Audubon Society's**   **Lorrimer Sanctuary** 790 Ewing Avenue, P.O. Box 125 Franklin Lakes, NJ 07417 201-891-2185    www.njaudubon.org | X | | | | | | | | | X | | | | | | | Y | Y | N | Y | Y | Y | P | |
| **The Palisades Nature Association**   **Green Brook Sanctuary** P.O. Box 155, Alpine, NJ 07620 201-768-1360 | | | X | X | X | | | | | X | | | | | | | Y | Y | Y | Y | Y | N | N | |
| **Tenafly Nature Center** 313 Hudson Avenue, Tenafly, NJ 07670 201-568-6093 www.tenaflynaturecenter.org | | | | X | X | | | X | | X | | | | | | | Y | Y | Y | Y | Y | Y | P | |

NEW JERSEY AUDUBON SOCIETY

## AVAILABLE SITES FOR HABITAT STUDY

Y = yes
N = no
P = partial
✻ = see comments

| | URBAN LANDSCAPE | VACANT LOT | FIELD | POND AND LAKE | RIVER AND STREAM | FRESHWATER MARSH | CEDAR SWAMP | SUGAR MAPLE/MIXED HARDWOOD FOREST | HEMLOCK FOREST | NORTHERN NEW JERSEY MIXED OAK FOREST | HARDWOOD SWAMP | SOUTHERN NEW JERSEY MIXED OAK FOREST | PINE FOREST | COASTAL DUNES AND FOREST | SALT MARSH | BEACH | BUS PARKING | RESTROOMS | PICNIC AREA | NATURALIST AVAILABLE | FEE FOR NATURALIST | SELF-GUIDED FIELD TRIPS | HANDICAP ACCESSIBLE | COMMENTS |
|---|---|---|---|---|---|---|---|---|---|---|---|---|---|---|---|---|---|---|---|---|---|---|---|---|
| **BURLINGTON COUNTY** **Camp Kettle Run**   Girl Scout Council of the South Jersey Pines 2944 Victoria Ave., P.O. Box 948 Newfield, NJ 08344-0948 856-697-3900 x 23 | | | X | X | X | X | | | | | | X | X | | | | Y | Y | Y | N | N | Y | P | |
| **Lebanon State Forest** P.O. Box 215 New Lisbon, NJ 08064 609-726-1191 | | X | X | X | X | | | | | | X | X | X | | | | Y | Y | Y | ✻ | N | Y | P | Seasonal Naturalist (Memorial Day to Labor Day) |
| **New Jersey Audubon Society's**   Rancocas Nature Center 1120 Rancocas Road, Mt. Holly, NJ 08060 609-261-2495 www.njaudubon.org | | | X | | X | X | | | | | | X | X | | | | Y | Y | Y | Y | Y | Y | P | |
| **Wharton State Forest** RD #4, Batsto Hammonton, NJ 08037 609-561-3262 | | | X | X | X | X | X | | | | | X | X | | | | Y | Y | Y | Y | N | Y | P | |
| **Woodford Cedar Run Wildlife Refuge** 4 Sawmill Road, Medford, NJ 08055-8132 856-983-0326 | | | | X | X | X | | | | | X | X | X | | | | Y | Y | Y | Y | Y | N | Y | Live animals in wildlife compound |
| **CAMDEN COUNTY** **Berlin Park** Camden County Environmental Studies Center Park Drive at Estaugh Avenue Berlin, NJ 08009 609-767-7275 | | | | X | X | | | | | | | X | | | | | Y | Y | Y | N | N | Y | Y | |
| **CAPE MAY COUNTY** **Cape May Point State Park** P.O. Box 107, Cape May Point, NJ 08212 609-884-2159 | | X | X | X | | X | | | | | | X | | X | X | | Y | Y | Y | Y | Y | Y | Y | World famous fall bird migration |
| **The Wetlands Institute** 1075 Stone Harbor Boulevard Stone Harbor, NJ 08247-1924 609-368-1211 www.Wetlandsinstitute.org | | | | | | | | | | | | | | | X | | Y | Y | Y | Y | Y | Y | Y | |

Bridges to the Natural World

NEW JERSEY AUDUBON SOCIETY

# AVAILABLE SITES FOR HABITAT STUDY

Y = yes
N = no
P = partial
✳ = see comments

| | Urban Landscape | Vacant Lot | Field | Pond and Lake | River and Stream | Freshwater Marsh | Cedar Swamp | Sugar Maple/Mixed Hardwood Forest | Hemlock Forest | Northern New Jersey Mixed Oak Forest | Hardwood Swamp | Southern New Jersey Mixed Oak Forest | Pine Forest | Coastal Dunes and Forest | Salt Marsh | Beach | Bus Parking | Restrooms | Picnic Area | Naturalist Available | Fee for Naturalist | Self-Guided Field Trips | Handicap Accessible | Comments |
|---|---|---|---|---|---|---|---|---|---|---|---|---|---|---|---|---|---|---|---|---|---|---|---|---|
| **New Jersey Audubon Society's Nature Center of Cape May** 1600 Delaware Ave., Cape May City, NJ 08204 609-898-8848 www.njaudubon.org | | X | X | X | | | | | | | | | | X | X | X | Y | Y | Y | Y | Y | Y | Y | Model Habitat Gardens |
| **CUMBERLAND COUNTY** **Delaware Bay Schooner Project** 2800 High Street, Port Norris, NJ 07626 856-785-2060 x 101 www.ajmeerwald.org | | X | | | X | | | | | | | | | | X | | Y | Y | Y | Y | Y | Y | P | Schooner trips on the bay available by appointment |
| **ESSEX COUNTY** **Cora Hartshorn Arboretum & Bird Sanctuary** 324 Forest Drive South, Short Hills, NJ 07078 973-376-3587 www.hartshornarboretum.com | | | | | | | | | | X | | | | | | | Y | Y | N | Y | Y | N | N | |
| **GLOUCESTER COUNTY** **Scotland Run Park Nature Center** **Gloucester County Parks and Recreation** 6 Blackwood - Barnsboro Road Sewell, NJ 08080 856-881-0845 | X | | | X | X | | | | | | | X | | | | | Y | Y | Y | Y | N | Y | Y | Pre-registration required. (Beach and dune are not handicap accessible) |
| **HUDSON COUNTY** **Liberty State Park Interpretive Center** Morris Pesin Drive, Jersey City, NJ 07305 201-915-3409 www.state.nj.us/dep/forestry/parks/liberty.htm | | X | X | X | | | | | | | | | | | X | | Y | Y | Y | Y | N | Y | Y | |
| **HUNTERDON COUNTY** **Hunterdon County Department of Parks and Recreation** 1020 Route 31, Lebanon, NJ 08833 908-782-1158 www.co.hunterdon.nj.us | | | X | X | X | X | | X | X | X | X | X | | | | | Y | Y | Y | Y | Y | Y | Y | |
| **MERCER COUNTY** **Hamilton/Trenton Marsh** **c/o Delaware & Raritan Greenway** 1328 Canal Road Princeton, NJ 08540 609-924-4646 | | | | X | | X | | | | | X | | | | | | Y | Y | Y | Y | Y | Y | N | Part of the Marsh study area is also in Burlington County |

Y = yes
N = no
P = partial
✱ = see comments

AVAILABLE SITES FOR HABITAT STUDY

| Site | Urban Landscape | Vacant Lot | Field | Pond and Lake | River and Stream | Freshwater Marsh | Cedar Swamp | Sugar Maple/Mixed Hardwood Forest | Hemlock Forest | Northern New Jersey Mixed Oak Forest | Hardwood Swamp | Southern New Jersey Mixed Oak Forest | Pine Forest | Coastal Dunes and Forest | Salt Marsh | Beach | Bus Parking | Restrooms | Picnic Area | Naturalist Available | Fee for Naturalist | Self-Guided Field Trips | Handicap Accessible | Comments |
|---|---|---|---|---|---|---|---|---|---|---|---|---|---|---|---|---|---|---|---|---|---|---|---|---|
| **The Nature Center** **Washington Crossing State Park** 355 Washington Crossing-Pennington Road Titusville, NJ 08560-9643 609-737-0609 | | | X | X | X | | X | | | X | | | | | | | Y | Y | Y | Y | N | Y | Y | |
| **Stony Brook-Millstone Watershed Association** **Buttinger Nature Center** 31 Titus Mill Road, Pennington, NJ 08534 609-737-7592 www.thewatershed.org | | X | X | X | X | X | | | | X | X | | | | X | | Y | Y | Y | Y | Y | Y | Y | Trails are not handicap accessible |
| **MIDDLESEX COUNTY** **Cheesequake State Park Interpretive Center** Gordon Road, Matawan, NJ 07747 732-556-3208 www.cheesequakestatepark.com | | | X | X | | X | X | | | X | | X | | | X | | Y | Y | Y | Y | N | Y | Y | Wed. - Sun., 10 to 3 |
| **New Jersey Audubon Society's** **Plainsboro Preserve** 80 Scotts Corner Road, Plainsboro, NJ 08536 609-897-9400 www.njaudubon.org | | X | X | X | X | | | | | | | X | | | | | Y | N | N | Y | Y | Y | Y | |
| **MONMOUTH COUNTY** **Allaire State Park** P.O. Box 220 Farmingdale, NJ 07727 732-938-2371 | | | X | X | X | | | | | X | X | X | | | | | Y | Y | Y | Y | N | N | P | |
| **Holmdel Park Activity Center** **Monmouth County Park System** 805 Newman Springs Road Lincroft, NJ 07738 732-842-4000 Ext. 4256 | | | X | X | X | X | | | | X | | | | | | | Y | Y | Y | Y | Y | Y | P | |
| **Huber Woods Environmental Center** **Monmouth County Park System** 805 Newman Springs Road Lincroft, NJ 07738 908-872-2670 | | | X | | | | | | | X | | X | | | | | Y | Y | Y | Y | Y | Y | Y | |

NEW JERSEY AUDUBON SOCIETY

AVAILABLE SITES FOR HABITAT STUDY

Y = yes
N = no
P = partial
* = see comments

| Site | Urban Landscape | Vacant Lot | Field | Pond and Lake | River and Stream | Freshwater Marsh | Cedar Swamp | Sugar Maple/Mixed Hardwood Forest | Hemlock Forest | Northern New Jersey Mixed Oak Forest | Hardwood Swamp | Southern New Jersey Mixed Oak Forest | Pine Forest | Coastal Dunes and Forest | Salt Marsh | Beach | Bus Parking | Restrooms | Picnic Area | Naturalist Available | Fee for Naturalist | Self-Guided Field Trips | Handicap Accessible | Comments |
|---|---|---|---|---|---|---|---|---|---|---|---|---|---|---|---|---|---|---|---|---|---|---|---|---|
| **Kateri Environmental Education Center** Conover Road, Wickatunk, NJ 07765, 732-946-9694 Ext. 45 | | X | X | X | X | X | | X | | X | | | X | | | | Y | Y | Y | Y | Y | N | Y | |
| **New Jersey Audubon Society's Sandy Hook Bird Observatory** 20 Hartshorne Drive, Fort Hancock, NJ 07732, 732-872-2500, www.njaudubon.org | | | | | | | | | | | | | | X | X | X | Y | Y | Y | Y | Y | N | Y | |
| **Ocean Institute Brookdale Community College** P.O. Box 533, Sandy Hook, NJ 07732, 732-224-2435, www.brookdale.cc.nj.us/staff/sandyhook/index.html | | X | X | X | X | X | X | | | X | | | | X | X | X | Y | Y | Y | Y | N | Y | Y | Programs scheduled by mail ONLY |
| **Poricy Park** P.O. Box 36, Middletown, NJ 07748, 732-842-5966, www.monmouth.com/~poricypark | | | X | X | X | | X | | | X | | | | | | | Y | Y | N | Y | Y | Y | P | Programs scheduled by mail |
| **Sandy Hook Environmental Center Gateway National Recreation Area** P.O. Box 530, Sandy Hook, NJ 07732-0530, 732-872-5970 | | X | X | X | | | | | | | | | | X | X | X | Y | Y | Y | Y | N | Y | P | |
| **Seven Presidents Oceanfront Park Monmouth County Park System** 805 Newman Springs Road, Lincroft, NJ 07738, 732-842-4000 Ext. 4256 | | | | | | | | | | | | | | X | | X | Y | Y | Y | Y | Y | Y | Y | |
| **Shark River Park Monmouth County Park System** 805 Newman Springs Road, Lincroft, NJ 07738, 732-842-4000 Ext. 4256 | | | X | X | X | X | | | | X | X | | | | X | | Y | Y | Y | N | Y | Y | P | Trails are not handicap accessible |
| **Thompson Park Monmouth County Park System** 805 Newman Springs Road, Lincroft, NJ 07738, 732-842-4000 Ext. 4256 | | | X | X | X | | | | | X | X | | | | | | Y | Y | Y | Y | Y | * | Y | 50 or more must call ahead |

COMMENTS

NEW JERSEY AUDUBON SOCIETY

# AVAILABLE SITES FOR HABITAT STUDY

Y = yes
N = no
P = partial
✲ = see comments

| | URBAN LANDSCAPE | VACANT LOT | FIELD | POND AND LAKE | RIVER AND STREAM | FRESHWATER MARSH | CEDAR SWAMP | SUGAR MAPLE/MIXED HARDWOOD FOREST | HEMLOCK FOREST | NORTHERN NEW JERSEY MIXED OAK FOREST | HARDWOOD SWAMP | SOUTHERN NEW JERSEY MIXED OAK FOREST | PINE FOREST | COASTAL DUNES AND FOREST | SALT MARSH | BEACH | BUS PARKING | RESTROOMS | PICNIC AREA | NATURALIST AVAILABLE | FEE FOR NATURALIST | SELF-GUIDED FIELD TRIPS | HANDICAP ACCESSIBLE | COMMENTS |
|---|---|---|---|---|---|---|---|---|---|---|---|---|---|---|---|---|---|---|---|---|---|---|---|---|
| **Turkey Swamp Park**    Monmouth County Park System   805 Newman Springs Road   Lincroft, NJ 07738   732-842-4000 Ext. 4256 | | | X | X | | | | | | | X | X | X | | | | Y | Y | Y | N | Y | Y | P | |
| **MORRIS COUNTY**   **Great Swamp Outdoor Education Center**   247 Southern Boulevard   Chatham, NJ 07928   973-635-6629 | | | X | X | X | X | | | | X | X | | | | | | Y | Y | N | Y | Y | Y | Y | |
| **Hacklebarney State Park**   119 Hacklebarney Road   Long Valley, NJ 07853   908-879-5677 | | | X | | X | | | | X | X | | | | | | | Y | Y | Y | N | N | Y | N | |
| **Jockey Hollow Environmental Studies Center**    Morris Area Girl Scout Council   1579 Sussex Turnpike   Randolph, NJ 07869   973-927-7722 | | | | | X | | | X | | X | | | | | | | Y | Y | Y | ✲ | Y | Y | N | Scout groups ONLY |
| **OCEAN COUNTY**   **Cooper Environmental Center**   1170 Cattus Island Boulevard   Toms River, NJ 08753   732-270-6960 | | | X | | | | | | | | X | X | | X | | | Y | Y | Y | Y | N | N | Y | |
| **Island Beach State Park**   P.O. Box 37   Seaside Park, NJ 08752   732-793-0506 | | | | | X | | | | | | | | | X | X | X | Y | Y | Y | ✲ | N | Y | P | Seasonal naturalist |
| **PASSAIC COUNTY**   **John J. Crowley Nature Center**    Passaic County Parks Department   317 Pennsylvania Avenue   Paterson, NJ 07503   973-523-0024 | | | | X | | | | | | | X | | | | | | Y | Y | Y | N | N | Y | P | Restrooms are not handicap accessible |
| **New Jersey Audubon Society's**    **Weis Ecology Center**   150 Snake Den Road, Ringwood, NJ 07456   973-835-2160   www.njaudubon.org | | | X | X | | X | | | | X | | | | | | | Y | Y | Y | Y | Y | Y | Y | Day use and residential programs by advance registration only |

NEW JERSEY AUDUBON SOCIETY

**AVAILABLE SITES FOR HABITAT STUDY**

Y = yes
N = no
P = partial
✻ = see comments

| Site | Urban Landscape | Vacant Lot | Field | Pond and Lake | River and Stream | Freshwater Marsh | Cedar Swamp | Sugar Maple/Mixed Hardwood Forest | Hemlock Forest | Northern New Jersey Mixed Oak Forest | Hardwood Swamp | Southern New Jersey Mixed Oak Forest | Pine Forest | Coastal Dunes and Forest | Salt Marsh | Beach | Bus Parking | Restrooms | Picnic Area | Naturalist Available | Fee for Naturalist | Self-Guided Field Trips | Handicap Accessible | Comments |
|---|---|---|---|---|---|---|---|---|---|---|---|---|---|---|---|---|---|---|---|---|---|---|---|---|
| **SALEM COUNTY** **Parvin State Park** 701 Almond Road Pittsgrove, NJ 08318 856-358-8616 | | X | | X | X | X | X | | | | | X | X | | | | Y | Y | Y | Y | N | Y | P | |
| **SOMERSET COUNTY** **New Jersey Audubon Society's Scherman Hoffman Wildlife Sanctuary** 11 Hardscrabble Road, P.O. Box 693 Bernardsville, NJ 07924 908-766-5787 www.njaudubon.org | | | X | X | | | | | | X | | | | | | | Y | Y | N | Y | Y | Y | Y | |
| **Somerset County Park Commission's Environmental Education Center** 190 Lord Sterling Road Basking Ridge, NJ 07920 908-766-2489 | | | X | X | X | X | | | | X | X | | | | | | Y | Y | N | Y | Y | Y | Y | |
| **SUSSEX COUNTY** **Fairview Lake Environmental Education Center** 1035 Fairview Lake Road Newton, NJ 07860 973-383-9282 | | | | X | X | | | | | X | X | | X | | | | Y | Y | Y | Y | Y | Y | P | All courses aligned with NJ core curriculum standards |
| **High Point State Park** 1480 State Route 23 Sussex, NJ 07461 973-875-4800 | | | X | X | X | X | X | X | X | X | | | | | | | Y | Y | Y | Y | N | N | P | |
| **Ken Etiwa Pec YMCA Outdoor Center** 23 Birch Ridge Road, Hardwick, NJ 07925 973-300-0021 (April-October) 908-362-8217 (Winter) | | | X | X | X | X | X | | | X | X | | | | | | Y | Y | N | Y | Y | N | P | Residential facilities in Delaware Watergap N.R.A |
| **New Jersey School of Conservation** 1 Wapalanne Road Branchville, NJ 07826 800-624-7790 or 973-655-7614 http://csam.montclair.edu/njsoc | | | | X | X | | | X | X | X | X | | | | | | Y | Y | N | Y | Y | Y | Y | Residential facilities |

NEW JERSEY AUDUBON SOCIETY

**AVAILABLE SITES FOR HABITAT STUDY**

Y = yes
N = no
P = partial
* = see comments

| Site | Urban Landscape | Vacant Lot | Field | Pond and Lake | River and Stream | Freshwater Marsh | Cedar Swamp | Sugar Maple/Mixed Hardwood Forest | Hemlock Forest | Northern New Jersey Mixed Oak Forest | Hardwood Swamp | Southern New Jersey Mixed Oak Forest | Pine Forest | Coastal Dunes and Forest | Salt Marsh | Beach | Bus Parking | Restrooms | Picnic Area | Naturalist Available | Fee for Naturalist | Self-Guided Field Trips | Handicap Accessible | Comments |
|---|---|---|---|---|---|---|---|---|---|---|---|---|---|---|---|---|---|---|---|---|---|---|---|---|
| Walpack Valley Environmental Education Center, P.O. Box 134, Walpack, NJ 07881, 973-948-5749 | | | X | X | X | | | X | X | X | | | | | | | Y | Y | Y | Y | Y | N | P | Residential and day field trips by registration only |
| **UNION COUNTY** Reeves-Reed Arboretum, 165 Hobart Avenue, Summit, NJ 07901, 908-273-8787, www.reevew-reedarboretum.org | | | X | X | | | | X | X | X | | | | | | | Y | Y | N | Y | Y | Y | P | |
| Trailside Nature and Science Center, 452 New Providence Road, Mountainside, NJ 07092, 908-789-3670 from 9am to 1pm, www.unioncountynj.org | | | X | X | X | | | X | X | X | X | | | | | | Y | Y | Y | Y | Y | Y | Y | |
| **WARREN COUNTY** Mason YMCA Outdoor Center, 23 Birch Ridge Road, Hardwick, NJ 07825, 908-362-8217, www.CampMason.org | | | X | X | X | X | X | X | | X | X | | | | | | Y | Y | Y | Y | Y | N | P | Residential facilities and programs ONLY |
| Merrill Creek Reservoir, 34 Merrill Creek Road, Washington, NJ 07882, 908-454-3339, www.MerrillCreek.org | | | X | X | X | | | X | | X | | X | | | | | Y | Y | Y | Y | N | Y | Y | Picnic carry in/out |
| Pequest Trout Hatchery and Natural Resource Education Center, 605 Pequest Road, Oxford, NJ 07863, 908-637-4125, www.njfishandwildlife.com | | | X | X | X | X | | X | | X | | | | | | | Y | Y | Y | Y | N | * | P | Teacher orientation required |
| **PENNSYLVANIA** Pocono Environmental Education Center, Briscoe Mountain Road, RR #2, P.O. Box 1010, Dingmans Ferry, PA 18328, 570-828-2319, www.peec.org | | | X | X | X | X | X | X | X | X | X | | X | | | | Y | Y | Y | Y | Y | Y | P | Residential facilities available |

*Bridges to the Natural World*

Section

2

# NATURAL HISTORY LESSONS

## HOW TO USE THIS SECTION

Each habitat described in Section One has its own set of dynamics. The activities, games and simulations in Section Two also create a dynamic as they focus on fundamental learning concepts and exercise critical thinking skills as they relate to the habitat of study. Each lesson should be treated as a means to learning the structure, **indicator species**, and uniqueness of the habitat or natural community. Although each lesson can be used as a single experience to teach a concept, when used in conjunction with each other they open more possibilities for children to understand that they are part of a whole greater than themselves.

The activities treat the following environmental science concepts: habitats, natural communities, ecosystems, human ecological impacts, and human land stewardship practices. Each is defined in the Table of Contents.

GRADE LEVEL
Although the activities have been labeled for specific grade levels, the teacher often is given suggestions for extensions of, or adaptations to, the lesson that make them appropriate for higher or lower grade students.

LENGTH OF ACTIVITY
The time indicated represents only that used in the procedure of the main activity.

MISSION LOGO
Each lesson and activity has a mission logo. This indicates student participation in one or more of New Jersey Audubon's threefold mission areas of conservation, education, and research.
- Conservation - lessons and activities contain practice in the skills and behaviors that are applied in preserving or enhancing habitat.
- Education - students share what they learn with others in their class or school or members of the community.
- Research - skills within the activity or lesson are those practiced by scientists doing field research that lead to conservation practices.

BACKGROUND INFORMATION
Information is provided to help the teacher gain a broad understanding of the lesson's intent. All information supports the basic concepts taught in the lesson.

BASIC CONCEPTS
Lessons were developed to illustrate basic concepts in ways that relate to natural phenomena in New Jersey.

ASSESSMENT
Each lesson is designed to include ongoing assessment of student answers and student participation. Some lessons and activities include worksheets to evaluate student observations and application of critical thinking skills. Other assessment tools can be found in Section Four of this book.

NEW JERSEY CORE CURRICULUM CONTENT STANDARDS
All of the lessons are aligned with the standards and address all applicable content areas. A table of standards matching the lessons can be found on the education section of the NJAS website (www.njaudubon.org).

In an effort to address the cultural diversity and multitude of languages in New Jersey's schools, the authors have identified those lessons or activities that lend themselves to translation by mentioning same in Take Another Step.

Natural History Lessons

NEW JERSEY
AUDUBON
SOCIETY

## MATERIALS
The materials required for the activities are all things that could be found in the ordinary household or classroom. Care has been taken to direct, whenever possible, the re-use of materials that would ordinarily be discarded or recycled.

Special information cards are part of the publication. Photocopying these playing materials for student participation does not violate copyright restrictions.

## PREPLANNING
While effort has been made to keep preparation simple, extra time may be required to collect some materials.

## MOTIVATIONAL ACTIVITY
Motivational activities are designed to direct the student's mind toward the concepts to be learned. Questions or activities draw on the student's personal experience and arouse a curiosity and expectancy for learning something new. None should exceed five minutes. Possible answers for all questions are in parentheses ( ).

## PROCEDURE
Like a cookbook, each procedure takes the teacher through a step-by-step explanation of the activity as it is to be explained to the students.

## PUTTING IT ALL TOGETHER
A child stands little chance of converting facts and information into personal knowledge unless he or she can apply the information to personal experience. This part of the lesson helps make that application. Ten or fifteen minutes should be enough for this wrap-up session.

## TAKE ANOTHER STEP
Putting the knowledge to work through extended activities assures the development of new attitudes and new behaviors for the students, making the learning experience a part of life.

## THINKING SKILLS
Each lesson is designed to guide the students through a process that will allow them to demonstrate their understanding of the content matter, analyze information, and apply the knowledge they have gained to new or different situations. The skills are listed after the questions or activity directions in brackets [ ].

## FOR MORE INFORMATION
Titles and authors of supplementary works are listed at the end of most lessons. The expanded bibliography in the appendix supplies the complete bibliographic information for these works.

# INTERDISCIPLINARY MATRIX

Natural History Lessons

| | SCIENCE | MATH | LANGUAGE ARTS | READING | SOCIAL STUDIES | MUSIC | ART | PHYSICAL EDUCATION |
|---|---|---|---|---|---|---|---|---|
| **HABITATS** | | | | | | | | |
| Nature's House ............ p. 116 | X | | X | | X | | | |
| Squirrel Signs ............ p. 121 | X | X | X | | | X | | |
| It's All in the Name ............ p. 126 | X | | X | | | | | |
| From Basement to Attic ............ p. 129 | X | X | X | | X | | X | |
| Nature's Symphony ............ p. 133 | X | | X | | | X | X | |
| Smile, Please ............ p. 140 | X | X | X | | | | X | |
| An Eventful Journey ............ p. 143 | X | | X | X | X | | | X |
| Can't We Share? ............ p. 151 | X | | X | X | X | | | |
| **NATURAL COMMUNITIES** | | | | | | | | |
| Nature's Palette ............ p. 155 | X | | X | | | | X | |
| A Dawn Chorus ............ p. 159 | X | | X | | | X | | |
| Leaves on Parade ............ p. 165 | X | X | X | | | | X | |
| Windows on the World ............ p. 171 | X | X | X | | X | | | |
| Myths, Legends & Storytelling ... p. 175 | X | | X | X | X | | X | |
| What Is Your Niche? ............ p. 179 | X | | X | X | X | | | |
| **ECOSYSTEMS** | | | | | | | | |
| Energy Play ............ p. 183 | X | | X | | | | X | |
| The Eaters and the Eaten ............ p. 187 | X | X | X | | X | | | X |
| Great Growing Ground Stuff .... p. 192 | X | | X | | | | | |
| The Disappearing Leaf ............ p. 200 | X | X | X | | | | | |
| Birds in the Nest ............ p. 205 | X | X | X | | X | | | X |
| The Eco-Connection ............ p. 210 | X | | X | X | | | | |
| **HUMAN ECOLOGICAL IMPACTS** | | | | | | | | |
| Litter Bits ............ p. 217 | X | X | X | | X | | | |
| Go With the Flow ............ p. 221 | X | | X | | X | | | |
| Riverside Drive ............ p. 225 | X | | X | | X | | X | |
| As the Cookie Crumbles ............ p. 228 | X | X | X | | X | | | |
| **HUMAN LAND STEWARDSHIP PRACTICES** | | | | | | | | |
| Check, Inspect and Protect Our Birds ............ p. 232 | X | X | X | X | | | | |
| Habitat Helpers ............ p. 237 | X | X | X | | X | | | |
| Open Spaces, Wild places ......... p. 241 | X | X | X | | X | | X | |

LENGTH OF ACTIVITY
2 periods
20-30
minutes each

GRADE LEVELS
1 - 6

Natural History Lessons

# NATURE'S HOUSE

The earliest records of human history show that people seek or construct shelters for protection from precipitation, wind, and extreme temperatures. As civilization and societies change, some of these shelters also change in structure.

Many human shelters have names like apartments, town houses, duplex houses, and ranch houses. Shelters tend to fit the needs and purposes of diversified populations. A single student in the city who needs only room enough to sleep, eat, and study may prefer a studio apartment. A couple raising a young family will need more space to accommodate the individual needs of family members. The location, size of the structure, and arrangement of the space are determined by the needs and preferences of the inhabitants.

Many human needs are no different from the needs of plants and animals. We, like they, need food and fresh water, shelter from the elements, and sufficient space. Each wildlife or plant species is found in a specific habitat or natural community that fulfills its needs. Polar bears and monkeys will never meet in the wild. Palm trees will not survive the winter if planted in New Jersey. These species require their own climate and set of community interactions. They cannot adapt. Likewise, these habitats, or natural communities exhibit different structures. A salt marsh is different in structure from a forest or field or beach. Within these structures, many plants and animals find the materials and spaces they require to meet individual needs and preferences.

All living things share these commonalities. They need food, water, shelter and space in an arrangement that will support their life cycle and enable them to reproduce their own kind for the continuation of the species.

## PROCESS SKILLS

*Observing, classifying, communicating, comparing, inferring, collecting data, drawing conclusions, and evaluating.*

NEW JERSEY
AUDUBON
SOCIETY

**Bridges to the Natural World**

## BASIC CONCEPTS

☞ All living things need food, water, shelter, and space in an appropriate arrangement.

☞ People arrange their shelters according to need and preference.

☞ Plants and animals act as indicators that define a habitat.

☞ Habitat structure in the natural world meets the needs of the indicator plant and animal species.

## MATERIALS

**Lesson 1**

☐ chalk board or flip chart for brainstorming

**Lesson 2**

☐ Nature's House Data Sheet (Figure 1)

### PREPLANNING

1. Assemble the supplies.

2. Find a natural area to explore for part 2 of this lesson.

# LESSON 1: MOTIVATIONAL ACTIVITY

Ask the students, "What would it be like if there was no school building and we met for class outside every day? Let's list the advantages and disadvantages."

(Advantages - nice to be outside in the fresh air and sunshine, different scenery with each season, nice to hear the sounds of birds, and feel the breeze.
Disadvantages - Cold in winter, rain and snow would ruin paper and books, no control of the noises)

### PROCEDURE

1. Let's think about the different types of buildings in which people live. (Apartment, one-story, two-family, colonial, etc.)

2. Write the word *structure* on the blackboard. Let's describe these structures and discuss what makes them the same and what makes them different. Create a list on the blackboard. (Same: have roof, walls, doors, and windows, similar functions to the rooms - kitchen, bathroom, etc. Different: style, size, arrangement of rooms, colors, building materials, number of rooms and floors.)

3. Ask the students to think of one window in their house. Say, "If I looked into this window, tell me what *things* I would see?" (Be careful not to ask what *room* you would be looking into. We want the students to define the space by the indicators.) Call on one student to list the items in the room. When sufficient items are listed ask the other students to determine the use of the room. Say, "We know what the use of the room because of the indicators." Repeat the process with two or three other students. Write the word *indicators* on the blackboard. Categorize the items according to the rooms they represent. Ask, "What do these indicators tell us about the people who live there? What do they like to do? How do you know there are children in the house? Can you tell how many people live there?"

4. Lead an open discussion about the students' favorite room(s) in the house and why it is their favorite. Note the difference in *preference*. Some may prefer the rooms where there is always lots of activity while others have need for quiet. Write the word *preference* on the board and list some of the student answers.

5. Ask, "What reasons do people have for choosing where they live?" (close to job, food stores, mass transit, good schools).

NEW JERSEY AUDUBON SOCIETY

Natural History Lessons

## Putting It All Together

**?** Why do people build so many different kinds of structures for their homes? (Need for space, style, need for proximity to many other people, etc.)

**?** What arrangements of space are the same in most houses? (kitchen, bedroom, bathroom, etc.) How are they different? (Decorations, furniture, hobby tools)

**?** What clues are indicators for the special use of different rooms in the house? (kitchen: sink, stove, cabinets, refrigerator; bedroom: bed, chest of drawers, desk. etc.)

**?** How do these differences help us to understand the people who live there? (They tell us what kinds of things they like, if they prefer orderly or random arrangements, etc.)

**?** "Did we see any live squirrels?" (If yes) "What were they doing?" [Applies knowledge to practical situations] (If no) "Why did we not see any?" (Perhaps one or more of their needs is not being met.

---

## Take Another Step

✔ Describe the structure and use of other buildings (school, food store, department store, gas station).

✔ List some indicators that tell the use of the building (hydraulic lift - service station; desks and chalk - school classroom, etc.).

✔ What do the structure and indicators tell us about the people who work there and those who use their services?

✔ Have the students translate the indicators for each room into other languages.

---

## LESSON 2: **MOTIVATIONAL ACTIVITY**

Discuss the previous lesson to elicit the three important factors: structure, indicators and preference. Say, "All of the things we listed that are important to people are also true of plant and animal species. Today we are going to visit 'Nature's House'. We will identify different kinds of natural structures, the **indicator species** that tell us what type of habitat it is, and the preferences of the plants and the animals that live there."

**PROCEDURE**

Lead the students outside to the study area. Have them describe the overall structure of the natural site. The students form teams and explore the area to complete the Nature's House data sheet (Figure 1).

(Teacher's Copy)
1. Estimate the height of the tallest plants. [Translates material to mathematical formula.]

2. Name the most common plants you see (**indicator** plants: tree, grass, vine and similar

NEW JERSEY
AUDUBON
SOCIETY

generic names is sufficient for the introductory lesson. At a later time, or for older students consult field guides for individual species names. [Interprets visual indicators.]

3. List the evidence or clues left behind by animals that live here. (holes in the ground and in trees, vines climb up trees, etc.) [Interprets visual indicators and formulates a classification scheme.]

# Putting It All Together

**?** In order to live in this place what do you have to be able to tolerate? (exposed area- direct sun, lawn - crowded conditions, shady area - no direct sun, etc.) Have the students consider living conditions the plant or animal would meet at another season. [Appraises needs of species and relates them to habitat circumstances.]

**?** Compare natural habitats to human spaces. (Both contain built structures; you can infer something about the inhabitant's preferences by looking at the structure.) [Categorizes spaces in natural communities and compares them to similar spaces in human communities.]

## Take Another Step

✔ Have the students explore an area near their home asking the same questions. How do the different areas compare in structure? What indicators were the same? What new species were found?

✔ Draw pictures of at least four of the plants found on the habitat. Use a flower or tree identification book to learn their scientific names.

✔ Interview parents or caregivers and ask what benefits are gained by living in the house you occupy. How do their answers illustrate obtaining essentials? How do they illustrate preferences?

✔ Have the students translate the natural indicators into other languages.

**FOR MORE INFORMATION**

Hoberman, Mary Ann, "*A House Is a House for Me*"

# NATURE'S HOUSE
**Figure 1**

Name of Team: _____      Date: _____

Members: _____      Site: _____

_____

_____

_____

_____

PLANTS: Name or draw the most common plants you see (indicator plants).

ANIMALS: Name or draw evidence or clues left by animals that live here (indicator animals).

STRUCTURES: Describe or draw the structures these animals use for shelter.

*Natural History Lessons*

RESEARCH
CONSERVATION
EDUCATION

**LENGTH OF ACTIVITY**

**40** minutes

**GRADE LEVELS**
Pre-K - 2

Natural History Lessons

# SQUIRREL SIGNS

New Jersey is home to three **native** squirrel **species**: gray squirrel, red squirrel, and flying squirrel. Red squirrels are small animals usually found living in pine forests, and flying squirrels, being strictly **nocturnal**, are rarely seen. Of the three, the largest and most commonly seen is the gray squirrel.

None of the squirrels **hibernates**. Much of the winter food of gray squirrels comes from nuts and seeds they have buried or cached between late summer and autumn when food supplies are abundant. In the process, different things may happen: nuts and seeds may become food for animals other than squirrels, either immediately or during the winter months; food not found by the squirrel or another animal may germinate in the spring; or food items may decay, releasing plant **nutrients** into the soil. Regardless of what happens, the squirrel, in its need to find and store food for itself, plays a special role within its **habitat**. This role or position is called its **niche**. Although the gray squirrel is not the only gatherer and spreader of seeds in New Jersey, it is an important one. Loss of great numbers of these animals would alter the way seeds and nuts from certain plants (oaks, hickories, and pines) are dispersed.

---
**BASIC CONCEPTS**
---

☞ Animals need food, water, shelter, and space to live.

☞ Animals live in a certain place because there they can find the things they need.

☞ People share some of the same needs and preferences as squirrels.

## PROCESS SKILLS
*Communicating, observing, classifying, inferring, predicting, interpreting data.*

NEW JERSEY
AUDUBON
SOCIETY

---

**MATERIALS**

❏ Squirrel Signs worksheet (Figure 2)

❏ oaktag

❏ 1 crayon for each student

❏ stapler

❏ popsicle sticks

❏ tape

❏ picture of a squirrel

---

**PREPLANNING**

1. Make squirrel signs.
   a. Copy the sample (Figure 2).
   b. Cut each sheet of paper to produce two signs.
   c. Staple one sign to oaktag or other stiff paper.
   c. Tape a popsicle stick to the back of the paper.

2. Find pictures of squirrels or take pictures of squirrels seen near the school.

3. Determine an area for exploration. (possible areas:  park, vacant lot, woodlot, schoolyard)

# MOTIVATIONAL ACTIVITY

Show the gray squirrel picture to the students. Ask questions that encourage sharing of previous experience. (Have you seen this animal? What is its name? Where did you see it? Have you ever seen one eating? What food does it like? What kind of home does it have?)

Optional - This story may be used as an enrichment before or after the field trip. Say, "I'm going to tell you a story about a squirrel that lived right here in (your town). It is called 'The Squirrel Who Forgot'.

*In late November, right around Thanksgiving Day, Samantha Squirrel was returning to her nest in the big oak tree for the last time before dark. Between her teeth was the biggest acorn she had ever found and it would soon be stored with all the others she had gathered through the autumn weeks. Just as she arrived at the hole in the great tree, Samantha heard a startling cry from a higher branch. "Thief, thief!" It was Belinda Blue Jay and in her beak was a plump acorn.*

*"Oh, dear," said Samantha fretfully, "Has that pesky bird found my winter food?" This was always a worry for the animals that stored nuts and seeds. Blue Jays have been known for stealing from the gatherers for themselves. That's why they were given the cry of "thief"; so others would be warned that they were near. But it was too late for Samantha. Most of her precious food supply was gone from the nest in the oak tree. She would have to work harder now in the remaining weeks to fill up her store again. "But she won't get this prize," said Samantha with determination. She carried the acorn down the tree trunk to the ground. "I'll bury this one in the ground as well as all the rest I find from now on. Belinda Blue Jay doesn't like to dig in the ground."*

*For the next weeks Samantha worked harder than ever gathering nuts and seeds. She buried so many acorns that she was never hungry even once during the cold wintertime. When spring came and new buds popped out on the bushes and trees, Samantha munched on the new green leaves, happy for something different to eat. She forgot all about the biggest acorn that was still buried.*

*As the sun warmed the spring days and rain moistened the earth, the acorn began to swell. Soon it burst its shell and sent a small root down. It began to reach up toward the surface of the ground and soon a tiny stem appeared, stretching higher and higher toward the sun. Through the spring and summer it grew and by autumn it took its place among the other trees.*

*Many winters and summers went by. The tree grew and Samantha continued her gathering in the autumn. "It's wonderful how trees just keep growing out of the ground," she thought to herself. "I wonder where they come from."*

## PROCEDURE

1. Distribute one squirrel sign and one crayon to each student.

2. Explain that during the discovery walk they will be looking for "squirrel signs or clues." Each time a sign is found the student will fill in one box next to the appropriate symbol. A finished squirrel sign will resemble a bar graph.

## Ask:

1. "Where did the squirrel store her acorns and seeds?" (nest in oak tree and in the ground) [Recalls specific knowledge]

2. "Which place is better? Explain your answer." (If they are stored in the tree, the Blue Jay might take them. If they are stored in the ground they could be overlooked. There is risk in both places.) [Draws conclusions from data and justifies answers]

3. "How would you answer Samantha Squirrel's question, 'Where do trees come from?'" (Sometimes animals bury seeds and nuts and forget about them. When spring comes, they grow.) [Explains the process of spreading seeds]

*"Let's see if Samantha or one of her relatives is outside today."*

## Putting It All Together

**?** Why did we go outside to look for a squirrel? (Wild animal needs are best met there.) [Recognizes and defines animal needs.]

**?** How many live squirrels did we see? What were they doing? (If none were seen) Why did we not see any? (Perhaps one or more of the needs is not met: food, water, shelter, space.) [Analyzes and evaluates the information gathered.]

**?** What kinds of food did we find that squirrels would eat? (nuts, bread, seeds, pine cones, berries, leaves) [Applies knowledge of animal needs to new situations.]

**?** What are some things that could happen if a nut got buried by a squirrel? (It may grow into a new plant; other animals may eat it; it may rot.) [Integrates knowledge with practical application and generates new ideas.]

**?** What places did we find where squirrels could have their homes? (holes in trees, leaf nests in trees) [Applies knowledge to a practical situation.]

**?** How are squirrel needs the same as people needs? (both need food, shelter and space to move) How are they different? (people cultivate the soil, cook their food, etc., they require more space, and their houses are more complex - different rooms for different activities)

**?** Imagine what it would be like to be a squirrel. What part of the squirrel's life would you like best? What would you like least? [Applies knowledge to a new situation.]

NEW JERSEY AUDUBON SOCIETY

Natural History Lessons

## Take Another Step

✔ Take a bag of peanuts that are still in their shells to the area where the Gray Squirrel was seen. Scatter the nuts and watch what the squirrel does. If there is a school lawn, peanuts could be scattered and watched to see what other animals might gather them. DO NOT TRY TO FEED ANY WILD ANIMAL BY HAND.

✔ Do this activity with other animals. Make a bulletin board of the signs and the habitat where each animal lives. (pigeon, crow, worm, sparrow)

✔ Teach the students the Squirrel Song (Figure 3).

✔ Have the students watch for squirrel signs over a weekend. In addition to the information on Figure 2 worksheet have them give the date and place of sighting:

# Squirrel Signs

**Figure 2**

Photocopy two Squirrel Signs and trim on dotted lines. Position both pieces side by side on a standard sheet of 8½ x 11 paper and make additional photocopies for the students.

| | | | | |
|---|---|---|---|---|
| Homes | | | | |
| Food | | | | |
| Footprints | | | | |
| Live Squirrels | | | | |

NEW JERSEY
AUDUBON
SOCIETY

**Figure 3**

# The Squirrel Song (Author Unknown)

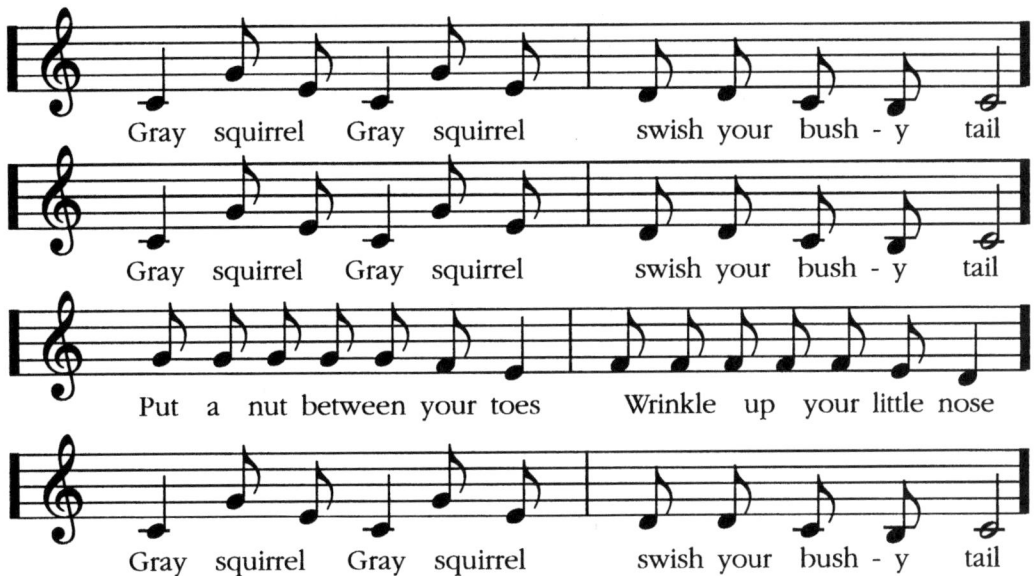

Gray squirrel Gray squirrel swish your bush - y tail

Gray squirrel Gray squirrel swish your bush - y tail

Put a nut between your toes Wrinkle up your little nose

Gray squirrel Gray squirrel swish your bush - y tail

(Hand motions can be used to involve the students during the singing of the song.)

1. Let's make ourselves look like a squirrel sitting on a branch. (Stoop slightly and put one hand at a time in front of your body so that you look like a squirrel in a sitting position with paws out in front of body.)

2. Make the squirrel swish its tail. (Move backside back and forth.)

3. How would the squirrel hold a nut in its paws? (Hold hands together pretending to hold nut, then stand up and wrinkle your nose.)

4. Go back to the beginning.

## FOR MORE INFORMATION

Ross, David, ed. "The Squirrel," *The Illustrated Treasury of Poetry for Children.*

NEW JERSEY AUDUBON SOCIETY

Natural History Lessons

**LENGTH OF ACTIVITY**

## 30 minutes

**GRADE LEVELS**
Pre-K - 6

Pitcher Plant

# IT'S ALL IN THE NAME

Classification as we know it today is relatively new. By the mid-1800s people were traveling more and information was shared on a wider scale through the printing of books. Interest in the interpretation of the natural world increased through the works of people like John James Audubon and others who explored new lands, finding plants, birds, and animals never before seen by Europeans. Problems arose when single species carried a variety of names.

For communication purposes, it fell upon the educated elite to decide on a single name for each known species. These people of letters, the writers of poetry and prose, people of medicine, and the clergy ascribed names that reflected elements of their own culture and background. As a result, we have such poetic names as maiden hair for the forest fern. We have bladder wort, given the name no doubt because of the capacity to retain water, and St. John's wort given its name because it blooms around June 12, the Feast of St. John the Baptist. And what about the cardinal? The red feathers reminded some clergyman of the prelate of the same name.

It is important to have accepted names for individual species so we can communicate and collect scientific data. The system has been refined even more through the works of Carolus Linneaus, eliminating some of the obstacles posed by the original poetic names. In the process of classification we need to remember that we always find new ways to clarify distinctions. DNA is revolutionizing classification altogether.

Although knowing the accepted name is important, strict identification does not necessarily encourage the observer to become keenly aware of the organism's physical characteristics and behaviors.

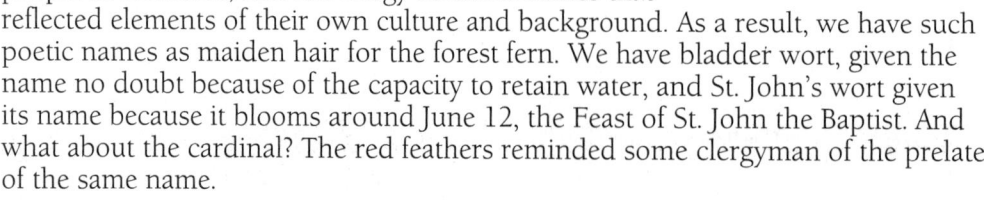

## PROCESS SKILLS

*Observing, analyzing, synthesizing, interpreting, communicating, justifying.*

## BASIC CONCEPTS

☞ Physical characteristics help distinguish similarities and differences in species.

☞ Classification helps people sort plant and animal species.

☞ Classification helps people share ideas and communicate.

## MATERIALS

no materials needed

### PREPLANNING

Find an area on the school grounds or in a park where students can make close observation of some plant or animal.

# MOTIVATIONAL ACTIVITY

Call a child to the front of the room. Ask, "Who can tell me this student's name?" (Response) "How do you know? Where did we learn the name? Who was first to call this child by name? Tell some ways that you always recognize this student."

Just as we name each other and know each other by certain characteristics, we can learn about the plants and animals in nature.

### PROCEDURE
LOWER PRIMARY VERSION

1. Take the students to a tree. Have them describe as many physical characteristics as they can observe. (broken branches, rough bark, twisted trunk, limbs like twisty fingers, scary holes)

2. When ideas are well run, ask the children to make up a name for the tree based on the things we saw and described. Allow for several imaginative names to emerge; ask each student who offers a name to give the reason for his or her answer.

3. "They are very interesting names, but if each of you went into the principal's office and named the tree by your own name, what problem will arise?" (The principal will think we are talking about as many different trees as we offer names.)

4. Ask, "How can we solve this problem?" (We need to decide on a single name. We can choose one of the names offered or we can make up another name.)

5. Have the children decide on a single name. Ask them if there are any other trees in the area with the same characteristics?

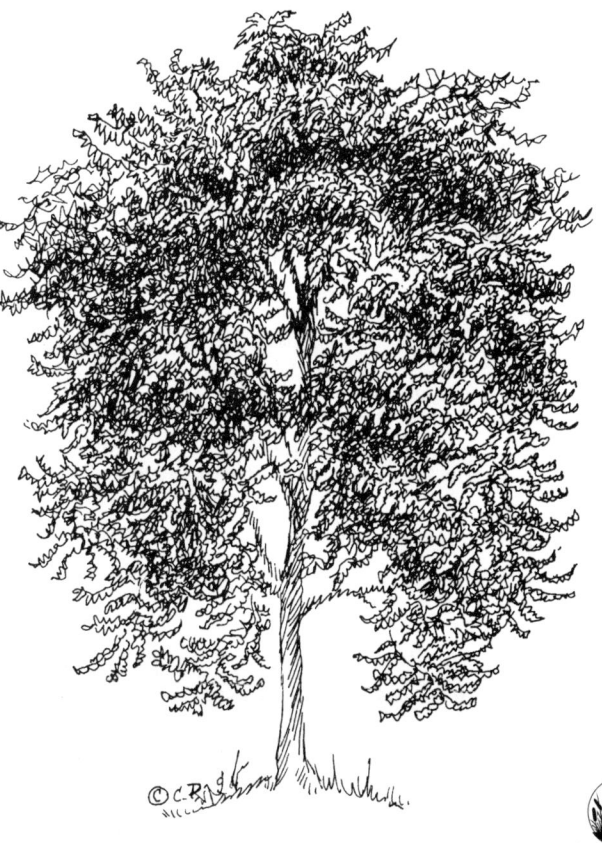

©C.B.

NEW JERSEY
AUDUBON
SOCIETY

Natural History Lessons

**PROCEDURE**
UPPER PRIMARY AND MIDDLE SCHOOL VERSION

1. Divide the class into pairs.

2. Ask the students to select a natural object. (three minutes for selection)

3. Tell them to observe as many different physical characteristics as they can experience through sight, smell, and touch.

4. Ask them to name the natural object according to the characteristics they observe. The name can be literal, poetic, or whimsical, but it must be based on some physical characteristic. (five minutes to observe and name the object)

After the allotted time, call the students back. Allow as many as possible to tell the story of how they named their object.

## Putting It All Together

**?** How does naming the plant or animal or natural object help you remember it? (investment of personal experiences) [Formulates a scheme for identification.]

**?** Are you able to identify other natural objects that are alike because of the name you have chosen?

**?** What would happen if everybody created their own names for things? (difficult to communicate, hard to compare information about some species) [Infers value of accepted scientific terms.]

**?** Why is it necessary for people to name things by the same name? (standardization aids in communication between scientists, researchers, and naturalists) [Recognizes value of scientific terms.]

**?** How can you find out what scientists call your object? ( ask them, use identification guides) [Recognizes appropriate resource for solving problems.]

---

## Take Another Step

✔ Create an identification booklet of trees and plants found in the schoolyard using the names assigned by the students. Beside the student assigned name, write the accepted name found in a field guide.

✔ Have the students name other plants or animals according to their characteristics.

---

**FOR MORE INFORMATION**

Carson, Rachel. *A Sense of Wonder*

NEW JERSEY
AUDUBON
SOCIETY

**Bridges to the Natural World**

LENGTH OF ACTIVITY

40 minutes

# FROM BASEMENT TO ATTIC

Plants help to define the structure of most natural habitats. They interact with each other and with animals to form a natural community. Deciduous forests, like those found in New Jersey exhibit distinct layers in vegetation. The forest floor is home to ground-hugging plants such as mosses, while the next layer up supports herbaceous vegetation such as ferns, wildflowers, and grasses. The understory includes shrubs and small trees such as spicebush and dogwood, and the canopy, that thick layer of leaves from the large deciduous trees, covers everything. These layers are seen easily, unless the forest has been manipulated by people or browsed by deer.

What can't be seen easily is the massive root structure that holds all these plants in place. These roots, much like pipes in a basement, are a hidden layer beneath everything.

## BASIC CONCEPTS

☞ Plants help define the structure of a natural habitat.

☞ Layers of a terrestrial habitat extend from the underground to the top of the tallest plant.

☞ Animal and insect activity can be observed at every layer of the habitat.

☞ Habitats support populations of animals.

## PROCESS SKILLS
*Observing, classifying, inferring, recording data, communicating.*

NEW JERSEY
AUDUBON
SOCIETY

Natural History Lessons

---

## MATERIALS

**For each student:**

☐ clipboard, *The Forest Is a House* (Figure 4) and a pencil

☐ clothesline or butcher cord at least 30' long

☐ clothespins or masking tape to fasten worksheets to line

## PREPLANNING

1. Make one copy of Figure 4 for each student.

2. Arrange for a field trip to a woodland habitat.

# MOTIVATIONAL ACTIVITY

Draw a simple picture of a one-story ranch house, a two-story colonial house, and a four-story apartment house. Discuss with the students how the building's size and structure determines the number of people or families that can live there comfortably. Discuss how space can be arranged to accommodate people's needs.

## PROCEDURE

1. Distribute a copy of Figure 4 to each student. Lead the students in a discussion about the functions of the different parts of a house.
   a. What might we find in the basement? (heater, water tank, pipes, etc.)
   b. What are some of the rooms that are usually on the first floor? (kitchen, living room, den) Second floor? (bedrooms)
   c. What is the attic for? (storage)
   d. What is the purpose of the roof? (protection from weather) [Recalls and applies previous knowledge.]

2. Have the students look at the woodland habitat from the edge. Ask the following:
   a. What part is like a basement? (underground) A basement in a house has pipes, a water tank, and heater. What is underground here that could compare with some of those things? (roots)
   b. In a house the food is stored in the kitchen. Where is the food stored in this house? (Food items are found and stored at all levels of the habitat.)
   c. Where is the first story of this habitat? (It includes the forest floor and plants that grow to your knees. These are all the small herbaceous plants like ferns, wildflowers, and mosses.)
   d. What about the second story? (It includes the shrubs or bushes or understory of the forest. They may grow as high as 10 or 12 feet.)
   e. Where would the attic or roof be located? (The attic is the space between the top of the understory and the top of the foliage. The roof is the very top branches of the tallest trees.) [Infers relationships and formulates judgments.]

3. Walk through the forest and have the students draw or name the animals or insects they see. Instruct them to insert the name or drawing on the corresponding floors of the house worksheet.

4. While the students are exploring, extend the clothesline tying each end to trees about twenty-five feet apart.

5. After a suitable time period call the students together and have them hang their worksheets on the line.

NEW JERSEY
AUDUBON
SOCIETY

**Bridges to the Natural World**

## Putting It All Together

**?** Let's look at the insects and animals we found in the basement or under the leaf litter. How many species are represented? (Examples: red ants, black ants, pillbugs, spiders) Total the numbers of species that are the same in each sheet. [Generalizes and summarizes data.]

**?** Repeat this procedure for each layer of the forest. How many of the same species have we found on more than one worksheet report? [Classifies and computes data.]

**?** When we find the same species on a number of report sheets and these are not the same individuals, we can say that this habitat has a population of ants, or woodpeckers, or chipmunks. From our observations, what is the most common population of animals in this forest? [Interprets and organizes data.]

**?** Why is it important for us to know what plants and animals live here? (to have a better understanding of the natural world around us, to gather basic information about the habitat for future conservation reference) [Understands and accepts responsibility toward natural systems.]

---

## Take Another Step

✔ Save the worksheets from different habitats and make comparisons.

---

Natural History Lessons

# THE FOREST AS A HOUSE
**Figure 4**

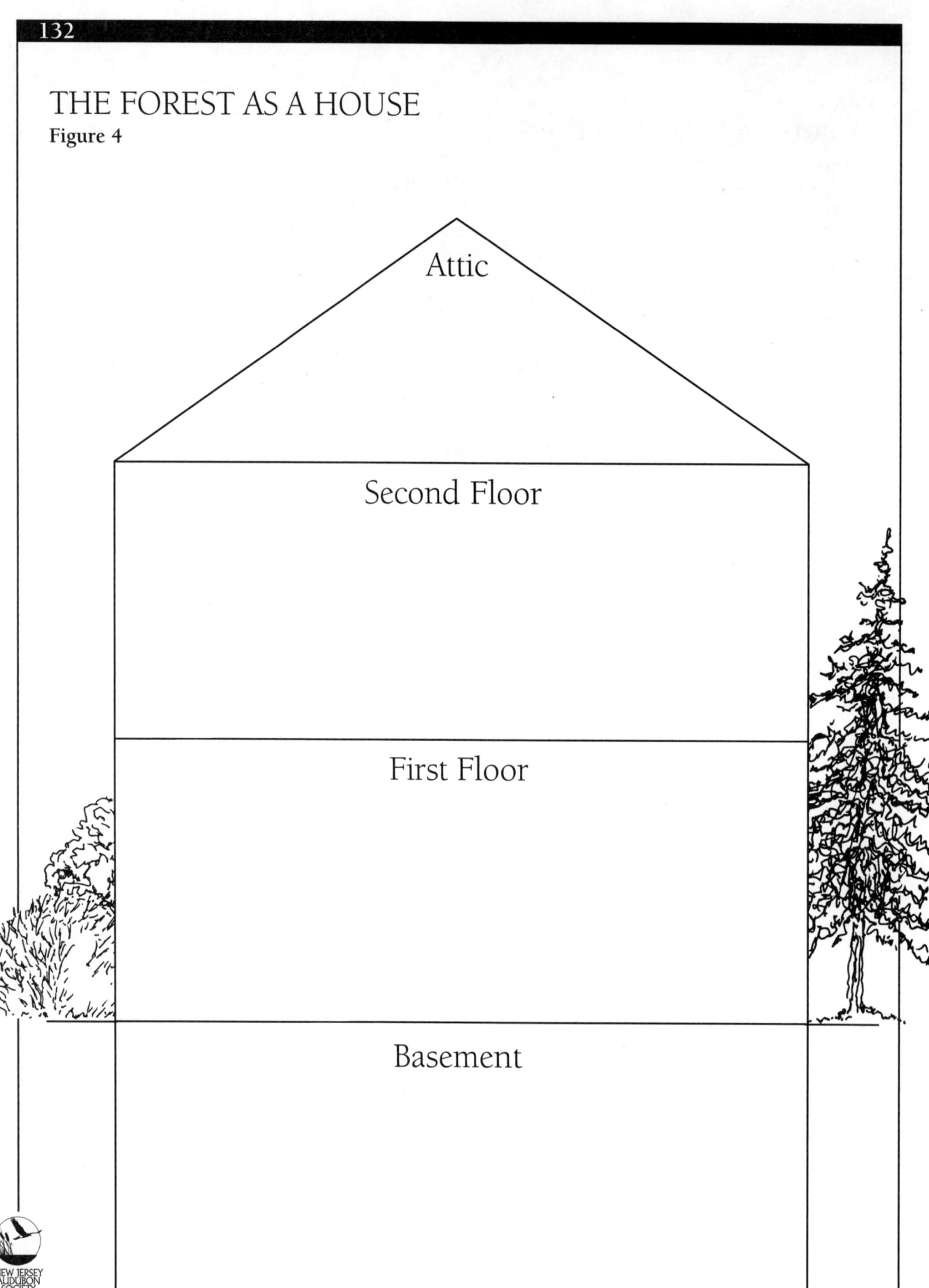

Attic

Second Floor

First Floor

Basement

NEW JERSEY
AUDUBON
SOCIETY

RESEARCH
CONSERVATION EDUCATION
**E**

RESEARCH
CONSERVATION EDUCATION
**R**

LENGTH OF ACTIVITY
5 periods
20-30
minutes each

GRADE LEVELS
Pre-K - 4

# NATURE'S SYMPHONY

The music of life is all around us. There is melody, rhythm, and mood in nature as it occurs every day. We hear melody in bird song, animal calls, wind, and the tide. The syllables and accents in the names we give things add rhythm, and the different weather patterns and animal behaviors add more rhythm and mood to a great symphony.

The earliest music reflected people's encounters with the natural world, as they imitated earth sounds with instruments taken from natural objects: reeds, wood, skins, and bone. Today these instruments are refined and manufactured with sophisticated technology, making them appear inaccessible to the average person. Likewise, the fact that music is written on a scale often intimidates teachers and students. This need not be the case. Anyone can explore the sounds of nature and interpret it by making music. This series of activities is a way to attune young listeners to what is happening all around them. It sharpens their senses and provides the opportunity to dramatize their own observations.

While the title and focus of this lesson is the forest, the theme can easily be adapted to fit any other habitat available for study.

## BASIC CONCEPTS

☞ Melody, rhythm, and mood are found in nature.

☞ Plants come in many sizes and shapes.

☞ Animals have unique and individual behaviors.

☞ Animals have ways of communicating.

## PROCESS SKILLS
*Communicating, using time and space, observing, classifying, inferring.*

NEW JERSEY
AUDUBON
SOCIETY

## MATERIALS

☐ rhythm band instruments, bought or homemade

☐ chalkboard or newsprint tablet

☐ writing implements for the teacher

### PREPLANNING

Arrange a field trip to a place where plants and animals can be observed. This may be on the school grounds or to one of the sites listed in the Habitats of New Jersey (Section One).

# PERIOD 1: SOUNDS ON THE NATURE WALK
## MOTIVATIONAL ACTIVITY

Have the students invent sounds that resemble a clock, barking dog, front doorbell, etc. (familiar sounds) Let's go outside and listen for some other sounds.

### PROCEDURE

Tell the children to close their eyes and listen to the sounds. What sounds do you hear that are made by people or by things that people make? (cars, sirens, trucks, airplanes, etc.) [Identifies and classifies sounds.] Keeping their eyes closed, children answer.

Open your eyes. Can anyone make a sound like the sounds we heard? (Children respond.) [Converts sounds heard to vocalizations.]

Now I want you to close your eyes again and listen for the sounds that are made by a bird's calling or singing. When you hear one, point toward the direction of the sound. After a suitable pause have the children open their eyes and discuss the number and kinds of sounds they heard birds make. Encourage the children to imitate the sounds with their own voices, matching as closely as possible the tone and rhythm of the call they hear. They may even use letter sounds or words to better imitate the song. (E.g., sssssssst; chuck, chuck; dee,dee,dee; I see, I see, I see; toodle-eet) What does it sound like the birds are saying? [Classifies and verbalizes birdsong.]

When the variety of sounds have been described and imitated, count how many different birds were heard.

Close your eyes once more. Are there any other sounds you hear? Do you think they were made by an animal or an insect? Is the sound a call or is it made by their movements? When you hear a noise, point toward the direction of the sound.

Again, after a suitable pause, have the children open their eyes and discuss the number and kinds of sounds they hear. Encourage them, as before, to imitate the sounds with their voices.

Repeat this procedure if there are other sounds to be noticed, such as wind, water in a brook, etc.

## Putting It All Together

Return to the classroom and create a list of all the sounds heard on the field trip. Write them in the syllables that the students created. [Recalls information.]

Natural History Lessons

# PERIOD 2: SIGHTS ON THE NATURE WALK
## MOTIVATIONAL ACTIVITY

Call on volunteers to imitate some behavior of a pet or some animal they have observed. Bring attention to the parts of the body used to correlate parts and shapes of the animal parts. (hands for paws, curled up body or wagging backside) [Demonstrates understanding of animal behaviors.]

Let's go outside and find other plants or animals to imitate.

### PROCEDURE

Take the children to a wooded area or a lawn where trees are growing. Tell them to look at all the things around them. What are the largest plants? (trees, bushes) [Interprets visual material.]

Direct the students' attention to a single tree. Use your pointing finger and in the air, trace the trunk of the tree from the ground to the very end of the first branch. Do the same with the second branch and each of the branches going up the tree always starting at the trunk and moving outward. Look at the base of the tree. Can you see any of the roots? With your hand, measure how far the roots reach out from the base of the tree...one length of your hand? two? three lengths? [Matches verbal description to practical experience.]

Have the children imitate the shape of the tree with their bodies. Let the body represent the main trunk, the arms as branches and feet as roots. Look at the shape of the tree. Use your body to make a shape like that of the tree. [Analyzes the tree structure and reconstructs through dramatization.]

Allow the students to select their own tree and repeat the process. Let them explain the positions they chose to imitate the tree. [Justifies interpretation.]

Next, look carefully through the different layers of the forest: middle section, up toward the tops of the trees. Watch the motion of a living creature or the branches of the trees blowing in the wind. Allow time for the children to imitate these movements. [Classifies observations and demonstrates understanding through dramatization.]

## Putting It All Together

Return to the classroom and create a list of the plants and animals seen. Encourage phrase descriptions. (the tree with the broken branch, the bird that hopped back and forth on the ground) [Creates descriptions of observations.]

Natural History Lessons

NEW JERSEY
AUDUBON
SOCIETY

# PERIOD 3: ROLE PLAYING
## MOTIVATIONAL ACTIVITY

Do you remember the trees we saw when we went outside? Let me see you stand and imitate one of those trees. [Demonstrates understanding through dramatization.]

### PROCEDURE

Recall that some of the plants were very large with many branches. Instruct the students to pick a partner and, together, create a plant they saw. (bush, vine, tree) [Reconstructs through dramatization.]

How can we make a tree taller? (Add a chair or a table for students to stand on.) Wider? (Have four or five students stand in a circle with backs to the center.) How can we show roots sticking up from the ground? (A few children sit on the floor, backs to tree trunk and legs extended.) [Combines information to create a new situation.]

Suppose we wanted to make a forest, how would we do it?

### Plants
A sapling could be one child. A large tree might involve three children with their backs to a common center and their arms extended. A larger tree might have six: three on chairs and three on the floor, all with backs toward the same center. A very large tree could have nine children: three on chairs, three standing and three as roots reaching out across the floor from the base.

### Animals
Name the animal seen. As the animal is named, have the children imitate the sounds and behaviors they remember. (E.g., woodpecker drums at the tree, squirrel scurries on forest floor, birds fly.) Some animals, like a centipede or a deer, might require more than 1 child.

### Weather
Change the weather patterns from fair weather to: slight breeze, clouds and wind, thunder, rain and wind, storm passing, storm just over, fair again. Allow children to dramatize each change as if they were the trees or animals of the forest. Where would the animals go? Would they try to protect themselves from the storm? [Integrates learning from different areas to a plan for problem solving.]

# PERIOD 4: SETTING IT TO MUSIC
## MOTIVATIONAL ACTIVITY

Introduce the rhythm instruments and allow students to explore the different sounds that can be made with them. The instruments selected can be used to imitate a sound in nature or the rhythm can remind the children of how the animals move. They also can be used to express the movements or sounds of weather and how they affect other creatures of the forest.

The following are examples of instruments that usually are found in rhythm bands. These examples were generated by children who attended New Jersey Audubon Day Camps. Under each instrument are listed possible sound or rhythm interpretations. Each class should be allowed time to experiment with the instruments and to invent its own sounds, rhythms, and interpretations.

1. **Wood Block** - Tap
   (Woodpecker at a tree.)

2. **Jingle tap** - Shake
   (Small animals hop, run, scurry and stop, scurry and stop.)

3. **Guiro** - Rub the stick against the ridged part of the instrument.
   (Different speeds produce different sounds and moods. They can remind you of a duck quacking or some noisy birds in a tree. They can also be like the buzz of an insect or like the movement of a snake slithering on the forest floor.)

4. **Loop bells** - Shake
   (At different speeds, the bells will sound like a chorus of spring peepers [frogs] or cicadas [late summer insects] or many birds gathering in the trees.)

5. **Triangle** - Hold the triangle by the loop so that it is suspended. Don't allow anything to touch it. Tap the triangle with the baton.
   (Soft strokes - first light of morning. As the tone gets louder and more intense, the sunlight gets stronger.)

6. **Cymbals** - Strike together
   (A storm: lightning or thunder.)

7. **Recorder** - Block all the holes with your fingers and blow softly. Move your fingers to alter tones. There is no need to know the notes or the scale. Just move your fingers and blow.
   (The wind blowing through the trees. The sound of wind can be made by individual voice or in chorus.)

8. **Tambourine** - Hold it at the space provided and shake.
   (Light rain increasing to heavy rain or a hot sizzling sun overhead.)

9. **Tick tock** - Strike the mallet on each side alternately.
   (Raindrops - play at different speeds according to the intensity of the storm.)

10. **Bongo drums or any kind of drum** - Strike
    (Tapping fingers lightly, the beginning of rain. Heavy hitting could be thunder ending in a loud BOOM!)

Natural History Lessons

**Natural History Lessons**

# PERIOD 5: PUTTING IT ALL TOGETHER - NATURE'S SYMPHONY
## MOTIVATIONAL ACTIVITY

Assign roles of plants and animals, or allow the children to choose the role they will each portray. Make certain that there is a good variety represented. Tell them that you are going to tell a story and as the character they are playing is mentioned, they are to perform their part and then take a place quietly on the stage until they hear another direction.

The teacher is the narrator and the director. The following is a suggestion as used in NJAS day camps.

## PROCEDURE

1. "Once upon a time there was a beautiful forest. In the middle of this forest stood a very large tree." (Enter the children who make the central tree.)

2. "There were other trees and bushes too." (Enter the children who make smaller trees and bushes.)

3. "Some trees that had died or were knocked down by storms lay on the ground where they nourish the forest by making new soil." (Enter the children representing dead logs.)

4. "It was a beautiful place where many animals found all the food and shelter and space that they needed. There were chipmunks scurrying along the ground looking for seeds" (Enter chipmunks playing instruments and imitating the animal's behavior) "and squirrels" (Enter squirrels) "and birds" (name individuals and allow each to perform) " and insects." Go on until all have been named who will perform in this category.

5. "Each morning the sun came up. It gave just a little bit of light at first" (child plays softly on the triangle) "but gave more and more light as the earth turned." (louder to loudest)

6. "During the day the animals would move about looking for food." (Name the animals again. This time they continue to play even

after the narration proceeds to another animal. The scene should be full of sound and activity.)

7. "All at once clouds gathered in the sky and a breeze began to blow." (Breezes make a soft sound.) "The trees and bushes waved their branches." (Trees and bushes begin to move gently.)

Natural History Lessons

8. "Soon the wind grew stronger. The trees and bushes bent their branches all around. In the distance was a soft roll of thunder." (Recorders or chorus gets stronger and there is a soft drum roll.)

9. "Rain began to fall... a few drops at first," (tick-tock soft and slow) "but then it came harder and faster." (tick-tock and any other instruments)

10. "Then came LOUD thunder!" (drum) "and STRONG wind" (recorder, chorus) "and HEAVY rain." (tick-tock and other instruments) "All the animals went for cover to protect themselves from the fierce storm." (Now the instruments of weather are played at their loudest until the teacher gives the signal to STOP.)

11. "The storm passed. The thunder was only a distant roll," (drum played softly) "the winds calmed down," (recorders or chorus softened) and the rain stopped. (tick-tock and other instruments gradually stop)

PAUSE

12. "The clouds passed and once again the sun came out." (triangle, gently) "Its warm rays came down to the forest floor and dried up all the rain." (tambourine, light sizzle)

13. "The creatures of the forest began to move about once again."

## Take Another Step

✔ Do an interpretation for another habitat.

✔ Add a variety of instruments from other cultures.

**FOR MORE INFORMATION**

Barnett, Elise Braun. *Montessori & Music: Rhythmic Activities for Young Children.*

Bisgaard, Erling, and Gulle Stehouwer. *Musicbook 0: Pulse, Pitch, Rhythm, Form, Dynamics.*

Glazer, Tom. *Happy Rhythms & Rhymes.*

Goss, Linda. *Afro-American Tales & Games.*

Heyge, Lorna Lutz, and Audrey Sillick. *Teacher's Guide Year One: Kindermusik for the Very Young; Teacher's Guide Year Two: Kindermusik for the Very Young; Kindermusik 1.*

Jenkins, Ella. *This is Rhythm.*

Palmer, Hap. *Hap Palmer Favorites: Songs for Learning Through Music and Movement.*

Natural History Lessons

CONSERVATION RESEARCH EDUCATION

**R**

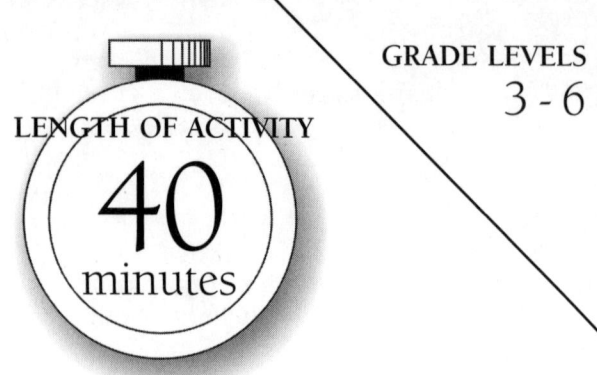

LENGTH OF ACTIVITY

**40** minutes

GRADE LEVELS
3 - 6

# SMILE, PLEASE

**C**areful observation of the smallest details can lead to new discoveries and a deeper understanding of the natural world.

Increasing and refining observation skills is an important first step in the scientific process.

Each **habitat** or natural community has distinctive characteristics. By observing rock types and landforms along with identifying plant and animal species, one can learn a great deal about the area. Recognition of these individual components and how they fit together within the habitat leads to a broader vision of the whole.

---

### BASIC CONCEPTS

☞ Natural areas and specific locations can be identified by carefully observing their components.

☞ Good research depends on precise observation.

---

## PROCESS SKILLS
*Communicating, using time and space, observing, classifying, inferring, predicting, interpreting data, formulating hypotheses.*

NEW JERSEY
AUDUBON
SOCIETY

**Bridges to the Natural World**

## MATERIALS

- ❏ camera and film or digital camera

- ❏ at least 10 or 12 photographs of an outdoor study area

- ❏ oaktag or cardboard for mounting pictures (optional)

- ❏ three pictures of famous locations: e.g., Grand Canyon, Epcot Center, local school

## PREPLANNING

1. Select a natural site on the school grounds that is available for the students to use. (courtyard, playground, field, woods)

2. Photograph special locations within the study area that show a variety of natural objects and landform configurations. (examples: tree trunk with special markings, a pile of rocks, part of a wall, exposed roots, etc.) Take photographs from different perspectives: ground-level, eye-level, panorama, close-up.

3. Mount the photos and number them.

# MOTIVATIONAL ACTIVITY

Show pictures of famous locations to the students. Ask the students to tell how they were able to recognize the locations. Discuss shape, arrangement, landform, landmark, and personal experience.

## PROCEDURE

1. Divide the class into groups of two.

2. Give a photograph to each pair. Show the students the designated study area and explain that they are to find the exact location of what is shown in the photograph.

3. Allow each pair time to find the location. [Analyzes data and relates it to practical situations.]

4. Ask each pair to describe the features and relationships that helped them identify the exact location of the photograph's site. [Justifies conclusions.]

5. Repeat the activity by giving each pair a new photograph.

NEW JERSEY
AUDUBON
SOCIETY

## Putting It All Together

**?** What special features in the photograph helped you locate the area in your photograph? [Analyzes data.]

**?** How did you know your location was identified correctly? (The shapes and arrangement of the actual objects matched the objects in the photograph.) [Integrates data into a plan for problem solving.]

**?** Display the pictures from the activity. What was the best representation and why? [Supports evaluation.]

**?** Create a checklist of important steps or pieces in identifying an area. [Analyzes and evaluates relevancy of data.]

## Take Another Step

✔ Discuss map making. Have students create a Habitat Map and include one of the sites from the photographs as the focal point. (see p. 258)

✔ Pretend you are a bird flying from Central America to New Jersey. How would you find your way without the help of a printed map? (Discuss what landmarks they may use for guidance: mountain ranges, coastlines, position of the stars, the sun, and the moon.)

✔ Have a photography display of school-site locations. Encourage other students to locate the exact sites.

✔ Repeat the activity in a different habitat. Make a collage of photographs from different habitats.

✔ Allow students to take the pictures and challenge their classmates.

NEW JERSEY
AUDUBON
SOCIETY

**Bridges to the Natural World**

LENGTH OF ACTIVITY
40
minutes

Natural History Lessons

# AN EVENTFUL JOURNEY

**B**ird **migration** refers to the regular seasonal movement of certain species of birds. Nearly all North American birds migrate between their breeding areas and their wintering areas. Each species has its own special requirements for food and time for breeding; hence, they migrate at different times (Figure 5). A major stimulus for bird migration is the seasonal change in the amount of daylight. In spring, lengthening days trigger hormonal changes in birds that prompt northward migration. In autumn, decreasing daylight effects similar changes that prompt southward migration. The benefits of migrating include increased availability of food and of nesting territories as well as escape from extremes of climate.

During migration birds encounter many obstacles. They need to rest and feed during their flight north or south. Severe weather, lack of food, destruction of prime **habitat** through alteration or pollutants, and human harassment are all problems which may result in diminished numbers. As a result of these obstacles, it is estimated that many species have a 50% mortality rate during migration and in young birds it may be as high as 80%.

**Ornithologists** study migration in several ways. One way is simple observation: count the number of birds that fly through a specific area during a specific time period. New Jersey Audubon Society conducts regular hawk and seabird counts in the fall. Ornithologists also study migration by banding birds. Bird banding involves catching birds alive and placing small, individually numbered aluminum bands on their legs. When banded birds are recaptured or found dead elsewhere, scientists gain facts about where they go, how long they live, and the **physiological** changes caused by their migration.

Scientists use the information they collect from counting and banding birds to detect upward and downward trends in bird populations. A declining trend will sometimes warn that there may be a problem in the environment.

New Jersey is in the heart of the Atlantic Flyway, one of the four major migratory pathways in North America. This makes New Jersey's habitats some of the most important habitats for migrating birds.

NEW JERSEY
AUDUBON
SOCIETY

## BASIC CONCEPTS

☞ Migration is a regular seasonal movement.

☞ New Jersey is in the Atlantic Flyway; birds that migrate through the state use its habitats as resting and feeding areas.

☞ Birds encounter obstacles created by natural phenomena and human behaviors.

☞ People have the ability to minimize some of these obstacles by preserving critical habitats, conserving open space, and planning new development that is compatible with our natural resources.

## MATERIALS

☐ 24 migration statements (Figure 6)

☐ ten risk statements (Figure 7)

☐ 34  3 x 5 index cards

☐ three gummed labels

☐ magic marker

☐ glue or stapler

☐ 24 clip-on clothespins (optional)

## PROCESS SKILLS

*Inferring, predicting, interpreting data, formulating hypotheses, communicating.*

### PREPLANNING

1. Prepare a set of journey cards. Copy the sample migration statements (Figure 6). Cut and attach each to an index card.

2. Clip one clothespin to each card to prevent the cards from blowing away (optional). These cards will be used to form a simulated migration path.

3. Prepare a set of risk cards. Copy samples (Figure 7). Cut and attach to index cards. Mark the back of each card with "RISK." Clip cards together with a clothespin.

4. Find an appropriate location for the game (indoors or outdoors). You will need approximately 100 feet of clear pathway for the students to follow with separate starting and ending points. The pathway does not have to be linear.

5. Mark each gummed label with an "x". Place them at the end of the pathway. (There are three mortality cards. The students who come to the finish line with these cards get a label stuck to their forehead and are asked not to divulge what happened to them.)

6. Wait until the game is about to begin before placing the cards on the pathway.

## MOTIVATIONAL ACTIVITY

Engage the students in a discussion about plans for a journey.
You are going on a trip to Florida. What are some things that would help you get there? (fair weather, car in good condition, fuel, airplane, money for fares, food, suitcases, place to sleep along the way)

What are some things that would upset your plans along the way? (flat tire, breakdown, accident, no places to eat or sleep on the way, lost or stolen money, plane crash) [Analyzes and classifies data.]

## PROCEDURE

1. Explain to the students that they are going to pretend to be migrating birds.

2. Create a migration path with the journey cards by placing each card face down at four-foot intervals along the pathway.

3. Risk cards should be set in a pile off to the side of the pathway.

4. The ideal number for this game is 12. When the class size is larger, students can travel in twos or threes and "fly" as a single unit with their group to each space.

5. Divide the class into three groups. As you designate a student or group to be an early, middle or late migrant, (Figure 5) show them a picture of the bird. Visit www.webshots.com for samples.

6. Beginning with the first group of migrants, assign each student/unit a number from one to four.

7. Start the game by sending the first group (early migrants) onto the pathway: first student/unit to card #1, second to card #2, etc.

8. Instruct the students to pick up the card, read it, replace it face down, and do what the card tells them to do. Anytime someone else is using the card they are sent to, they are to go to the risk pile and follow the instructions on the card that is picked. If a number along the migration path is missing or out of sequence, go to the next card in the path.

9. As the travel cards are vacated by the early migrants, middle migrants enter the pathway. Then repeat the procedure with late migrants.

10. When most have reached the finish, assemble for discussion. (Note: Some students may get caught in a holding pattern. This is not unusual as many young birds do not breed until their second year.)

## Putting It All Together

**?** Let's talk about your journey. What obstacles did you encounter as birds? [Describes specific events] Which of those obstacles were created by people? (powerlines, plastic fishing line, pollution, lighthouses, glass buildings) Which were natural phenomena? (hawks, cold snaps, difficult winds, storms) [Interprets data.]

**?** What things helped you complete your migration? Which of these were created by people? (bird feeders, wildlife refuges) Which were natural phenomena? (good winds, plenty of food) [Analyzes and classifies data.]

**?** Why didn't all of you finish at the same time? (Birds migrate at different times, birds were held back by obstacles, and they were advanced by helps.) [Draws inferences from unstated facts.]

**?** What do you think happened to the 'birds' with the 'Xs' on their foreheads? (They died.) [Draws conclusions.]

**?** What kinds of habitats would birds use as they migrate through New Jersey? (marshes, mountain ridges, fields, coastal areas, lakes, ponds, streams, rivers, swamps, woodlands) [Applies knowledge to practical situation.]

**?** What should people consider when altering a natural habitat by building and development? (Current use of the area by wildlife and migrating birds, what impact the development would have, and whether development would displace animals permanently.) [Identifies criteria and draws conclusions.]

NEW JERSEY
AUDUBON
SOCIETY

# Take Another Step

✔ Plant shrubs, trees, or vines that will produce wild food (seeds, berries, flowers, etc.) around the edge of your schoolyard or lawn. These will attract migrating birds.

✔ Evaluate your community. List the things that would help birds migrate and those which would interfere with migration.

✔ Erect and monitor a feeding station on the school grounds. Keep a daily log and make seasonal comparisons of the birds that come to feed. Note: A feeding station can be as simple as scattered seed on the ground near a tree or bush.

✔ Research the birds you have seen at the feeding station. Categorize them into winter visitors and year-round residents. Why are some birds able to survive the winter without migrating? (Winters are milder, birds change their diet or have a varied diet.)

✔ Make a list of winter birds other than those seen at your feeding station. Where do they come from and why are they here?

✔ On a map of New Jersey, locate all the sites mentioned on the journey cards.

## FOR MORE INFORMATION

Dunne, Peter J., Richard Kane, and Paul Kerlinger. *New Jersey at the Crossroads of Migration.* (text and video)

Brian Vernachio, Don Freiday and Dale A. Rosselet. *Wild Journeys: Migration in New Jersey.* NJ Audubon Society, 2003.

National Geographic Society. *Bird Migration in the Americas.* (map)

Opus and Massachusetts Audubon Society. *Audubon Alliance Bird Identifier.* (chart)

Peterson, Roger Tory. *Eastern Birds.*

Sutton, Patricia. *Backyard Habitat for Birds: A Guide for Landowners and Communities in New Jersey.*

NEW JERSEY
AUDUBON
SOCIETY

**Bridges to the Natural World**

**Figure 5**

# New Jersey Birds
# Migration Chart

The following is a partial list of birds that migrate to or through New Jersey.

**EARLY MIGRANTS**
*late February through mid-April*
Common grackle
Turkey vulture
Red-winged blackbird
Eastern bluebird
Yellow-shafted flicker
Red-tailed hawk
Saw-whet owl
Ring-necked duck
Pine warbler
Ruddy duck
American robin
Killdeer
Eastern phoebe
Northern harrier
Northern pintail

**MIDDLE MIGRANTS**
*mid-April through mid-May*
Field sparrow
Ruby-crowned kinglet
Solitary sandpiper
Least tern
Whip-poor-will
Eastern kingbird
House wren
Veery
Blue-winged warbler
Yellow warbler
Ovenbird
Northern oriole
Scarlet tanager
Rose-breasted grosbeak

**LATE MIGRANTS**
*mid-May through mid-June*
Willow flycatcher
Red knot
Mourning warbler
Blackpoll warbler
Bay-breasted warbler

**Figure 6**

## Migration Cards

Photocopy and mount on 3 x 5 index cards.

1. WATCH OUT !!! Power lines ahead in Long Valley. Don't hit them! Crawl ahead four spaces on your hands and knees.

2. Many berries and insects are available in this overgrown field in West Milford. Smack your lips four times and move ahead four spaces.

3. You land in a polluted marsh and become sick from the food you eat. Sit down, hold your stomach for a count of 30, groan ten times, then move ahead two spaces.

4. Watch out for the Sharp-shinned hawk! It wants to eat you. Freeze, count to 40, then move ahead three spaces.

Natural History Lessons

NEW JERSEY
AUDUBON
SOCIETY

5. You escape being caught by a cat in Freehold but slightly sprain your wing in the escape. Get it back in shape. Slowly swing your left arm around ten times and move ahead one space.

6. Scientists at the Cape May Bird Observatory catch you for research. After putting a numbered metal band on your leg you are set free. Move ahead three spaces.

7. You got tangled in a plastic fishing line near the Shrewsbury River. You can't eat and are weak from hunger. A kind person takes you to the nature center at Sandy Hook where the ranger cuts away the line. Hop on one leg in a circle, count to 40, then move ahead four spaces.

8. You find a bird feeder in a fifth-grader's backyard in Vineland. Spend a few days enjoying the free food. Chew 20 times and move ahead five spaces.

9. It's raining, it's pouring, and you don't want to fly in this rainstorm. Count to 50 while you wait for the storm to stop, then move ahead four spaces.

10. You can't find the spot you came to last year because a new shopping mall has been built on the site. Walk around in three wide circles searching for a place to rest and feed. Because you are still hungry you have only enough strength to move ahead one space.

11. While traveling at night, you become confused by the beam from Barnegat Lighthouse on the New Jersey coastline. You are tired from flying in circles and can't continue. Sit down, count to 40 and move ahead three spaces.

12. You arrive at the Delaware Bay shore when the horseshoe crabs lay their eggs in the sand. Yum! Rub your stomach 15 times and move ahead four spaces.

13. You are able to fly a long distance in one day because of good winds along the Kittatinny mountain ridges of western New Jersey. Move ahead four spaces.

14. It's hard to find caterpillars to eat because the forest was sprayed with an insecticide. Open and close your eyes 25 times while you look for food and move ahead one space.

NEW JERSEY
AUDUBON
SOCIETY

15. Strong winds from the wrong direction keep you from migrating. Go back three spaces.

16. You become covered with oil from a spill in the Arthur Kill near Newark Bay. Although rescued, you do not recover. The game is OVER for you. You died! DON'T TELL ANYONE. Take this card with you. Go to the finish and place a gummed sticker on your forehead. Sit down and wait for the others to finish.

17. You just flew into a tall glass building in Trenton. Sit down, hold your head, count to 35 and move ahead two spaces.

18. A good wind helps you fly. Move ahead four spaces.

19. You have been shot with a BB gun. The game is OVER for you. You're dead! DON'T TELL ANYONE. Take this card with you. Go to the finish and place a gummed sticker on your forehead. Sit down and wait for the others to finish.

20. After flying for several days you land in the Great Swamp National Wildlife Refuge. Spend time feeding on berries in a thicket. Pretend to pick 10 berries from a bush, then move ahead one space.

21. Oops! An unexpected freeze kills off all the insects that you usually eat. Go back two spaces as you try to find more food.

22. A hurricane blows you into the Atlantic Ocean off Mantoloking. You rest on the water, but get eaten by a gull. The game is OVER for you. You're dead! DON'T TELL ANYONE. Take this card with you. Go to the finish and place a gummed sticker on your forehead. Sit down and wait for the others to finish.

23. Strong winds along the Delaware River blow you off course. Go back six spaces.

24. Spend five days resting and feeding on the mudflats at Brigantine Wildlife Refuge. Count to 40. Because you are so strong you can fly to the finish!

Natural History Lessons

NEW JERSEY
AUDUBON
SOCIETY

**Natural History Lessons**

Figure 7

# Risk Cards

Photocopy and mount on 3 x 5 index cards.

Go to card #9

Go to card #23

Go to card #18

Go to card #3

Go to card #24

Go to card #6

Go to card #5

Go to card #15

Go to card #10

Go to card #17

NEW JERSEY
AUDUBON
SOCIETY

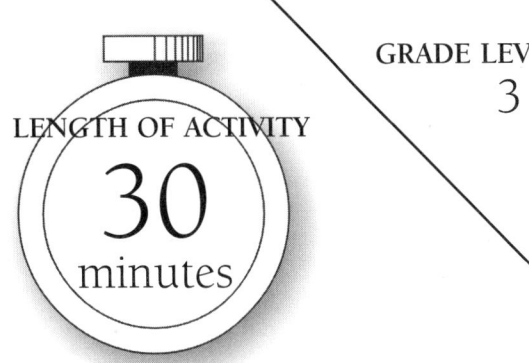

LENGTH OF ACTIVITY

**30**
minutes

**Natural History Lessons**

# CAN'T WE SHARE?

A balanced **ecosystem** is one that has adequate food, water, air, space, and shelter (**habitat**) for individual **species**, as well as population controls such as **herbivores** to maintain plant growth and **carnivores** to maintain animal populations.

Often human behaviors such as overdevelopment of open space, pollution, fragmentation of habitats, general misuse, and management for a single species upset this balanced ecosystem.

Natural conditions such as erosion, climate change, disease, flooding, and fire affect the balance of an ecosystem as well.

As a result of natural and human-related conditions, animals may die, relocate, or increase their populations by adapting to the new circumstances.

## BASIC CONCEPTS

☞ An animal's habitat includes food, shelter, space, water, and air.

☞ Animal populations respond to habitat loss.

## PROCESS SKILLS

*Communicating, using time and space, observing, inferring, predicting, interpreting data, identifying variables, formulating hypotheses.*

NEW JERSEY
AUDUBON
SOCIETY

Natural History Lessons

---

┌─────────────────────────┐
│      **MATERIALS**      │
└─────────────────────────┘

❑ 1 chair per student

❑ tape or CD of music

❑ index cards

❑ felt marker

❑ sticking tape

❑ 2 copies of the Environmental Events sheet  (Figure 9)

## PREPLANNING

1.  Select music and arrange the chairs in two rows back to back, as in musical chairs.

2.  Attach a habitat name to each chair, alternating the cards for equal distribution: woodland, wetland, field.

3.  Write a species name and habitat name on an index card. (See Figure 8). Make enough species cards so that each student has one. Be sure your selections match the number of habitat samples that are marked on the chairs, e.g., eight from field, eight from woodland, and eight from wetland.

4.  Make two copies of the Environmental Events sheet, cut them apart to individual events, and place them in a box for random selection.

# MOTIVATIONAL ACTIVITY

Make a class list of *basic life needs*. Lead a discussion on how these are provided.

## PROCEDURE

1.  Explain that each chair represents a specific habitat, such as a woodland, a wetland, or a field.  Each habitat supplies various plants and animals with their basic life needs.

2.  Hand out the species cards.  Have the students read the cards and tell what kind of animal or plant is represented and what habitat is required.

3.  Tell the students to stand in front of a chair representing their habitat

4.  Start the music and tell the students to *walk* around the chairs slowly.  When the music stops students should sit down in a chair representing their habitat.

5.  The teacher or a student chooses an "event" from the box, reads it aloud, and removes a chair representing the affected habitat.

6.  Continue the game, removing or adding one or more chairs at each stop in the music and as "events" are selected and read.

# Putting It All Together

**?** Students tell how an event affected their habitat. Of what basic needs were the plants and animals deprived? What will they do now? [Applies concepts and principles to new situations.]

**?** When more than one person was trying to take the same chair, what happened? How is this same behavior reflected in nature? (Some animals and plants will compete with each other within a habitat.) [Infers relevancy of new information.]

**?** Classify the events into natural phenomena and results of human behaviors. [Analyzes given data.]

**?** Which events can people do something to prevent? (Those that directly result from their own behavior) [Applies concepts to practical situations.]

**?** Which events cannot be controlled? (Natural phenomena.)

**?** What are some actions people can take to enhance habitats? (Replace grass with native plant species, create schoolyard habitats.) [Analyzes given data.]

**?** What can people do to correct disasters caused by natural phenomena? (Restore sand dunes and plant grass to secure them.) [Proposes a plan for problem-solving.]

**?** Tell the class the solution you would choose for the changes that took place in your habitat. Explain why. [Judges data and supports conclusions.]

## Take Another Step

✔ Research a plant or animal listed. Describe the food, shelter, space, and unique adaptations or behaviors associated with that species.

✔ Organize a town hearing. Choose one of the environmental events named in the game as the issue to be discussed. The mayor and council (four or five students) will listen to personal interest groups regarding a solution to the problem. (E.g., the 300 acres of field or the woodland that was developed. Personal interest groups should include people that hold different points of view regarding the land.)

**FOR MORE INFORMATION**

Dunne, Peter J., Richard Kane, and Paul Kerlinger. *New Jersey at the Crossroads of Migration.* (text and video)

NEW JERSEY
AUDUBON
SOCIETY

**Figure 8**

# SAMPLE SPECIES

FIELD HABITAT: sumac, dandelion, white-footed mouse, rabbit, eastern bluebird, blackberry, American goldfinch, garter snake, goldenrod, swallowtail butterfly, praying mantis, cricket, box turtle, honeybee

WOODLAND HABITAT: gray squirrel, white-tailed deer, American toad, downy woodpecker, sassafras, red oak, sugar maple, Jack-in-the-pulpit, American redstart, red-backed salamander, blue violet, daddy-long-legs, slug, poison ivy

WETLAND HABITAT: cattail, red-winged blackbird, green-backed heron, muskrat, cinnamon fern, green frog, snapping turtle, red maple, purple loosestrife, northern red salamander, northern water snake, mosquito, dragonfly, skunk cabbage, raccoon

**Figure 9**- *Make two photocopies of the Environmental Events list for use with the lesson.*

**Figure 9**

# ENVIRONMENTAL EVENTS

1. A town has 300 acres of old field habitat. A large shopping mall is built on one half of the property. Three years later an office complex is built on the other 150 acres. (Remove two chairs.)

2. Tanks of toxic chemicals buried in a field become corroded and the liquid seeps into the soil. (Remove one chair.)

3. In 50 square miles of continuous forest 20 private properties of two square miles each are sold. These properties, scattered throughout the area, are cleared and developed for homes, shopping malls, and a country club with golf course and tennis courts. (Remove one chair.)

4. At several new housing developments no silt retention barriers are erected. Rain sweeps soil into the waterways which fills in adjacent wetlands. (Remove one chair.)

5. A dam built across a river causes the surrounding wetlands and woodlands to be flooded. (Remove two chairs.)

6. A rural field is used for a local landfill. (Remove one chair.)

7. Unusual drought occurs. Freshwater wetland dries out. (Remove one chair.)

8. A disease-carrying insect infests the trees in a forest. (Remove two chairs.)

9. Rains flood lowland fields. (Remove one chair.)

10. Sparks from an abandoned campfire fly out on dry leaves and start a fire, destroying the surrounding woodland. (Remove two chairs.)

11. A hurricane blows away sand dunes, allowing ocean water to wash into the freshwater wetland. (Remove one chair.)

12. A large power company builds a dike to keep salt water out of a freshwater wetland area. (Add one chair.)

13. Local corporations stop mowing most of their extensive lawns. These are now managed for meadow and field habitat. (Add two chairs.)

14. Local school children replant a variety of trees along a water way. Eventually this will grow into a woodland. (Add one chair.)

15. A teacher works with her students and their parents to create a small wetland habitat on the school grounds. (Add one chair.)

© 2002 New Jersey Audubon Society

**LENGTH OF ACTIVITY**

**30 minutes**

**GRADE LEVELS**
Pre-K - 2

Natural History Lessons

# NATURE'S PALETTE

Our world is full of color. Color is the brain's interpretation of the frequency of light that is received by the eye. A **spectrum** is a series of colors (red, orange, yellow, green, blue indigo, violet, which can be remembered by the mnemonic ROY G. BIV), which is formed when light is refracted by something that acts like a **prism**. A droplet of water is a good example of something that acts like a prism. In a rainbow, each droplet of water acts as a prism and separates light into the spectrum of color.

Plants contain specific chemicals which produce colors, and people have learned how to obtain pigments from nature by rubbing, bruising, crushing, or boiling natural objects. These pigments have been used throughout history to produce paint, dye fabrics, and create face and body paint. Through years of experimentation it has been learned that the process by which the natural object is treated helps determine the resulting color. For instance, a green leaf rubbed on paper will produce a green color, but if the leaf is cooked it may produce a yellow color.

| BASIC CONCEPTS |
| --- |

☞ We identify colors of the spectrum as red, orange, yellow, green, blue indigo and violet. The colors grade into each other.

☞ The colors of the spectrum are found in nature.

☞ People use color to enhance and beautify their own environment.

## PROCESS SKILLS

*Communicating, using time and space, observing, classifying, inferring, predicting, interpreting data, formulating hypotheses, experimenting.*

NEW JERSEY
AUDUBON
SOCIETY

Natural History Lessons

## MATERIALS

**ACTIVITY A:**

☐ white unlined index cards

☐ markers or crayons the colors of the spectrum

**ACTIVITY B:**

☐ 1 support for drawing (clipboard or cardboard with paper clips) for each child

☐ white drawing paper

### PREPLANNING

There are two activities that teach the concepts. ACTIVITY A uses color cards. In ACTIVITY B each child creates a color palette.

Activity A:
Write a color of the spectrum on an index card using the same-colored crayon or felt marker. Continue through the spectrum until you have enough for each child to hold one card. (These cards could also be made of colored construction paper and covered with clear contact paper for future use.)

SUGGESTED COLOR DIVISIONS: Pre-K and K: Primary colors - red, yellow, blue; Grades 1 and 2: Primary and secondary colors - red, yellow, blue, orange, green, violet; Grades 3 to 6: Full spectrum plus tints and shades.

Activity B:
Secure drawing paper onto support.

TO DO AN OUTDOOR ACTIVITY: Find an area where the children will be permitted to gather and investigate samples of plants and other natural objects. Make sure you can identify poison ivy (see p. 84). Scout the area in advance for availability of berries, leaves, and flowers that will offer a variety of color.

TO DO AN INDOOR ACTIVITY: Collect organic materials from a variety of areas such as the grocery store, school lunchroom, or outdoor areas. Include leaves and vegetables (carrot roots and tops, beets, potato skins), fruits and berries (strawberries and orange skins), flowers, soil, and any other natural materials.

# MOTIVATIONAL ACTIVITIES

Have the students identify the colors of the spectrum.

1. Use spray from a garden hose or a plant mister to produce a rainbow. Do this in the morning or afternoon when the sun is not overhead. Stand with your back to the sun, adjust the nozzle to the finest spray and direct it away from the sun at a 45 degree angle above the horizontal. The rainbow will be easier to observe if the spray is directed toward a shaded or dark background.

2. Fill a large clear glass jar or fish bowl with water. Hold it in the direct sunlight and look for the spectrum reflected on the ceiling or wall of the classroom. Do the same with a glass prism.

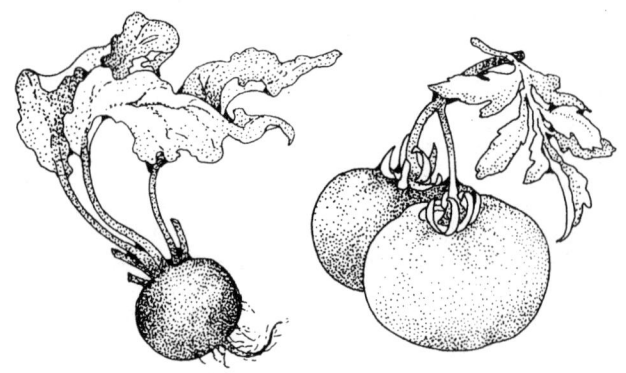

NEW JERSEY
AUDUBON
SOCIETY

**Bridges to the Natural World**

## PROCEDURE

### Activity A:

1. Mix the color cards thoroughly and distribute one to each child.

2. Take the students to the place you have prepared to find their colors.

3. Tell the students to match their color card to a natural object. It may not be an exact match, it may be lighter or darker than the color in hand. [Identifies and matches data.]

### Activity B:

1. Give each student a white paper and a support on which to draw.

2. Go to the selected study area. If indoors, spread the natural objects within reach of all students.

3. Each student should choose one piece of a natural object. When doing sampling in the outdoors it is important to stress SMALL amounts. Stress *use*, not *abuse*. Some plants can be shared by more than one student. [Practices discipline in gathering data.]

4. Direct the students to make a mark on their paper by using the chosen object. This can be accomplished by rubbing the object on the paper. Give assistance only if needed. [Analyzes relationships between organic material and color.]

5. Discuss the results and compare the shades and tints. [Combines and classifies data.]

6. Encourage the children to continue investigating by trying other objects. The teacher can guide each color and object or allow the students to explore and investigate on their own. [Creates a plan for problem solving; experiments and draws conclusions.]

## Putting It All Together

### Activity A:

**?** What colors did you see today? [Identifies color.]

**?** What objects were lighter than the color on your card? Darker? Just the same? [Analyzes data, makes comparisons, and draws conclusions.]

**?** Arrange the objects from lightest to darkest. [Rearranges data in a new pattern.]

**?** Look at your clothes. What colors are you wearing that are the same or nearly the same? [Uses data to make comparisons and draw conclusions.]

**?** Do your clothes have a color we did not see in our lesson today? [Integrates knowledge with practical situation.] Can you name something in nature that has the same color? [Demonstrates understanding by giving examples.]

**Activity B:**

**?** Label the colors on your paper. [Identifies color.]

**?** How many different colors were you able to reproduce? [Classifies data.]

**?** Did the color of the natural object always match the color it produced? [Compares differences and similarities.]

## Take Another Step

✔ Have the students prepare a bulletin board with their palettes.
    Pre-K and K: color palette
    Grades 1 and 2: picture of self or some article of clothing
    Grades 3 and up: landscape, favorite place in nature

✔ Have the students translate the colors into different languages.

✔ Use natural materials to make paint. Mix 1 cup flour and 1/4 cup liquid white soap together. Add natural pigment such as stain-making fruit or vegetable juice. Berries work best when they have been cooked, mashed, and strained.

✔ Label the colors of living things in the classroom.
(green leaves, violet flowers, orange fish)

✔ Identify seasons by color.

✔ Identify holidays by color.
(Christmas = red, green; Valentine's Day = red;
Halloween = orange, black, etc.)

✔ Name plant colors that you may get on your clothing without intending to do so.
(grass stains, tomato sauce, grape juice)

### FOR MORE INFORMATION

Duvoisin, Roger. *The House of Four Seasons.*

Grae, Ida. *Nature's Colors, Dyes from Plants.*

Kirkpatrick, Rena K. *Look at Rainbow Colors.*

O'Neill, Mary. *Hailstones and Halibut Bones.*

Simon, Hilda. *The Magic of Color.*

Yarrow, Ruth. *Exploring Environments.*

LENGTH OF ACTIVITY

# 30 minutes

GRADE LEVELS
Pre-K - 6

Natural History Lessons

# A DAWN CHORUS

**A**ll animals have developed ways to communicate with individuals of their own **species** and other animals with which they come in contact. In our own daily lives, pets make their needs clear through vocalizations and body language. A dog wags its tail, barks or growls. People learn to interpret and respond to these communications.

In the bird world, the most obvious signs of communication are through songs and calls. Birds sing to attract a mate, to continue the pair bonding that is required during the breeding season, to help delineate their nesting or feeding territory, and to warn competitors not to intrude. Bird calls are usually single notes that convey information about a bird's specific needs or concerns: the begging calls of **nestlings**, the alarm note of a bird that detects a **predator**, the insistent chirps of a bird that is defending its territory, or the flight call of a migrating bird.

### BASIC CONCEPTS

☞ Animals communicate with each other.

☞ Birds communicate through songs and calls.

☞ Each bird species has its own song or call.

## PROCESS SKILLS

*Communicating, observing, classifying, inferring, identifying variables, experimenting.*

NEW JERSEY
AUDUBON
SOCIETY

**Natural History Lessons**

---

## MATERIALS

❑ bird song sheet (Figure 10)

❑ cassette recorder

❑ blank cassette

❑ bird song tape or CD (optional)

❑ bird pictures

### PREPLANNING

Collect and mount pictures of the birds used in Figure 10.

# MOTIVATIONAL ACTIVITY

Lead the students in a discussion concerning the ways people communicate with each other about the events in their lives. Ask the students the following:
1. How do you introduce yourself? (Students say name.)
2. Why don't we all have the same name? [Analyzes relationships and makes inferences.]
3. How would you warn someone of danger? (shout, yell, scream) [Applies understanding to practical situation.]
4. Show how you would protect your favorite toy from a thief. (aggressive behavior)

If people communicate different messages in different ways, what messages might a bird want to communicate? (They identify themselves; they warn of danger, and they defend and delineate territory.) [Discriminates and makes inferences.]

## PROCEDURE

1. Tell the class that many birds like to sing in the morning and we call this "dawn chorus." As a class they are going to learn some bird songs and create a dawn chorus.

2. Divide the class into groups. Each group will represent a different bird. If working with very young students select only two or three birds for the entire class.

3. Show the students a picture of a bird, imitate its song, and have the students practice the song as a class.

4. Give each group a picture of one bird, imitate its song, and have the students repeat the song (see sample bird songs, Figure 10). Have students practice their songs. [Demonstrates understanding by imitation.]

5. Tell the students that a dawn chorus starts softly (predawn), gets louder (at dawn and shortly afterwards), then gets soft again (as the heat of the day sets in).

6. Arrange the students in a half circle. Explain to them that as you point to each of them, they are to begin their songs and continue until you point to them again.

7. Practice the songs. Have the entire group "sing" for about 10 seconds, then begin pointing to the students to stop.

8. Repeat the songs. Record the chorus on a cassette.

NEW JERSEY
AUDUBON
SOCIETY

**Bridges to the Natural World**

## Putting It All Together

**?** Do birds actually say words when they sing? (No. People have given human words to some birds' songs to help them remember.) [Distinguishes between fact and anthropomorphisms.]

**?** Why do birds sing? (Birds sing to communicate with other birds and animals.) [Demonstrates understanding by listing examples.]

**?** Why don't all birds have the same song? (Each species of bird has its own song so it is better able to communicate with its own species.) [Draws inferences.]

## Take Another Step

✔ Ask the students to listen to the bird songs around the school yard or their homes. See if they can recognize any of the ones used in the "dawn chorus".

✔ Listen to the "real" song of the birds used in the activity. Bird tapes and CDs are available in some libraries and can be purchased through NJ Audubon Society. There are also numerous "mood" tapes that include bird songs The Dawn Chorus tape can be purchased from NJAS Department of Education.

✔ Find out how other animals communicate.

✔ Research one of the birds in the Dawn Chorus. Find out what food it eats, where it nests, and some unique adaptation or behavior.

**FOR MORE INFORMATION:**

Walton, Richard K. and Robert W. Lawson. *Peterson Field Guides: Backyard Bird Song.*

Elliott, Lang and Marie Read. *Common Birds and Their Songs* (book and CD).

NEW JERSEY
AUDUBON
SOCIETY

### Figure 10 - **Bird Songs**

## Tufted Titmouse

Pe- ter, Pe- ter, Pe- ter

## Northern Cardinal

Cheer, Cheer, Cheer

## Red-winged Blackbird

Onk a Ree, Onk a Ree

## Yellow-shafted Flicker

Flick - a, Flick - a, Flick - a

## Blue Jay

Jay, Jay, Jay

## Black-capped Chickadee

Chicka Dee Dee Dee Dee Dee

NEW JERSEY AUDUBON SOCIETY

## American Goldfinch (Eastern)

Po ta - to - Chip,   Po ta - to - Chip

## White-throated Sparrow

O Sweet Ca - na - da Ca - na - da Ca - na - da

## Rufous-sided Towhee

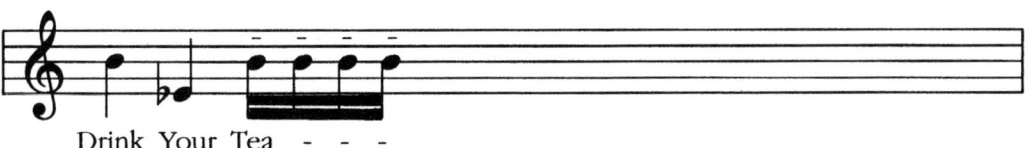

Drink Your Tea - - -

## Indigo Bunting

Fire    Fire    Where    Where    Here    Here

## American Robin

Cheer-y  Up,  Chee-ry  Up,  Cheer-up

## Red-eyed Vireo

Where am I?   Way up here,  see me!

## American (Common) Crow

C a w, C a w, C a w

## White-breasted Nuthatch

Yank, Yank, Yank, Yank, Yank
(Nasally)

## Gray Catbird

M e w, M e w, M e w, M e w

## Ovenbird

Teacher, Teacher, Teacher, Teacher

## Common Yellowthroat

Witch i ty, Witch i ty, Witch i ty, Witch

LENGTH OF ACTIVITY
3 periods
20
minutes each

**GRADE LEVELS**
Pre-K - 6

# LEAVES ON PARADE

New Jersey has five distinct **physiographic regions**. The geological **diversity** in regions determines the kinds of plants that grow and the types of forests that develop throughout the state. Consider trees alone. Even though New Jersey is the most densely populated state in the union per square mile, it is composed of 45% forest cover with 77 species of native trees. This is one of the features that gives New Jersey the descriptive title, "Garden State."

Learning to identify plants by leaves can lead to a broader understanding of the **habitat** in which they are found and consequently the kind of wildlife living there. Plants can be identified by their leaf edges, veins, petioles, and structure. The sugar maple, with its simple structure, lobed leaves, and palmate veins, is the **dominant** tree in the sugar maple/mixed hardwood forest. Knowing this, we can expect also to find tulip, sassafras, and several kinds of oaks. Among birds and animals will be great-horned owl, eastern chipmunk, wood turtle, and ring-necked snake.

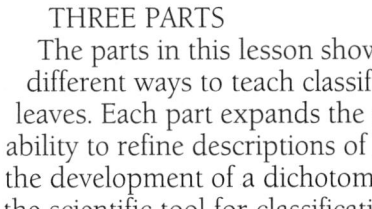

The chief function of leaves is to manufacture food for the plant through **photosynthesis**, but no other element of any **ecosystem** has a more vital interrelationship with the other creatures sharing the same habitat, since leaves are able to directly or indirectly satisfy those creatures' basic needs.

THREE PARTS
The parts in this lesson show three different ways to teach classification of leaves. Each part expands the student's ability to refine descriptions of leaves for the development of a dichotomous key, the scientific tool for classification.

NEW JERSEY
AUDUBON
SOCIETY

## BASIC CONCEPTS

☞ Leaf edges have different patterns.

☞ Leaves have veins and petioles.

☞ Leaves have different structures.

☞ New Jersey has a wide variety of deciduous plants.

## MATERIALS

☐ at least one deciduous leaf for each child

☐ display chart of leaf characteristics (Figure 11)

☐ comb for demonstration

# PROCESS SKILLS

*Communicating, observing, classifying, comparing and contrasting, inferring, interpreting data.*

### PREPLANNING

1. Prepare one display chart for each leaf characteristic (edges, veins, structure). (Figure 11).

2. Collect a variety of deciduous leaf samples from the schoolyard. (Options: Have students bring leaves from home or collect leaves from your own explorations.)

### FOR MORE INFORMATION

Kricher, John C., and Gordon Morrison. *Peterson Field Guides: Eastern Forests.*

Watts, May Theilgaard. *Tree Finder: A Manual for the Identification of Trees by Their Leaves.*

USDA Forest Service, Northeastern Research Station, *Trends in New Jersey Forests.* DEP Forestry Services, 501 E. State Street, P.O. Box 404, Trenton, New Jersey, 08625-0404. (609) 292-2531 (brochures free of charge).

# MOTIVATIONAL ACTIVITY

Ask the children to think of their best friend. "What words would you use to describe your friend's hair?" (long, short, brown, blonde, curly, braided, etc.) "What other words would you use to help describe what your friend looks like?" (short, tall, wears glasses, etc.) We can identify certain plants by describing their special features.

NEW JERSEY AUDUBON SOCIETY

# PERIOD 1
## Edges of Leaves

### PROCEDURE

1. Provide the students with a variety of leaves.

2. Direct the students' discoveries with the following questions. Use the edge chart to reinforce your descriptions.

### Smooth or straight

Trace the edge of your desk with your finger. How does it feel? (smooth or straight) Some leaves have smooth or straight edges. Point to the smooth edge of the Sour gum leaf on the diagram.

Ask the students to find leaves that have smooth or straight edges.

### Lobed

Run your finger along the bottom part of your ear. Do you know what that part of your ear is called? (lobe) Some leaves have parts that stick out just like your earlobe. At times they are so deeply notched, they almost look like fingers. Point to the lobed Post oak leaf on the diagram. Lobes can be pointed or rounded.

See if there are any lobed leaves in the collection.

### Toothed

Rub your finger along the edge of your teeth. How does it feel? (sharp, pointy) Can you think of anything else we use that has sharp pointy edges that we call teeth? Hold up the comb. Some leaves have sharp pointy edges just like teeth on a comb or a saw. Point to toothed leaf of the Sweet pepperbush on the diagram.

Find leaves that are toothed.

### Wavy

Sometimes the leaf looks as if it has teeth, but the points are not sharp. It's not really a smooth edge, it's kind of bumpy or like little waves. Have students use their hands to make an undulating motion in the air, like the track of a roller coaster. Point to the wavy leaf of the Blackjack oak on the diagram.

Ask the students to find leaves that have wavy edges. [Interprets verbal descriptions and applies concepts to practical situations.]

## Putting It All Together

**?** How can leaves be described? (by their edges: smooth, lobed, toothed, wavy) [Describes leaf edges.]

**?** How many different kinds of leaf edges did we find today? [Classifies and interprets data.]

**?** What can we suppose if there is no match for one of the descriptions? (There are other kinds of plants than what we have represented.) [Makes inferences and draws conclusions.]

NEW JERSEY
AUDUBON
SOCIETY

# PERIOD 2
## Leaf Veins

### PROCEDURE

Use the same selection of leaves, preparation, motivational, and extension activities as in Part 1. Refer to the veination chart for visual reinforcement.

### Pinnate

In some leaves, the main vein divides the leaf in half from top to bottom. Other veins reach from different points along the axis to the edges of the leaf. Ask the students for examples of things that are divided equally in half. (the human body, a pine cone, etc.) Point to pinnate American holly leaf on the diagram.

Ask students to find leaves that have a pinnate vein pattern. (Note: The pattern is the same on either side of the main vein but the secondary veins are sometimes exactly opposite each other and sometimes alternate.)

### Palmate

Hold up your hand stretching your fingers apart. Trace each finger from the base of your palm at the wrist to the tip of each finger. The palm is the center from which the fingers are attached. The veins of some leaves are arranged in much the same way. The bottom of the leaf attached to the stem is much like your palm at your wrist. The other veins, like your fingers, reach out to the end of the leaf from that point.

Point to the palmate Sugar maple leaf on the diagram.

Find any leaves that have a palmate arrangement to the veins.

### Parallel

Railroad tracks and steps in a ladder are good examples of parallel lines. Look around you right now and see if you see any other examples of parallel lines in any nearby structures. In leaves, while there is some point where the veins all come together, the pattern for the most part is parallel.

Point to the parallel Arrowhead leaves on the diagram.

Look for any leaves that have parallel veins.

*Note:*
Sometimes it is easier to see the vein pattern from the underside of the leaf.

## Putting It All Together

**?** What new way have we learned to describe leaves? (veins: pinnate, palmate, parallel) [Describes leaf veins.]

**?** Describe a leaf by its edge and by its veins. (e.g., lobed edge with pinnate veins of a white oak leaf) [Applies knowledge to a practical situation.]

**?** Sort the leaves into the descriptive categories we have named. (Edges and veins must be similar.) [Analyzes data and reorganizes for problem solving.]

**?** How many groups do we have now? How is this different from when we sorted only by leaf edge description? (The grouping will change because of new assortment. Some were eliminated from the original groups to form new groups.) [Uses definitions to rearrange materials into new categories.]

# PERIOD 3
## Leaf Structure

### PROCEDURE

Use the same selection of leaves, preparation, motivational, and extension activities as in Part 1. Refer to the structure chart to reinforce descriptions.

The way a leaf is attached to the branch determines its structure.

### Simple

Most leaves are attached directly to a branch by a single stem, or petiole. You can check to see if this is so by noticing the slight bump or wider part where the stem is attached to the branch. Such leaves are classified as simple in structure.

Point to the simple Lowbush blueberry leaves in the diagram.

### Compound

Some trees have leaves that are made up of leaflets attached to a stem which is attached to a branch. You can tell these by using the same clue in determining the simple leaf. Look at the end of the stem. There is a bump at the end of the main leaf. There is no bump at the end of the leaflets.

Point to the compound Ailanthus leaf on the diagram.

## Putting It All Together

**?** What new descriptions can we use to identify leaves? (leaf structure) [Describes leaf structure.]

**?** Pick one leaf. Describe it using the terms you have learned. (Example: A red maple leaf has a simple structure, a palmate vein arrangement, and a toothed edge.) [Integrates and combines information for new classification of leaves.]

**?** Observe the trees, vines, or shrubs in the schoolyard, on your way to school, and at home. Using the descriptions you have learned, how many are the same species? Different species? What does this tell you about the variety of plants in the area where you spend most of your time? [Applies new knowledge to practical situations.]

## Take Another Step

✓ Make a collection of leaves for a bulletin board. Classify them according to the descriptions learned.

✓ In autumn, have each child outline a leaf on a piece of construction paper that matches the color of the leaf. Tie a string to the stem and attach it to the classroom ceiling, creating a mobile.

✓ Construct a dichotomous key for the trees in your school or the site you are visiting (see Creating a Dichotomous Key, p. 276).

NEW JERSEY
AUDUBON
SOCIETY

**Natural History Lessons**

*Natural History Lessons* (sidebar)

**Figure 11**
# Leaf Characteristics

*Leaf Edges*

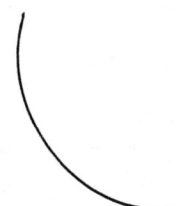

**SMOOTH**
(as in Sour gum - p. 67)

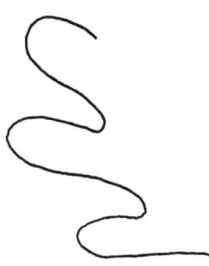

**LOBED**
(as in Post oak - p. 73)

**TOOTHED**
(as in Sweet pepperbush - p. 43)

**WAVY**
(as in Blackjack oak - p. 70)

**NEW JERSEY AUDUBON SOCIETY**

*Leaf Veins*

**PINNATE**
(as in American holly - p. 84)

**PALMATE**
(as in Sugar maple - p. 49)

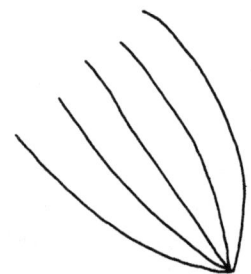

**PARALLEL**
(as in Broad-leaf plantain - p. 9)

*Leaf Structure*

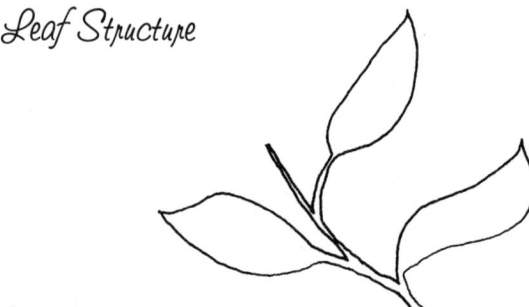

**SIMPLE**
(as in Lowbush blueberry - p. 78)

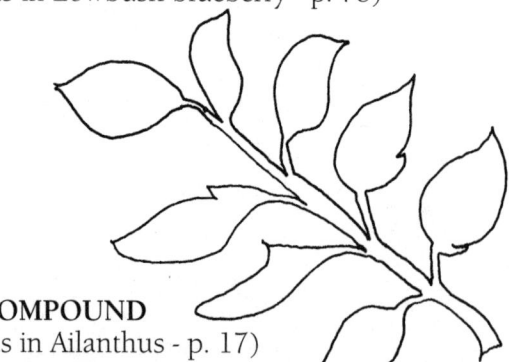

**COMPOUND**
(as in Ailanthus - p. 17)

RESEARCH
R
CONSERVATION
EDUCATION

**LENGTH OF ACTIVITY**
20 minutes

# WINDOWS ON THE WORLD

**Natural History Lessons**

Diversity of **species** can be observed in the most common places. A good example is a grassy area in a school yard or local park. A hasty glance gives the impression that grass seed is all that has germinated in the area, while closer observation reveals a wide variety of plants. Without cultivation through the use of **herbicides** and fertilizers, other plants will invade the area naturally.

The seeds of nearby plants are carried to the grassy area by way of wind, water, and animals. Some seeds have physical **adaptations** that make it easy for the wind to transport them. The fluff of dandelions and milkweeds provides more surface area for the wind to transport the seed, while the "wings" of a maple tree or tulip tree seed help carry it away from the parent plant. Rainstorms will dislodge seeds from its parent plant as well as force airborne seeds to the ground. Water run-off then moves the seeds to more distant areas. Again, animals transport seeds in a variety of ways. They collect and bury them to be eaten at some other time; they eat seeds which pass through their digestive systems and are deposited elsewhere; they carry seeds on their coats as hitchhikers. Many seeds are so hearty they can grow in the cracks and crevices of sidewalks, parking lots, macadam playgrounds, and building walls.

It is common to find monocultures in nature. More likely one will find a natural community that has several dominant species with a variety of other species that are adapted to the soil conditions and climate.

## BASIC CONCEPTS

☞ There are many different kinds of plants in a natural community.

☞ Some plants are more dominant than others.

☞ Seeds are dispersed by wind, water, and animal activity.

## PROCESS SKILLS

*Communicating, using time and space, measuring, observing, estimating, classifying, inferring, predicting, interpreting data, formulating hypotheses.*

NEW JERSEY
AUDUBON
SOCIETY

**Natural History Lessons**

## MATERIALS

For each student

☐ 1 wire hanger

☐ clip board

☐ paper and pencil

Natural History Lessons

### PREPLANNING

1. Form each hanger into a diamond-shaped frame. Bend the hook and tape to cover sharp edges.

2. Assemble clip boards, pencils, and paper.

3. Find a grassy area on the school grounds where the students will be able to kneel and examine the ground closely. This activity also can be done along cracks in a blacktop surface, or sidewalk where there are plants growing.

# MOTIVATIONAL ACTIVITY

Most people who live in America came here, or were brought, from some other part of the world. How did they get here? (They immigrated or traveled from another land.)

Let's talk about travel. What are some ways that people travel around the earth? Teacher leads a discussion of land, sea, and air transportation. [Defines modes of travel.] Plants that come from seeds travel in the same way. Some are planted by a farmer or gardener, but others travel by other means. How would they fly? Would they take an airplane? (carried by wind) By water? (transported in streams, rivers, etc., and by rain) And by land? (carried by people and other animals) [Demonstrates understanding of principle.]

## Lesson 1
### PROCEDURE

1. Bring the students to the area you plan to study. "What was planted here? Let's take a closer look."

2. Group the students into pairs.

3. Direct the students to form a circle, leaving at least an arm's length between each pair.

4. Have the students kneel on the ground. Distribute materials to students.

5. Tell the students to place their hangers on the ground in front of them. This space will be their "window."

6. Look very carefully at everything inside your window.

7. Direct the exploration. Ask the students to look at leaf shape, plant and leaf size, variety of plants, color, presence of flowers or seeds, etc. [Analyzes and classifies data.]

8. Direct the students to pick or draw one sample leaf for each different kind of plant they see. (When doing sampling activities pick only the leaf; be careful not to uproot the plant.)

*Optional*
Save the samples in an envelope for Lesson 2 or for extensions.

### Teacher Note
It is possible that students will select parts of, or smaller versions of the same plant and claim that they are different specimens. It is sufficient for this introductory lesson to recognize what is similar and what is different and to explain the differences in their own words. As students repeat the lesson at a later date, or learn from other students, they gain the opportunity to assess their own conclusions and adjust them accordingly.

NEW JERSEY
AUDUBON
SOCIETY

## Putting It All Together

**?** How many different kinds of plants did you see in your observation window? [Applies knowledge to classify and compute diversity of plants.]

**?** How could you tell if the plants were the same kind or different? (Leaf shapes were different, sizes will vary, colors will be different, and there were seeds or flowers on some of the plants.) [Analyzes the information found.]

**?** What kind of seeds do you think the grounds keepers planted to make this lawn? (grass) How do you think all these other plants got here? (wind, rain, carried by birds and other animals) [Evaluates and draws conclusions.]

## Lesson 2
**PROCEDURE**

1. Have students examine their original envelope of plant samples from Lesson 1. Arrange the plants in like categories on a desk.

2. Ask the students to create a visual diagram showing different plant species. (bar graph, drawings of the plants, leaf rubbings, pie graph, etc.) [Creates visual report of exploration.]

3. Label the diagram according to species dominance.

4. Leave the sample plants on the desk. Collect the completed data sheets, shuffle them, and redistribute one sheet to each pair of students. Students must find the correct sample based on the information described on the data sheet.

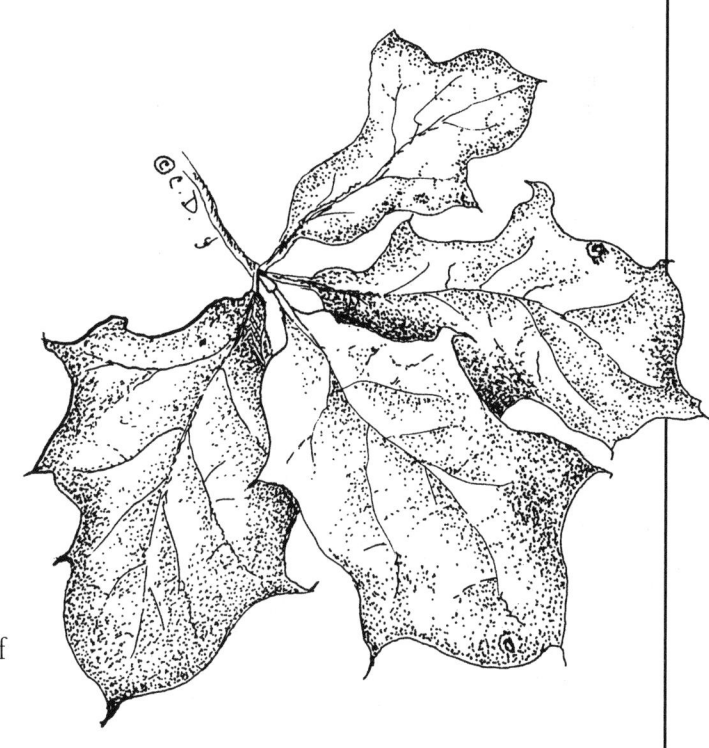

## Putting It All Together

**?** Ask the person who designed the data sheet to confirm the match made.

**?** How many samples among the groups had the same dominant plant?

**?** Which of the methods used to describe and illustrate plant diversity was most effective? Why? [Assesses methodology and justifies position.]

Natural History Lessons

## Take Another Step

✔ Have the students compare and classify all leaves according to similarity. [Classifies data.]

✔ Draw a picture of what this area might look like if no one cut the lawn. (The plants would grow taller; trees and shrubs eventually would grow.)

✔ Ask the maintenance personnel to leave a section of the grassy area unmowed. Monitor the type and growth of the plants that appear by taking pictures or having the students draw their observations.

✔ Have the students collect seeds from outdoors. Plant these seeds in a classroom planting box. Observe how many different kinds of seeds germinate.

✔ Pretend you are a seed. How did you make it to this grassy area? Tell your story to the rest of the class. Is your story possible or not possible?

✔ Transpose the data from the field sheets on to the computer. Create a more complete picture of the natural community's diversity by including all the students' information [Interprets and combines data to draw conclusions.]

✔ Use large round hoops (hoola-hoops) and have students explore the area in teams.

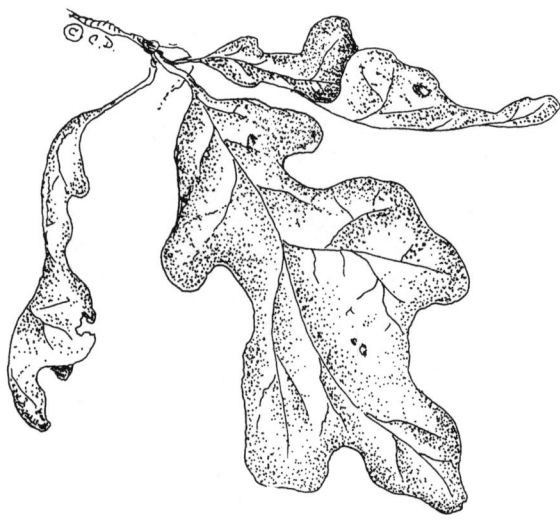

NEW JERSEY
AUDUBON
SOCIETY

**Bridges to the Natural World**

CONSERVATION RESEARCH
E
EDUCATION

LENGTH OF ACTIVITY
## 30 minutes

Natural History Lessons

# MYTHS, LEGENDS, AND STORYTELLING

Early Native Americans were keen observers of the natural world. Their culture had a familiarity with the plants and animals, weather systems, and seasonal changes. Their food, shelter, recreation, education, religion, and economy were developed out of their close relationship with nature.

The stories made up by indigenous peoples all over the world are reflections of nature and how nature works. They are also reflections on human behaviors. The stories that are passed from one generation to another are not intended to be literal scientific explanations of how things got that way. Instead, they communicate observations about relationships. They are intended to carry a message that speaks uniquely to each individual. The meaning is subjective and can be interpreted according to present need or perspective.

The myth or legend as we understand it today is not intended to carry historical or scientific truth.

Myths and legends are kinds of truth that help us form life-giving relationships with ourselves, with others, and with the world in which we live.

Developing a myth or legend requires a basic knowledge which is gained by careful observation and an imagination that leads to the invention of new or different ideas or points of view. Storytelling is therefore a great springboard for developing an inventive mind. Telling stories in the outdoors can stimulate children's imagination and inspire them to create their own (Figure 12).

---

### BASIC CONCEPTS

☞ Living things have characteristics or behaviors that make them unique.

☞ Humans have used myths and legends to explain natural phenomena.

☞ Oral communication is a traditional form of sharing information and fostering concern for natural systems.

---

NEW JERSEY
AUDUBON
SOCIETY

**Natural History Lessons**

# PROCESS SKILLS

*Communicating, using time and space, observing, classifying, inferring, interpreting data, formulating hypotheses.*

**MATERIALS**

❑ paper

❑ pencils or crayons

## PREPLANNING

1. Find an area to take the students on a nature walk. Choose places along the way where you can draw attention to some unique features of a tree, bird, animal, etc.

2. Single out a number of items: a tree with smooth bark, one with rough bark, a fuzzy item, special markings or sounds of birds and other animals.

# MOTIVATIONAL ACTIVITY

Tell the following story to the students.

## HOW THE CHIPMUNK GOT ITS STRIPES

When the world was new and only the animal people lived on the land, Bear fell asleep when it got cold and the sky turned deep blue as the night came. Bear slept all through the cold time of winter and never learned how night and day worked. When he woke up it was night.

"It's dark all the time," said Bear.

"No, sometimes it's light," said Chipmunk.

They argued for days and Bear became more and more impatient.

*Finally, Chipmunk shouted, "Light, I see light coming." Sure enough, at the far end of the valley, a thin stream of sunlight shot up and the darkness disappeared. Bear was so angry that he ran after Chipmunk and scratched him with his huge claws just as the little creature jumped out of sight. From that day to this Chipmunk carries the stripes on his back to show where Bear's claws scratched him.*

Tell the students that native peoples all over the world explain how nature works through legends. In legends some things are scientifically true and some things are imaginary.

In the story "How the Chipmunk Got Its Stripes" what things are true or factual? [Distinguishes between fact and fiction.]

1. There is such an animal as a chipmunk.
2. Eastern chipmunks have two white stripes on their backs.
3. There is such an animal as a bear.
4. Bears have claws.
5. There is such thing as darkness and the sun gives light.

What things are imagined?

1. What it was like when the world first began.
2. Bears and chipmunks argue with each other.
3. The stripes from a chipmunk come from a bear's claws.

To make up stories about how things came to be the way they are we must use our imaginations mixed with some actual facts that we can observe and measure.

**PROCEDURE**

Take the students outdoors to a natural habitat area. Draw attention to the unique characteristics of plants and animals along the trail. Invite the students to share their observations. Begin storytelling by encouraging the students to explain or invent why the plants and animals exhibit these unique characteristics.

# Putting It All Together

**?** Choose one special thing that everyone in the class saw. Have the students give a description of its size, color, special markings or sounds, behavior, etc. Choose one characteristic that was observed and write a class legend about how it came to be. (E.g., Some trees have smooth bark and some have rough, or wrinkled bark. Make up a story on how the tree got wrinkly bark.)

**?** Make a class list of all the plants, animals, minerals, and phenomena observed on the walk. Encourage the students to invent stories of their own about something on the list. The title should begin with "How the," or "Why the" and the story should be about origins.

## Take Another Step

✔ Enhance the written stories with the students' own illustrations.

✔ Develop the stories using pictures drawn in comic-strip style. Display these on a classroom or corridor bulletin board.

✔ Dramatize the stories for a school assembly.

### FOR MORE INFORMATION

Caduto, Michael J., and Joseph Bruchac. *Keepers of the Animals: Native American Stories and Environmental Activities for Children.*

Caduto, Michael J., and Joseph Bruchac. *Keepers of the Earth: Native American Stories and Environmental Activities for Children.*

Pellowski, Anne. *Hidden Stories in Plants.*

### Figure 12

## Sample Stories

These stories were created by children attending a New Jersey Audubon Summer Day Camp.

*Once scarlet tanagers were all red. Mr. Tanager was flying over the meadow. Mrs. Fox caught him and tied him down. She dropped him into a pot over the fire. He floundered about and singed his wings black and broke the string. Then he flew away. From that day on all male scarlet tanagers have black wings.*

Kristin Lamm, Age 7

*Scarlet Tanager picked a berry and flew away. He flew over a house but dropped his berry as he went over the chimney. He flew after the berry and fluttered around the chimney. The soot made his wings black. Ever since that time, scarlet tanager's wings are black.*

Emily Keber, Age 6

NEW JERSEY
AUDUBON
SOCIETY

CONSERVATION RESEARCH EDUCATION

LENGTH OF ACTIVITY
**45**
minutes

**GRADE LEVELS**
**4 - 6**

# WHAT IS YOUR NICHE?

In a natural community, a niche represents the role that a particular animal or plant occupies in that ecological community. Part of the role consists of obtaining or creating food. In the animal world **carnivores** and **omnivores** are hunters while **herbivores** become the hunted. Other important work for animals is to find or to build a shelter. These actions or works often have an impact on the community in general. They cause alterations: the woodpecker drills a hole to find insects, and the squirrel uses that hole for a nest. They can also affect the work of others in the community, as when the Blue Jay takes the squirrel's acorns or an egg from a bird's nest. These alterations influence other life forms that share the habitat. Through animal niches, plants and animals in any given natural community are linked together like strands in a spider's web.

Ecological niches can be compared to the jobs or occupations of humans. People work primarily to support themselves and their families and provide food and shelter, but the services they perform benefit different needs of the community. Wild animals work primarily for their own survival, but in that effort they often benefit or otherwise affect a wide variety of other animals and plants of the surrounding community. The various animals and their respective niches create the interrelationships and connections that allow any natural community to function as a defined ecological unit.

## BASIC CONCEPTS

☞ The roles that animals occupy in natural communities are called niches.

☞ These niches are similar to human jobs in the sense that they benefit other members of the community.

☞ Animal niches may relate to their food sources, shelter needs, or other self-preservation activities.

☞ Close observation of animals in their natural habitats may reveal significant information about their various niches.

## PROCESS SKILLS
*Observing, comparing and contrasting, inferring, communicating.*

NEW JERSEY AUDUBON SOCIETY

---

## MATERIALS

For each team of two students:

☐ job reference sheet (Figure 13)

☐ clipboard and pencil

Investigation tools:

☐ hand lenses

☐ containers for holding and observing small animals

☐ binoculars (optional)

---

**PREPLANNING**

1. Delineate the natural area where students will observe wildlife or look for evidence of their presence.

2. Assemble materials needed.

3. Read lessons, Crawlies in the Hand (p. 285), and Turning Logs and Rocks (p. 285) to help guide the exploration.

# MOTIVATIONAL ACTIVITY

Discuss various jobs or occupations of people in the local community. How do these jobs help other people in the community, the state, nation, and the world? What jobs are directly connected with food supply? With housing? With safety? With health? What would our lives be like if any of these services were not performed?

**PROCEDURE**

1. Assign teams of two, distribute the materials, and take the students to an outdoor natural community.

2. Tell the students, "The job list describes services offered by people in a human community. Your task is to observe similar jobs performed in the wild. For example, we see a squirrel burying an acorn. One job of the squirrel could be interpreted as a farmer planting a crop. Match as many job descriptions on your sheet with animal activity, or evidence of animal activity that you observe."

3. Hand lenses, observation containers and binoculars are placed in a central location for student use.

## Putting It All Together

**?** What evidence indicated hunting, gathering, or storage of food? (piles of seeds, holes in leaves, animal bones or fur, insects or animals feeding) [Analyzes evidence or behavior of animals.]

**?** What evidence of animal behavior did not relate to food? (holes in trees and in the ground and nests in trees; loud noises of alarm.) [Analyses evidence or behavior of animals.]

**?** How do animal niches in natural communities relate to jobs or occupations in human communities? (provide food for others, construct shelters intentionally or as a result of another activity, sound security alarms) [Identifies similarities and creates analogous situations.]

**?** Do any two animals occupy exactly the same niches in natural communities? Why or why not? (Yes, some creatures in the soil eat the rotting material and their excrement enriches the soil; bees and butterflies both pollinate flowers. No, if too many occupied the same niche the competition would be too great. E.g. – Deer browse is changing forest composition. Invasive plants are crowding out native species of plants.) [Compares similar situations and draws conclusions.]

## Take Another Step

✔ Have each student "adopt" an animal native to a local natural community and keep an ongoing journal record of the *niche characteristics* of that animal (perhaps spanning two or three seasons of the year)

✔ Have teams of students design an ad for employment in the *Animal Gazette*. Include qualifications necessary as well as working conditions.

✔ Teams of students design job posters for companies recruiting employees. The graphics should demonstrate how beneficial and rewarding it is to work for this company.

NEW JERSEY
AUDUBON
SOCIETY

Natural History Lessons

**Figure 13**

# JOBS IN THE COMMUNITY
## Human and Wildlife Niches

| HUMAN COMMUNITY | WILDLIFE COMMUNITY |
|---|---|
| **Sanitation Engineer**<br>Cleans up waste materials. | |
| **Earth mover**<br>Digs into the ground to prepare for construction of buildings or roads. | |
| **Manufacturer**<br>Takes raw materials and makes a product. | |
| **Security Guard**<br>Sounds an alarm when an intruder enters. | |
| **Construction Engineer**<br>Constructs a very solid structure to be used as a home by others in the community. | |
| **Farmer**<br>Cultivates the soil so water and air can assist plants to grow. | |
| **Delivery person**<br>Carries products from one place to another. | |
| **Rescue workers**<br>Help members of the community when there is an emergency or disaster. | |

NEW JERSEY
AUDUBON
SOCIETY

**Bridges to the Natural World**

LENGTH OF ACTIVITY

## 30 minutes

GRADE LEVELS

1 - 3

Natural History Lessons

# ENERGY PLAY

All living **organisms** require energy in order to live and grow. The sun is the basic source of almost all energy. Green plants use the sun's energy, air, water, and available **nutrients** (mineral elements) to make food. When animals eat plants, and in turn, are eaten by other animals, the energy passes from one organism to another. This is called a **food chain.**

To trace the sequence of energy flow, food chains are organized into **trophic levels**. This is the passage of nutrients from one organism to another. All green plants (**producers**) are members of the first trophic level; all plant-eaters (**herbivores**) constitute the second level (**primary consumers**), and all meat-eaters (**carnivores**) make up the third level (**secondary consumers**). In most cases **decomposition** begins to operate when organisms die. Decomposers, air, and water help to break down dead organisms, releasing nutrients from plant and animal matter so they can be used again.

If air is missing from this process putrification results. This outcome prevents the nutrients from being recycled back into the **habitat**.

## BASIC CONCEPTS

☞ All living organisms require energy.

☞ The sun is the basic source of almost all energy.

☞ All living things are parts of food chains.

☞ Decomposers recycle nutrients.

## PROCESS SKILLS

*Communicating, using time and space, observing, classifying.*

NEW JERSEY
AUDUBON
SOCIETY

---

## MATERIALS

☐ one plant or part of a plant that shows evidence of insect activity for each student. (Dry leaves are suitable for this lesson.)

☐ Optional - pictures to represent the players: sun, decomposers, plants, animals, and seeds (can be found in magazines or reproduced from this manual)

## PREPLANNING

1. Reserve an area large enough for the students to sit in a circle.

2. Find or collect necessary plant materials.

# MOTIVATIONAL ACTIVITY

As a group, look at a living plant or part of a plant. Discuss what helps it grow. (sun, water, soil nutrients, and air) [Lists necessary factors for growth of plants and animals] What do the holes in the leaves tell us about what happened to this plant? (The plant has been food for an animal.) [Makes inferences.] If an insect were eating the leaf, what other kind of animal may eat the insect? (a bird, a different kind of insect, a chipmunk, etc.) [Applies principle to practical situation.] What will happen to the plant as it dies? (Given the right circumstances of air, moisture, and decomposing animals, the plant will decay and release its nutrients back into the soil.) [Analyzes sequence of events and makes a new hypothesis.]

## PROCEDURE

1. Explain to the students that they will be using hand motions and words to show how energy from the sun is used by plants and animals.

2. Divide the class into the following groups:
   - one sun
   - three decomposers
   - two seeds
   - the rest of the class is divided into green plants, plant-eaters, and meat-eaters

3. Arrange the groups as in Figure 14.

4. Rehearse each group's words and hand motions.
   - The sun winds up like a baseball pitcher and pretends to throw energy to the plants while saying "Heeere's energy!"

- Green plants receive energy by holding both arms outstretched and folding them in one arm at a time while saying "hug in, hug in, hug in." [Dramatizes absorption process.]
- Plant-eaters "eat" plants by opening and closing hands near their mouth while saying "munch, munch, munch, munch."
- Meat-eaters "eat" plant-eaters by rubbing their own stomachs while saying "yum, yum, yum, yum."
- Decomposers wriggle their fingers all around themselves while chanting, "rot, rot, rot, rot."
- Seeds keep their bodies in a tucked position.

5. Begin narration:
T (teacher) - "In the morning when the sun comes up it throws energy to the earth..."
Sun - "Heeere's energy"... (repeat three times before the teacher begins the next line.)

T - "The growing plants gather in energy..."

Plants - "Hug in"... ( repeat three times)

T - "Along comes a hungry rabbit (or any other plant-eater) to eat the plants..."

Plant-eaters - "Munch, munch"... (repeat three times)

T - "Soaring overhead is a hawk looking for food. It swoops down, captures the rabbit and begins to eat it..."

Meat-eaters - "Yum, yum"... ( repeat three times)

T - "Some of the plants die. They begin to decay and become part of the soil..."

Decomposer 1 - "Rot, rot"...(repeat three times)

T - "Some of the plant-eaters die. They begin to decay and become part of the soil..."

Decomposer 2 - "Rot, rot"...(repeat three times)

T - "Some of the meat-eaters die as well and begin to decay and become part of the soil..."

Decomposer 3 - "Rot, rot"...(repeat three times)

T - "The plants and animals that died and decayed became part of the soil and new plants begin to grow from seeds..."

Seeds sprout silently.

## Putting It All Together

**?** How are people part of a food chain? (Humans eat plant and animal matter.) [Applies principle to practical situation.]

**?** Which living things get their energy directly from the sun? (plants) [Draws specific information from a sequence.]

**?** What would the world be like if there were no animals to eat plants? (The meat-eaters would disappear and only plants could live.) [Analyzes and reconstructs information to form a new hypothesis.]

**?** What would happen if there were no plants? (There would be no plant-eaters, meat-eaters, or decomposers.) [Analysis and reconstruction of information.]

**?** What would happen if there were no decomposers? (There would be a build-up of dead matter; the soil would not be replenished with nutrients.) [Reconstructs information and draws conclusions.]

**?** What would the earth be like if there were no sun? (There would be no life.) [Recognizes unstated assumptions.]

**?** What kind of world do you prefer? Explain your answer. [Makes comparisons and uses criteria for making judgments.]

Natural History Lessons

## Take Another Step

✔ Choose any meal of the day and have the students list all of the foods they ate. Trace the energy of the meal to the sun. Illustrate this chain for a bulletin board display.

✔ Play the game again, but make each trophic level a specific organism to illustrate food chains. Examples: sun-acorn-mouse-owl-(decomposers)-maggot; OR sun-algae-tadpole-water snake (decomposers)-bacteria.

✔ Use this activity as an assembly program.

✔ Translate names of the energy players to another language.

✔ Bury a chicken bone in soil. Wrap a chicken bone in plastic and bury it in soil. After one month, dig them up and compare the two bones.

**Figure 14**
## Game Set-up

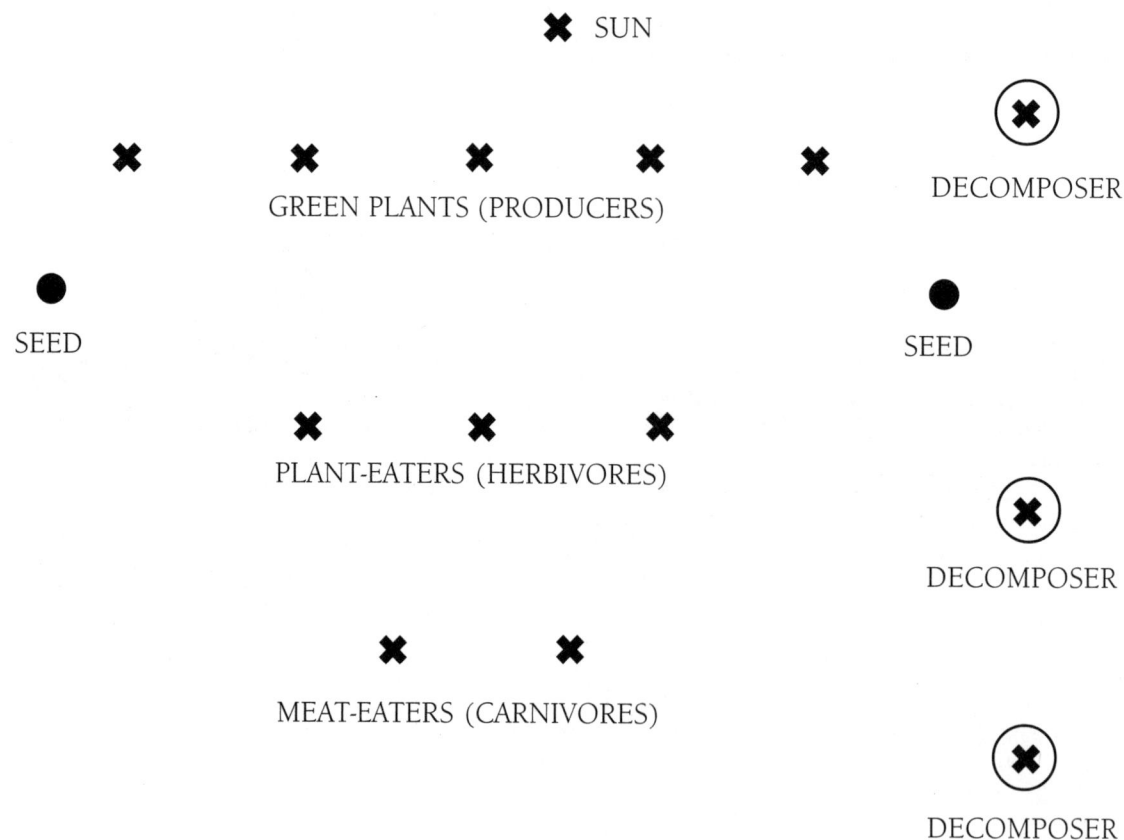

LENGTH OF ACTIVITY

**30**
minutes

**Natural History Lessons**

# THE EATERS AND
## THE EATEN

**A**ll animals require food and water to survive. They eat a variety of foods based on specific needs. Some animals are **carnivores**, some are **herbivores**, and some are **omnivores**.

**Predators** are animals that eat other animals. **Instinct** is the inner program that dictates the selection of **prey** and method of capture. Physical **adaptations** are the tools that enable an animal to be successful. The red fox, with its acute senses of sight, hearing, and smell, will track a field mouse, give chase, and capture it, using its strong jaws and sharp teeth. The sleek body of the river otter allows it to move swiftly through the water and its sharp teeth enable it to catch and hold fish. An individual animal that uses its instinct and physical adaptations to sharpen its skills will have the best chance of survival.

Another factor that has bearing on the amount of food an animal finds is the availability of that food. A harsh winter that impedes access to food supplies decreases population numbers by starvation, reproductive regulation, disease, and freezing.

---

### BASIC CONCEPTS

☞ Animals need food to live.

☞ Wild animals must find their own food.

## PROCESS SKILLS
*Communicating, using time and space, measuring, observing, classifying, inferring, predicting, interpreting data.*

NEW JERSEY
AUDUBON
SOCIETY

## MATERIALS

- ☐ mouse and fish sheet (Figure 15)
- ☐ fox and river otter sheet (Figure 16)
- ☐ stapler or glue
- ☐ clear contact paper (optional)
- ☐ 3 x 5 index cards
- ☐ one clip-on clothespin for each child

### PREPLANNING

1. Reserve the all-purpose room, playground, or similar area for this activity.

2. Make 10 copies of the mouse and fish sheet (Figure 15) per class of 25 students. Cut the pages into individual squares so that each square has a mouse or a fish on it.

3. The class will be divided into two groups; half will be river otters, half will be foxes. Make enough copies of the fox and river otter sheet (Figure 16) for the number of students in each of these groups. Cut the sheet into individual squares.

4. Mount the fox and river otter squares on 3 x 5 index cards. (Option: Cover the cards with clear contact paper for durability. The same might be done for the food pictures of mice and fish.)

# MOTIVATIONAL ACTIVITY

Ask the students:

1. "What does a dog eat?" "What does a cat eat?" "What does a goldfish eat?" "Why do these animals eat food?" "Where do these pets get their food?" (from people) [Lists appropriate animal food and identifies source.]

2. "What does a squirrel eat?" "What does an owl eat?" "What does a fox eat?" "Why do these animals eat food?" "Where do these wild animals get their food?" (They have to find it for themselves.) [Differentiates categories: wild from domestic.]

### PROCEDURE

1. Take the class to the playing area.

2. Divide the class into two groups.

3. Distribute the tags and as the students clip on their tags, introduce the predators.

The fox hunts for its food on the land. Which animal would it eat, the mouse or the fish? (mouse)

The river otter hunts for its food in lakes and rivers. Which animal would it prefer? (fish) [Makes inferences.]

4. While the students stand on the sideline, scatter the food cards (fish and mice) on the playing field. Spread them out so the students have to move all around the field to find the food cards.

5. At your signal, each student will collect as many food cards as he or she can. Foxes may pick up ONLY mice, river otters may pick up ONLY fish.

6. After all the food cards have been collected bring the students back to a central area to discuss what happened.

NEW JERSEY
AUDUBON
SOCIETY

**Bridges to the Natural World**

## Putting It All Together

**?** Name an animal that eats a fish. (river otter or equivalent) Name an animal that eats a mouse. (fox or equivalent) [Names predators.]

**?** When was it easy to find food? (at the beginning of the game when there were many food cards) When was it hard to find food? (at the end of the game when the food cards were more scarce) [Analyzes events and arranges in sequence.]

**?** Have each student count his own food cards. Those animals that satisfied their appetites hold four or more cards, those with fewer cards are still hungry. Ask, "Who are the foxes and river otters that are full?" [Computes and evaluates materials; relates to a plan for problem solving.] "Who are those that are still hungry?"

**?** Tell a story about what would happen to your animal if it did not find any food. Explain your reason. (It would get very hungry; it would move to a different hunting area; it might die.) [Predicts an outcome and justifies a conclusion.]

**?** What are some reasons why an animal would not find enough food? (severe weather such as drought, heat; storms have depleted prey; disease has depleted prey; injury to predator; too many seeking the same food, etc.) [Generates a new list of outcomes.]

---

## Take Another Step

✔ Play the game using other sets of animals. [Applies the principle to new data.]

✔ Vary the number of prey items.

✔ Give the river otters clothespins to pick up their food items and have the foxes wear socks or mittens on their hands.

✔ Watch a bird or an animal eat. Describe in detail all of the behaviors. Give examples of the sequence of actions. (E.g., bite, look up, chew, etc.)

✔ Translate animal names into other languages.

*Natural History Lessons*

**Figure 15**

## Mouse and Fish (Prey)

Photocopy the images below and trim. Mount on index cards. See Preplanning for details.

Mouse

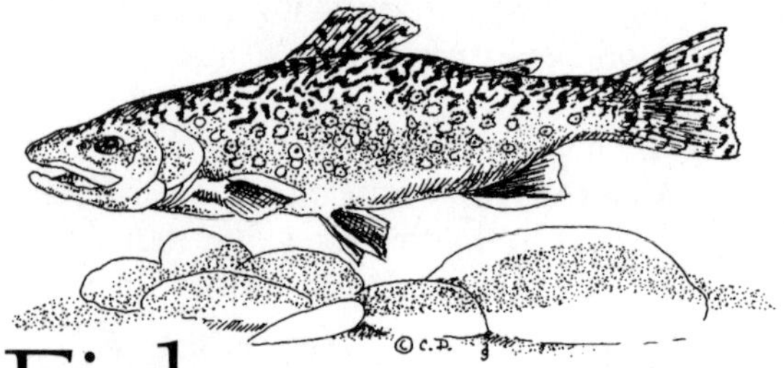

Fish

Mouse

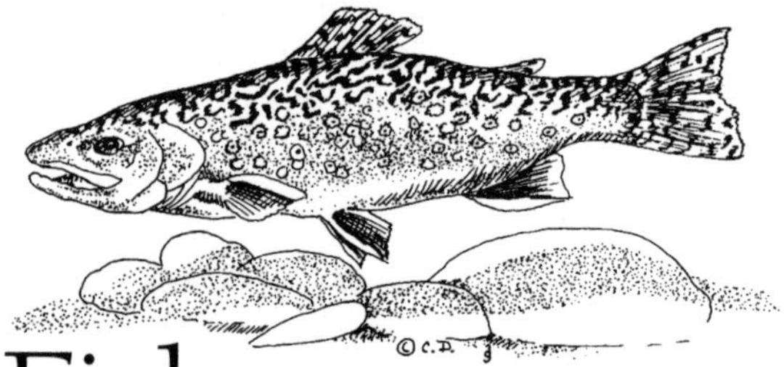

Fish

Mouse

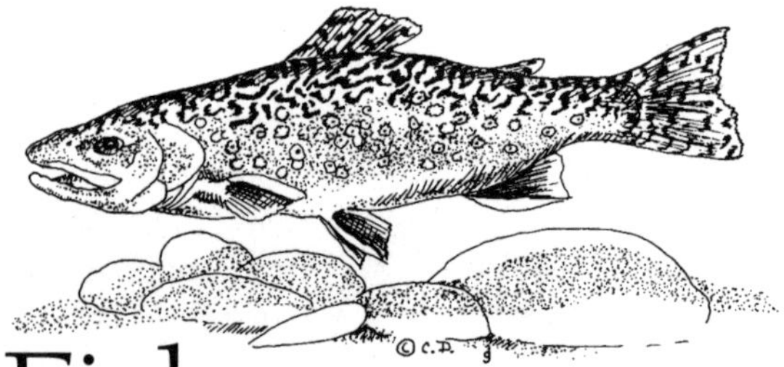

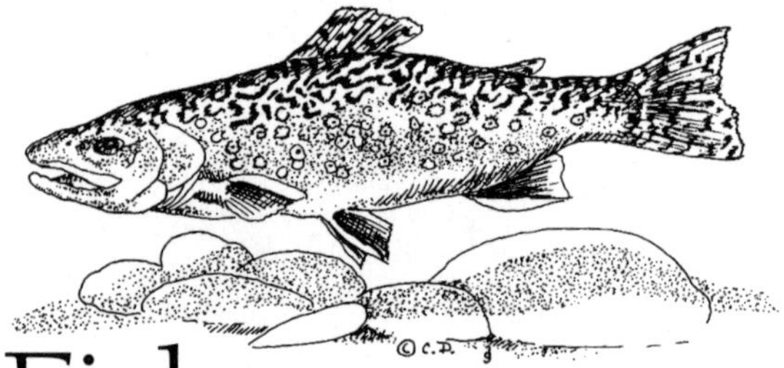

Fish

Mouse

Fish

**Figure 16**

# Fox and River Otter (Predators)

Photocopy the images below and trim. Mount
on index cards. See Preplanning for details.

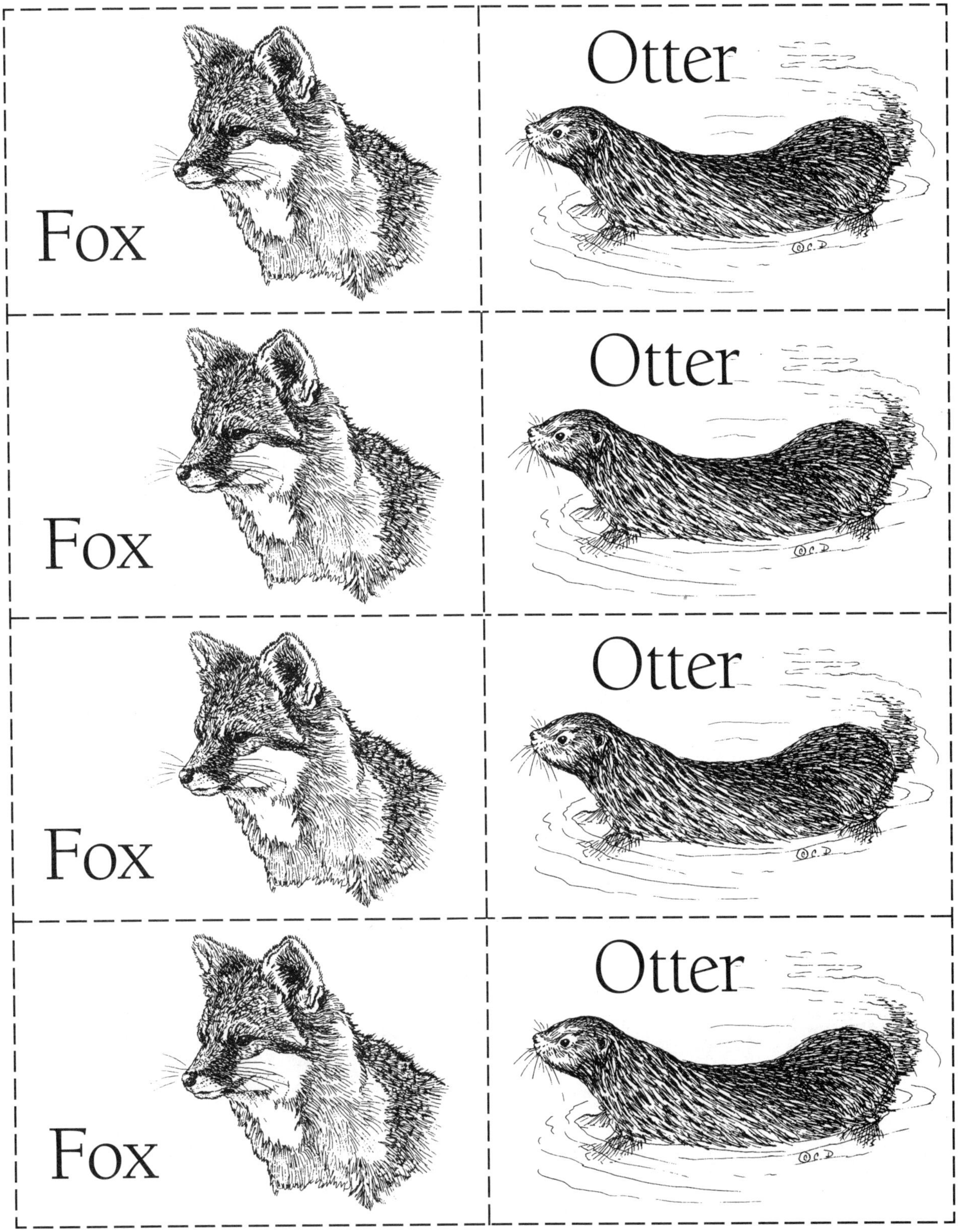

Fox

Otter

Fox

Otter

Fox

Otter

Fox

Otter

LENGTH OF ACTIVITY
45 minutes

Natural History Lessons

# GREAT GROWING GROUND STUFF

Soil is one of the least understood and appreciated of all earth substances because many people view it simply as dirt. Dirt is something to be excavated during construction; paved-over in commercial developments, or cultivated with fertilizers and pesticides as a part of gardening or agriculture. Soil, on the other hand, is something completely different. Few people understand that the overall health, stability, and productivity of natural ecosystems are directly related to the condition and quality of the soil. Soil, which may have taken eons to develop, can be destroyed overnight with surprising ease, and degraded soil quickly results in a degraded environment.

Soil is the foundation for terrestrial forms of life. It is a storehouse of nutrients, a medium for the growth of plants, and a habitat for a wide variety of animals. Soil is a vessel for surface water and acts as a sponge for runoff water. It is a pollution filter, and a site for critical chemical reactions that relate to air, water, and plants. Were it not for the extraordinary ability of soil to support the vegetation of the Earth, life, as we know it, would not exist.

For soil to be truly understood, it must be experienced firsthand, by observing, touching, smelling, and experimenting, just as an early farmer may have done in order to anticipate the ability of his land's soil to support crops. This kind of exploration on hands and knees offers deeper understanding of genuine, life-sustaining soil.

## PROCESS SKILLS

*Communicating, using time and space, observing, classifying inferring, predicting, formulating hypotheses, experimenting, drawing conclusions.*

NEW JERSEY
AUDUBON
SOCIETY

**Bridges to the Natural World**

## BASIC CONCEPTS

☞ Soil is a unique earth substance that supports life.

☞ Soil is made of many ingredients (some living [biotic], some nonliving [abiotic]).

☞ Soil forms in layers, combining minerals from weathered bedrock below with decaying organic matter from the ground surface.

☞ Most soil takes a long time to form; it can be damaged or destroyed by human activity.

## PREPLANNING

1. Define a site where a variety of soil properties may be investigated.

2. Assemble investigation tools.

3. Make one copy of each soil investigation sheet.

## MATERIALS

☐ clipboards

☐ pencils

☐ soil investigation sheets (copied from Figures 17 - 20)

☐ hand trowel

☐ shovel

☐ three open-ended cans (e.g. large juice cans)

☐ three empty coffee cans with plastic lids

☐ three clear plastic jars with lids

☐ felt marking pen

☐ small plastic cups or other containers for briefly containing and observing small soil animals

☐ time piece with second hand

☐ three rulers

☐ thermometer

☐ two gallons of water

☐ paper and/or hand towels (for clean-up)

Natural History Lessons

# MOTIVATIONAL ACTIVITY

Write the following list on the blackboard.
- dead plant and animal matter
- rocks
- green-leaved tree
- water
- clay

Ask: "All but one of the items on the blackboard has something in common to the rest of the list. What is it?" (Allow time for speculation. If any student says 'all are soil components except the green-leaved tree,' do not affirm at this time.) "Today's exploration will unlock the riddle to see if anyone had the right answer."

## PROCEDURE

This lesson requires students to work cooperatively with little teacher guidance. The teacher is advised to lend more assistance if necessary to assure success of the lesson.

1. Accompany students to a natural area where they can investigate soil conditions.

2. Divide the class into four teams and give each team a clipboard, pencil and one of the soil investigation sheets.

4. Place all investigation materials in a central area. Tell the students that their sheet describes an actual investigation they will carry out with their team. Their charge is:
   a. Define the site for investigation within the designated area.
   b. Decide on a strategy for carrying out the investigation and assign a task for each member of the team. (project coordinator, secretary, keeper/distributor of tools, experimentation coordinators) [Organizes investigation in sequential orderly system.]
   c. Select tools they will use for their investigation from the box of materials. [Chooses appropriate materials for collecting data.]

5. After a 30-minute investigation period, gather all teams together to share the observations and conclusions. [Interprets data and supports experiments with logical conclusions.]

6. Ask for an answer to the riddle. (The tree with green leaves uses soil, but is not a soil component.)

©'91 Carol Decker

NEW JERSEY
AUDUBON
SOCIETY

Bridges to the Natural World

## Putting It All Together

**?** What different ingredients did you find in the soils you investigated? (sand, loam, water, plant matter, animal matter, clay, living organisms) [Explains experiences.]

**?** What did each of these different ingredients have to offer to the soil as a whole? (**biotic** and **abiotic** elements determine the amount of nutrients and minerals, soil particle size determines water drainage, organisms manufacture soil) [Justifies data interpretation.]

**?** Which of your senses did you use in your soil investigations? [Relies on personal experience to draw conclusions.]

**?** What signs of human activity did you find in the study area? (cut plants, tamping of soil to form paths) [Interprets landscape and draws conclusions on human use.]

**?** What processes contribute to soil forming in layers? (each year new materials drop to the ground and the previous litter is processed into new soil) [Infers the sequences of the soil cycle from personal investigation and experimentation.]

**?** Why does good fertile soil take such a long time to form? (it takes seasons, life cycles, and different kinds of weather to provide the components of soil) [Draws inferences from experimentation and investigation.]

**?** What are some human activities that caused damage or destruction of the soil in the vicinity? (denude slopes of vegetation causing erosion, allow waste to accumulate on the site, paths hardened the soil preventing water penetration.) [Relates human behavior to negative consequences.]

**?** Name some ways that you think humans can help to protect or renew the soil in any location (check area for signs of soil erosion and create preventive barriers or plantings; write and circulate an information sheet about soil pollution and its prevention; add organic material back into the soil by using compost, grass clippings, and leaf mulch.) [Displays consciousness of human responsibility toward sustaining natural cycles.]

## Take Another Step

✔ Create a school exhibit that illustrates key soil properties in your investigation site(s) to better inform the overall school population about the values of soil in your area.

✔ Take only one soil investigation activity at a time and extend the activities to four lessons.

✔ Test the soil for PH. Research the plants that would grow best in your site. (Resources: library, internet, nurseries)

NEW JERSEY
AUDUBON
SOCIETY

Natural History Lessons

**Figure 17 -** SOIL INVESTIGATION SHEET

# Soil Thickness

Name(s) _____

### Investigation
1. Choose three separate sites to conduct your investigation. Each site should exhibit some visual differences. (E.g. field, forest edge, and forest.)
2. Dig a hole about 1-foot deep and define different layers of soil.
3. Remove elements from each layer noting visible changes in the materials as you go deeper into the hole.

### Conclusions
1. Describe the similarities and differences between your investigation sites.

2. How many layers were you able to uncover at each site?

   Site #1          Site #2          Site #3

3. Draw a cross-section of the soil at each site.

| Site #1 | Site #2 | Site #3 |
|---|---|---|
|  |  |  |

4. Measure the thickness of each layer at each site. Label each cross section.

   Site #1          Site #2          Site #3

5. List the specific materials you found at each level.

   Site #1

   Site #2

   Site #3

6. What tools did you use?

**Figure 18** - SOIL INVESTIGATION SHEET

# Soil Ingredients

Name(s) _____

**Investigation**
1. Choose three separate sites to conduct your investigation. Each site should exhibit some visual differences. (E.g.- field, forest edge, and forest.)
2. Scrape away the litter layer of the ground and scoop a handful of soil.
3. Hold the soil in your hand and squeeze it together. Does it hold together like clay or fall apart like dry coffee grounds? Smell the soil. Record observations below.
4. Spread the ingredients out. Categorize the visible contents.
5. Place a handful of soil from each site in three clear containers. Add water until half full. Close each container and shake vigorously. Watch the order in which soil particles settle.

**Conclusions**
1. Describe the similarities and differences between your investigation sites.


2. How many different ways can you describe the feel and smell of the soil?


3. What items did you find in the soil?

       Site #1

       Site #2

       Site #3

4. What particles settled in the water first? How long did it take for all to settle?

| Site #1 | Site #2 | Site #3 |
|---------|---------|---------|
| _____ | _____ | _____ |
| 1 First to settle | 1 First to settle | 1 First to settle |
| _____ | _____ | _____ |
| ⏱ Time to settle | ⏱ Time to settle | ⏱ Time to settle |
| _____ | _____ | _____ |

*Natural History Lessons*

NEW JERSEY
AUDUBON
SOCIETY

**Figure 19** - SOIL INVESTIGATION SHEET

# Water Absorption

Name(s) _____

### Investigation
1. Choose three separate sites to conduct your investigation. Each site should exhibit some visual differences. (E.g.- field, forest edge and forest.)
2. Push one open-ended can about 1 inch into the soil at each sample site.
3. Pour 1 quart of water into each collar.
4. Mark the water level of each can.
5. At two-minute intervals, draw a line on the can to record the water level for a total of six minutes at each site.
6. Record the inches of water absorbed at each time interval.

### Conclusions
1. Describe the similarities and differences between your investigation sites.


2. How much water was left in the can at the end of the time period?

        Site #1            Site #2           Site #3


3. How long did it take for each site to absorb the quart of water?

        Site #1

        Site #2

        Site #3


4. What prevents water from seeping into the soil?




5. What allows water to seep into the soil?

Natural History Lessons

**Figure 20** - SOIL INVESTIGATION SHEET

# Soil Animals

Name(s) _____

**Investigation**
1. Choose three separate sites to conduct your investigation. Each site should exhibit some visual differences. (E.g. - field, forest edge and forest.)
2. Explore the areas for living insects and creatures working in the soil.
3. Gather single samples of each animal long enough to observe all characteristics.
4. Write descriptions or draw pictures of each creature including: body parts, legs, distinctive colors, shape.
5. Summarize the total number of different species from each group.

**Conclusions**
1. Describe the similarities and differences between your investigation sites.


2. What is the total number of distinct creatures found?


3. How many of the same species were found in all three sites?


4. How many were found in only one site?


5. Count the number of species at each site. Mark this number on the graph below and then color in the space.

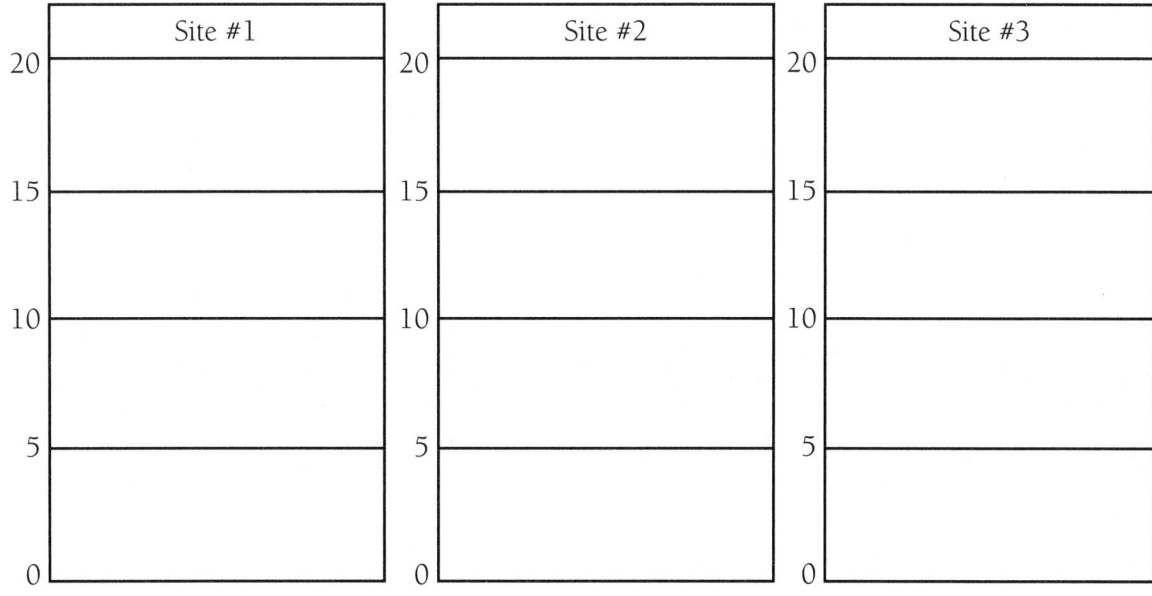

Natural History Lessons

RESEARCH
CONSERVATION
R
EDUCATION

LENGTH OF ACTIVITY
40 minutes

GRADE LEVELS
4 - 6

# THE DISAPPEARING LEAF

Soil is the fertile surface material of the Earth that is able to support plant growth. Composed of living and nonliving materials, it is essential to life. Living components include bacteria and fungi, while nonliving components include **inorganic** chemicals. Water and energy in the form of heat, light, and wind affect changes in matter contained in soil.

If we could watch for hundreds of years we would see soil form in this manner:
1. Rocks are broken down into smaller pieces by physical and chemical **weathering.**
2. Primitive plants (lichens, mosses, etc.) take hold, continue to break down the rock, *and* add **organic** materials to the surface of the rock.
3. Bacteria and fungi **decompose** organic materials into **humus.**

Soil is being formed constantly. It is difficult for us to see the microscopic events, but we can observe surface decomposition which results in a top layer of humus. In temperate latitudes like New Jersey, it takes approximately three years for a season's accumulation of leaf litter to break down and become part of the soil.

Decomposition is a natural recycling process. When plants and animals die, microorganisms and weathering reduce them into essential **nutrients.** Decomposers release enzymes into dead plants and animals. These partially broken down compounds then can be absorbed more readily by the decomposers and other parts of the soil system.

In addition to microorganisms, there are also important animals that facilitate soil formation: earthworms, slugs, millipedes, centipedes, pillbugs, and an amazing variety of other **detritus** reducers.

NEW JERSEY
AUDUBON
SOCIETY

**Bridges to the Natural World**

## BASIC CONCEPTS

☞ When leaves are separated from their source of nutrition, they change color and die.

☞ As plants decompose, they create humus and enrich the soil.

☞ Decomposition is nature's way of recycling nutrients.

☞ Soil is made up of living and nonliving parts.

# PROCESS SKILLS

*Communicating, using time and space, observing, classifying, inferring, predicting, interpreting data, formulating hypotheses.*

© C.D.

## MATERIALS

For each student:

☐ collecting bag

☐ Disappearing Leaf Chart (Figure 22) mounted on cardboard

☐ at least one tablespoon of soil

☐ paper towel or newspaper

For the class:

☐ glue or paste

☐ markers

☐ scissors

☐ green construction paper

For the teacher:

☐ one green leaf and one brown leaf from the same plant

### PREPLANNING

1. Copy The Disappearing Leaf Chart (Figure 22).

2. Create a Teacher Demonstration Chart (Figure 21).

3. Collect a soil sample.

4. Collect one green leaf and one brown leaf from the same type of plant.

5. Find an area on the school grounds where the students can collect samples of brown leaves and leaf matter.

NEW JERSEY
AUDUBON
SOCIETY

# MOTIVATIONAL ACTIVITY

Provide each student with a soil sample on a paper towel. Have the students examine and sort the particles. [Analyzes and classifies components.] Create a class list of the things found. (sand, clay, rootlets, broken leaves, bark, insects, etc.) [Lists categories.] Ask: "Which are living or came from a living organism?" (leaves, twigs, roots) [Rearranges for new classification.] "Which are nonliving?" (sand, clay) [Discriminates and reclassifies.]

## PROCEDURE

1. Hold up a green leaf and a brown leaf from the same type of plant. Ask the students to explain the reasons for the differences between the two leaves. (One is living, one is dead.) [Makes comparisons and explains differences.]

2. Show the Teacher Demonstration Chart (Figure 21). Tell the students that they will be making a similar chart to show how green leaves, after they die, contribute to the soil-making process.

3. Supply each student with a collecting bag.

4. On a walk outdoors, have the students collect the samples of brown leaves and leaf matter necessary to complete their chart. We discourage the removal of green leaves in preference to a construction paper shape of a local leaf. Ask the students why this is a good practice. (Green leaves are food factories of the plant. We do not interfere with this process when it is not necessary.)

5. Back at the classroom distribute a Disappearing Leaf chart and art materials to each student. Instruct the students to mount the chart on cardboard, cut out a green leaf of the same shape as their whole brown leaf, and glue or paste the collected items in the proper sequence to complete the chart. [Classifies and rearranges materials in a sequence.]

## Putting It All Together

**?** Why do leaves change color? (The leaf stops producing chlorophyll, allowing us to see other colors that are in the leaf.) [Makes inferences based on past experience.]

**?** If an ordinary autumn leaf fall deposits three inches of leaves on the ground, how many feet deep should the layer be after a hundred years? (25 feet deep) [Computes data.] What happened to all of those leaves? (They decomposed and were recycled in the soil.) [Applies principles to practical situation.]

**?** If all the dead leaves in an area are removed, what will happen to the soil? (It will lose its natural nutrients, it will be eroded by wind and rain, the animals dependent on the soil ecosystem would die.) [Analyzes data, formulates hypotheses, and draws conclusions.]

Natural History Lessons

## Take Another Step

✔ Make a list of all the things that contribute to the decomposition of a leaf. (snow, heat, fire, rain, animals, wind)

✔ Discuss how the leaves in the yard can be used to enrich the soil. (Compost them through personal, community, county, or state program.)

✔ Keep track of the decomposition rates of various types of materials. Examples: bread, fruit, leaf, rock. Place each item in a covered clear container. Regularly mist each item with water.

✔ Collect and compare different types of soil (sand, humus, and clay-based).

**FOR MORE INFORMATION**

Alexander, Taylor R. and George S. Fichter. *A Golden Guide: Ecology.*

Andrews, William, ed. *A Guide to the Study of Soil Ecology.*

**Figure 21**

# The Disappearing Leaf: Teacher Demonstration Chart

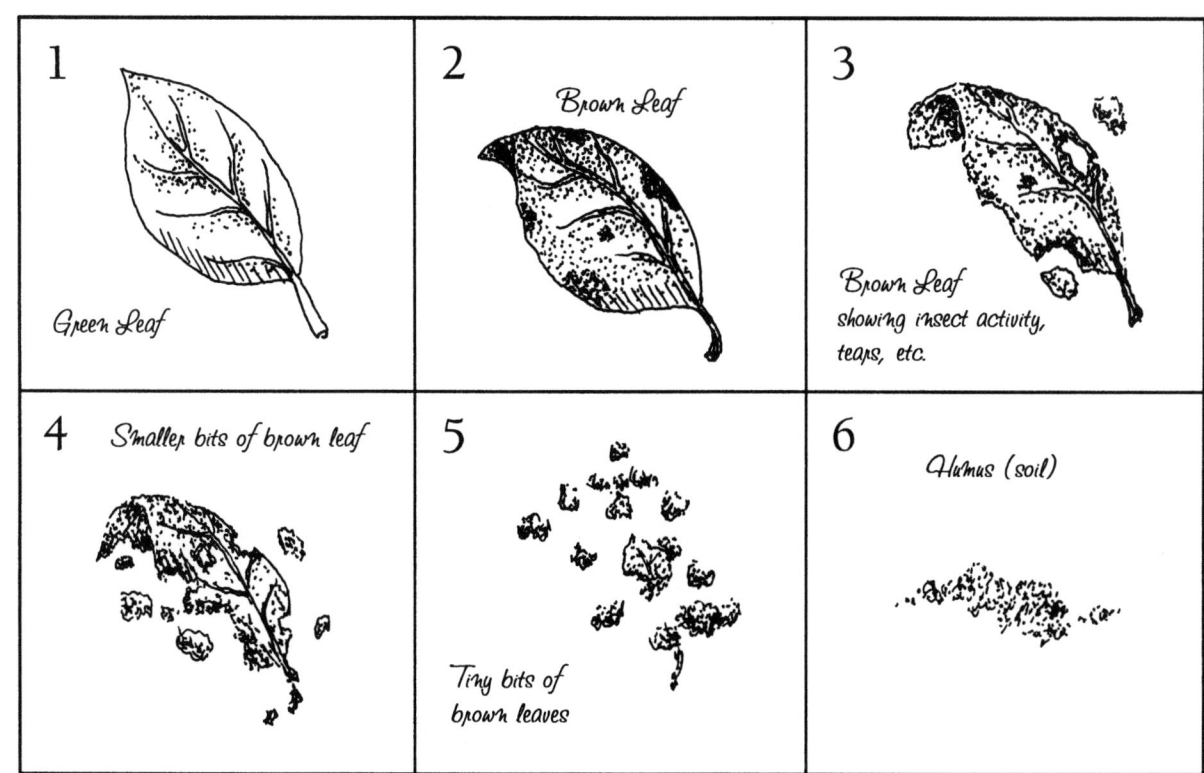

1. Green Leaf
2. Brown Leaf
3. Brown Leaf showing insect activity, tears, etc.
4. Smaller bits of brown leaf
5. Tiny bits of brown leaves
6. Humus (soil)

**Figure 22**

# The Disappearing Leaf Chart

| 1 | 2 |
|---|---|
| 3 | 4 |
| 5 | 6 |

NEW JERSEY
AUDUBON
SOCIETY

CONSERVATION RESEARCH
C
EDUCATION

Natural History Lessons

# BIRDS IN THE NEST

B irds establish breeding and wintering territories mostly on the basis of available food. During the breeding season they must have a constant supply of food for the young to survive. Some birds will exclude others of their own species from the territories in order to assure their own food supply. Birds that do not compete for the same food can coexist in the same territory.

**Figure 23**
## Interaction of Birds Within a Habitat

Some birds compete for food supplies and therefore need their own territory within a habitat.

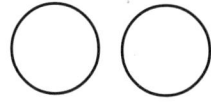

Some birds can share the same territory within a habitat because they use different food supplies.

Habitats that offer a wide diversity of food supplies can support many species of birds.

Over the years, bird species have adjusted the time of their breeding to coincide with the maximum availability of their preferred food. Warblers and other insect-eating birds rear their young at the height of the insect season in late May and June. Goldfinches do not breed until the summer months when thistle down is available for nest building and the seed is available for feeding young. Great-horned owls typically hatch their young in early spring. The owlets' **fledging** the nest coincides with the appearance of young mammals in late spring, providing an abundant food source.

Even during this time of plenty, the parents are under considerable stress to provide food for their growing young. At first, the **nestlings** require constant protection. One parent remains at the nest while the other searches for food. As the young mature there is less need for protection but a greater demand for food. Both parents share the task of feeding the nestlings. As an example, a cardinal nestling must be fed approximately every 20 minutes during daylight hours. If there are four young in the nest, the parent birds have to return to the nest every five minutes to feed one of the nestlings. If there are 12 hours of daylight, it makes a total of at least 144 trips per day for the 9 or 10 days the young are in the nest.

NEW JERSEY
AUDUBON
SOCIETY

Some birds have a single **brood** per season, but others, like cardinals, bluebirds, robins, and sparrows have two or three broods per season. Disturbance at this time by humans or by **predators** may cause a nest to fail. When the young leave the nest they are not skilled in flight and continue to be fed by their parents. At this time, baby birds may appear to be abandoned, but in fact, are closely observed by their parents. It is important that fledgling birds be allowed to develop without human interference. Often, people misinterpret this process and while intending to save the baby bird actually cause trauma and prevent the bird from learning life-saving skills. For more information see "About Orphaned and Injured Wildlife" on p. 323.

## BASIC CONCEPTS

☞ Many kinds of baby birds depend on their parents for food and protection.

☞ Birds have ways of communicating their needs.

☞ Parent birds are under considerable stress at nesting time.

# PROCESS SKILLS

*Communicating, using time and space, measuring, observing, classifying, inferring, predicting, interpreting data, identifying variables, formulating hypotheses.*

## MATERIALS

☐ one paper cup for each student: six per nest.

☐ four bowls to hold food supply

☐ 80 berries (or fruit pieces, popcorn, cereal, gummy worms, etc.)

☐ hoops or string to define each nest site

☐ measuring tape (optional)

## PREPLANNING

Each nest will be made up of two parents and at least four nestlings. The nestlings remain at the nest site. With a class of fewer than 24, reduce the number of nest sites and food sources.

1. Prepare the food supply by placing 20 pieces in each bowl.

2. Set up the activity's playing area (see Figure 24). Place a hoop or a circle of string to designate four nest sites. Place a food bowl at each food supply corner.

# MOTIVATIONAL ACTIVITY

Where does your food come from? (store, farms, dairies, etc.) Who provides food for you? (parent or guardian) What do they do to provide your food? (go to work, prepare meals) Do they ever get stressed from having too much to do? Today we will play a game that teaches us what it is like for birds during nesting time.

## PROCEDURE

1. Divide the class into teams. Assign two parents and four nestlings to each team. Let the students decide which bird species their team will represent.

2. Place the students at the nest sites (corners of the smallest rectangle). Show each team the location of its food source (the opposite corner of the larger rectangle). Each team may take food ONLY from its assigned bowl.

3. Demonstrate the procedure by walking one team through one round before the game begins.

4. At your signal, one parent runs to the assigned food supply, picks up a berry, places it in a cup, then carries a berry back to a nestling. When the first parent returns, the second parent leaves the nest to gather food while the first guards the nest. The parents take turns in the guarding, gathering, and feeding. With a very large class the teacher may assign a food monitor to make sure the parent birds take only the prescribed amounts.

5. The nestlings should invent sounds or motions to attract the attention of the parent with the food supply. The parents should feed the most insistent nestling. No one may eat the food until the game is over; they must keep it in their cup.

6. After a few rounds the teacher stops the game and says, "As the nestlings grow they don't need as much protection but they need more food. Now, both parents may leave the nest to gather food." The teacher may determine when the game ends. This may occur when one team uses the whole food supply or sooner. At the end of the game, have all the students count their food units.

NEW JERSEY
AUDUBON
SOCIETY

# Putting It All Together

**?** Which parents supplied the greatest amount of food to their nestlings? (Total the number of food units from each nest.) [Computes and compares for problem solving.]

**?** Which nestlings got the most food? The least? [Reclassifies for comparison.]

**?** Why did some nestlings get more than others? (In competition for food some nestlings attract more attention and therefore receive more food.) [Makes inferences.]

**?** How did the parent birds know which young to feed? (The parents will almost always go to the nestling making the most noise.) [Makes inferences.]

**?** What else did the parents do for the young besides feed them? (One parent stayed with the nest to protect the young.) [Analyzes, sequences, and describes behaviors.]

**?** List the tasks of the parent birds. (protect young, get food for the young and for themselves, fly back and forth from the nest to the food supply) Arrange the tasks from easiest to hardest. Which caused the most stress? [Organize information in new categories.]

**?** At what stage of the nestlings' development are both parents the most active? (when the nestlings got older and both parents went for food) [Arrange behaviors in sequence.]

**?** How is bird behavior different from human behavior in caring for young? (Humans care for young equitably. A weak child will receive special care to help make it well and strong.) [Uses information for making other comparisons.]

**?** What makes it possible for birds to raise their young at this time? (available food, nesting material, water, warm temperature.) [Infers interdependence of factors within the ecosystem.]

**?** How should humans behave when they know they are near a nest? (Do not interfere with parents sitting on eggs or feeding young. If the nest can't be viewed without chasing the parents away, it is best to stay away.) [Uses new knowledge to evaluate and modify personal behaviors.]

## VARIATIONS

**!** Put twice as many (40) food units in each bowl.

**!** Require that each nestling have at least five food units to fledge.

**!** Distribute the food unequally. Have the students make up a story about how this happened. (Drought, early frost killed the fruits, area is too built up.) [Reorganize data and predict an outcome.] What will happen next year? Explain your answer. (With normal rainfall and temperature an average crop will satisfy the birds' needs; birds will have to find a new place to nest; people will develop backyard habitats with plants that offset the overdevelopment.) [Sequence events and justify conclusions.]

**!** Move the food sources closer to or farther from the nests. Have someone time the games and compare the difference. [Measure differences and make comparisons.]

**!** Introduce a predator/human intruder into the game. The intruder stands between a nest and the food source. The parent may not move if the intruder is blocking the path. The intruder may move to block parents of any of the nests. How does this affect the parents? (more stress) Count the food supplies of the young. How did the intruder affect the food supply? (The nestlings did not get their food when they needed it and some didn't get the same amount as when there was no intruder.) [Revises experiment by changing variables, interprets outcome.]

## Take Another Step

✔ Have the students observe birds and keep a log on their observations. What bird? Where was it? What was it doing?

✔ Encourage birds to nest and raise young in the area by planting trees, shrubs, and flowers that provide food and nesting places.

✔ Arrange supplemental nesting materials (yarn, string, cotton, bits of material, etc.) on a peg board. Place the board outside in the spring and keep track of which materials the birds use for their nests.

✔ Build and erect bird houses.

✔ Make collages and/or mobiles of common birds and their foods.

**Figure 24**
# Game Set-up

● FOOD D          FOOD C ●

NEST A          NEST B
● ●

NEST C          NEST D
● ●

● FOOD B          FOOD A ●

**FOR MORE INFORMATION**

Dunne, Peter J., Richard Kane, and Paul Kerlinger. *New Jersey at the Crossroads of Migration.* (book and video)

Ehrlich, Paul R., David S. Dobkin, and Darryl Wheye. *The Birder's Handbook.*

Kress, Stephen W. *Audubon Society Guide to Attracting Birds.*

Martin, Alexander C., Herbert S. Zimm, and Arnold L. Nelson. *American Wildlife and Plants: A Guide to Wildlife Food Habits.*

McKinley, Michael. *How to Attract Birds.*

Stokes, Donald, and Lillian Stokes. *The Bird Feeder Book.*

Sutton, Patricia. *Backyard Habitat for Birds: A Guide for Landowners and Communities in New Jersey.*

NEW JERSEY
AUDUBON
SOCIETY

Natural History Lessons

LENGTH OF ACTIVITY

40 minutes

GRADE LEVELS

4 - 6

# THE ECO-CONNECTION

A natural community is sustained by the interaction and interdependencies among and between biological or living factors and abiotic or nonliving factors. This dynamic creates an ecosystem that is at the same time self-sustaining, yet ever-changing. The systems that make up an ecosystem include food chains, energy flow, and nutrient exchange, all of which take place within the various **trophic layers.**

Biological factors include plants and animals in all stages of their existence. From seed to rotting leaves and trunk, the tree and all its parts are fundamentally biological. Each stage contributes in some way to the functioning of the entire ecosystem.

Physical or abiotic factors never had the capacity of ingesting food, growing, or reproducing their own kind. These elements of an ecosystem impact the biological elements by creating structure, weather, and physical changes. Water sustains all life. Weathering rocks add minute particles to the soil and they release minerals into the soil for use by plants and animals. Rock composition helps determine the type of plant communities that will exist in an area. Sunlight and air along with geographic factors provide the temperature and weather that induces and regulates plant growth.

The interactions and interdependencies among biotic and abiotic factors are all linked together to form the complexities of an ecosystem. Recognizing these connections is a critical link to understanding how nature works and to living in harmony with the systems that sustain life on this planet.

## PROCESS SKILLS

*Observing, classifying, inferring, predicting, analyzing, communicating.*

Natural History Lessons

## BASIC CONCEPTS

☞ There are a number of interdependencies within an ecosystem.

☞ Biotic or biological factors in an ecosystem are those organisms that grow and reproduce their own kind.

☞ Abiotic or physical factors are minerals rocks, water, sun, and air.

☞ Biotic and abiotic factors work together to sustain the ecosystem.

## MATERIALS

For each student:

☐ clipboard

☐ pencil

☐ "Words for Understanding" and "Discovery" worksheets (Figure 25 and Figure 26, front and back)

### PREPLANNING

1. Duplicate the worksheets. Save paper by putting Figure 26 on both sides (front and back) of a sheet of copier paper.

2. Choose an outdoor natural area for exploration.

3. In presenting both activity sheets it may be necessary to model each section before the students do the exercise independently. It is better to do only a few examples well than try to complete all with less understanding. Some natural areas may not hold evident examples for each category. It is better to leave them blank. Continued practice will enhance proficiency.

# MOTIVATIONAL ACTIVITY

With the students, list five or six actions that they have performed today (selected clothes to dress, ate meals, talked with friends, rode to school by bus). Where did our clothes come from? (cotton, wool, petroleum/polyester) In what way have we interacted with plant or animal life to bring us clothes? How about when we get on a bus? What materials were used to make the bus? (metals: aluminum, steel) In what way have people interacted with minerals from the ground to bring us this transportation? All the interactions on earth take place among plants, animals and nonliving things.

NEW JERSEY
AUDUBON
SOCIETY

## PROCEDURE

1. Distribute "Words for Understanding."
Have students find examples of each definition
as found in the natural area.

2. Have each student or pair complete Figure 26.

## Putting It All Together

**?** Use the teacher answer sheets for
follow-up discussion. How many different
examples were the students able to find?
In what categories were the answers
consistently the same?

**?** How important are **abiotic** factors in
the life cycle of living things? (There
would be no life without them.) [Draws
conclusions from data collected.]

## Take Another Step

✔ Create a habitat bulletin board with
drawings of all the Eco-Connection
factors observed by the students: plants
and animals positioned and
demonstrating their natural behavior,
rocks, water, sunlight and air. Label the
factors as collected in the worksheets.

✔ Pair and share. Each student will
mime some behavior of a plant or an
animal observed during the investigation
and present it to the partner for
interpretation. If the action is not clear,
encourage the students to work together
to create a clearer demonstration. For
longer session, join pairs with another
pair and continue.

**Figure 25**

# The Eco-Connection: WORDS FOR UNDERSTANDING

What are BIOLOGICAL FACTORS?

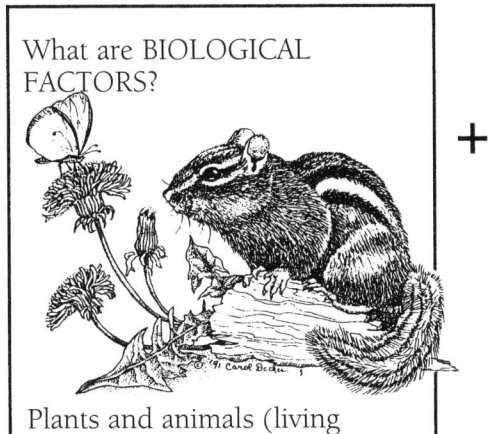

Plants and animals (living or having lived). Alive, they grow and reproduce their own kind.

**+**

What are PHYSICAL FACTORS?

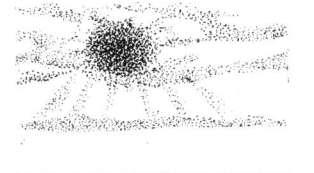

Rocks, water, sunlight, air.

**=**

Working together, these factors make an ECOSYSTEM.

What is an ANIMAL?

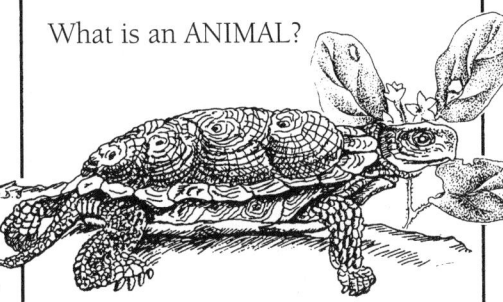

It has locomotion and eats plants and/or animals.

What is a PLANT?

Most plants stay in one place, are rooted in the ground, and make their own food from air and water and sunlight.

What is a HABITAT?

Wood Duck
Freshwater Marsh
New Jersey

Where a plant or animal lives; the ADDRESS.

What is a NICHE?

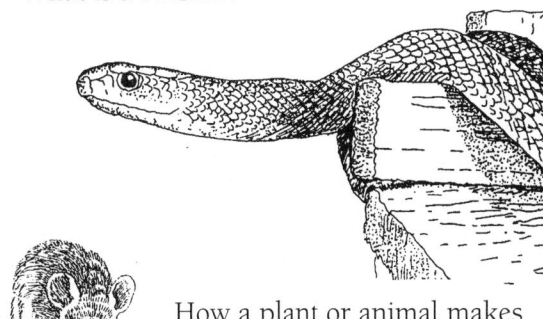

How a plant or animal makes a living in the habitat; what it does to live its life cycle; its PROFESSION.

NEW JERSEY
AUDUBON
SOCIETY

Natural History Lessons

**Natural History Lessons**

Natural History Lessons

**Figure 26** (Front)

**Name:** _____

# The Eco-Connection: DISCOVERY

Type of habitat: _____

Identify by description or sketch:

1. Two physical or abiotic factors

2. Two plants

3. Two animals

4. Plant or animal adaptation (*Hint:* Many animals eat the same food but gather it in different ways.  Also, look closely at a plant for evidence of how its seeds will be transported away from the plant.)

© 2002 New Jersey Audubon Society

**Bridges to the Natural World**

**Figure 26** (Back)

# The Eco-Connection: DISCOVERY

List examples of inter*action* that you find in this habitat.

*Hint* - Remember:    a. elements of a habitat (food, shelter, space)
                      b. things that cause change (minerals, rocks, sun, water, air are abiotic factors)
                      c. animal and plant adaptations

1. Evidence of action - *biotic factor on an abiotic factor.*

2. Evidence of action - *abiotic factor on a biotic factor.*

3. Evidence of action - *plant on plant.*

4. Evidence of action - *animal on plant.*

5. Evidence of action - *plant on animal.*

6. Evidence of action - *animal on animal.*

NEW JERSEY
AUDUBON
SOCIETY

Natural History Lessons

**Figure 26** (Teacher's Copy)

# The Eco-Connection: DISCOVERY

Type of Habitat: SUGAR MAPLE / MIXED HARDWOOD FOREST

Identify by description or sketch:

1. Two physical factors                        (ROCKS, WIND)

2. Two plants                                (TREE, VINE)

3. Two animals                             (CHIPMUNK, BLUE JAY)

4. Plant or animal adaptation          (MANY BIRDS EAT SEED, BUT THEY HAVE DIFFERENTLY-SHAPED BILLS TO CRACK OPEN DIFFERENT TYPES OF SEEDS.)

                                            (TREES HAVE A VARIETY OF WAYS TO DISPERSE THEIR SEEDS.)

List examples of inter*action* that you find in this habitat.
*Hint -* Remember:     a. elements of a habitat (food, shelter, space)
                    b. things that cause change (minerals, rocks, sun, water, air are abiotic factors
                    c. animal and plant adaptations

1. Evidence of action - *biotic factor on an abiotic factor*       (LICHEN'S ACID DISSOLVES ROCK. PLANT ROOTS WIDEN CRACKS IN ROCKS.)

2. Evidence of action - *abiotic factor on a biotic factor.*       (SEA SPRAY INHIBITS PLANT GROWTH. SUNLIGHT INDUCES PLANT GROWTH.)

3. Evidence of action - *plant on plant.*       (VINES USE TREES AS SUPPORT FOR GROWING. TALL TREES SHADE UNDERSTORY PLANTS.)

4. Evidence of action - *animal on plant.*       (INSECTS EAT LEAVES. BIRDS USE PLANTS FOR NEST MATERIAL.)

5. Evidence of action - *plant on animal.*       (FLOWER COLOR AND SMELL ATTRACT POLLINATORS AND SEED DISBURSERS.)

6. Evidence of action - *animal on animal.*       (BLUE JAYS TAKE EGGS FROM OTHER BIRDS; FEMALE MOSQUITOES FEED ON HUMAN BLOOD.)

NEW JERSEY AUDUBON SOCIETY

Natural History Lessons

LENGTH OF ACTIVITY
# 20
minutes

Natural History Lessons

# LITTER BITS

According to Webster's *New World Dictionary* litter is the careless or untidy disposal of used materials. When applying the word to the environment, almost every living thing is responsible in some way for littering the earth. The tallest trees drop their needles and leaves to the ground, creating a ground cover of litter. Microscopic plants and animals die and become part of the floor of the **habitat**. All of nature's litter becomes part of a recycling process that returns **nutrients** to the soil when these plants and animals **decompose**, giving way for new life through the rejuvenated soil.

Litter created by people, however, is not ordinarily part of that process. While some of our refuse is **organic**, most is not and does not readily decompose.

In recent years, solid waste disposal has become a worldwide problem. Landfills reach capacity and new sites are not readily available. The **resources** used for manufacturing the products we use, though sometimes **renewable**, are being consumed faster than natural processes require for replacement. People are more conscious of the need to recycle our used products instead of consigning them to the trash barrel.

## BASIC CONCEPTS

☞ Litter is a disorderly arrangement of used materials.

☞ Some litter is recycled more easily than others.

☞ Various manufactured materials can be recycled.

## PROCESS SKILLS

*Communicating, using time and space, observing, classifying, inferring, predicting, interpreting, experimenting.*

NEW JERSEY
AUDUBON
SOCIETY

Natural History Lessons

## MATERIALS

For full class participation:

☐ samples of ground litter: leaves and twigs.

☐ samples of manufactured litter: candy wrappers, boxes, soda bottles and cans, popsicle sticks, newspaper, etc. (Half of the items should be products that are recycled in the local community.)

☐ 10 coffee cans with plastic lids

☐ 10 clear plastic jars: peanut butter, jelly, etc.

☐ half gallon of water

☐ newspaper

### PREPLANNING

1. If leaf litter is not available near your school, plan to gather this material at the nearest park or woodland.

2. Collect materials.

Note: The activity is best suited for a classroom with desks or tables.

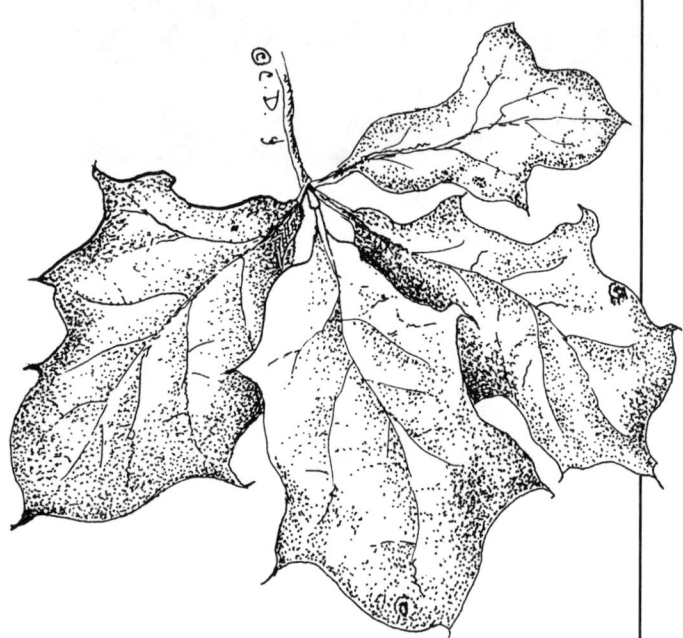

# MOTIVATIONAL ACTIVITY

Tell the students to look at the classroom floor. What do you see that does not belong there? (paper, pencils, etc.) [Recognizes disorder.]

The teacher leads a discussion on how the objects got on the floor and what they were once used for. Can they be used again or should they be put in the waste basket? [Describes sequence of events.]

What should we do with the things that are on the floor? (Put them away or throw them away.) [Distinguishes useful from not useful.]

Give students time to pick up objects from the floor that are out of order and return them to the appropriate place or discard them in the waste basket. [Applies principle to a practical situation.]

When things are scattered on the ground or on the floor it is called "litter". Litter is found in many different forms. Sometimes it can be "recycled" or made into something else, and sometimes it must be put in the garbage. Let's look at some kinds of litter and decide what should be done with them.

NEW JERSEY AUDUBON SOCIETY

Bridges to the Natural World

## PROCEDURE

1. Show the students the different kinds of litter that you have collected. Tell me where I might have collected this litter. (woods, park, backyard for leaves and twigs; home, lunchroom, schoolyard, etc. for wrappers, cans, etc.) [Matches objects with events or circumstances.]

2. Instruct five students to place a handful of plant litter in five coffee cans. Be sure the lids are on tightly. Place some of the leftover leaves and twigs out on a table.

3. What might happen in the woods that would cause the leaves to break up or fall apart? (People or other animals might walk on them. Wind blows them around, rain softens them and they break apart.) [Analyzes a sequence and forms a hypothesis.]

4. Shake the cans as hard as you can. After a reasonable time have the students empty the cans onto newspaper and compare their litter with the control sample.

5. What are some changes that have taken place? (Pieces are smaller, broken apart.) [Classifies and makes comparisons.]

6. Let's do the same thing to some of the litter that people have left.

7. Ask another five students to place paper, drink containers, etc., into five coffee cans. What might happen to these things that would cause them to break up while they are left on the ground? (People walk on them, wind blows them around, cars run over them.) [Analyzes sequence and forms hypothesis.]

8. Have the students shake the cans and compare the results with the control samples. Did these items break up as much as the leaves and sticks? Explain. (No, they are harder, stronger.) [Reclassifies and makes comparisons.]

9. Let's see what water will do to the litter.

10. Place leaf litter in five clear containers and manufactured litter in the other five clear containers. Add about two cups of water to the jars and close the lids tightly.

11. How can we make a storm happen in these jars? (Shake them hard.) [Recognizes simulation of natural phenomena.]

12. Instruct students to shake the jars as hard as they can. Compare the outcome with all former experiments and the control groups. [Analyzes data and makes comparisons.]

# Putting It All Together

**?** When we compare the leaf or ground litter with the litter that people leave, which kind is broken up more easily by air and water and crushing? (leaf litter) [Evaluates comparisons and draws conclusions.]

**?** Let's go back again and tell the story of how the other litter gets on the ground or on the floor. (People drop it or throw it there. The wind blows it away from where people put it.) [Creates a sequence of events.]

**?** What are some things that people can do to keep their litter off the ground or floor? (Put things away securely or place them in the trash.) [Identifies responsible behavior.]

**?** Can any of the items that we experimented with today be recycled and made into something else? (newspaper, metal and glass containers, etc.) [Classifies and identifies recyclable materials.]

**?** Name some ways that you can help prevent the scattering of litter. (proper disposal of waste materials and proper sorting of recyclables) [Evaluates behaviors.]

## Take Another Step

✔ At the end of the day of the lesson, collect all the trash items from the floor and tape them to a poster board. Label them with the day of the week. Do the same at the end of every day for a week. How long does it take before there is no litter left on the floor when the students have left for the day?

✔ Use old milk cartons of all sizes as building blocks.

✔ Create a bird feeder from a plastic detergent bottle.

**FOR MORE INFORMATION**

NJDEP, Division of Solid Waste Management Education Program. *Here Today, Here Tomorrow - Revisited.*

(The Division can also be contacted for latest lists of county recycling coordinators and recyclable materials.)

NEW JERSEY AUDUBON SOCIETY

LENGTH OF ACTIVITY
**30** minutes

GRADE LEVELS
2 - 6

Natural History Lessons

# GO WITH THE FLOW

**H**istorically, water has been a universal cleanser. Visible **pollutants** are washed from one area to another by rain, other kinds of precipitation, and human activities. Water is also a universal solvent; therefore, water is used for diluting many things including chemicals, paints, **pesticides**, and fertilizers.

Pollutants are contaminants generally made and introduced into the environment by humans. Macro pollutants are visible and easily removed. Micro pollutants are invisible, such as organic and **inorganic** chemicals. These are not always as evident and more difficult to filter out. Many of them either dissolve into or mix with surface and **groundwater**. The separation process is difficult, technical, and often extremely costly.

With foresight and planning, litter and recyclable materials can be reduced to a minimum through community clean-up projects, aggressive town and statewide recycling programs, and education.

Eventually, waterways empty into the ocean **ecosystem** which seems to have an unlimited ability for **regeneration**. Evidence from oceanic research in the last 50 years proves this to be untrue. This degradation of ocean ecosystems is related directly to human behaviors.

© Carol Decker

NEW JERSEY
AUDUBON
SOCIETY

Natural History Lessons

---

## BASIC CONCEPTS

☞ Water follows a natural course which leads eventually to the ocean.

☞ Many pollutants can be carried by water.

☞ Humans play a major role in controlling the amount of pollutants found in water systems.

---

# PROCESS SKILLS

*Communicating, using time and space, observing,
classifying, inferring, predicting,
interpreting data, formulating hypotheses.*

## MATERIALS

☐ 30 samples of trash and pollution (liquid soap, paint thinner and oil in sealed unbreakable containers, plastic bags, aluminum cans, toy pieces, paper, etc.)

### PREPLANNING

1. Collect materials.

2. Arrange for an outdoor area or all-purpose room suitable for the game.

# MOTIVATIONAL ACTIVITY

Say to the students, "Which one of these things is out of place: lace, silk, satin, empty can? Explain why. Ice cream cone, cake, popcorn, candy wrappers? Explain why. Flowers, stream, fish, old tire? Explain why." (Empty can, candy wrappers and old tire are out of place. They are items that usually we discard.) [Analyzes relationships.]

NEW JERSEY
AUDUBON
SOCIETY

## PROCEDURE

1. Distribute one pollutant sample to each student. Allow the students time to prepare stories about how the pollutants were deposited in the water. For example: Oil: "I was having a good day, tumbling over the rocks, when I noticed a man with a bucket walking along beside me. All at once he stopped, looked all around, then poured this thick, black, yucky stuff all over me and I haven't felt the same since."

2. Ask for 15 volunteers to represent "streams," standing them in line abreast.

Four more volunteers represent "rivers" and form a line 10 feet away from the streams and have one student in front of them to represent the ocean. (extrovert recommended for this role) Adjust the numbers to suit the class size.

3. As each pollution story is told by a "stream," the pollutant object is passed to the nearest river. When the stream pollutants have all been passed, the rivers tell their stories and pass pollutants on to the ocean.

4. Lastly, the ocean tells its story.

## Putting It All Together

? Trace the movement of the pollutants. (They moved from streams to rivers to the ocean.) [Describes sequence of events.]

? What other water bodies might be included in this path? (ponds, lakes, swamps, marshes, reservoirs) [Applies principle to a new situation.]

? If we were a volunteer clean-up crew for a local body of water, what items would be the easiest to remove? Explain. (cans, paper items, litter items) [Classifies data and justifies interpretation.] Which would be more difficult? (soap, oil, fertilizers, etc.) "Why?" (These pollutants dissolve into the water.) [Applies principle to a practical situation.]

? Which pollutants do more harm to the environment? Why? (The dissolved pollutants do more harm because they are taken up into the ecosystem and get into the food chain.) [Makes inferences.]

? What can be done to minimize the amount of pollution in our waterways? (recycle, don't litter, make sure that toxins are disposed of properly) [Integrates learning into a plan for problem-solving.]

NEW JERSEY
AUDUBON
SOCIETY

**Natural History Lessons**

Natural History Lessons

# Take Another Step

✔ Play the game with the following variation. Place a recycling bin between the stream and river lines. As the children move pollutants, put the recyclables in the bin. [Arranges materials into new categories.] "How much does this lighten the load for the ocean?" [Makes comparisons for value judgments.]

✔ Do a stream cleanup in a local neighborhood.

✔ Do a townwide campaign on non-point source pollution. For example: Stencil a fish on all the storm drains to remind people that what is disposed of in these drains can affect aquatic systems.

✔ Translate the pollutants into other languages.

## FOR MORE INFORMATION

Hollings, Holling Clancy. *Paddle to the Sea.*

Seager, Fortner, Taylor. *Supplemental Curriculum Activities for use with Paddle to the Sea.*

Ziff, Cindy. *Storm Drain Stenciling Project.*

**Bridges to the Natural World**

RESEARCH

**C** CONSERVATION EDUCATION

LENGTH OF ACTIVITY

**40** minutes

GRADE LEVELS
4 - 6

# RIVERSIDE DRIVE

**A** river is part of an intricate **ecosystem**. We see the running water, the banks, and the associated animal and plant life. Not so obvious, though, are other important interactions which create a distinct character for each waterway. Variables such as riverbed slope, bottom type, velocity of water flow, amount of sediments the river carries, the river's water temperature, and the amount and type of riverbank vegetation — all contribute to the make-up of a particular river ecosystem.

Floodlands and marshes adjacent to rivers act like sponges and slow turbulent floodwaters. Any precipitation that seeps into **groundwater** reservoirs flows through sediments and rockbeds which help in the cleaning process.

Human practices influence the effectiveness of these natural processes. Clearing riverbanks of vegetation causes erosion and sediment build-up in the water. These excessive sediments cloud the water, cause the flow of the river to lessen, and increase the temperature of the water. Additionally, channel alteration can interfere with fish migration and may decrease species diversity. To maintain and protect the quality of our drinking water all these processes must be considered in the land-use decisions that concern sensitive river ecosystems.

---

## BASIC CONCEPTS

☞ Alteration or destruction of a river ecosystem in one area will have impact on other areas.

☞ Individual decisions have an impact on the quality of the environment.

## PROCESS SKILLS

*Communicating, using time and space, observing, classifying, inferring, predicting, interpreting data, formulating hypotheses, experimenting.*

NEW JERSEY
AUDUBON
SOCIETY

---

## MATERIALS

☐ one piece of paper for every two students in the class

☐ crayons/pencils

☐ tape

### PREPLANNING

1. Tape the individual sheets of paper together into one long strip.

2. Draw two parallel lines two-inches apart across the entire strip, simulating a winding river. Leave enough room on either side of the lines for the students to draw.

3. Number the back of each sheet from 1 to n (n = the number of student pairs in the class).

4. Reserve a wall or floor space long enough to display the entire river, about 13 feet for a class of 25.

5. Separate the papers. At the left side of each paper draw a small arrow pointing to the right to show the direction of water flow.

6. Shuffle the sheets to mix.

## MOTIVATIONAL ACTIVITY

Ask the students, "How do people use rivers?" (for transportation, recreation, power generation, drinking water) "List the kinds of development or facilities you have seen along riverbanks." (marinas, waterparks, canoe rentals, houses, parks, power plants, bridges, beaches) [Describes previous experience.]

Ask, "How do wild animals use rivers and river banks?" (for drinking water, holds food supply, transportation, shelters) [Classifies and lists animal use.]

Continue with a teacher-led discussion eliciting river and riverbank uses mentioned in the background information.

### PROCEDURE

1. Pair the students off and give one sheet of paper with a portion of the river drawn on it.

2. Tell the students that each team represents a town that exists along the river. Instruct them to consider the uses mentioned in the discussion and draw on their part of the riverbank what the people of their town would want to have along their riverbank. [Applies principle to practical situation.]

3. After the students have drawn all of their ideas, tell them to arrange a linear display of their papers in numerical order.

4. Instruct the students to examine the length of the river and list the different uses in each frame. [Gathers and classifies new data.]

NEW JERSEY
AUDUBON
SOCIETY

**Bridges to the Natural World**

## Putting It All Together

**?** Have each team briefly describe how his or her town land was used. [Reports on reorganization.]

**?** How many of the uses drawn into the plans were duplicated? (power plants, marinas, etc.) [Matches similar developments.]

**?** How has the collective use of the land affected the wildlife habitat along the river? (Are there places for wildlife to hide, to find food, etc.?) [Makes judgment based on collected data.]

**?** If the towns had worked together to plan development along the river, would it look different than it does when each worked individually? Explain. [Draws inferences and justifies interpretations.]

**?** Which is a better plan? Explain. [Appraises value of the river ecosystem and supports conclusions.]

## Take Another Step

✔ Enact a planning board hearing to debate developments along a river system. Divide the class into special interest groups, e.g., environmentalists, energy company, department of recreation, developers, and citizen group. Use a map similar to the one in the initial activity. Have the class draw in the revised plan and compare it with the original.

✔ Repeat the initial procedure using a river that branches in three different directions.

✔ Plan a field trip to a center that has a river or stream habitat.

**FOR MORE INFORMATION**

Hollings, Holling Clancy. *Paddle to the Sea.*

Hynes, H.B.N. *The Ecology of Running Waters.*

Rosselet, Anderson, Vernachio, Risdon, Barnes. *New Jersey WATERS: A Watershed Approach to Teaching the Ecology of Regional Systems.*

NEW JERSEY
AUDUBON
SOCIETY

LENGTH OF ACTIVITY

**30** minutes

GRADE LEVELS
4 - 6

Natural History Lessons

# AS THE COOKIE CRUMBLES

Humans share some of the same needs as other animals in the natural world. In order to survive we require food, shelter, clean water, clean air, and space in an interrelated **ecosystem**. Throughout human history the evolution of different cultures was determined by the creative use of available **natural resources** to meet these basic needs.

The methods and rate at which we harvest these natural resources can cause either minimal or extreme impact on the ecosystems in which they occur.

Strip mining for coal and ores or clear-cutting for timber can destroy **habitats** beyond recovery. On the other hand, shaft mining and select forest harvesting cause less impact.

No matter how we live, as part of the earth's system, we will have an impact on it. As humans we have the capacity for making informed decisions. It is to our best advantage to develop and choose strategies that are compatible with the cycles and systems that sustain life.

"Treat the earth well. You did not inherit it. It was loaned to you by your children." (Kenyan proverb)

---

### BASIC CONCEPTS

☞ Natural resources are used by humans.

☞ There are different methods for harvesting natural resources.

☞ Some harvesting methods of natural resources affect natural habitats more than others.

---

NEW JERSEY
AUDUBON
SOCIETY

**Bridges to the Natural World**

# PROCESS SKILLS

*Communicating, using time and space, measuring, observing, inferring, predicting, identifying variables, formulating hypotheses, experimenting.*

## MATERIALS

☐ one crisp chocolate chip cookie per two students

☐ napkins

☐ one toothpick per student

### PREPLANNING

1. Assign partners among the students. Partners should be able to work together on a flat surface.

2. Assemble cookies, napkins, and toothpicks.

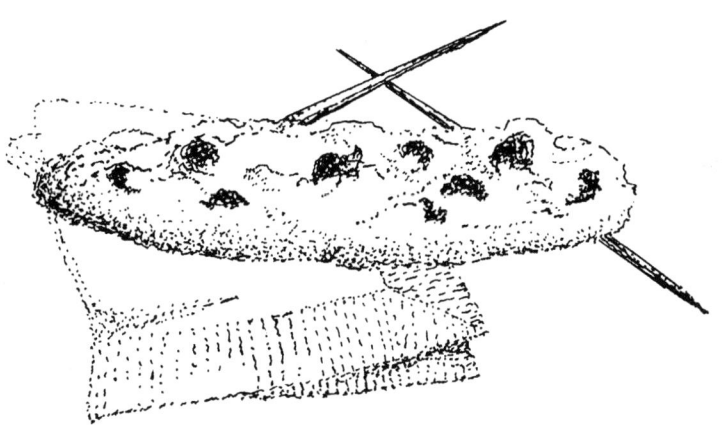

# MOTIVATIONAL ACTIVITY

There are three things you have your heart set on: going to see that new movie with a friend, renting a video game for the weekend, and buying the latest CD of your favorite music group. List the items according your preference. [Classifies according to personal criteria.]

The movie with a soda and popcorn will cost $15.00. Video rentals are $2.00, and the CD costs $18.00. If you get $5.00 a week for allowance and chores, how long will it take you to get each item separately? (movie, etc. = three weeks; video = now; CD = four weeks) [Applies mathematical principles to a practical situation.]

Does this change your order of priorities? Will you change your goals for an immediate reward or do you wait and stick to a plan? [Evaluates by using personal criteria and forms a conclusion.]

Just as you planned the spending of your money, we must plan for the use of the earth's resources.

NEW JERSEY
AUDUBON
SOCIETY

## PROCEDURE

1. Give the materials to each pair.

2. Explain that the cookie represents a stone quarry and the land surrounding it. The chocolate chips represent the stone. The toothpicks represent the tools to remove the stone. The students may change the form of the toothpicks any way they wish, but may not use any additional tools.

3. Tell the students they have ten minutes to excavate the stone. Any crumbs produced from the operation represent destruction of habitat. ALL residue (cookie, crumbs, and chips) must stay on the napkin. [Invents tool to achieve desired outcome.]

4. After five minutes announce the time left.

# Putting It All Together

? What natural resources were affected other than the stone? (plants, animals, and soil) [Explains the outcome of the experiment.]

? Describe the method you used to remove the stone. (dig, shave, drill) Which method created the least amount of crumbs? [Devises a plan for problem solving and evaluates an outcome.]

? What kind of tool was your toothpick? (pick, brace, drill, etc.) If you altered the toothpick in any way, explain why. [Establishes criteria, applies principle to practical situation, makes adjustments, and justifies conclusions.]

? What other type of tool would you want to use? Explain. (water to dissolve the surrounding area, heat to soften the chip) [Proposes a plan for experimentation based on personal criteria.]

? What was the impact of your mining on the surrounding land? (little difference, considerable difference, completely destroyed) [Makes comparisons and evaluates conclusions.]

? What does the earth (cookie) look like now? (the same, holes filled in with residue, total destruction) [Describes outcome.]

? How can you restore the disturbed habitat? (Put the residue crumbs back in the holes.) [Integrates learning experience into a plan for problem solving.]

? If you did this activity again how would you change your methods? [Appraises problem solving process and reconstructs a new sequence.]

NEW JERSEY
AUDUBON
SOCIETY

## Take Another Step

✔ List ten things you use every day and trace them to their original natural resources. How can you use these products in a way that demonstrates a concern for natural systems?

✔ Create a bulletin board display connecting everyday products to their natural resources.

✔ Research industries in New Jersey that are connected with harvesting natural resources. How do they impact on the environment?

✔ Play the video, "New Jersey at the Crossroads of Migration." Research some of the birds mentioned in the film to find out what habitats they depend upon to live out their life cycle.

## FOR MORE INFORMATION

Dunne, Peter J., Richard Kane, and Paul Kerlinger. *New Jersey at the Crossroads of Migration.* (text and video)

**LENGTH OF ACTIVITY**
**40 minutes**

**GRADE LEVELS**
**K - 6**

# CHECK, INSPECT AND PROTECT OUR BIRDS

In 1993 New Jersey Audubon Society embarked on an ambitious research project that extended over a period of five years – the New Jersey Breeding Bird Atlas. Over 550 volunteers monitored bird activity throughout the state. The volunteers were assigned to areas of approximately ten square miles where they observed and noted breeding bird activity, as well as sightings of birds that occurred regularly, occasionally, or rarely throughout the year. The work of the volunteers was compiled into a book. Anyone searching information relating to the occurrence, distribution, and status of the 440 birds recorded, can find it in the pages of *Birds of New Jersey*.

What we know about birds in New Jersey is constantly changing. Even now, only a few years after its publication, new data about birds is being recorded. Citizen scientists continue to monitor portions of New Jersey and report sightings regularly. These records reveal patterns of migration and the effects of habitat loss or alteration on bird populations. They also show recovery of bird populations where there have been habitat restoration efforts.

New Jersey residents have a richness of bird life that compares in number with very few states. Diversity of forests and wetlands make New Jersey a crossroad for migratory flocks. Some species are winging their way from farther north to tropical lands for winter. Others, like the hundreds of thousands of shorebirds, pass through our Delaware Bayshore area on their way to the tundra to breed. Many birds of the tropics come to our forests, fields, and wetlands for summer nesting.

Individuals who keep records of these birds help us understand our changing world, the impact of natural disasters and of human behaviors. Everyone can be a volunteer citizen scientist and keep track of our natural treasures.

NEW JERSEY
AUDUBON
SOCIETY

## BASIC CONCEPTS

☞ Birds occur in all areas of New Jersey.

☞ Birds come to New Jersey to breed.

☞ Birds can be seen during every season of the year.

☞ Birds are indicators of change.

## MATERIALS

Field records for each student:

☐ Bird Behavior Data sheet (Figure 27)

☐ Data Collection sheet (Figure 28)

☐ clipboard

☐ pencil

For future comparisons

☐ computer data program

## PROCESS SKILLS

*Observing, classifying, inferring, measuring, predicting, interpreting data, communicating, using time and space.*

# MOTIVATIONAL ACTIVITY

Ask the students, "How many of you ever marked your growth on a doorjamb? When did you start? How often did you check your growth?" Discuss how this bit of information changed gradually and could not be collected in one day. Some information we learn about the natural world takes time. It can't be collected in one day or even one year. This is the way scientists work when they want to learn about how nature works. We will observe and record certain bird behaviors in our school yard.

## PROCEDURE

1. Create a list of different things the students have seen birds doing.

2. Categorize these into major topic areas. (e.g., flying, feeding, nest building, courting, perching, bathing, etc.) [Recalls previous experience.]

3. Distribute the Bird Behavior Data Sheet to each student or pair of students. Discuss the categories listed and the instructions for the activity.

4. Take the students to the outdoor observation area and discuss the best methods for seeing birds. (Be quiet, move slowly, and listen attentively.)

5. Have the students watch birds in the defined area and record behaviors that match those on the behavior description sheet.

6. During the exploration, call attention to the different species of birds. How many are the same? How many are different? (You may want to incorporate the lesson, How to Identify Birds found on page 267.)

7. Create a method for sharing the data with other students in the school. Have students create graphs and charts using traditional methods or using computer programs.

NEW JERSEY
AUDUBON
SOCIETY

Natural History Lessons

## Putting It All Together

**?** How many different bird species did you see? [Distinguishes physical characteristics as indicators of different species.]

**?** What were they doing? [Generalizes observed behaviors.]

**?** What role do plants play in sustaining birds? [Infers plant use by association.]

**?** What difficulties did you encounter in gathering your data? (Heard birds, but couldn't see them; foliage prevented clear observation; birds moved too fast.)

**?** How did you overcome the obstacles? (Waited for the bird to move; changed angle of observation.) [Defines a problem and reorganizes for solution.]

**?** What tools would make the study easier? (Binoculars, telescope, observe at a different season.) [Appraises situation and seeks new solutions.]

**?** What would we learn from repeating this study over the full school year? What if it were part of an ongoing study? (Observe different birds and different behaviors.) [Predicts and gives examples of possible solutions.]

**?** How can we prepare a report that would have long-term value? (Design a data base program that allows us to compare species and behaviors over the years.) [Uses technology to support investigation and recognizes long term value of observations.]

**?** How does preservation of open space depend on knowing about the birds that nest in a particular area? (Research data may be required as evidence for habitat preservation agreements.) [Infers conservation practice from scientific data.]

---

## Take Another Step

✔ Repeat the gathering of data on a regular basis to determine which behaviors are seasonal.

✔ An interesting experiment may be to erect a pegboard near your area of study. Attach varying thickness of string and yarn, tufts of hair saved from your hairbrush, and bits of cotton. Any nappy materials are suitable. Note if any of the materials get taken. You may find them in a nearby nest.

---

**FOR MORE INFORMATION**

Joan Walsh, Vince Elia, Rich Kane, and Thomas Halliwell. *Birds of New Jersey*. NJ Audubon

NEW JERSEY
AUDUBON
SOCIETY

Bridges to the Natural World

**Figure 27**

# BIRD BEHAVIOR DATA SHEET

Name: _____

Date of observation: _____

Season: _____

Observation Site (describe): _____

_____

_____

_____

Weather (describe): _____

Evidence of human activity: _____

_____

_____

_____

Things to remember:

1)  Birds build their nests with a variety of materials

✔  Grass – you may observe varying lengths of grass hanging from the birds bill

✔  Thread or string

✔  Animal fur or human hair

✔  Moss

✔  Mud – robins and swallows may be observed in mud puddles or flying with globs of mud in
    their bill.

2)  Different birds eat different foods.  Some food items include:

✔  Insects

✔  Caterpillars

✔  Worms

✔  Seeds

NEW JERSEY
AUDUBON
SOCIETY

Natural History Lessons

Natural History Lessons

**Figure 28**

# DATA COLLECTION SHEET
## Bird Behaviors
Draw a hatch mark for each bird's action(s). – e.g., ////

FLYING
    Nothing in the bill _____

    Nesting materials in the bill _____

    Food in the bill _____

PERCHED ON A BRANCH
    Nothing in the bill _____

    Nesting material in the bill _____

    Food in the bill _____

FEEDING OR SCRATCHING ON THE GROUND _____

BUILDING A NEST
    In a tree _____

    In a bush or shrub _____

    On the ground _____

FEEDING YOUNG
    At the nest _____

    On a branch _____

    On the ground _____

    Bathing
        In a puddle_____

        In a bird bath _____

OTHER (describe): _____

_____

_____

_____

NEW JERSEY
AUDUBON
SOCIETY

LENGTH OF ACTIVITY

## 40 minutes

Independent group work
Ongoing wildlife habitat development

Natural History Lessons

# HABITAT HELPERS

A habitat is the natural environment of an organism where it most typically finds the food, water, shelter, and space it needs to live its full life cycle and reproduce others of its kind. Throughout the world and in New Jersey animal habitats are being threatened by land-use practices that eliminate or **fragment** valuable habitats or replace them with features that can no longer sustain life.

Renewing wildlife habitat in any given area involves research and conservation measures. Research specialists need to study particular forms of wildlife that may be native to a region and determine their habitat needs. Conservation specialists need to decide on specific strategies to return or restore those habitat features to an area to support the wildlife species whose restoration is being encouraged. In many cases, this involves the introduction or restoration of vegetation that plays an important role in providing food and/or protective shelter to the wildlife species in question. In other cases, these conservation measures may involve improving wildlife access to water, or perhaps roosting, resting, or nesting space.

Not all wildlife habitats need to be large, so some small habitat sites can be improved on school or community park sites, or even backyards.

### BASIC CONCEPTS

☞ Habitats are vital to wildlife.

☞ Wildlife habitats are being threatened in New Jersey.

☞ Restoring habitats involves research and conservation practices.

☞ Vegetation is important to most habitat restoration projects.

☞ Small habitat restoration projects may be valuable.

NEW JERSEY
AUDUBON
SOCIETY

**Natural History Lessons**

# PROCESS SKILLS

*Observing, analyzing, measuring, evaluating, communicating, using time and space, estimating, comparing and contrasting.*

## PREPLANNING

1. Copy habitat pictures from *Bridges to the Natural World* habitat section.

2. Seek appropriate permission for habitat restoration project on the school grounds.

3. Determine source of gardening materials.

4. Schedule volunteers for assistance in collection/donation of materials and construction of the garden.

## MATERIALS

Part 1 - Planning a habitat garden

❑ *Bridges to the Natural World* habitat pictures.

❑ graph paper

Part 2 - Plotting a habitat garden

❑ measuring tape

❑ stakes

❑ hammer

❑ fluorescent ribbon

Part 3 - Building a habitat garden

❑ native, drought resistant plants (see Appendices p. 325)

❑ garden tools

❑ community volunteers

# MOTIVATIONAL ACTIVITY

Decide on a plant and animal with which all students have had personal experience. (E.g., squirrel, crow, tree, grass) Ask the students to list the things these organisms need in order to survive. [Recalls previous observations.]

## PROCEDURE

## Part 1 - **Planning a habitat garden**

1. Students discuss similarities and differences in habitat pictures. How do these habitats indicate the different needs and preferences of the plants and animals that use them? [Able to infer plant and animal needs by physical features.]

2. Tell the students that they are going to enhance a portion of the schoolyard to benefit wildlife.

Bridges to the Natural World

3. List the features that should be included so a variety of species will benefit. [Recalls elements of a complete habitat.]

4. Have groups of four or five students use graph paper to create a scale map of the garden, plotting placement of plants and pathway access. [Acts cooperatively to solve problem by creating graphic design.]

5. Students choose final plan or construct another composite of submitted plans. [Appraises scientific and aesthetic value. Uses objectivity in problem solving.]

6. Design a flyer describing the goals of the project to attract volunteers and support. [Synthesizes goals and needs to gain support.]

## Part 2 – **Plotting a habitat garden**

1. For first time efforts it's advisable to begin with a small manageable area. Measure and mark with stakes. Tie a fluorescent ribbon on the stakes to enhance visibility of the perimeter. [Applies skills to new situation.]

2. Plan a list of community helpers. Invite parents and grandparents to offer advice to the class on the tools and materials that will be needed. Contact Coalition for Schoolyard Habitat for available support. For best results, plant native, drought resistant plant species. [Compiles an organized list of resources to solve problem.]

3. Schedule and invite helpers for suggestions and sign-up dates for building the habitat. [Integrates learning from different areas into a plan for solving a problem.]

## Part 3 – **Building a habitat garden**

1. Work with the students to involve parents, grandparents, maintenance staff, local businesses, and other community members in construction of the habitat.

2. Students collect on-going baseline data: pictures of progress, dates of germination, growth measurements, budding/flowering/ fruiting of plants, wildlife attraction. [Analyzes and organizes data.]

© carol Decker

NEW JERSEY
AUDUBON
SOCIETY

## Putting It All Together

**?** Describe the major differences between the before and after habitat site. What role did the enhancement project play? (Created more opportunities for wildlife to find food, shelter and water.) [Evaluates and justifies conclusions.]

**?** What are the major challenges in creating a wildlife habitat? How were these challenges met?

**?** What changes/additions would you like to see to the site now that it has been started? [Recognizes need for flexibility in making decisions.]

## Take Another Step

✔ Call upon the assistance of a habitat restoration expert from the Coalition for Schoolyard Habitats (an affiliate of the Alliance for New Jersey Environmental Education-ANJEE).

✔ While the garden is growing, examine other parts of the school grounds to see how plants assist wildlife.

**FOR MORE INFORMATION**

Coalition for Schoolyard Habitat
NJAS/ANJEE
PO Box 693
Bernardsville, NJ 07924

Food requirements of most common birds and mammals (and limited food information on fish, amphibians and reptiles), consult *American Wildlife and Plants: A Guide to Wildlife Food Habits*, Martin, Zim, and Nelson, Dover Publications, Inc., NY, 1961.

Habitat features and indicators for many common eastern species of wildlife, consult *The Field Guide to Wildlife Habitats of the Eastern United States*, Janine M. Benyus, Simon and Schuster, NY, 1989.

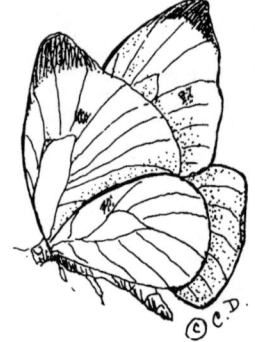

NEW JERSEY
AUDUBON
SOCIETY

**LENGTH OF ACTIVITY**
2 periods
**40**
minutes each

**GRADE LEVELS**
3 - 6

# OPEN SPACES, WILD PLACES

Open space is that land not covered by pavement or by buildings. Open space can be cultivated, disturbed by human activity, or left wild. It can be thousands of acres or only a small plot of land. A nature sanctuary is a protected, safe place for wildlife and all that the wildlife needs in order to grow and reproduce others of its kind. The New Jersey Audubon Society (NJAS) maintains and protects over 30 sanctuaries throughout the state that range in size from only a few acres to many hundreds of acres.

If a sanctuary is large, it may include many plant and animal members of a **natural community** and contain **habitat** features that support many species of wildlife. Nature sanctuaries provide visitors the opportunity to observe and study first hand the important interrelationships and living and nonliving elements of **ecosystems.** Finally, wildlife sanctuaries often serve as islands of protection, where many species of birds and other animals can find refuge during migration.

Private citizens set portions of their property aside, creating habitats for wildlife in their own backyards. Municipalities recognize that open space is not only good for wildlife, but provides an improved quality of life for its citizens. New Jersey Audubon Society played a major role in the state plan for purchasing one million acres of open space land in New Jersey in order to preserve the natural treasures that are the heritage of every citizen.

Stewardship includes the ability to evaluate land use and determine the benefits to all forms of life. The ideal is to live in harmony with nature.

## PROCESS SKILLS
*Observing, classifying, measuring, communicating, creating models.*

NEW JERSEY
AUDUBON
SOCIETY

**Natural History Lessons**

## BASIC CONCEPTS

☞ Land that is not occupied by human structures is open space.

☞ Open space can be cultivated, disturbed by human activity, or left wild.

☞ A nature sanctuary is a protected, safe place for wildlife

☞ Humans can choose to live in harmony with natural systems.

## MATERIALS

❏ clipboards

❏ pencils, crayons or felt markers

❏ rulers

❏ measuring tapes

❏ worksheet (Figure 29)

❏ masking tape

❏ paper

### PREPLANNING

Define the outdoor area that will be studied by the students. The group should be able to observe the full area in a ten-minute walk.

# MOTIVATIONAL ACTIVITY

Have each child place one of their feet on a piece of paper and trace an outline. Say, "We will use this as a symbol of human activity. Architects and planners use this term to describe the built environment (school, roads, playground). The areas not covered by a human footprint are open spaces.

### PROCEDURE

## Period 1 Exploring Open Spaces

1. Lead the students around the entire designated area. As you encounter a part of the built environment, tape to it one of the "footprints." [Distinguishes categories.]

2. Discuss different categories of open space available: Cultivated - controlled regularly by humans; disturbed - shows evidence of human activity; wild - shows no evidence of human activity.

3. Categorize the open space types.

NEW JERSEY
AUDUBON
SOCIETY

**Bridges to the Natural World**

## Period 2 **Mapping Open Spaces**

1. Return to the designated area. Divide the students into groups of five. Each team will develop a land-use map that shows the difference between the footprints of the built environment and open spaces. This map will also classify the open spaces according to cultivated, disturbed, or wild.

2. Each team works independently to plan how they will construct a graphic that represents the designated area. [Creates graphic of defined area.]

3. Help the students choose color codes for the categories of open spaces and the built footprints. Discuss these choices so that there is agreement on the code. [Ascribes meaning to color symbols.]

4. Instruct the students to make a SYMBOL KEY in the corner of their paper so they will remember the symbols in use.

5. Ask the students to create maps of the area. [Creates interpretive chart.]

6. When the students finish, allow them to exchange maps. See if they agree with the areas in the maps of fellow students. [Judges logic of symbols.]

7. Have students create a visual for the hallway or other venue to educate fellow schoolmates about the school's open spaces.

## Putting It All Together

**?** What kinds of built footprints did you find? Which ones take up the most space? [Interprets compiled data.]

**?** How does the amount of open space compare with built space? [Interprets, organizes and explains data.]

**?** What fraction of the open space could be considered wild? [Estimates number from a symbol.]

**?** What alterations would you suggest to make the cultivated and disturbed areas more useful to wildlife? [Prepares and explains critique.]

**?** What areas would you set aside as a wildlife sanctuary? [Applies new knowledge to problem solving.]

NEW JERSEY
AUDUBON
SOCIETY

**Figure 29**

# Footprints Worksheet

Name of team _____

Members of the team _____

_____

---

## Area Map

MAP KEY

Footprints – ☐

Cultivated – ☐

Disturbed – ☐

Wild – ☐

# NOTES

# NOTES

*Bridges to the Natural World*

Section

3

ACTIVITIES

Skill Activities

# NATURE ORIENTATION
# AND SKILL-BUILDING

# HOW TO USE THIS SECTION

The activities in Section Three are offered to assist the teacher who will use the school grounds or visit one of the natural communities in Section One for outdoor study. These activities are primarily skill-building exercises that engage the student in observing multiple facets of a unique natural community by viewing it from both objective and subjective perspectives.

Becoming involved is the key to knowledge and understanding of the natural world. As soon as they step outside, students need to be drawn into some activity that will focus their attention and start them on a pattern of thinking and doing.

A.  Transitional Activities: taking that first step into the outdoors.
B.  Discovery–Awareness Activities: getting involved with natural habitats.
C.  Classification Activities: sorting things out.
D.  Developing an Environmental Ethic: walking lightly on the planet.

Twenty-three transition, discovery, and classification activities and six teacher-directed environmental ethic activities are offered. Although each one lists the grades appropriate for the activity, with minor adjustments, these activities can be used at multiple levels. While the activities are not as developed as the lessons, they do list teaching objectives and materials needed, describe the study site and procedure, and with some, offer a follow-up activity.

Skill Activities

NEW JERSEY
AUDUBON
SOCIETY

**Nature Orientation and Skill Activities**

# INDOORS TO OUTDOORS
# TRANSITIONAL ACTIVITIES

## THE CENTIPEDE

GRADE LEVELS
Pre-K - 1

OBJECTIVE
**To simulate the movement of a centipede.**

MATERIALS
• 50-foot clothesline rope or the equivalent

PREPLANNING
Tie 12" loops tied at 12" intervals. The number of loops should equal the number of students. The loops should be large enough for each student to slip a hand through and hold.*

PROCEDURE
Tell the students, "We are going to make a giant centipede. All stand and form a single line. As I come to you take hold of the rope loop I offer you."

When all have a loop of the rope, lead a discussion on the best way to make this giant centipede move. (Discuss cooperation; all move left foot forward first, then right foot forward so that feet are together.) Try a few steps to assure understanding.

Use this activity to move from the classroom to the outdoors or from a place in the schoolyard to the study site.

*Note*:  The students are NOT tied to the rope.  Each should hold a loop so that by simply opening the hand the rope would drop.

## THE WONDERFUL PICNIC

GRADE LEVELS
Pre-K - 3

OBJECTIVE
**To recognize an animal's need for food.**

MATERIALS
• crumbs saved from students' lunch or snack
• napkins for collecting crumbs

PREPLANNING
Tell the students before lunch or a snack to save the crumbs that are left. Arrange to use a section of the school grounds for the experiment.

PROCEDURE
Each child wraps the crumbs in a napkin or lunch bag. At a suitable time, take the crumbs outdoors and place them in an area where an animal or insect might find and eat them.

Leave the crumbs for a 24-hour period. Go back and examine whatever activity can be observed. If the crumbs have disappeared ask: "What might have happened to them?" (Animals came and ate them, wind blew them away, someone swept them away, etc.)

**CHILDREN'S BOOK**
Baines, Chris. *The Picnic.*

NEW JERSEY
AUDUBON
SOCIETY

# SNAKE WALK

GRADE LEVELS
Pre-K - 6

OBJECTIVE
**To demonstrate the effect of protective coloration in wildlife**

MATERIALS
• pipe cleaners of various colors. (There should be twice the number of pipe cleaners as students in the class.)

PREPLANNING
Twist two pipe cleaners together (use the same color or different colors to get a striped effect). At one end, create a space between the pipe cleaners to resemble an oval head (Figure 1). Place the "snakes" along a chosen trail at a habitat site or on the school grounds.

PROCEDURE
Take the students to the prepared trail and tell them they are looking for make-believe snakes that are hidden along the path. When any student sees one of these creatures he or she is to call out "SNAKE" and point to the site. When the class confirms the claim, the "snake" is removed. Continue until all have been removed. Tell the students, "When you are looking for wildlife, you must look very carefully. Animals are sometimes hard to see because their colors blend in with the colors that surround them, just as the make-believe snakes were not easy to find."

**Figure 1**

# FOOD SHOPPING

GRADE LEVELS
K - 3

OBJECTIVE
**To recognize food supplies for wildlife and to compare them to food used by humans**

MATERIALS
• empty boxes, cans, or bottles that represent the kinds of foods the students would eat.

SITE
School grounds or habitat study site.

PREPLANNING
Set materials on a table or desk as they might appear on a supermarket shelf.

PROCEDURE
Before going outside, lead a discussion on food shopping. Use the props to identify the preparation and packaging of food for people. In the outdoors, instruct the students to examine a habitat site as though they were going food shopping for wild animals. What is in this market? What might an animal use for food? Is there any evidence that some animal has been feeding here? (broken shells, seeds, holes in leaves) Collect samples. Ask the students, "What animals have we seen that might eat these foods?"

FOLLOW-UP
Back in the classroom, have the students compare the kinds of food that people eat with the kinds of food eaten by wildlife. How are they the same? How are they different?

**Skill Activities**

**Nature Orientation and Skill Activities**

# TOUCH AND REMEMBER

**GRADE LEVELS**
K - 6

**OBJECTIVE**
**To recognize natural objects by using the sense of touch.**

**MATERIALS**
• one natural object from the study site for each child in the class (e.g., shells, rocks, pine cones, sticks). The objects collected and distributed can be similar (e.g., all rocks, all sticks) or dissimilar (e.g., stick, rock, shell).

**PREPLANNING**
Collect from the site the objects that the students will study.

**PROCEDURE**
Have the students stand in a circle with their faces to the center and their hands behind them. Place an object in the hand of each student. Say, "Without looking, examine the object in your hands thoroughly. Become familiar with its shape, its texture, and any distinctive marks. When you are sure that you know your object, hold it in one hand and raise the other hand above your head."

At the appropriate time collect the objects and place them in the center of the circle. Tell the students to look at the objects. One at a time, have the students pick out their object and explain to the group how they know it is theirs. If a choice is challenged, defer until all other objects have been selected.

For older children, observation skills are sharpened if the activity is played first with dissimilar objects followed by a second round of similar objects.

**FOLLOW-UP**
While investigating a habitat site, have the students find a match for the objects identified in the group.

# DO YOU SEE WHAT I SEE?

**GRADE LEVELS**
1 - 6

**OBJECTIVE**
**To demonstrate how people think in different ways about the things they observe in the natural world.**

**MATERIALS**
• five natural objects for each student.

**PREPLANNING**
If natural objects are available, use the schoolyard. If this is not possible, the teacher could collect things from another neighborhood, park, or nature center.

**PROCEDURE**
Instruct each student to choose five objects and arrange them in any pattern they like. They must be able to explain why they have chosen their arrangement (e.g., colors from light to dark, similar shapes together, arrangement in the shape of a star). No answer is incorrect. The teacher should note the variety of arrangements and point out to the students that there are many different ways of looking at things and that we increase our own knowledge when we share ideas.

# HABITAT ENCOUNTERS OF THE SENSORY KIND

## GRADE LEVELS
4 - 6

## OBJECTIVE
**To use the senses of sight, hearing, smell, and touch to become familiar with natural surroundings**

## MATERIALS
• Notepad
• Pencil
• "Habitat Encounters of the Sensory Kind" worksheet (Figure 2) (optional)

## PREPLANNING
Arrange a trip to a habitat site or to an area of the school grounds.

## PROCEDURE
During your visit to a study area have the students form a circle with their backs to the center. Ask them, "How do people learn about each other?" (We listen to their stories, watch their behavior, etc.) Ask, "How do we learn about nature?" (We use our senses.)

Today we are going to pretend that we have come to the earth for the first time. We do not know the language or the people. At my signal you will take 25 steps straight out from where you are currently standing. That is your landing spot. You may stretch out in any direction but you may not move your feet from that place. There is to be no contact with any other of your own species. You are on a fact-finding mission and will have to report your findings when you return. Stand quietly, trying to understand all that is around you. Listen for every sound, gather every scent, feel all that your body experiences. What can you learn about the life on this planet by observing the activity or stillness around you? Your signal to leave and to return will be (teacher's choice).

Time allotted for this activity is determined by the attention span of the class. We suggest a brief period, three minutes or so, for the first experience.

The teacher may wish to direct the activity verbally or to copy the direction sheet (Figure 2) for the students' reference while on their fact-finding mission. The experience is then divided into four activities. The students return and share their findings after exercising each of the senses. Save any descriptive vocabulary they generate for use in creative writing.

NEW JERSEY AUDUBON SOCIETY

**Nature Orientation and Skill Activities**

**Figure 2**
# Habitat Encounters of the Sensory Kind

## HOW TO LOOK

Focus on one object with HARD EYES. That means notice everything about it: color, shape, special marks, and place in the habitat. Does it stand alone or is it part of something else? How does the light shining on it create different shades and tints of color? Does it move?

Without moving your head or your eyes, broaden your vision by looking with SOFT EYES; what can you see, though not clearly, without moving any part of your body? Can you identify other things around you without looking directly at them?

Next, move your head from your left to your right shoulder and take in the FULL PAN-ORAMA of the habitat in front of you.

CLOSE YOUR EYES. In your mind's eye, look at the panorama before you. Do you remember the first thing you saw and each thing after that?

OPEN YOUR EYES. Focus on the first image. Move your head slowly and look at other things in front of you. Did you forget anything? Is there something you see now that you did not notice the first time?

## HOW TO TOUCH

Sit down and close your eyes. Focus your attention on any area of your skin that is exposed to air. How does the temperature make your skin feel? Are you aware of any movement of the air (suggestions: wind, breeze)? Place your hands out in front of you and compare the temperature away from your body. Are there any differences in the movement of the air or the temperature?

Imagine how it would feel if a storm were coming. Imagine standing in heavy rain, fog, or snowfall. How would any exposed areas of skin feel?

Put your hands on the ground. Press the ground hard. Move them lightly over the surface. Pick up any loose material and try to identify it without looking at it. Feel the surface of any objects around you. Notice any difference in textures. Find things that are smooth, bumpy, soft, rough, and hard.

Open your eyes and examine the things you have just felt. Evaluate your identifications.

## HOW TO SMELL

Put your nose to the ground and smell the soil. Describe the smell. (suggestions: sweet, sour, sharp, mellow, bitter)

What does the smell remind you of? Is it a smell you will remember?

Stand up. Breathe in through your nose. Try to single out a scent that will help you remember this special place.

Are there any other scents in the air? How would you describe them? Can you identify the source?

## HOW TO LISTEN

Close your eyes and listen. Do you hear any sounds that are made by people or by things people use? Put them in an imaginary box and set them aside. Focus on the sounds made by things in nature.

What sounds are caused by the weather? (suggestions: wind, rain, snow) What sounds are made by mammals, birds, or insects? (suggestions: calls and songs as well as behavior)

Skill Activities

# DISCOVERY-AWARENESS ACTIVITIES

## STREAM STUDY

### GRADE LEVELS
Pre-K - 1 (with assistance)
2 - 6 (independently)

### OBJECTIVE
**To discover and study behavior of stream animals.**

### MATERIALS
- holding pan (dishpan size)
- gathering containers
- seine or net (See "Making Field Study and Nature Investigation Tools" p. 299)
- field guide to stream and pond

### PREPLANNING
1. Gather and prepare materials needed for the stream study.
2. Inform the students to dress in shorts and old sneakers without socks. They should bring extra clothing, shoes and socks and towel for drying and changing after the field trip.
3. Assemble parent or other adult volunteers to help lead discovery and to chaperone.

### PROCEDURE
Bring the materials to the edge of the stream. Have the students arrange their towels and extra shoes so they will be able to find them when the session is over.

### ENTERING THE STREAM

The teacher enters the stream first and calls the students one at a time to an assigned place along the edge. When everyone has a place, review the safety regulations for stream activity:
- Under NO CIRCUMSTANCES is any object to be thrown. Students who forget will be required to return to the shore.
- Do NOT RUN.
- There is to be NO splashing of anyone or anything. (When the lesson is over you may want to do a splashing activity described at the end of this lesson or assign a supervised area for splashing downstream from those who are still exploring. If you do allow the students to splash at all, save this activity until after the lesson.)

### EXPLORING THE STREAM

1. *Holding tank.* Distribute a holding tank (deli container) to each student. They are in charge of their own tank. Warn them not to let it get away in the current, which would litter the stream. Inform them that the stream is another kind of habitat for many different kinds of animals.

2. *Observation tank.* When the students find a creature they may gather it as carefully as possible in their holding tank and bring it to the larger container (dishpan or equivalent) on the bank of the stream. The creatures will be held in that container until the lesson is over. This gives the whole class an opportunity to observe the behavior of the different animals caught.

NEW JERSEY
AUDUBON
SOCIETY

**Skill Activities**

**Nature Orientation and Skill Activities**

Be sure to release the captured animals back into the stream before you leave. Under NO circumstances are any of these animals to be kept as pets.

3. *Things to discuss.*

A. ***What's here?*** Animals are on top of the stream in quiet places, in the water, near and under the rocks and plants on the stream bottom. Caddisfly larvae make cases of tiny pebbles or sticks, which sometimes are found attached to the rocks. Watch for these interesting structures. The crayfish is probably the most exciting creature of the stream. Their pinch is not very strong; it feels like a pinch with fingernails. They are not easy to catch because they hide under rocks and move *backwards* when they try to escape. It takes a quick hand to catch one, but students, even first and second graders, can be successful if they are patient.

B. ***How do I find them?*** Tell the students to move slowly as they observe and gather the animals. Moving in the stream, kneeling in the water, or lifting and turning rocks should be undertaken carefully. Many of the creatures are wary and when uncovered will move away as fast as they can. Slow movements will at least allow the students to get close to these animals.

C. ***Rocks.*** Many insect larvae, nymphs, and adult water insects eat the tiny organisms that adhere to streambed rocks. Students should lift a rock gently, turn it over and wait. As the water drains off the rock, the larvae move around on the rock. They can be picked off and placed in the holding tank.

D. ***Quiet places.*** Away from the swift current students may find the insects that travel on top of the water, newts that live under the water near rocks, and some fish.

E. ***I'm finished now.*** Student interest will vary. Some will want to stay all day to explore, others will begin to look for another activity. Suggestions:
- Students can go to the holding tank and watch the animals that the class has caught. If the water level is getting too high someone could be appointed to scoop out some of the excess.
- Assign a supervised area downstream from the rest of the class for building structures with the rocks or for splashing. Repeat the "no throwing" rule.
- A Group Splash - Have all of the students line up at the edge of the stream as they were when you first assigned places. Open with a discussion of the water cycle. Where did this water come from? (other smaller streams, rain) Where is it going? (to a larger stream or river) Which way? (direction of stream flow) Where will it go eventually? (into the ocean, soak into soil for plants, be drunk by animals, evaporate into the atmosphere, come down again as rain)

**Let's make some raindrops.**
1. Put your hands into the water, lift them up high, let your fingers dangle and watch the droplets fall off.
2. Make your hands into cups and lift up handfuls of water. Let it fall from your hands. The rain is getting heavier. The storm is getting stronger. How can we make a big storm in the stream? (Splash as hard as you can.)

FOLLOW-UP
Have the students dramatize or draw some of the creatures they observed.

# TEMPERATURE PLEASE!

GRADE LEVELS
1 - 6

OBJECTIVE
**To compare different temperature readings at a single site.**

MATERIALS
• outdoor thermometers

PREPLANNING
This activity can be done at any habitat site or in the classroom. If you cannot provide a thermometer for each child, provide one for each pair. If only one thermometer is available, assign pairs of students to take readings from different places.

PROCEDURE
1. Have the students designate a variety of locations in the habitat to be studied where the air temperature might vary.
2. Send the students to the spots they identify to take and record the temperatures. Stress that the thermometer needs to remain in the site for at least three minutes to get an accurate reading.
3. Discuss the possible causes of similarities or differences in temperatures recorded.

FOLLOW-UP
Design bar and line graphs demonstrating the similarities and differences in temperatures.

# SOIL ANALYSIS

GRADE LEVELS
2 - 6

OBJECTIVE
**To analyze the contents of soil and discover how long it takes nature to make soil**

MATERIALS
• soil (If you purchase potting soil, be sure it contains humus.)
• a light-colored piece of material approximately 18" x 18"

PREPLANNING
Ideally, this activity is done at a habitat site.

PROCEDURE
1. Have each student pick up a handful of soil and spread it around on their palm.
2. Encourage the students to examine the small particles carefully.
3. List the soil's contents.
4. Ask, "How can we make soil?" and suggest, "Let's try."
5. Put a light-colored piece of material on the ground.
6. Challenge the students to find some of the things they found in the soil. Ask them to place these things on the material. Warn against collecting live animals or live plants. These organisms were found living in, not part of, the soil.
7. Does the collection look like soil? (no) What can we do to make it soil? (pound it, break the things up into little pieces, grind it)
8. Close the corners of the material. Allow each student the opportunity to pound, break, or grind the contents.
9. Open up the material. Assess the results. Why does it not look like soil? (Not enough time has passed for the organic materials to decompose and the inorganic materials to weather.)

FOLLOW-UP
In a small plastic jar, keep samples of different kinds of soil taken from each habitat you visit. List the contents and compare the differences.

NEW JERSEY
AUDUBON
SOCIETY

**Skill Activities**

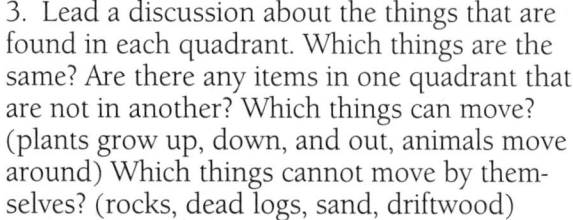

# HABITAT MAP

GRADE LEVELS
3 - 6

OBJECTIVE
**To create and recognize map symbols**

MATERIALS
For each student:
• paper
• clipboard
• pencil
For the class:
• 20 colored ribbons about 12 inches long

PREPLANNING
Choose a habitat site to be studied.

PROCEDURE
1. Divide the students into teams of five. Have each team measure off a quadrant, each side 10 paces long. Mark each corner of the quadrant with a colored ribbon. The quadrants should not overlap.
2. Tell the students to explore their quadrant for several minutes.

3. Lead a discussion about the things that are found in each quadrant. Which things are the same? Are there any items in one quadrant that are not in another? Which things can move? (plants grow up, down, and out, animals move around) Which things cannot move by themselves? (rocks, dead logs, sand, driftwood)
4. Help the students choose symbols for the items in their quadrants. Discuss these choices so that everyone understands how the symbols are to be drawn. For example, students can be shown that a large circle denotes a large old tree, while a small circle denotes a small young sapling. The same applies to other objects and their symbols.
5. Instruct the students to make a SYMBOL KEY in the corner of their paper so they will remember the symbols in use.
6. Ask the students to create maps of their quadrants and give them 10 minutes to do so. When they finish, allow them to exchange quadrants and maps. See if they can find the items in a different quadrant as represented on the maps of fellow students.

FOLLOW-UP
1. Ask each team to choose a hand-sized object from their quadrant. Hide the object near something that is represented on that team's map.
2. Write a description of the object and its location on a separate sheet of paper. Exchange maps, quadrants, and the object information with another team. The exchange team must find the item using the map of the original team.

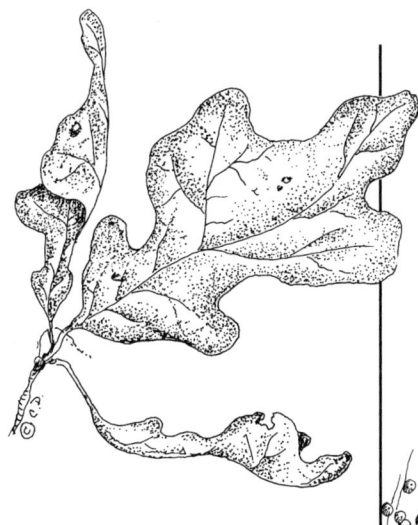

# HABITAT EXPLORATION: SCAVENGER HUNT

GRADE LEVELS
3 - 6

OBJECTIVE
**To apply descriptive words to natural objects.**

MATERIALS
For each student:
• "Habitat Exploration: Scavenger Hunt" worksheet (Figure 3)
• clipboard
• pencil

PREPLANNING
1. Arrange a field trip to one of the habitat sites.
2. Duplicate the "Habitat Exploration: Scavenger Hunt" worksheet (Figure 3).

PROCEDURE
1. Distribute the materials.
2. Instruct the students to find and draw objects in the habitat that match the description in each square. There must be a different object for each entry, so that at the end of the exercise 20 different items are named.
3. Give the students time to compare and explain their selections.

FOLLOW-UP
Have each student write a poem about the habitat using at least three or four of the descriptive words and their objects.

# LOOKING AT OPPOSITES

GRADE LEVELS
4 - 6 (Modify for younger students)

OBJECTIVE
**To evaluate natural objects by using a variety of criteria.**

MATERIALS
• natural objects collected from different habitats
• "Looking at Opposites" worksheet (Figure 4).

PREPLANNING
1. Arrange the natural objects on a table where all students can examine them. (This activity can be done outdoors as well.)
2. Duplicate the "Looking at Opposites" worksheet (Figure 4).

PROCEDURE
1. Have each student select a natural object from the collection and complete the worksheet.
2. Discuss the responses on each student's worksheet.

FOLLOW-UP
Students should be encouraged to invent new categories of opposites.

Skill Activities

NEW JERSEY
AUDUBON
SOCIETY

**Nature Orientation and Skill Activities**

**Figure 3**

**Name:** _____

# Habitat Exploration: Scavenger Hunt
**FIND SOMETHING:**

| | | | |
|---|---|---|---|
| curved | tiny | sharp | warm |
| not living | rough | rotted | hard |
| living | smooth | thin | straight |
| wet | light | house-like | new |
| cold | dry | old | round |

NEW JERSEY
AUDUBON
SOCIETY

**Bridges to the Natural World**

Skill Activities

**Figure 4**

Name: _____

## Looking At Opposites

| Name of the Object: | |
|---|---|
| What about it is... | |
| beautiful? | ugly? |
| hard? | soft? |
| peaceful? | threatening? |
| straight? | curved? |
| exciting? | boring? |

© 1992 New Jersey Audubon Society

NEW JERSEY
AUDUBON
SOCIETY

Skill Activities

# BE A HISTORY DETECTIVE

**GRADE LEVELS**
4 - 6

**OBJECTIVE**
**Interpret the signs of people's past activities by reading the landscape.**

**MATERIALS**
• none required

**SITE**
Old fields, forests, overgrown home sites.

**PROCEDURE**
As the recommended sites are investigated look for the following clues that are evidence of past human activities:

• Rock walls usually outline former fields.
• A mound or depression in the ground may indicate an old dump site. (With permission, use gloves and a trowel to dig lightly around the area to reveal remnants of another lifetime.)
• A row of trees or shrubs along a field edge may have replaced an old fence. This happens because birds ingest seeds when they eat berries. While sitting on the fence they defecate and the seeds drop to the soil and grow. The new plants cover and hide the old fence.
• Long dirt mounds may be the remains of a railroad bed or an elevated roadway.
• Out-of-place plants, such as daffodils in the woods, lilac bushes in an old field, or clusters of apple trees, may hint at old homestead sites.

• Nails or old pieces of barbed wire embedded in trees show where a field fence might have been.
• Rock walls along riverbanks may tell of past use as a dam for a mill.
• Rock walls in a river or stream may be the sites where Native Americans or early settlers built a fish trap.
• The branches of the trees growing on the edge of a field give clues to the field's age. If all of the branches face the field, it is an old field. If they do not, it is a new field. How can you tell? Tree branches grow toward the sun. Branches of trees on the edge of an old field grew out into the open field to receive sunlight, and as the tree grew its branches continued to grow in the same direction. In a new field, however, the nearest sunlight comes from the sky. The branches, in growing toward that light, would not be concentrated on one side of the tree.

*Note*: Some of the centers listed in Section One, Habitats of New Jersey, contain such remnants of the past. If you tell the naturalist you are interested in this type information, these remnants can be included in the regular lesson.

NEW JERSEY
AUDUBON
SOCIETY

**Bridges to the Natural World**

Skill Activities

# CLASSIFICATION ACTIVITIES

## HITCHHIKERS

GRADE LEVELS
Pre-K - 2

OBJECTIVE
**To recognize plant parts and plant diversity.**

MATERIALS
For each student:
• 12-inch square of felt (the nappier the better)
• tie a 2-ft. piece of butcher cord through a hole at the edge of the felt square
• weighted fishing sinker (optional)
• one sheet 8½ x 11 white paper

SITE
Field or overgrown brushy area.

PREPLANNING
Schedule a trip to the exploration site.

PROCEDURE
1. Lead the students in a line through the study site, dragging the felt for about five minutes.* Integrate other observational activities and skills as the students are walking. Call attention to sounds, sights, and smells of the area.
2. At the end of the walk have the students fold the felt square so the particles that have adhered will remain inside.
3. Distribute the sheets of white paper. Have the students sit down and carefully turn the felt out again, brushing the particles of plant and other debris onto the paper.

4. Have the students sort, classify, and count the particles. Are there any seeds? How many different types of particles were found by each student? By the whole class? What other plant parts can be identified? Can any of the parts be matched with a plant still standing?

FOLLOW-UP
Save some of the seeds. Plant them in a container in the classroom and see what grows.

* Option – Tie a sinker on to the other end of the felt. Have the students line up along the edge of an overgrown field. Have them cast their felt pieces into the field and then reel them back in.

NEW JERSEY
AUDUBON
SOCIETY

**Skill Activities**

**Nature Orientation and Skill Activities**

# WHAT A BUGGY IDEA

GRADE LEVELS
Pre-K - 6

OBJECTIVE
**To closely observe insects, spiders, and other creatures for the numbers and kinds of body parts and behavior.**

MATERIALS
• magnifying glasses
• magnifying boxes (optional)*
• observation containers

PREPLANNING
Schedule a field trip to an outdoor area or explore your own classroom.

PROCEDURE
Almost all habitats include insects, spiders, and other small creatures. During your investigation of a habitat, have students observe these creatures by carefully turning over the leaf litter on the forest floor or by examining the underside of a dead log or rock.

Remind the students that they are visiting the home of another creature. To learn about the natural world people need to investigate, but they should be very careful in handling even the smallest of creatures.

The teachers of young students might use the story of Giant Thoughtless presented in this section under Developing an Environmental Ethic (p. 282) to help make this point.

When an animal is found it can be placed in a holding container for observation of behavior and parts (see discussion of Making Field Study and Nature Investigation Tools. p. 299). How many legs does it have? Where is its head? Does it have any other visible body parts? Does it have any special markings or color patterns? Some students may want to draw the creature.

At the end of the activity be certain that all of the animals have been returned to the places where they were found or one that is similar. Discuss why this is the best thing to do with the animals. (We cannot provide for the animals' life needs as well as their habitats can.)

FOLLOW-UP
Make drawings for exhibit of the small creatures studied. Compare them with studies of creatures found in other habitats. Use a field guide to identify the creatures observed.

*Magnifying boxes can be purchased through science supply companies.

NEW JERSEY
AUDUBON
SOCIETY

# IDENTIFYING VINES

GRADES LEVELS
1 - 6

OBJECTIVE
**To identify distinguishing characteristics of common vines for classification.**

MATERIALS
• vine information sheet for each student (Figure 5)

SITE
Woodland habitat or forest edge where a variety of vines can be found.

PREPLANNING
1. Schedule a field trip to a forest or forest edge.
2. Duplicate "Most Common Vines of New Jersey" (Figure 5)

PROCEDURE
1. Find a vine in the habitat and ask, "What makes this plant a vine?" (A vine is a plant whose stem requires support. Vines are successful because they are able to climb. They climb using several methods: draping over other plants, sending out tendrils, entwining with other plants, growing aerial rootlets.)
2. Distribute the vine information sheet and instruct the students to match the descriptions with vines in the study area, and then to draw pictures of the vines.

FOLLOW-UP
Have the students draw the three most common vines in New Jersey. Identify other habitats in which these plants are found. Display the drawings on a school bulletin board.

NEW JERSEY
AUDUBON
SOCIETY

Skill Activities

**Nature Orientation and Skill Activities**

**Figure 5**

Name: _____

# MOST COMMON VINES OF NEW JERSEY

WILD GRAPE (grape family)
• Fairly large, lobed, or heart-shaped leaves.
• Bark that shreds and peels easily; commonly used in bird nests.
• Large vine stems usually are unattached to tree trunks and hang freely.
• Clusters of purple fruit are eaten by birds and a variety of mammals.

POISON IVY  (cashew family)
DO NOT TOUCH
• Grows as a vine, shrub, or low-growing ground cover.
• As a vine it sends out small hair-like aerial rootlets that cling to tree bark and other upright structures.
• Has three leaflets; the end leaflet's stem is longer than those for the side leaves.
• All parts of the plant can be toxic to humans.
• Clusters of gray-green berries that ripen in the fall are food for many animals, including migrating birds.

VIRGINIA CREEPER
(grape family)
• Has five leaflets arranged in a circular design.
• Grows by sending tendrils and by aerial rootlets that have small pads at the ends.
• Has clusters of dark purplish blue berries that ripen in the fall.

© 1992 New Jersey Audubon Society

**Skill Activities**

**Bridges to the Natural World**

# HOW TO IDENTIFY A BIRD

GRADE LEVELS
1 - 6

OBJECTIVE
**To gather data for the classification of bird species.**

MATERIALS
For each student:
• Bird Data worksheet (Figure 6)
• Bird Identification Marks worksheet (Figure 7)
• clipboard
• pencil

PREPLANNING
1. Make one copy each of Figures 6 and 7 for each student in the class.
2. Make a larger teacher's copy of the Bird Data worksheet to which the students may refer. It should include the explanations of each classification category (noted below for teacher reference).
3. Arrange for a class field trip to one of the recommended habitats or set up bird feeders on the school grounds so that a variety of birds are attracted.

PROCEDURE
1. Discuss the classification categories with the class. Use the teacher's copy of the Bird Data worksheet.
2. Have the students observe at least one bird and complete the descriptions in each category. Continue making observations of other birds for comparison.
3. Using the descriptions, identify the species in a field guide to birds.

FOR TEACHER REFERENCE —
EXPLANATIONS FOR CLASSIFICATION CATEGORIES:
**Compare sizes.** Use a familiar bird for comparison: small - sparrow; medium - robin or pigeon; large - crow. Observe the new bird and compare. This bird is "larger than," "smaller than," "same as" a sparrow, or robin, or crow.

**Note shapes.** Is the bird chunky or slender? Does it have long or short legs? What shape is the bill? What shape is the tail?

**Note field marks** (Figure 7). What marks, patterns, or colors does the bird have that are unique and identifiable?

**Note flight.** What type of flying is the bird doing? Is it soaring, or undulating, or diving? Is there a pattern to its flight? For example, does it flap, sail, flap, sail?

**Note sounds.** What does the song or the call sound like?

**Note behavior.** What is the bird doing? Is it scratching on the ground or pecking at buds on a tree?

**Note site.** In what type of habitat did you see the bird? Where exactly was it? For example, a bird might be on the beach, wings tucked and facing the wind.

**Note season.** What season is it?

**Accepted species name**: What name is given to this bird in the field identification guide?

FOLLOW-UP
Keep a class list of birds observed and identified.

FOR MORE INFORMATION
Peterson, Roger Tory. *Birds of Eastern and Central North America*: Peterson Field Guide Series.

Latimer, Jonathan P. and Karen Stray Nolting. *Songbirds*: Peterson Field Guides for Young Naturalists. Note: This series also includes *Backyard Birds, Birds of Prey*, and *Shorebirds*.

**Skill Activities**

NEW JERSEY
AUDUBON
SOCIETY

**Figure 6**

Name: _____

# Bird Data

| Bird Name: | |
|---|---|
| **Size** | **Shape** |
| **Field Marks** | **Flight** |
| **Sound** | **Behavior** |
| **Site** | **Season** |

Skill Activities

**Figure 7**

Name: _____

# Bird Identification Marks

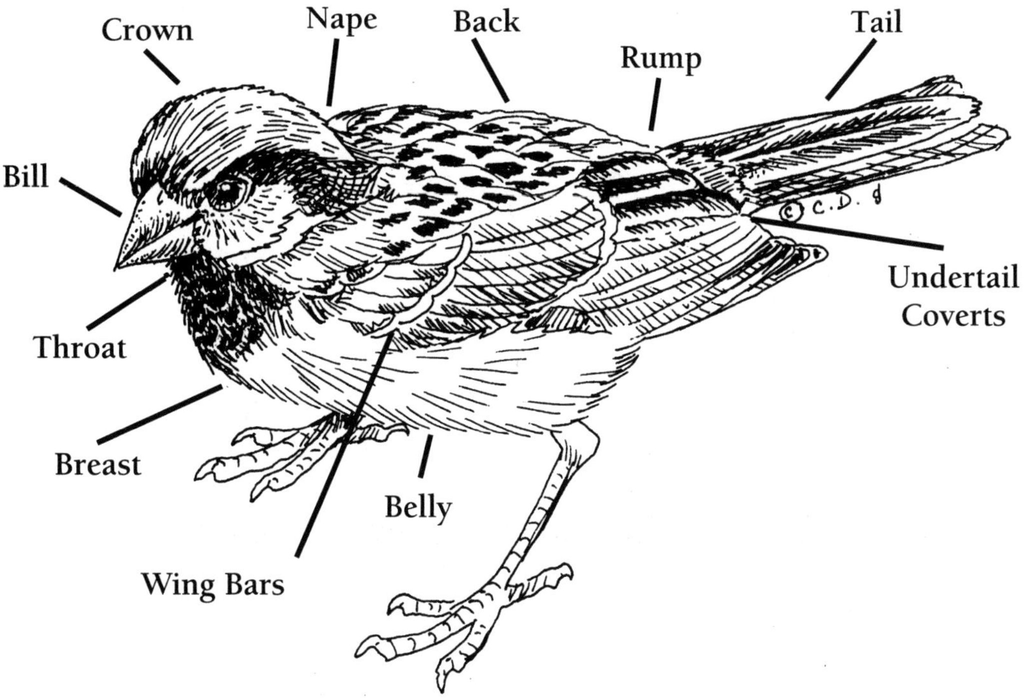

Crown    Nape    Back    Rump    Tail

Bill

Throat

Breast

Wing Bars    Belly

Undertail
Coverts

© C.D. ♂

Skill Activities

NEW JERSEY
AUDUBON
SOCIETY

Nature Orientation and Skill Activities

# HOW TO IDENTIFY A FLOWER

GRADE LEVELS
1 - 6

OBJECTIVE
**To gather data for the classification of flower species.**

MATERIALS
For each student:
- Flower Data worksheet (Figure 8)
- Flower Characteristics sheet (Figure 9)
- clipboard
- pencil

PREPLANNING
1. Make one copy each of Figures 8 and 9 for each student in the class.
2. Make a larger teacher's copy of the Flower Data worksheet (Figure 8) to which the students may refer. It should include the explanations of each classification category (noted below for teacher reference).
3. Arrange for a class field trip to one of the recommended habitats or use the school grounds.

PROCEDURE
1. Discuss the classification categories with the class. Use the teacher's copy of the Flower Data worksheet.
2. Have the students observe at least one flower and complete the descriptions in each category. Continue making observations of other flowers for comparison.
3. Using the descriptions, identify the species in a field guide to flowers.

FOR TEACHER REFERENCE –
EXPLANATIONS FOR FLOWER CLASSIFICATION CATEGORIES:

## Petal type:
- Regular – petals arranged in circular pattern around the center. Petals are the same shape and size.
- Irregular – petals are asymmetrical, may be different shapes and sizes.
- Indistinguishable – petals are too small or don't fit either of the other categories.

## Color:
Flowers run every color of the spectrum.

## Stem:
- **Texture**. Stems can be described as smooth, round, ridged, hairy, prickly, etc.
- **Flower arrangement**. Some flowers can be arranged singly on the stem. Sometimes they are in clusters along the length of the stem, or form large umbels on top of the stem.

## Leaves:
- **Leaf shape.** Leaves can be long and pointed, round, scalloped, etc.
- **Leaf texture.** Leaves can be smooth or hairy.
- **Leaf arrangement**. Leaves are arranged opposite, alternate, whorled, or wrapped around the stem (perfoliate).

**Site.** In what type of habitat did you see the flower? Where exactly was it? For example, a flower might be growing on the side of a road at the edge of a field.

**Season.** What season is it?

**Sketch/Photograph.** Naturalists identify species based on field identification sketches.

**Accepted Species Name.** What name is given in the flower field guide?

FOLLOW-UP
1. Keep a class list of flowers observed and identified.
2. Have the students draw a picture of their flower.
3. Have the students write a poem about their flower. Each line of the poem describes how the flower looks from different perspectives: from close up with hand lens, from above looking down on the flower, from eye level, and from six feet away.

FOR MORE INFORMATION
Newcomb, Lawrence. *Newcomb's Wildflower Guide.*

Zim, Herbert S., PhD. and Alexander C. Martin, PhD. *Flowers: A Golden Guide.*

NEW JERSEY
AUDUBON
SOCIETY

**Bridges to the Natural World**

Skill Activities

**Figure 8**

Name: _____

## Flower Data

| Petal type: | Color: |
|---|---|
| **Stem:**<br>  Texture:<br><br><br>  Flower Arrangement: | **Leaves on flower stem:**<br>  Shape:<br><br>  Texture:<br><br><br>  Arrangement: |

**Site:**

**Season:**

**Sketch/Photograph:**

**Accepted Species Name:**

Skill Activities

**Figure 9**

Name: _____

## Flower Characteristics

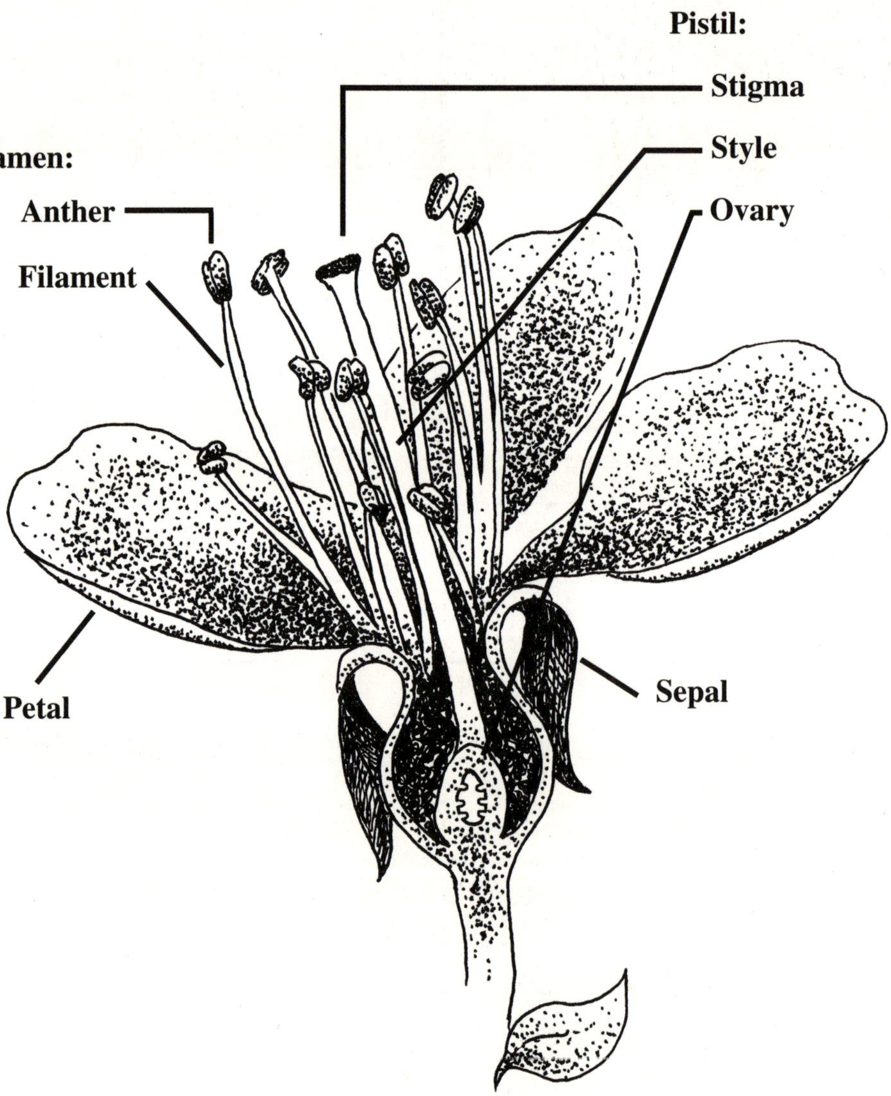

**Pistil:**

**Stigma**

**Style**

**Stamen:**

**Ovary**

**Anther**

**Filament**

**Petal**

**Sepal**

**Skill Activities**

# HOW TO IDENTIFY A BUTTERFLY OR MOTH

GRADE LEVELS
1 - 6

OBJECTIVE
**To gather data for the classification of moth and butterfly species.**

MATERIALS
For each student:
• Butterfly and Moth Data worksheet (Figure 10)
• Butterfly and Moth Identification Marks worksheet (Figure 11)
• clipboard
• pencil

PREPLANNING
1. Make one copy each of Figures 10 and 11 for each student in the class.
2. Make a larger teacher's copy of the Butterfly and Moth Data worksheet to which the students may refer. It should include the explanations of each classification category (noted below for teacher reference).
3. Arrange for a class field trip to one of the recommended habitats, school yard garden, or available open space.

PROCEDURE
1. Discuss the classification categories with the class. Use the teacher's copy of the Butterfly and Moth Data worksheet.
2. Have the students observe at least one butterfly or moth and complete the descriptions in each category. Continue making observations of other butterflies or moths for comparison.
3. Using the descriptions, identify the species in a field guide to butterflies and moths.

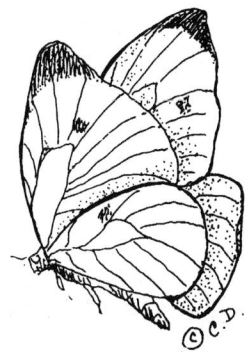

FOR TEACHER REFERENCE –
EXPLANATIONS FOR BUTTERFLY/MOTH CLASSIFICATION CATEGORIES:

**Compare sizes.** Is the butterfly/moth bigger or smaller than a penny, a quarter, the palm of your hand?

**Wing shape.** Are the wings *rounded* or *angular*?

**Field marks and colors.** What stripes, dots, or other shapes do you see on the butterfly/moth? Describe the colors you see. Which is dominant?

**Behavior.** Is the butterfly/moth nectaring, resting, or flying?

**Site.** Where did you see the butterfly/moth?

**Season.** What season is it?

**Sketch/Photograph.** Naturalists identify species based on field identification sketches.

**Accepted species name**: What name is given in the butterfly/moth field guide?

FOLLOW-UP
Keep a class list of butterflies and moths observed and identified.

FOR MORE INFORMATION
Glassberg, Jeffrey. *Butterflies through Binoculars: The East.*

Mitchell, Robert T. and Herbert S. Zim. *Butterflies and Moths*: A Golden Guide.

Latimer, Jonathan P. and Karen Stray Nolting. *Butterflies*: Peterson Field Guides for Young Naturalists.

Latimer, Jonathan P. and Karen Stray Nolting. *Caterpillars*: Peterson Field Guides for Young Naturalists.

NEW JERSEY AUDUBON SOCIETY

**Skill Activities**

**Figure 10**

Name: _____

# Butterfly and Moth Data

| Size: | Wing shape: |
|---|---|
| Field marks: | Behavior: |

Site:

Season:

Sketch/Photograph:

Accepted Species Name:

Skill Activities

Figure 11

Name: _____

# Butterfly and Moth Characteristics

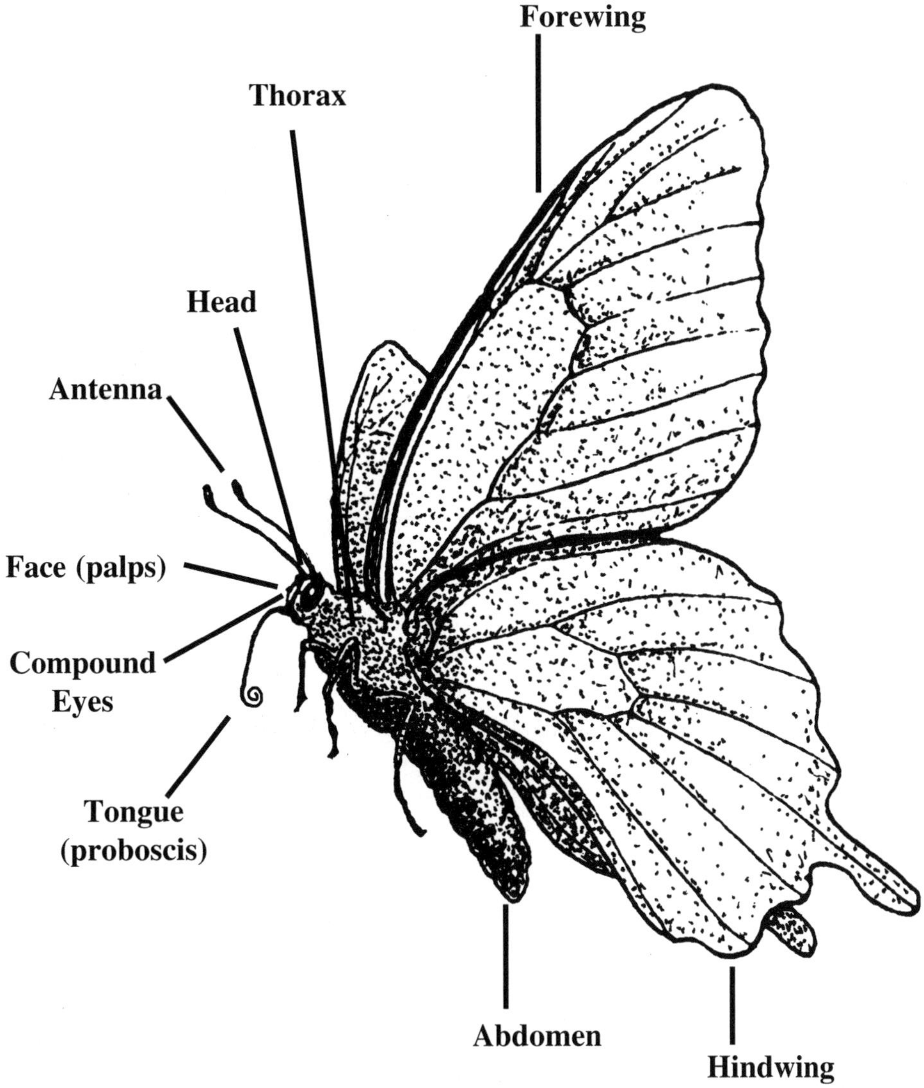

**Forewing**

**Thorax**

**Head**

**Antenna**

**Face (palps)**

**Compound Eyes**

**Tongue (proboscis)**

**Abdomen**

**Hindwing**

Skill Activities

# CREATING A DICHOTOMOUS KEY

## GRADE LEVELS
1 - 6

## OBJECTIVE
**To classify objects by distinctive characteristics.**

## BACKGROUND INFORMATION
A dichotomous key provides a method for distinguishing between species of animals or plants. An observer creates a dichotomous key by separating species initially into two all-inclusive categories according to distinctive characteristics. These categories are then repeatedly subdivided so as to more specifically describe the initial categories.

## MATERIALS
• chalkboard
• chalk
• Making A Dichotomous Key (Figure 13)*

## PREPLANNING
1. Assemble the class in an area where they can all stand in a large group.

2. Tell the students they will be learning how to create a dichotomous key, which is a tool that people use to help organize scientific information so it can be identified more easily.

3. Lead the students through this process in the following way:
   A. Ask the students to divide themselves into two groups. The two groups must include all students. (For example: boys and girls, or people with shoelaces and no shoelaces.) The categories must always be observable. Qualities such as age, virtues, etc., do not apply.
   B. Ask each group to divide itself into two subgroups. Each subgroup must include all members of the main group. Let the students decide on the criteria. (For example: boys with brown eyes and boys with different eye color or girls with slacks and girls with dresses.) Call on each group to define themselves by the criteria.

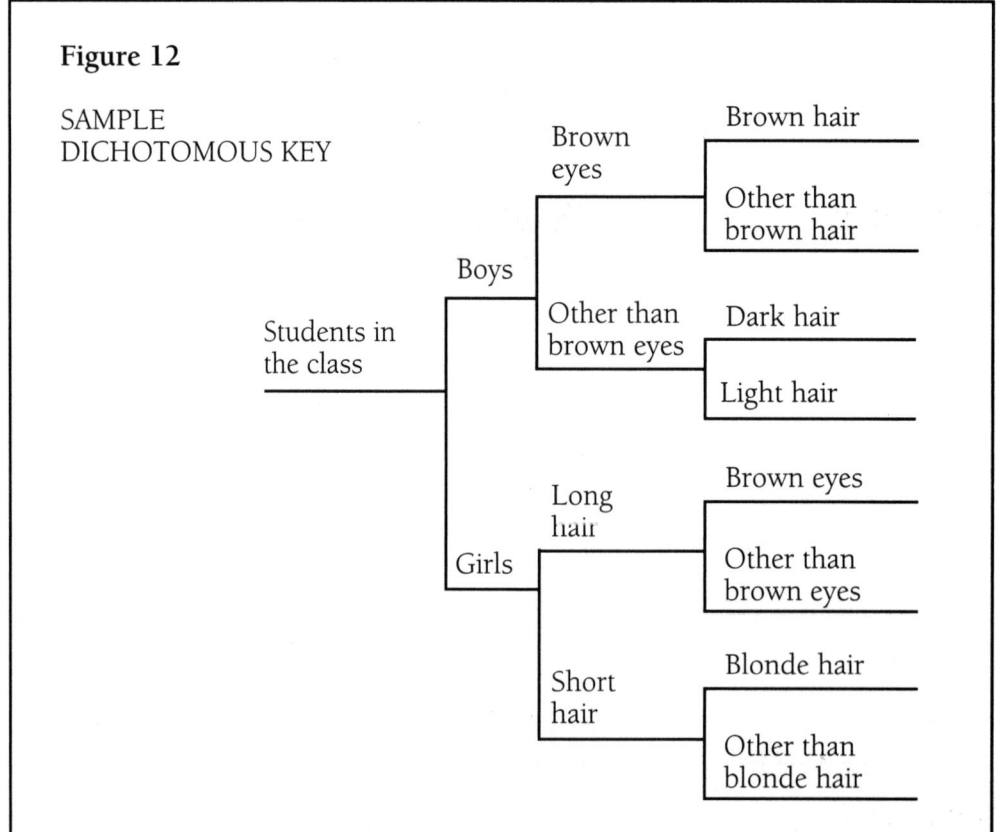

**Figure 12**

SAMPLE
DICHOTOMOUS KEY

C. Each of these subgroups must divide into two more subgroups. As before, these smaller groups must contain all members. (For example: brown-eyed boys with button shirts and those with no-button shirts.) Again, have the groups define themselves by the criteria they have chosen.

4. On the chalkboard, create the dichotomous key using the divisions that the students made.

5. To practice further, divide the students again by a different observable characteristic. Allow the groups to divide themselves again and have the opposite teams try to determine the physical feature that divides them. Continue with one or two more divisions.

(See Figure 12 for a sample dichotomous key for this activity.)

FOLLOW-UP
LEAF KEY
1. Have each student collect eight different leaves from the ground. (This activity works well in autumn.)

2. Provide each student with a blank dichotomous key (Figure 13).

3. Guide the students into creating a key for their leaves in the following way:
A. Divide your eight leaves into two categories of your choice. Base your decision on the leaves' characteristics. (E.g., leaves may be divided into groups by color, shape, texture, size, etc.) Write a simple description of each category on the lines marked #1.
B. Look at each of your main groups of leaves separately. Take each group and divide it into two subgroups. Write these descriptions on the lines marked #2.
C. If possible, divide each of these subgroups one more time. Write these descriptions on the lines marked #3.

SCHOOL YARD IDENTIFICATION KEY
Challenge the students to create a dichotomous key for the school grounds. Ask them to follow these steps:

1. Collect a sample leaf from the different trees on the property.

2. Identify each leaf using a tree identification guide.

3. Create a key using the categories suggested in the activity Leaves on Parade (p. 165).

NEW JERSEY AUDUBON SOCIETY

Figure 13

Name: _____

# MAKING A DICHOTOMOUS KEY

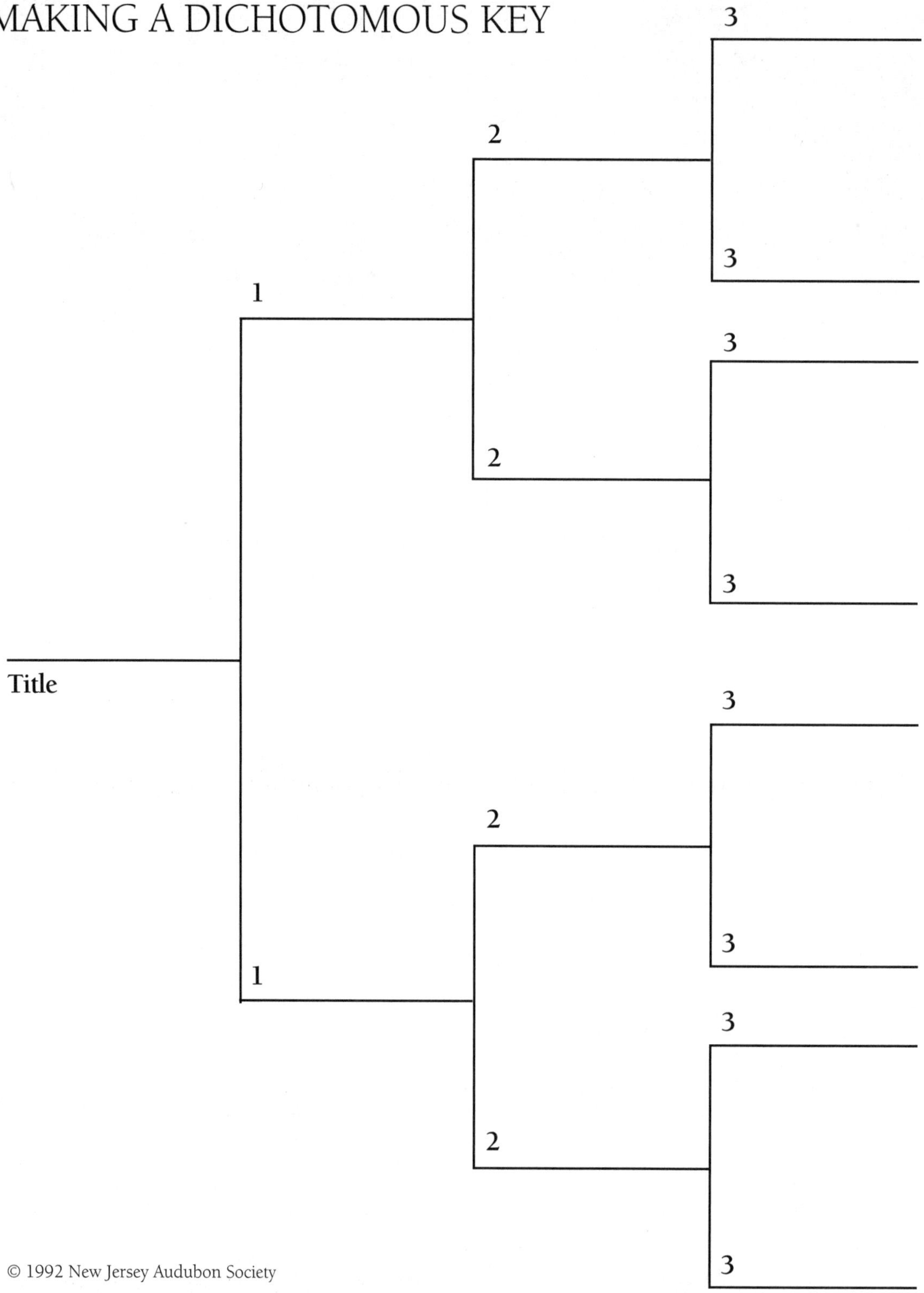

Title

1

2

3

3

2

3

3

1

2

3

3

2

3

3

Skill Activities

# FUNGUS HUNT

## GRADE LEVELS
4 - 6

## OBJECTIVE
**To recognize fungi and understand their role as decomposers.**

## BACKGROUND INFORMATION
Fungus is the most common type of decomposer. Because a fungus contains none of the green pigment chlorophyll, it cannot make its own food. Instead, a fungus gets nourishment by releasing chemicals that digest the organic material on which it grows.

Fungi occur in a variety of forms, including the familiar toadstools, puffballs as small as a dime or as large as a football, shelf fungus on tree trunks, molds on food, and netted fungus under tree bark. Any moist, organic (living or once-living) surface provides an excellent habitat for fungus. By contrast, dry, sandy habitats retard fungus growth and decomposition takes place much more slowly.

## MATERIALS
For each student:
• one 5 x 8 file card
• one 6-inch ruler
• pencil

## PREPLANNING
Select a natural, somewhat moist area where the students can spread out and do their own searching for a variety of fungi.

## PROCEDURE
1. Tell the class that they are going to explore the role of fungi in decomposition.
2. Have each student prepare a file card to resemble Figure 14.
3. Walk to the selected area and encourage the students to use their observation skills to locate different fungi to share with the group. **Remind the students that they are not to pick or damage the fungi.**

4. Discuss the natural process of decomposition. Note the spongy texture of decomposing wood.
5. Have each student locate, draw, and record the measurements of three species of fungi.
6. Bring the class together. Allow the students to share their findings.

## FOLLOW-UP
Return to the same site three weeks later. Which fungi remain and which have disappeared? What new fungi have appeared?

## Figure 14
# Fungi I.D.

| 1. |
| --- |
| 2. |
| 3. |

Name:

Skill Activities

NEW JERSEY
AUDUBON
SOCIETY

# WHAT IS A LICHEN?

GRADE LEVELS
4 - 6

OBJECTIVE
**To recognize the symbiotic relationship between fungi and algae that creates lichens.**

BACKGROUND INFORMATION
Lichen is composed of two plants: a fungus and an alga. The two plants work together to produce a mutually beneficial situation called a symbiotic relationship. The fungus, a nongreen plant, provides the moist structure that enables the lichen to adhere to a surface. The alga, a green plant, provides the chlorophyll that produces food for the lichen. Most lichens are very sensitive to air pollution. Generally, lichens have not been studied as comprehensively as many other families of plants. Therefore, very few lichens have standard common names. To minimize confusion most scientists refer to lichens by their scientific name. Lichens are divided into three main groups according to structure:

CRUCTOSE:  Lichens that grow tightly pressed against rocks and other surfaces and look crusty. Examples:
* *Zoned lichen* looks like a gray target-shaped smudge on rocks.
* *Pearl button lichen* looks like a white stain on rocks.

FOLIOSE:  Lichens that adhere to surfaces but tend to grow in thicker mats or look leafy. Examples:
* *Green shield lichen* almost always grows on deciduous trees and is a mat of light green, mossy-looking lichen.
* *Rock tripe* is a leathery, leafy lichen that grows on rocks.

FRUTICOSE:  Lichens that tend to look branched and hang from trees or grow on land. Examples:
* *British Soldiers lichen* grows in mats on the ground or on decaying logs. It is characterized by a light green stem with a tip of red.
* *Old man's beard lichen* is a feathery light green lichen which hangs from tree branches.

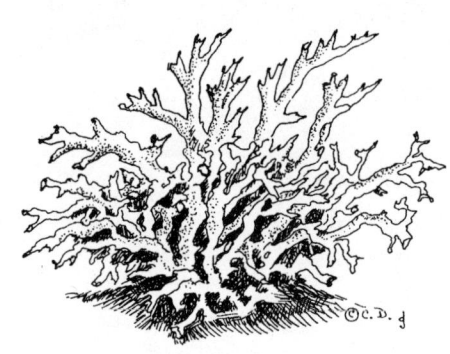

MATERIALS
For each student:
* magnifying glass
* Lichen Discovery worksheet (Figure 15)

SITE
Forest habitat or other area where a variety of lichens are present.

PREPLANNING
1. Schedule a field trip.
2. Copy Figure 15 for each student.

PROCEDURE
1. Tell the students the following story:

*THE STORY OF FRANNIE AND AL*
*This is the story about Frannie Fungus and Al Alga. Now, Frannie Fungus was an excellent carpenter. She took great pride in building wonderful and sturdy structures. And Al Alga, well, Al was a world-class chef. He enjoyed cooking all different types of dishes.*

*One day Frannie and Al met each other and took an immediate "lichen" (pronounced li-ken) to each other. They decided to spend the rest of their lives together. So, Frannie built and maintained their home while Al spent his time preparing all their meals. (Source unknown)*

2. Discuss the definition of lichen.

3. Tell the students that they will be looking for examples of lichens during their investigations and recording their findings on the lichen discovery sheet.

FOR MORE INFORMATION
Alexander, Taylor R., R. Will Burnett, and Herbert S. Zim. *Botany.*

NEW JERSEY
AUDUBON
SOCIETY

Skill Activities

**Figure 15**

**Name:** _____

# LICHEN DISCOVERY

Use your magnifying glass to look at lichens. Name each lichen you find based on the lichen's visual characteristics. Draw a picture of the lichen and write its name in the appropriate box.

CRUCTOSE LICHENS grow tightly against rocks and other surfaces. They look crusty.

FOLIOSE LICHENS grow on many surfaces. They tend to grow in thick mats or are leafy.

FRUTICOSE LICHENS are many-branched. They hang from trees or grow on land.

© 1992 New Jersey Audubon Society

NEW JERSEY
AUDUBON
SOCIETY

# DEVELOPING AN ENVIRONMENTAL ETHIC

Skill Activities

## GIANT THOUGHTLESS

GRADE LEVELS
Pre-K - 2

OBJECTIVE
**Provide a model for behavior while investigating a habitat.**

PRE-PLANNING
This story can be told at the habitat site or before an outdoor investigation.

## *GIANT THOUGHTLESS*

*Once upon a time there was a small village nestled in a valley between two great mountains. It was a beautiful place where the people were very happy. The villagers had small patches of garden in their yards where they grew every kind of fruit and vegetable. Children played and danced in the streets without fear. Men and women whistled and sang as they went about their daily business. In the evenings and on holidays, everyone came to the square in the center of the town to play games and tell stories. They all knew each other and they all helped each other. No one was ever in need.*

*On the far side of one of the great mountains lived a huge giant. When he stood tall, he nearly reached the top of the highest trees. He was a playful fellow, full of curiosities and great energy. Every morning, no matter what the weather, he would hike all over his side of the mountain. He hopped across streams, waded through the rivers, and shook the branches of huge trees, his huge feet thumping across the land. His days were full of marvelous discoveries and happy adventures.*

*One day in the spring, the giant woke up, rubbed his eyes and said to himself, "I have explored every part of this whole mountainside. I wonder what I would find if I climbed over the top?" After he ate his breakfast and washed his face in the river, he started up the mountain. Up, up, up he went, over rocks and boulders. It seemed as though he would touch the sky itself. At last he stood at the top and Thoughtless gave out a roar of delight, for he was certain that he was the first to have climbed so high. "Hurray for me! Hurray for me!" he shouted and waved his arms. His long shadow stretched down the mountain for many miles. At the foot of the mountain in the small village the people stood in shocked amazement. They had never before seen or heard such a large fellow. The giant gazed all around the countryside and finally his eyes rested on the people of the small village.*

*"Ohh ho," he roared. "What is this?" His curiosity sent him bounding down the mountain to the village. KA-BOOM, KA-BOOM, KA-BOOM, and BOOM! Down he came with such a noise that the children of the village froze in terror. Mothers and fathers snatched them up and ran for the shelter of the houses. They slammed shutters and stood*

NEW JERSEY
AUDUBON
SOCIETY

**Bridges to the Natural World**

behind locked doors armed with guns and pitchforks. With a great KA-BOOM, the giant landed on the bottom of the valley. He gazed at the village, which was now silent and still. "Aww. Where did they all go? I wanted to play with them," he said sorrowfully. The giant began to crawl about the streets of the village looking for the little people. He poked his finger in every opening he could find. He turned over horse carts, shook bins and boxes, and crunched small things that he didn't even see. The people trembled behind the doors, too afraid to go out and chase away the creature that was so destructive.

Thoughtless sat in the village square scratching his head and tapping on the roofs of the houses. Then he got an idea. He lay down in the middle of the village square, and brought his eye close to a window of one of the little houses. With his fingernail he pried open a squeaky shutter and peered inside. There, under a tiny bed, was a girl child of the little people. The giant reached inside and with one finger drew her out from under the bed. He lifted Awaria into the sunlight and placed her on his giant hand. The little girl began to kick, scratch, and punch every part of the giant that she could reach. Awaria screamed and shook her fists at him and bit him hard on the thumb.

"Ow," shouted the Giant, as he shook the little girl off his hand onto a pile of hay. "What did you do that for?"

"What for? What fooor! You drag me out of my house, lift me up into your hand, scare me half to death and when I bite you, you ask what for? What would you do if someone a zillion times bigger than you came to your house and did that to you?"

"But I didn't mean any harm. I was just playing."

"Just playing? Look what you did! You have destroyed a whole week's work by upsetting all of those boxes and bins. The carts are broken into pieces, half the roofs in town will have to be replaced, and you knocked off porches and knocked down street lamps. You've terrorized everyone in town, and YOU are just playing? You break things before you even know what they are for or what they mean. Don't you have any respect for other people's belongings?"

The giant's eyes filled with tears and he began to cry. "I only wanted to play. I only want to find out about things. I want everybody to like me and be friendly."

"Good grief," said Awaria. "Stop crying. You are getting me all wet." Each giant-sized tear was equal to a tub full of water and she was afraid he might cause a flood. "If you want to be a friend, you should come quietly the first time, come and ask to see, be gentle when you are in our village. Watch out where you put those big feet! Don't break things when you don't even know what they are. If you are polite, you will be a much better friend."

"Ooh," whimpered the giant as he wiped the last tear from his eyes.

In the following days, the giant returned, but this time he was different. He helped them rebuild their village by carrying wood and helping to make bricks. He enjoyed many happy days playing with the little people and watching them at play. He came often, but he came quietly and he was much, much more polite.

After a while the people changed his name from Giant Thoughtless to Giant Thoughtful.

— by Patricia Kane

THOUGHTFUL QUESTIONS
1. What happened in the story that disturbed the lives of the people? (The giant destroyed part of the village.)
2. Was Thoughtless an evil giant? Was he deliberately hurtful? (No, he didn't understand that he was causing harm.)
3. What did Awaria do when Thoughtless plucked her from under her bed? (She scratched and kicked and bit him.)
4. What did Awaria say to Thoughtless that let him know he did something wrong? (You break things before you even know what they are for or what they mean.)
5. Did the story have a happy ending? Explain. (Yes, the giant helped rebuild the village and after that was more careful.)
6. How could we be like Giant Thoughtless when we visit a wild area? (We are bigger than many of the creatures living there. We can destroy things that they work hard to create in order to live.)
7. Let's describe a way to act when we visit nature's house outdoors. (Walk carefully, don't poke fingers or sticks into small holes, leave the area the way you found it.)

NEW JERSEY
AUDUBON
SOCIETY

# SAFE HABITAT SPACES

GRADE LEVELS
Pre-K - 6

OBJECTIVE
**To develop an attitude of respect for all living things and their life support systems**

MATERIALS
• none required

PREPLANNING
Schedule a field trip to one of the habitat sites.

PROCEDURE
Before directing the students in exploration activities, use the following analogy to motivate behavior toward demonstrating a concern for living things.

How many of you know how to play baseball? Suppose you just hit the ball out into the field. What will you do next? (Run to first base.) Why do you run to the *base*? (The player is safe when he or she is on the base.) A base, then, is a safe place. You can't be put out of the game as long as you are on base. That's what a wildlife sanctuary is, a safe place for wildlife and all that the wildlife need in order to live and grow and reproduce others of their own kind. Remember that the plants and animals are protected. People come to sanctuaries to learn about nature, but not to change it. Most changes in a sanctuary are made by time and weather.

# COLLECTING SAMPLES

GRADE LEVELS
Pre-K - 6

OBJECTIVE
**Develop an attitude of concern for living things.**

MATERIALS
• none required

PREPLANNING
When visiting a nature center or wildlife sanctuary, one often will see a sign that says:

### TAKE ONLY MEMORIES
### AND LEAVE ONLY FOOTSTEPS

With the heavy use that most of these areas experience it would be detrimental if visitors took samples of plant life or wildlife.

PROCEDURE
Instruct the students to observe, describe, or sketch living organisms on-site rather than collect them. Nonliving objects and ground litter (fallen leaves, seeds, cones) may be taken for collections with the approval of the teacher/naturalist or park ranger.

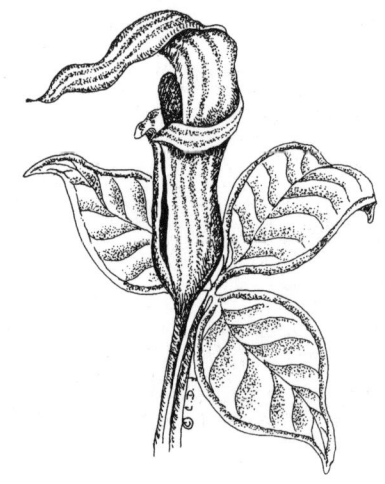

# TURNING LOGS AND ROCKS

## GRADE LEVELS
Pre-K - 6

## OBJECTIVE
**Develop an attitude of respect for all living creatures and for the habitats in which we find them.**

## BACKGROUND INFORMATION
There are many creatures that spend their entire life cycle underground. Turning a rock or a log is like opening the door to their micro-habitat. While we observe to learn, it is important that we cause as little disturbance as possible.

## MATERIALS
• none required

## PREPLANNING
Schedule a field trip to an area that has rocks or fallen logs on the ground.

## PROCEDURE
1. Grasp the log or rock from the farthest side and pull it toward you.
2. Observe the behavior of the animals you find: small creatures such as centipedes, millipedes, and sow bugs; also, slugs, earthworms, spiders, ants, and salamanders.
3. Replace the log or rock gently to the original spot. Pull leaves around the edges to add insulation.

# CRAWLIES IN THE HAND

## GRADE LEVELS
Pre-K - 6

## OBJECTIVE
**Handle small animals with care and concern for their well-being.**

## PROCEDURE
Handling small animals such as spiders, worms, sow bugs, and salamanders should be entirely voluntary. Students who choose to hold these animals should be careful not to mutilate them in any way. Allow the animal some movement in the hands.

If the creature is to be viewed by the entire class, it is better to put it in an observation container and pass it around than to pass it from one hand to another. (See "Making Field Study and Nature Investigation Tools" p. 299.)

Students who have sprayed insect repellant on their hands should not be allowed to handle small creatures. The chemicals in the repellant could be fatal to animals with which they come in contact.

Skill Activities

**Nature Orientation and Skill Activities**

# THE EARTH AS AN APPLE
(Author unknown)

GRADE LEVELS
4 - 6

OBJECTIVE
**Demonstrate the need for conservation of resources that sustain life**

MATERIALS
• apple
• paring knife

PREPLANNING
This teacher-led demonstration can be done in the classroom.

PROCEDURE
Say to the students, "Consider the earth as an apple."

1. Slice the apple into quarters. Set aside three of the quarters. "These represent the oceans of the world. The fourth quarter roughly represents the total land area that remains."

2. Slice this land quarter in half, giving you two 1/8th world pieces. Set aside one of the pieces. "This land is inhospitable to people: the polar areas, deserts, swamps, very high or rocky mountainous areas. The other 1/8th piece is the land area where people live, but not necessarily where they grow the foods needed for life."

3. Now slice this 1/8th piece into four sections, giving you four 1/32nd pieces. Set aside three of these pieces. "These are areas too rocky, too wet, too cold, too steep, or with soil too poor to actually produce food; they include the areas of land that have been used for highways, suburban developments, shopping centers, and other structures that people have built."

4. This leaves us with a 1/32nd slice of the earth. Carefully peel this slice. "This tiny bit of peeling represents the surface, the very skin of the earth's crust upon which humans depend. Less than five feet deep, it is a fixed amount of food-producing land."

5. "Now you realize that protecting our land resources is important too. Advanced agricultural technology has enabled the world to feed many of its people, but erosion, pollution, and overdevelopment are an abuse of our soil resources. We must protect the environmental quality of our air, water, and land."

FOLLOW-UP
Find out what soil conservation programs there are in your county.

*Skill Activities*

# NOTES

# NOTES

NEW JERSEY
AUDUBON
SOCIETY

**Bridges to the Natural World**

*Bridges to the Natural World*

Section 4

# HELPFUL HINTS

## FOR OUTDOOR NATURE AND ECOLOGY INVESTIGATIONS

Helpful Hints

# HOW TO USE THIS SECTION

"If a child is to keep an inborn sense of wonder without any such gift from the fairies, there needs to be the companionship of at least one adult who can share it, rediscovering the joy, excitement and mystery of the world we live in."

This bit of wisdom is taken from Rachel Carson's *The Sense of Wonder*. It sprang from her profound love of the earth, which she shared with her nephew, Roger, on so many excursions into wild places.

Children have a natural curiosity for the world around them. They find fascination in the wanderings of insects. There is intimacy with the land through exploration of small places. Allowed to wander, they create their own learning experiences. What is more important, they establish a connection with the natural world that provides a stability which cannot be taught and which sustains them through life's journey.

A few summers ago, two children were observed playing in a stream. The boy hopped over rocks and gazed into a pool where he found a frog. The girl, stooped at the muddy edge, dipped her finger into the bottom of the water, creating circular cloud patterns of mud. Both were intent and very quiet, steeped in their own fascinations. From the path above their mother shouted, "Come up here. There are a bunch of plants with all the names written on them. You could learn something." Obediently, they clambered up to the path, but the look of disappointment spoke of different lessons that met an untimely end.

Real life is not held within four walls. It is uncontained and spontaneous. While we depend on technology to control much of our indoor climate and provide us with instant information, our five senses are still our fundamental learning tools. In their developmental process, there is no better arena than the outdoors for honing observation skills, expanding imagination, applying and exercising critical thinking.

"...There is a sense of continuity and truth in the world of nature. Although a changing balance constantly presents us with newness, nature still functions according to the same laws that have ruled the wilds for centuries. Go outside. Take your group with you, and if anyone asks you why you are going out, reply that the outdoors is where life is, and where learning should take place."

*From an Anonymous Source*

This section is divided into the things you may want to consider when taking students into the outdoor classroom.

HOW TO USE THE SCHOOL GROUNDS AS AN OUTDOOR CLASSROOM
Onsite schoolyard investigation allows the teacher to be flexible in presenting content and giving ongoing discovery experiences rather than waiting for the next field trip.

NATURAL COMMUNITY LEARNING LOOPS
Create a learning circle that enables students to build on existing knowledge, experience new discoveries, and transfer that knowledge to new situations.

HOW TO KEEP A JOURNAL
Journals can be an effective method for assessing student understanding and growth.

Helpful Hints

NEW JERSEY
AUDUBON
SOCIETY

SAFETY IN THE OUTDOOR CLASSROOM
Preparation is the best prevention of problems in the outdoors. Following outdoor investigation guidelines can help avoid discomfort or injury.

MAKING FIELD STUDY AND NATURE INVESTIGATION TOOLS
Household throw-aways and recyclables become useful and inexpensive tools.

TEACHER AND STUDENT ASSESSMENT
*Rubrics*
Gauging the immediate effectiveness of the lessons and activities in *Bridges to the Natural World* may be a challenging endeavor due to the spontaneity of outdoor investigations. Evaluation tools for the teacher and the student in the form of rubrics help assess whether the objectives of the outdoor activity were achieved.

*I Can Teach Myself (KWL Chart)*
Give students a chance to take responsibility for their own learning by having them list what they already know, what they want to learn, and after the field trip, what they actually learned.

TECHNO-TIPS
Suggestions for enhancing and sharing the outdoor experience using technology.

# HOW TO USE THE SCHOOL GROUNDS AS AN OUTDOOR CLASSROOM

If the school grounds have never been used as a learning area, the transition from classroom to outdoor teaching can be a dramatic change for any teacher regardless of the student's age or grade level. Loss of ability to discipline and inability to identify flora and fauna are the two main reasons why most teachers do not go outside to teach.

From their earliest training children are taught the difference between inside and outside behavior. Inside is for restrained activity and quiet conversational tones; outside is for large muscle exercise and loud vocal exclamations. At school, children go outside for recess or to abandon restrained classroom behavior, and for most, the thought of going outside for lessons is as alien as food shopping in a farmer's field. In addition, the culture of our society regards the natural world as a place to be used, controlled, or manipulated. The time it will take to overcome these attitudes will vary with each class, but recognizing that they exist is half the battle.

No teacher should be intimidated by the size and complexity of the outdoors. Everything out there *does* have a name, but triple doctorates in botany, zoology, and ecology are not necessary to teach some of the basic concepts. "I don't know" is a perfectly acceptable answer to "What is that?" Better still, "I don't know, but I wonder why it is here?" puts the question to both teacher and student, leading into a dialogue of "how come," "why," "what if," and "suppose." Of course there is always a guide book for identification, but knowing the names of things is not as interesting or as important as knowing about them: what they need, what makes them flourish, why they live in this particular place. It's like getting to know new friends: we are not attracted by a name as much as we are by unique characteristics, behavior, or similar interests.

Any field trip to the schoolyard can be successful, and the secret to that success is preparation.

PRETRIP ORIENTATION
Lead a classroom discussion on going outdoors to learn about nature. This can be started by using the story "Giant Thoughtless," found on p. 282 or by getting the students to describe how they act when visiting someone's house for the first time. Start by discussing their arrival at the front door. (Knock or ring the bell and wait for someone to open the door and invite you in.) Continue with a tour of the house, an invitation to play a game, and maybe have some refreshments. At each place, have the students give their interpretation of polite behavior. At the end, ask what they would do with someone who came into their house without knocking, who went through the house helping themselves to food in the refrigerator, who dumped clothes out of drawers and closets, or who broke games and toys because they didn't understand their proper use. When there is agreement on good visiting behavior, say, "Going outside to explore nature is much like visiting someone's house. Everything means something, has a purpose. Just because we do not understand it or don't like it doesn't mean it is useless. Each person has the power to be a destroyer of life or a nurturer of life. The choice is yours, but you have to live with that choice." Make it clear that each child is to make a silent decision and that you do not want to know the answer.

NEW JERSEY
AUDUBON
SOCIETY

**Helpful Hints for Outdoor Nature and Ecology Investigations**

## INITIAL OUTDOOR EXPERIENCE

Choose an activity from the Natural History Lessons in Section Two or from the list of Transition Activities in Section Three. The importance of the initial activity is to draw the student's attention immediately to a specific task that will involve as many of the senses as possible. During this first experience some classes will be able to focus for only 20 minutes. That's fine. If the class seems unable to focus on the activity you have selected, it is better to do only part of the activity and return to the classroom than continue with constant admonition. A good rule of thumb is that it is always better to bring the class inside while interest is high rather than push toward a conclusion when enthusiasm has waned.

A note of caution: Suppose you have planned your schoolyard field trip for a specific day. You are well prepared. The children are prepared. The day arrives and the fire department makes a surprise visit complete with fire drills. After the drills it is time for your class to go to lunch, then recess. Later in the afternoon an unscheduled assembly program occurs. Please cancel your field trip. It is better to wait for a more normal school day to initiate outdoor teaching. The main point in this transition process is take your time and don't hurry the children.

## HOW TO MAKE UP YOUR OWN QUESTIONS

It would be a mistake to think that naming the plants and animals is all that is needed to know and understand our natural world and the systems that sustain life on this planet. Describing and naming is only the first step toward understanding. Just as our human relationships develop and are enriched by repeated interactions in different circumstances, so too our understanding of natural communities evolves from seeing the plants and animals within the context of all the interdependencies of their life cycles.

Questions that involve simple "Yes" or "No" answers, or one-word naming answers, are necessary for getting started, just as our, "Hi, my name is ," gets us introduced in social settings.

Questions that are directed to behaviors, foods, and types of shelter, or that compare similarities and differences are more likely to lead students to use the critical thinking skills that help them make evaluations and judgments.

Questions about the habitat –
  Think of yourself as a plant or animal living here. What is it like to live here?
  What do you have to like or be able to tolerate?
  How are you structured to get the things you need?
Other thought starters –
Allow the children to make up a question about each habitat you visit that begins with:
  What if all the...
  Why isn't...
  Where would...
  Suppose the...
  When did the...

## FIELD TRIPS FOR DISCOVERY AND INVESTIGATION

Determine the natural community type(s) that can be found on the school grounds by reading through Section One, Habitats of New Jersey. Begin to journal each area or choose activities from other sections of the manual.

Helpful Hints

# NATURAL COMMUNITY LEARNING LOOPS

Learning in the outdoors is an ongoing process focused on the ecological systems and interdependencies found within natural communities. The fundamental concepts taught and developed through the lessons and activities have relevance only if they loop back and connect to the context in which they are learned; that is, the natural community.

The habitat of a plant or animal is an important natural science concept, but it loses much of its meaning if taught as separate from the myriad interdependent relationships in the larger community. Just as people can't exist in a meaningful way apart from human support systems, plants and animals with all their behaviors and adaptations should be taught within the context of the systems that sustain them.

The following outline is offered as a framework for planning the outdoor lessons. Remember, *less is more*. It is better to teach one concept well than rush through many.

## SENSORY INVESTIGATION

### Experience
- Engage students in a personal way. Relate learning activities to past personal experiences.
- Provide experience *before* instruction. Offer simple, necessary directions, but save lectured explanations about nature.
- Allow students to make personal responses.

### Reflection
- Share personal perceptions of the experiences.
- Summarize and compare similarities and differences of perception and opinion.
- Clarify reasons for learning about this place.

## MAKING CONNECTIONS

### Conceptualization
- Blend the affective with the cognitive by alternating experiences that use both convergent and divergent thinking skills. This deepens the connection between the concept and the learners' life.
- Offer a brief, sequential explanation of facts that tie the experiences back to the reason for the study, the natural community. Don't overwhelm students with a lot of information.

### Application
- Encourage students to organize what they learn and share new discoveries.
- Facilitate transfer of knowledge by connecting students' exploratory experiences and findings to other disciplines.
- Be open to opportunities for students to apply the skills and knowledge gained to life outside of school.

Helpful Hints

NEW JERSEY
AUDUBON
SOCIETY

Helpful Hints for Outdoor Nature and Ecology Investigations

# NATURAL COMMUNITY LEARNING LOOPS

Helpful Hints

# HOW TO KEEP A JOURNAL

Keeping a record of observations can play a significant role in helping students remember what was unique about each habitat or study site. It is recommended that a portion of the time spent at each site be given to creating a journal. Drawing or writing in nature provides a personal, illustrated record of a special event in the student's life and reinforces a sense of place and belonging. Nature becomes the teacher; unfolding lessons that can be taught only when paying careful attention to lines that define an object or choosing words that describe a scene.

### Ideally...

Each student should have a pencil, paper, and a clipboard. At a given signal, they disperse within a designated area and are allowed to spend time alone, reflecting and recording. The teacher circulates among the students, offering assistance as needed.

### But if time is limited...

After a habitat site has been visited the teacher directs the students to reflect on the experience.

Suggestions:
>  What animals were seen?
>  What were they doing?
>  What plants were seen?
>  How were they arranged?
>  Describe something that was: beautiful, ugly, joyous, scary, familiar,
>       comforting, disturbing.
>  Why will your visit to this habitat be memorable?

If you are using the journal as part of the Habitat Passport program, include at least one full page of reflection for each habitat, or each session on the study area. Reflections may be written, drawn, or used in combination. Duplications of the illustrations and lists of flora and fauna may be copied and distributed to the students, but they should not be part of the journal submitted afterwards.*

Journals submitted for New Jersey Audubon Society's JUNIOR NATURALIST CERTIFICATE must have a cover sheet that includes the student's name. Teachers submitting journals from a full class should include a typed list with all student names, and the name of the school as it should appear on the award. Journals will be returned to the students after review. **Please include a check for $5 (payable to NJAS) for return postage.**

*Copies made for student use do not violate the copyright.

NEW JERSEY
AUDUBON
SOCIETY

# SAFETY IN THE OUTDOOR CLASSROOM

Preparation is the best prevention of problems in the outdoors. With a few precautions most people are able to explore the outdoors without fear or anxiety. We don't need to be *afraid* as much as we need to have *respect* for nature and wildlife.

**Dress**
In field, forest, or grassy areas in New Jersey:
• Long pants tucked into socks will protect skin from scratches and insect bites.
• Light colors are helpful for spotting any insects that might decide to explore people.
• Long-sleeved shirts minimize exposure to thorns and insects.
• A hat or bandanna deters insects from hiding on the scalp.

PLANTS – DO'S AND DON'TS

*Poison Ivy* - The most common poisonous plant in New Jersey is Poison Ivy (p. 86). It can be found in almost any habitat in the state and grows as a ground plant, vine, and shrub. Birds eat its berries and deposit the seeds in their droppings. All parts of the plant that come in contact with a person who is allergic can produce an itchy rash. Proper clothing can help a person avoid contact, but if contact is suspected, wash with brown soap or detergent as soon as possible to minimize the spreading of the oil which produces the rash. Poison ivy oil remains on clothing, so that too should be washed out with detergent.

Mushrooms, berries, other plants and their products (seeds, flowers, etc.) The best rule is, DON'T EAT IT. Unless you have a teacher or naturalist with you who identifies the plant and gives permission to taste, there is risk involved. Most of these plants are not fatally poisonous, but they can cause discomfort. It is best not to take any chances.

WILD ANIMALS

No matter how cute the chipmunk, raccoon, or squirrel may appear, NEVER TRY TO HOLD, PET, OR FEED A WILD ANIMAL. If a wild animal appears to be tame or friendly it is either an inexperienced young of the species or a sick animal.
1. Human handling of a healthy adult or baby wild animal is stressful to the animal.
2. Human handling of a sickly wild animal may invite bites or scratches that could be infectious to the human.

For further information about humans and wild animals, see *About Orphaned and Injured Animals* in the appendix of this book.

For information about Lyme Disease or rabies contact:
New Jersey Department of Health,
Environmental Health Services
CN 360
Trenton, NJ 08625-0360
(609) 633-2043

NEW JERSEY
AUDUBON
SOCIETY

Helpful Hints

# MAKING FIELD STUDY AND NATURE INVESTIGATION TOOLS:
# HOW TO GIVE THROW-AWAYS A SECOND CHANCE

## CARDBOARD MILK CARTONS
(half-gallon size)

STUDY SITE
Land or water

PREPARATION
Staple the spout shut. Cut out one of the side panels 1/4 inch from the edge to retain the stability of the carton.

USES
**Planter** - Gather seeds from weedy places in the school yard, take a handful of birdseed, plant them in potting soil and see what comes up.

**Observation box** - holds crawling insects, worms, salamanders, small reptiles or, with water, aquatic creatures. Place the animal in the box and pass it around for all to see. This is safer and less stressful for the creature observed.

## CARDBOARD PANELS
(from the milk cartons)

STUDY SITE
Land or water

USE
**Signage** - These leftovers make good labels along a school nature trail. They also can be used for flash cards. The teacher records the name of a plant or an animal on each card as it is discovered. This vocabulary can be used later in developing a report or other follow-up lessons back in the classroom.

## STYROFOAM TRAYS
(from meat packaging)

STUDY SITE
Land

USE
**Observation trays** - Instead of passing delicate samples of leaves or flowers for all to see, place them on the tray and pass it around the class or leave them along the study trail as a message that says to other members of the class, "This is worth noting."

NEW JERSEY
AUDUBON
SOCIETY

Helpful Hints

**Helpful Hints for Outdoor Nature and Ecology Investigations**

**Helpful Hints**

## COFFEE CANS
(13 oz. size)

STUDY SITE
Land

PREPARATION
Puncture the plastic lid with a paper punch or other device. Make enough holes so small particles can be shaken through like salt through a saltshaker.

USE
**Sieve** - Dig up some ground material from the habitat you are studying and put it in the can. Secure the lid to the can. Gently shake the can so the small particles land on a styrofoam tray. Separate the materials and determine their source: plant matter, insects, seeds, soil. List the findings. Examine other areas in the habitat and compare the sample trays. What is the same? What is different?

## COFFEE CAN AND AN OLD NYLON STOCKING

STUDY SITE
Water

PREPARATION
Cut off both ends of the can. Cut an old nylon stocking about 18" from the toe. Stretch the open end over one end of the coffee can and secure it with a rubber band or cord to make a seine.

USE
**Seine** - Anchor the can in a stream so the stocking end catches the water running downstream. Leave it alone for ten or fifteen minutes before checking to see if anything is caught. Never leave the seine overnight and, after observation, be sure to release any creatures that are caught.

## PLASTIC BOTTLES
(two- or three-liter size) and
## FABRIC SOFTENER SHEETS
(the kind without slits)

STUDY SITE
Land

PREPARATION
Cut off the top of the bottle just where the curve ends. You will also need a rubber band or cord that will fit around the bottle.

USE
**Classroom terrarium** - Gather ground litter during the winter from about four or five different habitats. Place each sample in its own bottle. Label each bottle according to habitat, date, and exact site from which the sample was taken. Stretch a fabric softener sheet over the top of each bottle and secure it. Bring the bottles into the classroom and add water regularly so that the litter is kept moist. Observe changes and keep a record. Are there any larvae that hatch or seeds that sprout? What does this tell you about the floors of the habitats?

## SMALL CLEAR PLASTIC CONTAINERS
(such as breath mint containers, some prescription boxes)

STUDY SITE
Land or water

PREPARATION
Some uses require cotton balls.

USES
**Observation box** - Students will stuff the container with cotton and deposit a seed so it can be seen. Moisten the cotton and seal the container. Students keep a record of the germination process in their own container.

**Observation tank** for very small water creatures. Tiny water creatures put in a flat box with a small quantity of water can be placed for limited time on an overhead projector. The entire class is then able to observe the physical characteristics and behavior of the creature.

## PLASTIC CONTAINERS
(One and two pound size)

STUDY SITE
Water

PREPARATION
These containers usually are obtained from delicatessen salads or margarine tubs. When doing a stream study, it is recommended that there be one for each student.

USE
**Observation and transport tank** - When the students discover and collect water creatures these containers enable close examination and transportation of the animal to the class holding tank (plastic dishpan) so all may observe.

## PLASTIC FILM CANISTERS
(from 35mm film)

STUDY SITE
Land

PREPARATION
Collect a variety of small objects, such as pebbles, seeds, or paper clips. Make two sets of each item and place the sets in the canisters so that one pair represents each object.

USE
**Sound canisters** - The students must shake the canisters and match the ones that produce the same sound. Open the canisters to check.

## WHITE BED SHEET
(any size)

STUDY SITE
Land - trees with low branches, shrubs, field

USE
**Insect observation sheet** - Spread the sheet under a tree or shrub. Shake the branch and watch the sheet to see if any insects drop. This provides a good insect observation area. Teams of students may be in charge of moving the sheet to test different areas. When placing the sheet in an open field, leave it alone for a while. Insects will hop onto the sheet.

## CARDBOARD ROLLS
(from paper towels or bathroom tissue)

STUDY SITE
Land

MATERIALS
• two rolls measuring four to six inches in length
• 24-inch length of butcher cord
• contact paper to cover cardboard rolls (optional)
• tool to puncture cardboard rolls
• masking tape

PREPARATION
The two rolls may be covered with contact paper for durability. Tape the rolls together lengthwise. At one end of the binoculars, puncture a hole on the outer rim of each roll large enough to slip the butcher cord through and knot the ends. The cord is slipped over the student's head so hands can be free.

USE
**Binoculars** - While these binoculars do not provide any magnification they are a good tool for teaching students how to focus their observation.
A. Use them to scan an area. This helps students examine details that might ordinarily be overlooked.
B. Draw the students' attention to a specific feature. Instruct them to raise the binoculars to their eyes while they continue to look at the object, which can then be seen through the binoculars but in a smaller field of vision. (This is not as easy as it sounds and the lesson should be repeated until the students are successful. The skill is an important preparation for the use of optics with magnification.)

Helpful Hints

NEW JERSEY
AUDUBON
SOCIETY

**Helpful Hints for Outdoor Nature and Ecology Investigations**

## TEACHER AND STUDENT ASSESSMENT

# HOW TO USE THE RUBRIC

Generally rubrics specify the level of performance expected for several levels of quality. These levels of quality may be written as different ratings (e.g., Best, Good, Fair) or as numerical scores (e.g., 4, 3, 2, 1) which are then added up to form a total score associated with a grade (e.g., A, B, C, etc). The following models are designed for upper elementary, Grades 4 to 6 using information from Rubistar: http://rubistar.4teachers.org

### TEACHER RUBRIC

The teacher rubric is a measure of the overall success of the outdoor learning lesson. It is a tool to help determine whether the methods used in presenting the information were effective, whether the goals of the lesson were met, and whether the students were engaged in learning.

Each category describes an aspect of the outdoor experience. Success is measured by matching achievements described in the columns with the achievements of the students. Under each category choose only one level of the lettered criteria. No total score should exceed 75 points.

### STUDENT RUBRIC

Given the right circumstances students can learn to take control of their own success in the outdoor classroom. Levels of achievement progress from understanding fundamental skills and knowledge to exhibiting advanced leadership skills. Give the students this rubric before they begin their work in the outdoors. They understand ahead of time what is expected to achieve excellence in knowledge, understanding, skills, attitudes and behaviors.

**Figure 1** (page 1 of 3)

# TEACHER RUBRIC
## FOR EVALUATING SCHOOLYARD OR HABITAT FIELD TRIP

Class: _____ Date: _____

| Teacher Criteria | | Exceeds Expectations | | Meets Expectations | | Does NOT Meet Expectations |
|---|---|---|---|---|---|---|
| **Lesson Concepts:** (list) _____ _____ _____ _____ _____ _____ _____ | ☐ | A. At least 75% of the students can discuss items of learned information with confidence. (3) | ☐ | A. About 50% of the students demonstrate understanding of at least 2 items of learned information. (2) | ☐ | A. Students repeat facts of at least some items of learned information, but are unable to explain the concept in their own words. (1) |
| | ☐ | B. At least 75% of the students seek further subject information independently and share that information with the class. (3) | ☐ | B. About 50% of the students ask questions related to the subject and share learned information. (2) | ☐ | B. Students do not refer to the lesson concepts in other situations or subject areas. (1) |
| **Materials/tools:** Investigations enabled students to learn how to use new materials/ tools/technologies. (Such as measuring, probing, photographic equipment, computer software) | ☐ | A. Tools helped all students to be fully engaged, rather than detracting from the experience. (3) | ☐ | A. Tools helped most students to be fully engaged. (2) | ☐ | A. Materials / tools were underutilized by most students. (1) |
| | ☐ | B. Use of tools led to further investigation and sharing of information with others through technological means. (3) | ☐ | B. Use of tools led to further investigation and sharing of information with others. (2) | ☐ | B. Use of tools led to further investigation. (1) |
| **Natural History Learning Loop:** Investigations lead students to build upon past knowledge and apply to new situations. | ☐ | A. At least 75% of the students recognize more than 5 indicator species of the habitat. (3) | ☐ | A. At least half the students recognize at least 3 indicator species of the habitat. (2) | ☐ | A. Most students can name 2 indicator species of the habitat but only with help. (1) |
| | ☐ | B. At least 75% of the students can name 3 physical characteristics that help define the habitat. (3) | ☐ | B. At least half the students can name 3 physical characteristics of the habitat. (2) | ☐ | B. Most students can name 2 physical characteristics of the habitat but only with help. (1) |
| | ☐ | C. Students are able to compare habitat components to those found in other habitats and explain why present species are indicator species. (3) | ☐ | C. At least half the students are able to make comparisons between habitats and discuss. (2) | ☐ | C. Most students can list differences between habitats. (1) |

Helpful Hints

NEW JERSEY AUDUBON SOCIETY

Helpful Hints for Outdoor Nature and Ecology Investigations

**Figure 1** (page 2 of 3) **TEACHER RUBRIC**

| Teacher Criteria | Exceeds Expectations | Meets Expectations | Does NOT Meet Expectations |
|---|---|---|---|
| **Investigation Skills:** Lessons promoted student driven investigations. | ☐ A. At least 75% of the students choose appropriate materials and organize the investigation independently. (3) | ☐ A. At least half of the students choose appropriate materials, but require assistance in organizing the investigation. (2) | ☐ A. Most students require guidance in organizing an investigation and choosing appropriate tools. (1) |
| | ☐ B. At least 75% of the students gather information without teacher assistance. (3) | ☐ B. At least half of the students require teacher instruction throughout the lesson. (2) | ☐ B. Students share information as the result of a question. (1) |
| | ☐ C. Students initiate discussion without prompting and are eager to share learned information. (3) | ☐ C. Students share learned information during teacher-led discussion. (2) | ☐ C. Students find it difficult to articulate what they have learned. (1) |
| **Cooperative Learning Skills:** Investigations encouraged students to exhibit team-building qualities such as cooperation, tolerance, and flexibility. | ☐ A. Students work as a cohesive unit coming to consensus by including all team members in the investigation. (3) | ☐ A. Students work as a team, and form consensus with some guidance. (2) | ☐ A. Students require teacher direction to achieve team participation. (1) |
| | ☐ B. Group members show interest in contributions of team members and work to include many opinions in the final product. (3) | ☐ B. Group members listen to other team members. (2) | ☐ B. Students share, but lose interest when others are sharing information or opinion. (1) |
| **Problem-solving:** Investigations encouraged students to participate in the problem-solving process – (such as posing questions, seeing patterns, generating new ideas, being detailed in description and explanation). | ☐ A. More than 75% of the students pose an original question about the habitat. (3) | ☐ A. About half the students are able to pose an original question about the habitat. (2) | ☐ A. Most students need assistance in forming a question about the habitat. (1) |
| | ☐ B. More than 75% of the students can organize a method for answering their question. (3) | ☐ B. About half the students are able to organize a method for answering their question. (2) | ☐ B. Most students need help organizing a method for answering their question. (1) |
| | ☐ C. More than 75% of the students are innovative and willing to take appropriate risks to answer questions/ solve problems. (3) | ☐ C. About half the students are willing to take appropriate risks to answer questions/solve problems. (2) | ☐ C. Most students are challenged to be innovative beyond getting the "right" answer. (1) |
| | ☐ D. More than 75% of the students generate ideas from a variety of approaches. (3) | ☐ D. About half the students generate ideas from a variety of approaches. (2) | ☐ D. Most students are challenged to generate ideas from more than one approach. (1) |
| | ☐ E. More than 75% of the students can justify their problem-solving approach. (3) | ☐ E. About half the students can justify their problem-solving approach. (2) | ☐ E. Most students are challenged to justify their problem-solving approach. (1) |

**Helpful Hints**

NEW JERSEY AUDUBON SOCIETY

**Figure 1** (page 3 of 3) **TEACHER RUBRIC**

| Teacher Criteria | | Exceeds Expectations | | Meets Expectations | | Does NOT Meet Expectations |
|---|---|---|---|---|---|---|
| **Time Management:** Investigations were well-paced and kept students engaged in learning. | ☐ | A. There is balanced time between lesson introduction, procedure, and discussion. (3) | ☐ | A. All concepts were covered, but parts of the lesson were rushed. (2) | ☐ | A. Sections of the lesson were left out due to lack of focus or interest. (1) |
| | ☐ | B. At least 75% of the students organize their investigation, remain focused and complete the process to solution. (3) | ☐ | B. About half the students are able to follow instructions and complete the process to solution. (2) | ☐ | B. Students require constant refocusing. (1) |
| | ☐ | C. At least 75% of the students use extra time to expand on investigation and exploration while waiting for others to finish. (3) | ☐ | C. About half the students complete their tasks without distracting other students who are still working. (2) | ☐ | C. Most students are challenged to complete their tasks. (1) |
| **Safety in the Outdoor Classroom:** Investigations promoted student, teacher, and chaperone safety. | ☐ | A. Over 75% of the students and chaperones wear appropriate shoes and clothing. (3) | ☐ | A. More than half the students and chaperones wear appropriate shoes and clothing. (2) | ☐ | A. Most students and chaperones do not wear appropriate shoes and clothing. (1) |
| | ☐ | B. Over 75% of the students follow all safety behaviors outlined by the teacher or chaperone. (3) | ☐ | B. Most students follow all safety precautions outlined by the teacher, but not their chaperone. (2) | ☐ | B. Students listen to safety precautions outlined by the teacher, but need to be reminded. (1) |
| | ☐ | C. Over 75% of the students understand and can explain reasons for being cautious and respectful in natural areas. (3) | ☐ | C. Most students do not harass wildlife or pick plants. (2) | ☐ | C. Most students need to be reminded not to harass wildlife or pick plants. (1) |
| **Environmental Ethic:** Investigations gave students ample opportunities to demonstrate their level of concern for the well being of other life form and natural systems. | ☐ | A. Over 75% of the students can articulate and demonstrate the need for care toward animals and plants in the habitat during their investigations. (3) | ☐ | A. More than half the students can articulate the need for care toward animals and plants in the habitat during their investigations. (2) | ☐ | A. Less than half the students can articulate the need for care toward animals and plants in the habitat during their investigations. (1) |
| | ☐ | B. Over 75% of the students understand and practice the phrase "take only photographs and leave only footprints." (3) | ☐ | B. More than half the students replace soil, leaf litter, and other natural materials after investigation. (2) | ☐ | B. Students need to be told why they may not remove plants or animals from the habitat. (1) |

Total Score _____
(All columns all three pages)

**POINT RANGE**
0 – 25 ...... Field trip does not meet with expectations for outdoor explorations; reassess techniques, length of time outside, etc..
26 – 50 ...... Field trip meets expectations; work to increase those areas that scored lower.
51 – 75 ...... Field trip exceeds expectations for outdoor explorations.

NEW JERSEY AUDUBON SOCIETY

Helpful Hints

**Figure 2** (page 1 of 2)

# STUDENT RUBRIC
# FOR EVALUATING PERSONAL ACHIEVEMENT

## In the Outdoor Classroom I am a Success

Name: _____ Date: _____

| Criteria | | Leader | | Discoverer | | Explorer |
|---|---|---|---|---|---|---|
| **Habitat:**<br>Each habitat or natural community has unique landscape features as well as different plants and animals that behave according to their needs. | ☐ | A. I can list ten new items of knowledge gained by studying this habitat. (3) | ☐ | A. I can name five new items of knowledge gained by studying this habitat. (2) | ☐ | A. I can name three new items of knowledge gained by studying this habitat. (1) |
| | ☐ | B. I can accurately describe and name three plants and three animals in this habitat. (3) | ☐ | B. I can accurately describe and name two plants and two animals in this habitat. (2) | ☐ | B. I can accurately describe and name one plant and one animal in this habitat. (1) |
| | ☐ | C. I can explain why indicator plants and animals are suited to this habitat. (3) | ☐ | C. I can explain the difference between this habitat and others. (2) | ☐ | C. I can recognize that this habitat is different than another habitat. (1) |
| **Cooperation:**<br>We can learn by sharing our ideas and discoveries with others. | ☐ | A. I shared at least three new ideas I had with others in my group. (3) | ☐ | A. I shared at least two new ideas I had with others in my group. (2) | ☐ | A. I shared at least one new idea I had with others in my group. (1) |
| | ☐ | B. I listened to the ideas and information from at least three different students. (3) | ☐ | B. I listened to the ideas and information from two different students. (2) | ☐ | B. I listened to the ideas and information from one other student. (1) |
| | ☐ | C. I respectfully stated a difference of opinion with justification. (3) | ☐ | C. I stated a difference of opinion. (2) | ☐ | C. I shared my opinion. (1) |
| | ☐ | D. I admitted when I made a mistake and thanked the student who offered new information to make that possible. (3) | ☐ | D. I did not make fun or ridicule any student's observation or opinion. (2) | ☐ | D. I did not make fun or ridicule a student when I disagreed. (1) |
| **Time:**<br>Staying focused and using time wisely. | ☐ | A. I did not allow distractions to keep me from my work. (3) | ☐ | A. I was distracted, but went back to the task assigned. (2) | ☐ | A. This is an exciting place and it was hard to stay on task. (1) |
| | ☐ | B. I finished all tasks given and used the extra time to explore the habitat for more information. (3) | ☐ | B. I finished more than half the tasks given. (2) | ☐ | B. I finished at least one of the tasks given. (1) |

**Helpful Hints**

NEW JERSEY
AUDUBON
SOCIETY

**Bridges to the Natural World**

**Figure 2** (page 2 of 2) **STUDENT RUBRIC**

| Criteria | | Leader | | Discoverer | | Explorer |
|---|---|---|---|---|---|---|
| **Tools:** A scientist uses tools to learn more about the world in which we live. | ☐ | A. I learned how to use the available tools the right way to help me learn at least five new facts about the habitat. (3) | ☐ | A. I used the available tools to help me learn at least four new facts about the habitat. (2) | ☐ | A. I used the available tools to help me learn at least three new facts about the habitat. (1) |
| | ☐ | B. I invented new tools in order to learn about the habitat. (3) | ☐ | B. I discovered how to use the tools in different ways in order to learn about the habitat (2) | ☐ | B. I found other tools to help me learn about the habitat. (1) |
| **Environmental Ethic:** We share the earth with many different life forms. | ☐ | A. I stay on the trails and am careful not to pick or step on living plants when I am exploring a habitat. (3) | ☐ | A. I stay on the trails and am careful not to pick any living plants when I am in exploring a habitat. (2) | ☐ | A. I stay on the trails while exploring a habitat. (1) |
| | ☐ | B. I keep from making loud noises or interfering with animal activity. (3) | ☐ | B. I try not to disturb animals by making loud noises or interfering with their activity. (2) | ☐ | B. I try not to disturb animals by interfering with their activity. (1) |
| | ☐ | C. I leave a natural area so you would never know that people had been there. (3) | ☐ | C. I replace rocks, logs, and leaves after I explore a natural area. (2) | ☐ | C. I leave a natural area without leaving anything behind. (1) |

**Total Score** _____

(All columns both pages)

**POINT RANGE**

0 – 14 ...... I know how to explore this habitat.

15 – 28 ...... I am learning how to discover many things about the habitat.

29 – 42 ...... I have taken a leadership role in the outdoor classroom.

Helpful Hints

NEW JERSEY AUDUBON SOCIETY

# I CAN TEACH MYSELF
## (KWL Chart)

It is the teacher's role to provide opportunities where students can take responsibility for their own learning. In early years of development it is critical to apply the natural curiosity of childhood to positive learning experiences. Curiosity needs to be exercised in order to stay fit, just as muscles of the body need exercise. Without it, both will atrophy. The worksheet that accompanies this exercise places the responsibility of learning squarely on the student. The natural world is their inheritance. Knowing and understanding its value is the first step to preserving it for the future. Measuring their personal progress in knowing about their world increases personal self-esteem and sense of accomplishment.

MATERIALS
• worksheet in Figure 3

PREPLANNING
Discuss learning in the outdoors and the site that will be visited.

PROCEDURE
Distribute the worksheets. Instruct the students to write in the first column the things they already know about the outdoors and the site they will visit. When they have completed this, instruct them to write the things they would like to learn about the site in the second column. After the field trip have the students write in the things they learned.

FOLLOW-UP
Lead a class discussion comparing the columns. Were expectations met? Were there surprises or disappointments? Create a compiled list of KWL columns by having students write their comments on the blackboard. Notice how much more we learn when we share our reflections.

**Helpful Hints**

NEW JERSEY
AUDUBON
SOCIETY

**Bridges to the Natural World**

**Figure 3**

# I CAN TEACH MYSELF (KWL Chart)

Name: _____

Habitat I will investigate: _____

| What I know | What I want to learn | What I learned |
|---|---|---|
|  |  |  |

NEW JERSEY
AUDUBON
SOCIETY

Helpful Hints

# TECHNO-TIPS

Technology can be a wonderful tool for the advancement of learning in the natural world. As a companion to outdoor investigations recording devices can serve as records for a series of different studies. Some computer programs tie into satellite information that describes land use and natural conditions. These records afford opportunities for comparison over time and seasons. Records can be studied by students over subsequent years to build a history of how areas change or remain the same.

During recent years, teachers have offered suggestions and records of their use of technology in the classroom. We pass these suggestions on to you to enhance the outdoor classroom experience.

## CAMCORDER
Patti Pfeiffer of Winfield Elementary School takes her camcorder with her kindergarten class when they do their habitat studies. She records some of the unique features of each natural community. Along the way, teacher-naturalist leaders explain some aspect of the area as well as plant or animal behavior. Student responses and comments are interspersed at appropriate intervals. Back in the classroom, students review the tapes. This inspires further discussion and reinforces the concepts taught. It also helps students recall the experience when reviewed later in the school year.

For older students, images from the camcorder can be used to design Power Point presentations and habitat web sites.

## DIGITAL CAMERA
Pictures that can be transferred into a computer program facilitate the development of visual presentations. The digital camera makes it easy to combine a variety of snapshots with printed information on a computerized presentation. They also personalize a report when pictures of classmates and observations appear on the printed page.

An album of habitat observations saved on the computer is a permanent record for future use in later years by other students.

## POWER POINT
Students prepare presentations of their outdoor experiences. They begin with lists of what they already knew about the natural area, list the things they wanted to learn, and then conclude with pictures, captions, graphs and information about the site visited and studied.

## DATABASE PROGRAMS
Theresa Santiago of Edward Patten Elementary School in Perth Amboy teaches a special needs class. As part of a bird study unit her students record the number of species they recognize and then create a database from which she had the students make graphs. A bar graph showed the number of each species observed, while another depicted a class vote on the most popular bird.
Keeping a census count of species is a valuable tool for monitoring a natural community of plants and animals. Daily, weekly, or monthly records lead to an accumulation of data that is valuable in noticing changes. This data raises questions as to the cause of change. Is it caused by seasonal cycles, or is there some other explanation? Students become involved in real scientific research that relates to their personal lives.

# NOTES

Helpful Hints

# NOTES

NEW JERSEY
AUDUBON
SOCIETY

Bridges to the Natural World

*Bridges to the Natural World*

Section 5

# TOOLS FOR BUILDING 'BRIDGES' OF UNDERSTANDING AND REFERENCES

APPENDICES

Appendices

# GLOSSARY

## A

**abiotic:** Nonliving substances

**adaptation:** Any physical or behavioral characteristic of a plant or animal that enhances the species' ability to survive. Adaptations do not occur because a species decides it would be more advantageous to change, but rather because a beneficial variation improves its ability to survive.

**alga:** One of a group of nonflowering plants, usually green and lacking a true vascular (conducting) system.

**amoeboid:** Like an amoeba. Usually refers to an organism's movement. Amoebas are simple, single-celled microscopic organisms.

**annual:** A plant species that completes its life cycle from seed to mature, seed-bearing plant in a single growing season and then dies.

**aquatic:** Living mostly or all the time in water. Opposite is terrestrial.

**arboreal:** Adapted for and living in trees.

**arthropod:** An animal belonging to the phylum of invertebrates which characteristically has an exoskeleton, a jointed body, and segmented limbs. This group includes insects, spiders, and crustaceans.

## B

**backwater:** The area in a river or stream in which the velocity of the water slows down enough to allow a different community of plants and animals to occur than that allowed by fast-moving water.

**ballast plants:** Introduced species of plants that arrived in North America in the soil or rocks used as ballast in cargoless ships.

**barrier island:** Islands in the ocean that are close to the coast and parallel to it. They act as natural buffers to ocean storms and tides. Long Beach Island is an example of a barrier island.

**biennial:** A plant species that has a two-year life cycle only. Biennials grow from seed and produce just leaves the first year; the second year they flower, bear fruit, and die.

**biomass:** The dry weight of an organism.

**biotic:** Composed of living substances

**bivalve:** A mollusk having a hinged, two-sided shell, such as a clam.

**bog:** A permanently wet area that gets its water only from precipitation. Usually it lacks drainage and is characterized by an accumulation of organic matter, extreme acidity, and low fertility.

**botany:** The study of plants.

**brood:** The eggs or young of birds and reptiles that are hatched, or born, and cared for at one time.

**bryozoan:** An aquatic invertebrate animal that often forms colonies of thousands of individuals. Such colonies appear in the water as large, gelatinous masses or mossy, brownish mats.

## C

**camouflage:** Specific colors and/or patterns in an animal that enable it to blend into its surroundings and be less visible to its predators or prey.

**canopy:** The layer formed by the upper branches of the trees in a forest.

**carnivore:** A meat-eating animal that feeds exclusively or primarily on prey animals.

**climax:** Theoretically, the final, mature, stable, self-maintaining and self-reproducing state of vegetational development that culminates plant succession on any given site.

**colonize:** The process by which a species of plant or animal enters an area not previously occupied by that species and establishes itself.

**community:** An association of plants and animals that inhabit a common environment and interact with one another.

**commensals:** Animals that happen to live in the same habitat, but do not interact or depend on one another such as house mouse and Norway rat.

NEW JERSEY
AUDUBON
SOCIETY

**compound leaves:** Leaves having two or more leaflets originating out of one leaf stem.

**conifer:** A needle-bearing evergreen tree, the fruit of which is usually a cone.

**consumer:** An organism that feeds on plants or animals, living or dead, to fuel its metabolism.

**crustacean:** A member of the subphylum of the arthropods characterized by mandibles, antennae, and modified appendages. Included in this category are lobsters, crabs, barnacles, and shrimp.

**cyclic:** A pattern that is repeated. The seasons are cyclical, as are some animal populations.

# D

**deciduous:** Plants that drop their leaves annually.

**decomposers:** Plants or animals (mostly fungi and bacteria) that, as a by-product of their metabolism, reduce organic material to simpler organic and inorganic forms.

**defoliate:** The removal of the leafy growth of plants. In the summer, gypsy moths can defoliate entire forests. White-tailed deer and other herbivores may defoliate ground cover and shrubs to the browse line, the line marking their furthest reach.

**detritus:** Dead and decomposing organic material.

**diversity:** The variety of different species in a community.

**dominant species:** A plant or animal species, or group of species, that exerts the major control on its community. Generally, plant dominants have the greatest biomass of the species in the community.

**dormant:** The condition in which there is absence of activity or growth in or of an animal or plant.

**dorsal:** Pertaining to the back (as opposed to the belly). Opposite is ventral.

# E

**ecology:** The study of the relationships between organisms and of the relationships between organisms and their nonliving environment.

**ecosystem:** An ecological unit in nature created by the interaction between living organisms and the nonliving physical environment.

**emergent:** Vegetation rooted at the bottom of and rising above the surface of a body of water.

**endangered species:** A species threatened with extinction or extirpation.

**endemic:** A species restricted in range to a particular area under consideration.

**environment:** An organism's living and nonliving surroundings that affect and influence it.

**epaulets:** Originally, shoulder pads worn by soldiers and later ornaments worn to signify military officers. Here, the brightly colored wing bars on the male red-winged blackbirds. The extent of the wing bar and the degree of color is associated with the most successful male in attracting mates and establishing territory.

**ephemerals:** Organisms or stages in their life cycles that are visible only for a short period of time.

**extinct:** Describes a plant or an animal no longer existing as a living species. Extinction occurs when the last individual of the species dies.

**extirpated:** Locally extinct, that is, extinct in a particular state or country, but perhaps still present elsewhere.

# F

**fauna:** Animals, as opposed to plants. (See flora.)

**filter feeder:** An organism that screens or filters water and extracts microscopic animals or plants for its food.

**fledging:** The production of a complete set of flight feathers which enable the young bird to leave the nest.

**floodplain:** The low-lying land along a river or stream that is inundated regularly when water levels are high.

**flora:** Plants, as opposed to animals. (See fauna.)

**foliage:** The leaves or needles of a plant.

**food chain:** A series of organisms in which energy and materials are transferred from a producer to successive consumers. Producers (plants) are eaten by a herbivore (rabbit), the herbivore is eaten by a carnivore (fox), and the carnivore is eaten by a larger carnivore (mountain lion). The largest carnivore is either eaten by a competitor of the same species or dies and is eaten by scavengers and decomposers, ultimately returning resources to the system.

**forage:** The act of an animal searching for food.

**forest fragmentation:** Division of a contiguous, undeveloped forest into smaller sections through the building of roads, towns, power lines, etc. These smaller, unconnected areas are not able to support as large a diversity of species, thus compromising the interrelationships of the ecosystem. Research has indicated that forests smaller than 40 acres are compromised for many species.

# G

**glacier:** A thick sheet of ice formed when successive snowfalls accumulate at a rate exceeding the rate of melting. As these ice sheets move they alter the landscape by carving valleys, moving boulders, and making sand and gravel. Glaciers have covered part of New Jersey at least three times in the last 100,000 years.

**groundwater:** Precipitation that soaks into the ground and recharges aquifers or moves in the water table until it returns to surface water.

# H

**habitat:** The natural environment of an organism where it most usually finds the food, water, shelter, and space it needs to live its full life cycle and reproduce others of its kind. In a broad sense habitats are unique areas defined by **indicator species**.

**hardwood:** Broad-leafed, deciduous trees.

**herbaceous:** Nonwoody.

**herbicide:** A chemical or combination of chemicals that kills plants.

**herbivore:** An animal that eats plants.

**hibernation:** The phenomenon by which some animals avoid the extreme conditions of winter by finding a suitable place to sleep for months. Their metabolic rate, temperature, and respiration decrease and these functions are maintained by metabolizing body fat.

**Highlands:** A physiographic region in New Jersey characterized by a belt of old mountains extending southwest from Bergen and Passaic Counties to the Delaware River.

**humus:** The organic, dark soil material that forms as plant and animal remains decompose.

# I

**indicator species:** Plant or animal that is found in a specific kind of geological and geographical location.

**infestation:** An animal population that, in a particular location and in given proportions, can be injurious to another organism.

**Inner Coastal Plain:** A physiographic region in New Jersey that is generally flat and somewhat less sandy than the Outer Coastal Plain, and mostly drains to the Delaware River. It is located west and immediately north of a low ridge that runs from Gloucester County to Atlantic Highlands.

**inorganic:** Not of, or from, living material. Does not contain carbon. (See organic.)

**instinct:** A behavior that is innate, not learned. Some instinctive activities may be modified by learning. A bird instinctively builds a nest, but learns from trial and error which materials work best.

**intergrade:** The gradual change in the dominant species in a community that reflects the effect both of the natural environmental changes and human-induced influences through land use.

**introduced species:** A non-native species. Species that are introduced either intentionally or inadvertently have been known to displace and/or eradicate native species, thus disrupting a local ecosystem.

**invasive:** Describes a species increasing its historic range of distribution, usually to the detriment of other species.

**invertebrate:** An animal that lacks a backbone, as opposed to a vertebrate, which has a backbone. (See vertebrate.)

**isopod:** An aquatic or terrestrial animal possessing seven pairs of walking legs, a rounded back, and flattened belly. These include sow bugs, pill bugs, etc.

# K

**kettle hole:** A depression in the ground formed when a large block of ice breaks free from a receding glacier. The land around the ice block is built up as glacial debris is deposited; when the ice block melts the depression remains. Often a kettle hole becomes a pond, or, in a seasonally wet area, a vernal pond.

NEW JERSEY
AUDUBON
SOCIETY

Appendices

larva: An immature animal before it metamorphoses into its pupal form.

larval: The stage of an animal's life prior to undergoing metamorphosis to its pupal form.

leaf axil: The point on the upper side of a leaf stem where it meets the main branch and where a bud is located.

leaf litter: The fallen leaves and organic material on the forest floor.

loam: Soil consisting of crumbling clay, silt, and sand.

lobes: The short, rounded, finger-like projections of a leaf edge.

# M

marsh: A nonwooded, permanent, usually well-drained wetland.

microclimate: A smaller area within a larger, relatively uniform, area where local conditions cause a different climate from that of the surrounding area.

midden: A mass of organic material, such as bones and shells, which is the refuse at an animal or animal's feeding station. A midden accumulated by successive generations of a species can give clues to the natural history of an area.

migration: The seasonal movement of populations of a species from one location to another.

mollusk: An animal belonging to the phylum of soft-bodied invertebrates that possess a hard, calcarious shell. Clams, mussels, and snails are in this phylum.

# N

native species: An indigenous, as opposed to introduced, species.

natural community: An association of plants and animals that inhabit a common environment and interact with one another.

natural resources: A term often applied to anything from which people can benefit in nature, the physical properties including plants and animals of the area.

naturalized alien: An introduced species that has become established and now occurs regularly.

nestling: A recently-hatched bird that has not yet abandoned the nest.

niche: The special role in a community assumed by a particular species of plant or animal.

nocturnal: Active at night.

nonvascular: As applied to plants, those groups that do not contain internal tubes for transporting water and nutrients from one part of the plant to another. Nonvascular plants include mosses, algae, lichens, and fungi.

nutrient: A substance necessary for growth.

# O

omnivore: An animal that eats both plant and animal materials.

organic: Material that contains carbon.

ornithologist: A scientist who studies birds.

outcrop: A naturally occurring exposed view of bedrock.

Outer Coastal Plain: A physiographic region in New Jersey that is generally flat, sandy, and drains to the Atlantic Ocean. It lies east of a low ridge that runs from Gloucester County to the Atlantic Highlands.

# P

parasite: An animal which, by living in or on another animal, benefits at the expense of the other animal.

pathogenic: Disease-causing.

pelagic: Of the free or open ocean water.

perennial: A plant that lives for several years, usually producing flowers and fruit each year.

pesticide: A chemical or combination of chemicals that kills both plant and animal "pests."

photosynthesis: The process by which a green plant, in the presence of chlorophyll, uses the sun's energy to convert water and carbon dioxide to carbohydrates (food), releasing oxygen as a by-product.

physiographic region: An area described largely by its geology and soil type. New Jersey has five physiographic regions.

physiological: Pertaining to the internal functioning mechanisms of an organism.

Piedmont: A physiographic region in New Jersey that is underlain by Triassic rocks, and includes the Watchung Mountains. It is located north of the coastal plains and extends as a belt from Bergen to Hunterdon counties.

NEW JERSEY AUDUBON SOCIETY

Appendices

**pioneer trees:** The trees that are first to grow in a disturbed area.

**plankton:** Microscopic aquatic organisms which, having limited mobility, are transported by water circulation, tides, and currents.

**pollutant:** A by-product of human activity that is detrimental to the ecosystem.

**predator:** An animal that kills and eats other animals.

**prey:** Any animal eaten by another organism.

**primary consumer:** A herbivore or animal that eats plants (primary producers).

**prism:** A piece of glass that bends light and separates it into the colors of the spectrum.

**producer:** Organisms that do not get their energy from eating other plants or animals. Producers are primarily green plants.

**propagation:** The planting of seeds, or the reproduction of plants by spreading root systems and adventitious leaves and stems.

**protozoan:** An invertebrate; a single-celled animal.

# R

**ravine:** A narrow valley between two steep slopes, formed by erosion from run-off during heavy rains.

**regeneration:** The act of an organism replacing a lost organ.

**renewable:** Something that can be replaced after it has been used. Paper comes from a renewable resource: trees.

**resources:** A term often applied to anything from which people can benefit, or, in nature, the physical properties including plants and animals of the area.

**Ridge and Valley:** A physiographic region in New Jersey that is characterized by a narrow belt of ridges and interconnecting valleys that run from northeast to southwest. It is located in the extreme northwestern portion of the state.

**riverine:** Along, in, or of a river.

**runoff:** Water that is not absorbed by the soil because the soil already is saturated, or is impermeable, or because the slope of the land is too steep to permit total absorption. The water runs directly into a drainage system, such as storm drain, river, stream, lake, or ocean.

# S

**scavenger:** An animal that eats dead plants or animals. For example, turkey vultures eat road kills.

**secondary consumer:** A carnivore or an omnivore that eats the primary consumer (planteaters).

**sepal:** The leaf-like structure beneath a flower. A sepal encases the flower bud before the flower opens.

**shrub:** A woody plant, normally growing with multiple stems and branching almost from ground level, and usually not reaching more than 10 feet in height.

**soluble nitrates:** Forms of nitrogen capable of being dissolved in water and that can be absorbed by plants. Nitrogen is a natural, necessary, and often limiting nutrient to the ecosystem.

**spathe:** A large leaf-like structure (or pair of structures) that protects or encases a flower, such as in skunk cabbage.

**species:** A population of individuals that are more or less alike and are able to interbreed and produce fertile offspring under natural conditions.

**species diversity:** The total number of different species found in an area and their frequency in the community. Species diversity is dependent upon the availability of resources and the variety of spatial habitats available.

**spectrum:** The range of color from red to blue, as seen in a rainbow.

**sponge:** An animal belonging to the phylum Porifera. The most primitive of multicellular animals characterized by their lack of true tissues or organs. Mostly marine, some fresh water, they are sessile, or attached.

**structure:** The layers of a habitat. Plants are the dominant species of a habitat and their formation defines the structure of the natural community.

**subadult:** An individual of a species that, despite its adult appearance, has not reached sexual maturity.

**subordinate:** A lower level or a lower life form.

**subsoil:** The layer of soil beneath the topsoil.

**substrate:** The surface on which an organism lives, grows, or to which it is attached.

**succession:** The slow, orderly progression of changes in a community from initial colonization of an area to the attainment of a climax typical of the area.

NEW JERSEY AUDUBON SOCIETY

Appendices

**swamp:** A seasonally flooded, wooded wetland.

# T

**tannic acid:** An acid produced by woody plants that reduces herbivore activity. Tannic acid produces the characteristic brown color of the water in the Pine Barrens and in bogs.

**temperate zone:** The climatic zone in which North America is located. The zone has a mean annual temperature of 10° - 13° degrees Celsius (50° - 55° degrees Fahrenheit).

**terrestrial:** Living mostly or all the time on dry land. Opposite is aquatic.

**thicket:** An impenetrable tangle of shrubs, vines, briars, and/or trees. Thickets are found commonly along hedgerows, field edges, and stream banks where sunlight penetration affords uninhibited growth. They provide excellent protective cover for many nesting and denning animals.

**threatened species:** A species whose survival is in danger of becoming endangered or extirpated.

**toxic:** Something that is poisonous or reduces the functions of an organism.

**toxin:** A poison produced as a product of metabolism.

**tree:** A woody plant having a single main stem and a more or less distinct crown of branches and usually reaching a height of 10 feet or more.

**trophic levels:** Levels in the food chain pyramid. Producers (green plants) form the base, herbivores are the next level, with carnivores and omnivores occupying the next successive levels.

**tundra:** A biome type characterized by a very short growing season, very low precipitation, and low growth. Tundra is found in arctic and high alpine areas.

**tunicate:** Primarily marine filter feeders in the phylum Chordata that are named for their tunic-like covering. The group includes sea squirts.

**turbid:** A description of the degree of organic and/or inorganic material suspended in a body of water. High turbidity limits sunlight penetration.

# U

**underlayer:** The layer beneath the canopy or highest layer of foliage in the forest. Other layers include the shrub and groundcover layer.

**understory:** A layer of plants growing beneath another, taller, group of plants.

**univalve:** A mollusk, such as a snail, that has a one-piece calcarious protective shell.

**upland:** An area that is high and dry. Excessive amounts of rainfall run off upland areas into streams or swampy areas.

# V

**vascular:** Applied to plants having internal tubes to conduct water and nutrients from one part of the organism to another. All flowering plants, ferns, and conifers are vascular.

**venomous:** Pertaining to animals that possess a gland for secreting poison or venom. The poison enables the animal, through a bite or sting, to catch its prey.

**vermifuge:** A deworming agent used to eliminate internal worms or parasites.

**vernal pond:** A pond that fills up only in the spring; in dry years a vernal pond may have little or no water at all.

**vertebrate:** Having a backbone or spinal column. Opposite of invertebrate.

**vertical zonation:** In terrestrial habitats, highest points are dominated by trees. Lower levels are occupied by shorter, shade-tolerant trees. Lower still are shrubs, and, finally, groundcover. Some animals will feed in one or several zones and nest or roost in another.

# W

**weathering:** The effect on rocks, soil, wood, etc., of being exposed to the elements: sun, wind, rain, snow, frost, or other agents of the local climate. The weathering of rocks produces sand and gravel.

# THREATENED AND ENDANGERED WILDLIFE SPECIES OF NEW JERSEY

ENDANGERED SPECIES are those whose prospects for survival in New Jersey are in immediate danger because of a loss of or change in habitat, over-exploitation, predation, competition, disease, disturbance, or contamination. These species need assistance if extinction in New Jersey is to be prevented.

THREATENED SPECIES are those who may become endangered if conditions surrounding them begin to or continue to deteriorate.

## BIRDS

### Endangered
Bittern, American *
Eagle, bald  BR**
Falcon, peregrine
Goshawk, northern*
Grebe, pied-billed*
Harrier, northern*
Hawk, red-shouldered
Owl, short-eared*
Plover, piping**
Sandpiper, upland
Shrike, loggerhead
Skimmer, black
Sparrow, Henslow's
Sparrow, vesper
Tern, least
Tern, roseate**
Wren, sedge

### Threatened
Bobolink
Eagle, bald NB**
Hawk, Cooper's
Hawk, red-shouldered NB
Night-heron, black-crowned*
Night-heron, yellow-crowned
Knot, red
Osprey*
Owl, barred

Owl, long-eared
Rail, black
Skimmer, black NB
Sparrow, grasshopper*
Sparrow, Savannah*
Sparrow, vesper NB
Woodpecker, red-headed

## REPTILES

### Endangered
Rattlesnake, timber
Snake, corn
Turtle, bog**
Atlantic Hawksbill **
Atlantic Leatherback**
Atlantic Loggerhead**
Atlantic Ridley**

### Threatened
Snake, northern pine
Turtle, Atlantic green**
Turtle, wood

*Continued on next page*

* Only breeding population considered
  endangered or threatened
** Federally endangered or threatened
BR – Breeding population only
NB – nonbreeding population only

Reprinted with the permission of the New Jersey Endangered and Nongame Species Program.

NEW JERSEY
AUDUBON
SOCIETY

Appendices

**THREATENED AND ENDANGERED WILDLIFE SPECIES OF NEW JERSEY**
*Continued from previous page*

## AMPHIBIANS

**Endangered**
Salamander, blue-spotted
Salamander, eastern tiger
Salamander, Tremblay's
Treefrog, pine barrens
Treefrog, southern gray

**Threatened**
Salamander, eastern mud
Salamander, long-tailed

## MAMMALS

**Endangered**
Bat, Indiana**
Bobcat
Whale, black right**
Whale, blue**
Whale, fin**
Whale, humpback**
Whale, sei**
Whale, sperm**
Woodrat, Allegheny

## FISH

**Endangered**
Shortnose sturgeon **

## INVERTEBRATES

**Endangered**
Beetle, American burying**
Beetle, northeastern beach tiger**
Copper, bronze
Floater, brook (mussel)
Floater, green (mussel)
Mussel, dwarf wedge**
Satyr, Mitchell's (butterfly)**
Skipper, Appalachian grizzled (butterfly)
Skipper, arogos (butterfly)

**Threatened**
Elfin, frosted (butterfly)
Floater, triangle (mussel)
Fritillary, silver-bordered (butterfly)
Lampmussel, eastern (mussel)
Lampmussel, yellow (mussel)
Mucket, tidewater (mussel)
Pondmussel, eastern (mussel)
White, checkered (butterfly)

* Only breeding population considered endangered or threatened
** Federally endangered or threatened
BR – Breeding population only
NB – nonbreeding population only

Lists of New Jersey's endangered and nongame wildlife species are maintained by the Department of Environmental Protection in the Division of Fish and Wildlife's Endangered and Nongame Species Program. These lists are used to determine protection and management actions necessary to insure the survival of the state's endangered and nongame wildlife. This work is made possible through voluntary contributions received through the Wildlife Check-off on the New Jersey State Tax Form. The Wildlife Check-off is one of the funding sources for the protection and management of the State's endangered and nongame wildlife resource. For more information about the Endangered and Nongame Species Program or to report a sighting of endangered or threatened wildlife contact the: Endangered and Nongame Species Program, P.O. Box 400, Trenton, NJ 08625 or call (609) 292-9400.  www.state.nj.us/dep/fgw
This list was revised 9/12/02.

Reprinted with the permission of the New Jersey Endangered and Nongame Species Program.

# ABOUT ORPHANED AND INJURED WILDLIFE

Young animals, particularly birds, often are discovered alone and apparently orphaned. Wild animals of all ages are found injured. Accidents on highways, encounters with family pets, and collisions with picture windows account for many of these injuries. In these situations, most people feel an instinctive urge to help the injured bird or mammal. However, even well-intentioned actions may prove disastrous to the creatures. Deprived of parental guidance and thus lacking the foraging or hunting skills necessary to survive, the released bird or mammal may starve. Since they lose part of their innate wariness, there is great probability that such animals will fall prey to people, cats, dogs, or even natural predators, which they fail to recognize as enemies. The following information may be all that is needed to lend assistance. Knowing what to do can prevent further stress to the creature.

## CATS INDOORS!

"Cats are the most popular pets in the United States. Their fascinating behavior and physical beauty endear them to their owners. But inside every cat are the genes of an efficient, prolific, and non-native predator. Scientists estimate that free-roaming cats kill hundreds of millions of birds and probably more than a billion other small wild animals in the United States yearly." (American Bird Conservancy)

It is highly probable that some of the injured wildlife encountered by students will have been caught and released and/or injured by neighborhood cats. Usually, the wild animals will not survive a cat's assault because of trauma or more obvious wounds. By keeping cats indoors, it not only protects neighborhood wildlife, but also protects the cats from disease and other harm. To learn more visit: www.njaudubon.org/conservation/cats.

NEW JERSEY AUDUBON SOCIETY

Appendices

## BABY BIRDS

### MOST YOUNG BIRDS DISCOVERED OUT OF THE NEST ARE NOT ORPHANS.

Young songbirds leave the nest before they are capable of extended flight and may remain essentially flightless for ten days or more. During this time the parents, who spend much of their time away from the young, gather food. The young of precocial birds (shorebirds, ducks, pheasants, and grouse), leave the nest immediately after hatching and go through a longer process of learning to forage for themselves before they can fly.

## BABY MAMMALS

### BABY MAMMALS ARE EVEN MORE VULNERABLE THAN BIRDS TO HUMAN INTERVENTION.

Perhaps because wild mammals are furry, warm, and cuddly, it is often assumed that they will respond to care, as would humans. The care of mammals, however, is fraught with the same problems as is the care of birds.

### ADULT MAMMALS MAY LEAVE THEIR YOUNG FOR RELATIVELY LONG PERIODS OF TIME.

This habit leads many people to believe the young are abandoned when actually they are not. It is best to leave the young where they are as the parents may be merely waiting for the human intruder to leave. This is especially true of young deer and rabbits.

### THE SURVIVAL CHANCES OF CAPTIVE MAMMALS ARE GREATLY DIMINISHED UPON THEIR RELEASE.

## CALL THE EXPERTS

Federal and state laws regulate the handling and rehabilitation of wildlife. The best procedure is to contact those who hold licenses to perform these services. One rehabilitation organization of world renown is located in New Jersey, The Raptor Trust. Information and field trip experiences can be found on their web site. (www.theraptortrust.org)

# CREATING A HABITAT FOR WILDLIFE

As stewards of our land, we can help to ensure that birds, butterflies, and other animals find favorable habitat. We can make a difference in our backyards, schoolyards, and community open spaces. These creatures' needs are basic: food, water, and a place to forage and rest that is safe from weather and predators. The vegetation we choose to plant or protect will benefit not only migrants, but resident species as well.

Native trees, shrubs, and vines are the key to successful habitats, offering critical food and cover to wildlife. Native vegetation will thrive with the least amount of care. This should be a prime consideration when in a drought cycle with water shortage problems. If an area is not mowed or left brushy, native trees, shrubs and vines will flourish on their own. As the untended area evolves, it is beneficial in all stages of its growth. Even early on, its brushy character offers important cover and food. A successful schoolyard habitat provides FOOD, COVER/SHELTER, WATER, and SPACE.

## FOOD

When planting to improve or create a habitat for wildlife, choose a variety of native trees, shrubs, and vines with different flowering and fruiting periods to provide food at different times of the year (e.g., nuts, berries, buds, catkins, fruits, nectar, and seeds). See the accompanying list of plants for suggestions.

Insects are also an important food source for wildlife. Most birds feed their young on insects, and species like swallows, flycatchers, and woodpeckers eat insects throughout their lifetime. Birds play a significant role in regulating insect populations. Avoid the use of insecticides and ensure a safe area for wildlife in your school community. Winter bird feeders filled with sunflower, thistle, mixed seed, suet, and fruit will offer an opportunity for students to observe birds close-up.

## COVER and SHELTER

Evergreen trees provide cover year-round. Brushy thickets of densely planted shrubs or overgrown areas provide a protected place for birds and small mammals to hide from predators and build their nests. A brush pile placed near winter feeders provides important cover. Birds take seed from the feeders and fly to a protected area to feed. The brush pile makes this process easy and less stressful in severe weather. Small mammals, reptiles and amphibians will also find homes in these structures. After the first of the year, Christmas trees make good brush piles for winter bird feeding.

Nest boxes for hole-nesting birds like screech owl, American kestrel, chickadee, bluebird, wren, and purple martin will also attract wintering birds seeking shelter. Dead or hollow trees are important to hole-nesting birds like woodpeckers, bluebird, screech owl, and chickadee as well as flying squirrel, and raccoon. Leave them standing, unless they are in danger of falling, to provide cavities for nesting, roosting, and winter shelter. The insects inhabiting the wood also serve as a food source.

## WATER

A birdbath is a simple way to provide water, important for drinking and bathing.

NEW JERSEY'S NATIVE TREES, SHRUBS and VINES THAT ARE BENEFICIAL TO BIRDS
These are some of the most important species along with the number of New Jersey bird species that feed on their nuts, berries, buds, fruits, seeds, nectar, or catkins. Some of these may already be present on your school grounds.

NEW JERSEY
AUDUBON
SOCIETY

Appendices

Appendices

# NEW JERSEY'S NATIVE TREES AND SHRUBS THAT ARE BENEFICIAL TO BIRDS

These are some of the most important species along with the number of bird species that feed on their nuts, berries, buds, fruits, seeds, nectar, or catkins. Some of these may already be present on your school grounds.

**Trees**
Red Cedar, *Juniperus virginiana* ...................... 32
OAKS, *Quercus* spp. ............................................. 29
Sassafras, *Sassafras albidum* ........................... 23
Wild Black Cherry, *Prunus serotina* ................ 53

**Shrubs**
Common Spicebush, *Lindera benzoin* ............ 15
Red Chokeberry, *Aronia arbutifolia* ................ 12
Black Chokeberry, *A. melanocarpa* ................... 7
VIBURNUMS, *Viburnum* spp. ............................ 23

Besides birds, a well-designed schoolyard habitat will also attract a variety of butterflies. Caterpillars will eat the leaves from some of these plants, while adult butterflies will come to the flowers for nectar. Some of these flowers are also appealing to hummingbirds!

# PLANTS TO ATTRACT HUMMINGBIRDS AND BUTTERFLIES

To attract nectar-loving species, think about planting these low maintenance and drought-resistant plants.

KEY:  A/P – Annual/Perennial, 1 = spring, 2 = summer, 3 = fall, 4 = until frost, S/sh – Sun/shade

## FLOWERS: PERENNIALS & ANNUALS

| Common Name | Botanical Name | A/P | 1/2 3/4 | S/sh | Color |
|---|---|---|---|---|---|
| Aster, New England | *Aster novae-angliae* | P | 2-4 | S | purple |
| Anise Hyssop | *Agastache foeniculum* | P | 2-3 | S | purple |
| Bee Balm / Monarda: | | | | | |
| Bee Balm | *Monarda didyma* | P | 2 | S/sh | purple, red, white |
| Wild Bergamot | *Monarda fistulosa* | P | 2 | S/sh | pale pink |
| Boltonia / "Snow Bank" | *Boltonia asteroides* | P | 2-3 | S | white |
| Butterfly Weed | *Asclepias tuberosa* | P | 2-3 | S | orange |
| Columbine, Wild | *Aquilegia canadensis* | P | 1-2 | S/sh | red w/yellow |
| Coral-bells | *Heuchera* | P | 1-2 | S/sh | pink, coral |
| Four O'Clock | *Mirabilis jalapa* | A/P | 2-3 | S/sh | # colors |
| Joe pye-weed | *Eupatorium purpureum* | P | 2-3 | S | pink |
| Milkweeds: | | | | | |
| Butterfly weed | *Asclepias tuberosa* | P | 2-3 | S | orange, yellow |
| Common Milkweed | *Asclepias syriaca* | P | 2-3 | S | pink |
| Scarlet Milkweed | *Asclepias currassavica* | A | 2-3 | S | red |
| Swamp Milkweed | *Asclepias incarnata* | P | 2-3 | S | pink |
| Mountain Mint | *Pycnanthemum muticum* | P | 2-3 | S | white |
| Purple Coneflower | *Echinacea purperea* | P | 2-4 | S | pink |
| Sedum | *Sedum spectabile* | P | 2-3 | S/sh | pink |
| Verbena | *Verbena bonariensis* | P | 2-4 | S | purple |
| Zinnia | *Zinnia elegans* | A | 2-4 | S | # colors |

Appendices

NEW JERSEY AUDUBON SOCIETY

**Bridges to the Natural World**

# PLANTS TO ATTRACT
# HUMMINGBIRDS AND BUTTERFLIES Continued

### FLOWERING VINES (great for schoolyard sites on a trellis or arbor)

| Common Name | Botanical Name | A/P | 1/2/3/4 | S/sh | Color |
|---|---|---|---|---|---|
| Cardinal Climber | *Ipomoea x multifida* | A | 2-3 | S | red |
| Scarlet Runner Bean | *Phaseolus coccineus* | A | 2-3 | S | red |
| Trumpet Honeysuckle | *Lonicera sempervirens* | P | 1-4 | S | red |

### FLOWERING SHRUBS

| Common Name | Botanical Name | A/P | 1/2/3/4 | S/sh | Color |
|---|---|---|---|---|---|
| Abelia, Glossy | *Abelia grandiflora* | P | 2-4 | S | white |
| Butterfly Bush | *Buddleia davidii* | P | 2-4 | S | # colors |

# RECOMMENDED "Caterpillar Foodplants,"
# also known as HOST PLANTS,
# TO BENEFIT SOME BUTTERFLIES AND MOTHS

These are some of the many plants sought by adult butterflies and moths for egg laying ...they are necessary to create the next generation of adult butterflies or moths.

Clover .............................................................................. sulphurs, Eastern Tailed Blue
Dill ................................................................................................... Black Swallowtail
Everlasting, Pearly .................................................................................. American Lady
Everlasting, Sweet .................................................................................. American Lady
Fennel, Bronze ..................................................................................... Black Swallowtail
Fennel, Green ...................................................................................... Black Swallowtail
Milkweed: Common, Butterfly Weed, Scarlet, & Swamp ................................................ Monarch
Parsley ............................................................................................. Black Swallowtail
Red Cedar (TREE) ................................................... Olive 'Juniper' Hairstreak, Imperial Moth
Sassafras (TREE) ................................................... Spicebush Swallowtail, Imperial Moth
Spicebush (SHRUB) ...................................................... Spicebush Swallowtail
Tomato .............................................. Five-spotted Hawk Moth (Tomato Hornworm),
Carolina Sphinx (Tobacco Hornworm)
Arrowwood (SHRUB) ............................................ Hummingbird Clearwing (moth)
Violets ...................................................................................... Fritillaries
White Pine (TREE) ............................................ E. Pine Elfin, Imperial Moth
Wild Black Cherry (TREE) ....................... E. Tiger Swallowtail, Coral Hairstreak,
Striped Hairstreak, Red-spotted Purple, Cecropia Moth,
Promethea Moth, & Hummingbird Clearwing (moth)

NEW JERSEY AUDUBON SOCIETY

**Appendices**

NEW JERSEY
AUDUBON
SOCIETY

Bridges to the Natural World

# BIBLIOGRAPHY AND RESOURCE LIST

## ACTIVITY BOOKS

Bowden, Marcia. 1989. *Nature for the Very Young: A Handbook of Indoor & Outdoor Activities.* New York: John Wiley & Sons, Inc.

Braus, Judy. *Ranger Rick's NatureScope.* Washington, D.C.: National Wildlife Federation.

Caduto, Michael J., and Joseph Bruchac. 1991. *Keepers of the Animals: Native American Stories and Environmental Activities for Children.* Golden, Colo.: Fulcrum Publishing.

——. 1988. *Keepers of the Earth: Native American Stories and Environmental Activities for Children.* Golden, Colo.: Fulcrum Publishing.

Council for Environmental Education. 2002. *Project Wild.* Council for Environmental Education and Western Association of Fish and Wildlife.

——. 1983. *Project Wild: Elementary Activity Guide.* Boulder, Colo.: Western Regional Environmental Education Council.

Cornell, Joseph Bharat. 1979. *Sharing Nature With Children.* Nevada City, Calif.: Ananda Publications.

Creative Educational Society. 1973. *How to Have Fun With an Indoor Garden.* Chicago: Children's Press.

Criswell, Susie Gwen. 1986. *Nature With Art.* New York: Prentice-Hall, Inc.

DeVito, Emile, PhD., ed. 1994. *The Songbird Connection.* Far Hills, NJ, New Jersey Conservation Foundation.

De Zeeuw, Maureen. 1998. Arctic-Nesting Shorebirds: Curriculum for Grades K-12. Anchorage, AK: U.S. Fish and Wildlife Service.

Heyge, Lorna Lutz, and Audrey Sillick. 1988. *Teacher's Guide Year One: Kindermusik for the Very Young.* Walton, N.Y.: Music Resources International.

——. 1988. *Teacher's Guide Year Two: Kindermusik for the Very Young.* Walton, N.Y.: Music Resources International.

——. 1988. *Kindermusik 1.* Walton, N.Y.: Music Resources International.

Hickman, Pamela M. 1990. *Bird Wise.* New York: Addison-Wesley Publishing Company, Inc.

Hunken, Jorie. 1992. *Birdwatching for All Ages: Activities for Children and Adults.* Chester, Conn.: Globe Pequot Press.

Hunken, Jorie, and The New England Wild Flower Society. 1989. *Botany for All Ages.* Chester, Conn.: Globe Pequot Press.

Kesselheim, Alan S., et al. 1995. *WOW! The Wonders of Wetlands.* St. Michaels, MD: Environmental Concern, Inc. and The Watercourse.

Knapp, Clifford. 1988. *Creating Humane Climates Outdoors: A People Skills Primer.* Charleston, W. Va.: Appalachia Educational Laboratory.

Lingelbach, Jenepher, ed. 1986. *Hands-On Nature: Information and Activities for Exploring the Environment with Children.* Woodstock, Vt.: Vermont Institute of Natural Science.

McGlauflin, Kathy, et al. 2001. *Project Learning Tree: Environmental Education Activity Guide Pre-K-8.* Washington, D.C.: American Forest Foundation and Council for Environmental Education.

Nelson, Denis, et al. 1995. *Project Wet: Water Education for Teachers.* Bozeman, MT: The Watercourse and Western Regional Environmental Education Council.

New Jersey Division of Solid Waste Management. 1988. *Here Today, Here Tomorrow.* Trenton: New Jersey Department of Environmental Protection and Energy.

New Jersey Office of Communications and Public Education. 1991. *Beneath the Shell.* Trenton: New Jersey Department of Environmental Protection and Energy.

Raabe, Christine R., ed. 1999. *Down Jersey: Celebrating Our Sense of Place.* Millville, NJ: Citizens United to Protect the Maurice River and Its Tributaries, Inc.

Rockwell, Robert E., Elizabeth A. Sherwood, and Robert A. Williams. 1983. *Hug a Tree and Other Things to Do Outdoors With Young Children.* Mt. Rainier, Md.: Gryphon House, Inc.

Appendices

Rosselet, Dale A., et al. 1999. *New Jersey WATERS: Watershed Approach to Teaching the Ecology of Regional Systems.* Bernardsville, NJ: New Jersey Audubon Society.

Seager, Marcia L., Rosanne W. Fortner, and Timothy A. Taylor. 1988. *Supplemental Curriculum Activities for use with Paddle to the Sea.* Columbus: Ohio State University Research Foundation.

Shaffer, Carolyn, and Erica Fielder. 1987. *City Safaris.* San Francisco: Sierra Club Books.

Sherwood, Elizabeth A., Robert A. Williams, and Robert E. Rockwell. 1990. *More Mudpies to Magnets: Science for Young Children.* Mt. Rainier, Md.: Gryphon House, Inc.

Sisson, Edith A. 1982. *Nature With Children of All Ages.* Englewood Cliffs, N.J.: Prentice-Hall, Inc.

Williams, Robert A., Robert E. Rockwell, and Elizabeth A. Sherwood. 1987. *Mudpies to Magnets: A Preschool Science Curriculum.* Mt. Rainier, Md.: Gryphon House, Inc.

Yarrow, Ruth. 1978. *Exploring Environments.* Staten Island, N.Y.: High Rock Park Conservation Center of the Staten Island Institute of Arts and Sciences.

Zipf, Cindy. 1989. *Storm Drain Stenciling Project.* Highlands, N.J.: Clean Ocean Action.

# VISUAL AND AUDIO AIDS

*Bird Migration in the Americas.* Washington, D.C.: National Geographic Society, 1979. (map).

Elliot, Lang. *Know Your Bird Sounds,* Vols. 1 and 2. Post Mills, Vt.: NatureSound Studio/Chelsea Green Publishing Co., 1991. (audio cassette).

Elliot, Lang and Donald and Lillian Stokes. 1997. *Stokes Field Guide to Bird Songs: Eastern Region.* New York: Time Warner AudioBooks. (audio cassettes)

Glazer, Tom. *Happy Rhythms & Rhymes.* New York: CMS Records, Inc., 1980.

Golden, David M. and John F. Bunnell. nd. *Calls of New Jersey Frogs and Toads.* Trenton, NJ: New Jersey Division of Fish and Wildlife. (compact diskette)

Goss, Linda. *Afro-American Tales & Games.* New York: Folkways Records, 1980.

Jenkins, Ella. *This is Rhythm.* New York: Folkways Records, 1961.

*New Jersey at the Crossroads.* Franklin Lakes, N.J.: New Jersey Audubon Society/Altered Image and Terra Communications, Inc., 1990. (video)

Peterson, Roger Tory. *A Field Guide to Bird Songs: Eastern and Central North America.* Boston: Houghton Mifflin Co., 1990. (audio cassette).

Thayer Birding Software. nd. *Our Birds: New Jersey.* (software)

Walton, Richard K., and Robert W. Lawson. *Peterson Field Guides: Backyard Bird Song.* Boston: Houghton Mifflin Co., 1991. (audio cassette).

Walton, Richard K. 1996. *Common Butterflies of the Northeast.* Concord, MA: author. (video)

Walton, Richard K. and Richard A. Forster. 1997. *Common Dragonflies of the Northeast.* Concord, MA: author (video).

# CHILDREN'S BOOKS

Baines, Chris. 1990. *The Flower.* New York: Crocodile Books/Interlink Publishing Group, Inc.

——. 1990. *The Picnic.* New York: Crocodile Books/ Interlink Publishing Group, Inc.

Brennan, Matthew J. 1972. *The Environment and You.* New York: Grosset & Dunlap.

Cochrane, Jennifer. 1978. *Animals and Their Homes.* New York: Grosset & Dunlap.

——. 1987. *Land Ecology.* New York: Bookwright Press.

——. 1988. *Urban Ecology.* New York: Bookwright Press.

Cook, David. 1985. *Birds.* New York: Crown Publishers, Inc.

——. 1985. *Environment.* New York: Crown Publishers, Inc.

Creative Educational Society. 1971. *The Ecology of North America.* Mankato, Minn.: Creative Educational Society, Inc.

Duvoisin, Roger. 1956. *The House of Four Seasons.* New York: Lothrop, Lee, & Shepard Books.

Geisel, Theodor Seuss [Dr. Seuss]. 1971. *The Lorax.* New York: Random House, Inc.

Guilbeau, Honore. 1971. *Mrs. Magpie's Invention.* Reading, Mass.: Addison-Wesley Publishing Company, Inc.

Hollings, Holling Clancy. 1969. *Paddle to the Sea.* Boston: Houghton Mifflin Co.

Kirkpatrick, Rena K. 1978. *Look at Rainbow Colors.* Milwaukee: Raintree Children's Books.

O'Neill, Mary. 1961. *Hailstones and Halibut Bones.* Garden City, N.Y.: Doubleday & Co., Inc.

Ross, David, ed. 1970. *The Illustrated Treasury of Poetry for Children.* New York: Grosset & Dunlap.

# FIELD GUIDES

Borror, Donald J., and Richard E. White. 1970. *Peterson Field Guides: Insects of America North of Mexico*. Boston: Houghton Mifflin Co.

Boyd, Howard P. 1991. *A Field Guide to the Pine Barrens of New Jersey*. Medford, N.J.: Plexus Publishing, Inc.

Boyle, William J., Jr. 2002. *A Guide to Bird Finding in New Jersey*. New Brunswick: Rutgers University Press.

Burt, William H., and Richard P. Grossenheider. 1980. *Peterson Field Guides: Mammals of North America*. Boston: Houghton Mifflin Co.

Conant, Roger. 1986. *Peterson Field Guides: Reptiles and Amphibians Eastern/Central North America*. Boston: Houghton Mifflin Co.

Dickinson, Mary B., ed. 1999. *Field Guide to the Birds of North America*. Washington, D.C.: National Geographic Society.

Dunkle, Sidney W. 2000. *Dragonflies through Binoculars*. New York: Oxford University Press.

Elphick, Chris, Johan B. Dunning, Jr. and David Allen Sibley, eds. 2001. *The Sibley Guide to Bird Life & Behavior*. New York: Alfred A. Knopf.

Glassberg, Jeffrey. 1999. *Butterflies through Binoculars: The East*. New York: Oxford University Press.

Gosner, Kenneth L. *Peterson Field Guides: Atlantic Seashore*. Boston: Houghton Mifflin Co.

Ehrlich, Paul R., David S. Dobkin, and Darryl Wheye. 1988. *The Birder's Handbook*. New York: Simon & Schuster, Inc.

Elbroch, Mark and Eleanor Marks, PhD. 2001. *Bird Tracks & Signs*. Mechanicsburg, PA: Stackpole Books.

Kaufman, Kenn. 2000. *Birds of North America*. New York: Houghton Mifflin Co.

Klots, Alexander B. 1979. *Peterson Field Guides: Eastern Butterflies*. Boston: Houghton Mifflin Co.

Kricher, John C., and Gordon Morrison. 1988. *Peterson Field Guides: Eastern Forests*. Boston: Houghton Mifflin Co.

McElroy, Thomas P., Jr. 1974. *The Habitat Guide to Birding*. New York: Lyons & Burford, Publishers, Inc.

McKnight, Kent H., and Vera B. McKnight. 1987. *Peterson Field Guides: Mushrooms*. Boston: Houghton Mifflin Co.

Morris, Percy A. 1975. *Peterson Field Guides: Shells of the Atlantic*. Boston: Houghton Mifflin Co.

Murie, Olaus J. 1974. *Peterson Field Guides: Animal Tracks*. Boston: Houghton Mifflin Co.

Niering, William A. 1985. *The Audubon Society Guides: Wetlands*. New York: Alfred A. Knopf, Inc.

Nikula, Blair, et al. 2002. *Stokes Beginner's Guide to Dragonflies*. New York: Little, Brown and Company.

Page, Lawrence M., and Brooks M. Burr. 1991. *Peterson Field Guides: Freshwater Fishes*. Boston: Houghton Mifflin Co.

Peterson, Roger Tory and Virginia Marie Peterson. 2002. *Peterson Field Guides: Eastern Birds*. Boston: Houghton Mifflin Co.

Peterson, Roger Tory, and Margaret McKenny. 1968. *Peterson Field Guides: Wildflowers Northeastern/North Central North America*. Boston: Houghton Mifflin Co.

Petrides, George A. 1986. *Peterson Field Guides: Trees and Shrubs*. Boston: Houghton Mifflin Co.

Robbins, C. Richard, G. Carleton Ray, and John Douglass. 1986. *Peterson Field Guides: Atlantic Coast Fishes*. Boston: Houghton Mifflin Co.

Schwartz, Vicki, PhD. and David M. Golden. 2002. *Field Guide to Reptiles and Amphibians of New Jersey*. Trenton, NJ: New Jersey Division of Fish and Wildlife.

Sibley, David Allen. 2002. *Sibley's Birding Basics*. New York: Alfred A. Knopf.

Sibley, David Allen. 2000. *The Sibley Guide to Birds*. New York: Alfred A. Knopf.

Stokes, Donald, and Lillian Stokes. 1986. *Stokes Nature Guides: A Guide to Animal Tracking and Behavior*. Boston: Little, Brown, & Co.

Sutton, Ann, and Myron Sutton. 1986. *The Audubon Society Nature Guides: Eastern Forests*. New York: Alfred A. Knopf, Inc.

Sutton, Clay and Patricia Taylor Sutton. 1996. *How to Spot Hawks & Eagles*. New York: Houghton Mifflin Company.

Sutton, Clay and Patricia Taylor. 1994. *How to Spot an Owl*. New York: Houghton Mifflin Company.

Sutton, Patricia Taylor and Clay Sutton. 1999. *How to Spot Butterflies*. New York: Houghton Mifflin Company.

Watts, May Theilgaard. 1986. *Tree Finder: A Manual for the Identification of Trees by Their Leaves*. Berkeley, CA: Nature Study Guild.

White, Richard E. 1983. *Peterson Field Guides: Beetles of North America*. Boston: Houghton Mifflin Co.

NEW JERSEY AUDUBON SOCIETY

Appendices

# GENERAL INFORMATION

Alexander, Taylor R., and George S. Fichter. 1973. *A Golden Guide: Ecology.* New York: Golden Press.

Anderson, Karl. 1983. *A Checklist of the Plants of New Jersey.* Mount Holly, N.J.: New Jersey Audubon Society.

Andrews, William, ed. 1973. *A Guide to the Study of Soil Ecology.* Englewood Cliffs, N.J.: Prentice-Hall, Inc.

Burnie, David. 1988. *Eyewitness Books: Bird.* New York: Alfred A. Knopf, Inc.

——. 1988. *Eyewitness Books: Tree.* New York: Alfred A. Knopf, Inc.

Collins, Beryl Robichaud and Karl H. Anderson. 1994. *Plant Communities of New Jersey.* New Brunswick, NJ: Rutgers University Press.

Dunne, Peter J., Richard Kane, and Paul Kerlinger. 1989. *New Jersey at the Crossroads of Migration.* Franklin Lakes, N.J.: New Jersey Audubon Society.

Ehrlich, Paul R., David S. Dobkin, and Darryl Wheye. 1988. *The Birder's Handbook.* New York: Simon & Schuster, Inc.

Garland, Mark. 1997. *Watching Nature: A Mid-Atlantic Natural History.* Washington: Smithsonian Institution Press.

Grae, Ida. 1974. *Nature's Colors, Dyes from Plants.* New York: Macmillan Publishing Co.

Hynes, H.B.N. 1970. *The Ecology of Running Waters.* Toronto: University of Toronto Press.

Kress, Stephen W. 1985. *Audubon Society Guide to Attracting Birds.* New York: Charles Scribner's Sons.

Martin, Alexander C., Herbert S. Zim, and Arnold L. Nelson. 1951. *American Wildlife and Plants: A Guide to Wildlife Food Habits.* New York: Dover Publications, Inc.

McKinley, Michael. 1983. *How to Attract Birds.* San Ramon, Calif.: Ortho Books, Division of Chevron Chemical Company.

Parker, Steve. 1988. *Eyewitness Books: Ponds & Rivers.* New York: Alfred A. Knopf, Inc.

Pellowski, Anne. 1990. *Hidden Stories in Plants.* New York: Macmillan Publishing Co.

Robichaud, Beryl, and Murray F. Buell. 1989. *Vegetation of New Jersey.* New Brunswick, N.J.: Rutgers University Press.

Rue, Leonard Lee, III. 1964. *New Jersey Out-of-Doors: A History of its Flora and Fauna.* Columbia, N.J.: Leonard Lee Rue Enterprises.

Sibley, David. 1993. *The Birds of Cape May.* Franklin Lakes, N.J.: Cape May Bird Observatory/New Jersey Audubon Society

Simon, Hilda. 1981. *The Magic of Color.* New York: Lothrop, Lee & Shepard Books.

Stokes, Donald, and Lillian Stokes. 1987. *The Bird Feeder Book.* Boston: Little, Brown, & Co.

Sutton, Patricia. 1989. *Backyard Habitat for Birds: A Guide for Landowners and Communities in New Jersey.* Cape May, N.J.: Cape May Bird Observatory/New Jersey Audubon Society.

Terborgh, John. 1989. *Where Have All the Birds Gone?* Princeton, N.J.: Princeton University Press.

Vernachio, Brian, Don Freiday and Dale A. Rosselet. 2003. *Wild Journeys: Migration in New Jersey.* Bernardsville, NJ. New Jersey Audubon Society.

Walsh, Joan, Vince Elia, Richard Kane, and Tom Halliwell. 1999. *Birds of New Jersey.* Bernardsville, N.J: New Jersey Audubon Society.

# ABOUT THE AUTHORS

**Pat Kane** was an elementary school teacher before coming to New Jersey Audubon in 1975. During her tenure she coauthored the original version of *Bridges to the Natural World*, developed school and day camp programs as well as professional development programs for teachers. She advanced to Director of Education and NJAS Vice President for Education. Now retired, she lives with her husband in Stewartsville, New Jersey, but is still engaged in environmental education through teacher education at Cook College, professional development in-service workshops for teachers, and storytelling.

**Dale Rosselet** gained experience in elementary education as a science teacher, resource room teacher and classroom teacher before beginning as a teacher naturalist for New Jersey Audubon Society in 1983. During her tenure she co-authored *Bridges to the Natural World*, and *New Jersey WATERS: A Watershed Approach to Teaching the Ecology of Regional Systems*. She is the sole author of *Linking Our Treasures*, a bilingual student guide about the New Jersey Highlands and *Fishing for Answers in an Urban Estuary*, a cooperative curriculum project done with the NJ Department of Environmental Protection. Dale now serves as NJAS Vice President for Education out of NJAS's Center for Research and Education in Cape May County.

**Karl Anderson** leads national and international botany and birding tours. He came to New Jersey Audubon in 1975 and now serves as the director of the Rancocas Nature Center and the NJAS Travel Program. His great expertise is botany and is co-author of *Plant Communities of New Jersey* as well as numerous other published natural history articles. Karl is responsible for writing the Habitats of New Jersey section of *Bridges to the Natural World*.

**Jerry Schierloh** is a retired professor of the School of Conservation, an outreach campus of Montclair University where he taught environmental education for over twenty-five years. Currently he is an environmental education consultant leading teacher workshops and working with school districts to integrate environmental education into their curricula and implementing a nationwide education reform project entitled "Using the Environment as an Integrating Context for Learning" (EIC). Jerry serves on the New Jersey Audubon Society's Board of Directors and chairs the Society's Education Committee.

**Carol Decker,** wildlife artist, sees the life in her subjects and captures it with her brush and pen. "I want my work to stand for more than its esthetic value. Environmental education is so important to maintain our outdoor space and its wildlife; it quiets and enriches our lives. I want people to see what I see, like being there looking over my shoulder." For over forty years this self-taught artist has been sharing her love of the natural world. She has painted eighty covers for *New Jersey Outdoors*, and illustrated five books. The Girl Scouts of America named her Woman of Distinction, recognizing her as an outstanding role model for young women in the world of the arts and environmental conservation. Carol lives in Branchville, N.J., with her husband, Roy. They have two grown sons and three grandchildren.

NEW JERSEY AUDUBON SOCIETY

Appendices

# ENDORSEMENTS

"New Jersey is a state that takes great pride in its natural resources. We know that we all have to work hard to protect our birds, animals and plant life so that our children and their children can enjoy the same wonder and beauty that we have come to treasure. The more we learn through groups like the New Jersey Audubon Society, the greater strides we make in protecting our natural heritage."

— Jim Florio,
Former Governor of New Jersey

"...Encouraging young New Jerseyans to be aware of and care for the state's delicate habitats should be one of our top educational priorities. *BRIDGES TO THE NATURAL WORLD* goes a long way toward meeting that goal."

— Bill Bradley,
Former New Jersey Senator

## What Teachers Say about *Bridges to the Natural World...*

### North Brunswick School District
"The lessons have real educational value and capture the attention of young children."

— Sharon Peisecki,
First Grade Teacher

"Fantastic, new and fresh approach to looking at the world around us!"

— Patricia Sacco,
Fifth Grade Teacher

### Bayonne School District
"Hands-on lessons make it interesting and fun for students to learn."

— Angela Henderson,
Special Ed Teacher

### Manalapen-Englishtown School District
"Excellent! Hands-on lessons and activities can be used by any kind of learner."

— Toby Kaster,
Resource Center

"Eye-opening."

— Carrie Jacobson
Fourth Grade Teacher

"A wonderful way to guide students in making connections with the nature that is all around us."

— Janice McDowell,
Fourth Grade Teacher

### Jersey City School District
"Exceptional! Lots of inexpensive ways to expand student understanding of nature in their everyday lives."

— Charlene D. Shariff,
Teacher of the Handicapped Grade 8

"Inspiring. It is so hard to get the attention of students who have had negative learning experiences in their past. I think they will definitely be turned on to science through these activities."

— Special Ed. Teacher,
Grades 6-8

### South Brunswick School District.
"Incredible! Not only did I find new lessons to teach, but I learned more about the world and how to help kids have a better sense of well-being."

— Shanna M. Spence,
Resource Center Teacher, Grade 6